Shylock Reconsidered

Published with the cooperation of the

CENTER FOR MEDIEVAL AND RENAISSANCE STUDIES

University of California, Los Angeles

Shylock Reconsidered

Jews, Moneylending, and Medieval Society

Joseph Shatzmiller

UNIVERSITY OF CALIFORNIA PRESS

Berkeley   Los Angeles   Oxford

University of California Press
Berkeley and Los Angeles, California

University of California Press, Ltd.
Oxford, England

Library of Congress Cataloging in Publication Data

Shatzmiller, Joseph.
   Shylock reconsidered : Jews, moneylending,
   and medieval society /
Joseph Shatzmiller.
      p.   cm.
   Bibliography: p.
   Includes index.
   ISBN 0-520-06635-9 (alk. paper)
   1. Jews—France—Marseille—Economic conditions. 2.
Bondavid, of Draguinan—Trials, litigation, etc. 3. Debtor
and   creditor—France—Marseille—History.   4.   Jewish
bankers—France—Marseille—History. 5. Usury laws. 6.
Marseille (France)—Ethnic relations. I. Title. II. Title:
Jews, moneylending.
DS135.F85M377   1989
332.7′43′089924044912—dc20   89-4970
                                                  CIP

Printed in the United States of America

1   2   3   4   5   6   7   8   9

The paper used in this publication meets the minimum
requirements of American National Standard for
Information Sciences—Permanence of Paper for Printed
Library Materials, ANSI Z39.48-1984

Contents

Acknowledgments   vii
Introduction   1

1   The Trial of Bondavid—Marseilles, 1317   5

The Dispute: Did Bondavid Claim a Debt
   Twice?   5
The Value of the Sixty Shillings Involved   8
Claiming Unpaid Debts in Medieval Marseilles   9
Retaining Promissory Notes: Suspicions against
   Moneylenders   14
"Faulty Creditor" and His Punishment   20
"Usurers" and "Manifest Usurers" in the
   Medieval City   22
Bondavid's Insistence on a Trial   25

**2   The Adversaries: Two Marseilles
Portraits**   27

Bondavid of Draguignan: A Wealthy Jew
   of Marseilles   28
A "Laborer": Petrus Guizo   35
The Credibility of the Depositions concerning
   the Two Men   40

**3   Opposition to Jewish Moneylending: Between
Theology and Politics**   43

Theologians, Lawyers, and Jewish
   Moneylending   44
Violent Opposition, Private and Collective   47

Debtors Cry for Help: The Role
   of Public Authorities   49
Aragon: The Government's Commitment to the
   Official Rate of Interest   55
France: Campaigns against Usury and Capetian
   Propaganda   58
"Ameliorating the Jews": A Prelude to Their
   Expulsion   62
The Politics of Expulsion   65
Indecisiveness: The Usages of *Usura*   67

4   **Indebtedness in Medieval Society: Need,
    Habit, and Equanimity**   71

The Universality of Indebtedness: Some
   Quantitative Assessments   72
Can Society Function without "Usury"?   79
Jewish and Non-Jewish Moneylenders   84
Choosing among Moneylenders   93
Ma'arufia: Preferred Customers   99
Marseilles 1317: Clients in Defense of Their
   Moneylender   103

5   **Shylock Reconsidered: Bondavid Seen by His
    Friends**   104

The Document, Once Again   104
Bondavid's Witnesses   107
Praise for Bondavid   112
The Shadows of the Council of Vienne   119

Conclusion   123
Appendixes
   1. Minutes of the Trial of Bondavid   127
   *2. Abraham of Draguignan's Last *Will*   163
Notes   167
Bibliography   225
Index   248

Acknowledgments

In the summer of 1972, as I was going through the court registers of Marseilles for the fourteenth century, I first came across the documentary record of a lawsuit of 1317 which involved the Jewish moneylender Bondavid (written also Bondavit, Bondavi, Bondavin, Bonus Davinus, etc.). It was only two years later, however, after deciphering the approximately fifty folios pertaining to the case, that I began to appreciate its importance. In order better to understand the case and its dramatis personae, I decided to survey all the surviving documents of the city for the period. The first three volumes of the catalog of Janine Sornay and R. H. Bautier, *Les sources de l'histoire économique et sociale du moyen âge*,[1] greatly facilitated this enterprise. It quickly became clear, though, that owing to the sheer number of documents, it would require a lifetime of nothing but academic sabbaticals to fulfill such an ambition. Eventually a much narrower project, covering only the twenty years from 1307 through 1327, was decided upon. Even this required many months of work in the archives. Fortunately, the Social Sciences and Humanities Research Council of Canada generously supported this study from beginning to end. I should like to express my gratitude to the Council for making this project possible.

In the course of almost twenty years' work, I have benefited from the help and advice of many colleagues. I should especially like to acknowledge the courteous and helpful reception I was given by the director of the Archives municipales de Marseille, M. Arnoud Ramière de Fortanier, and by the director of the Archives de Provence, M. P. Santoni. I am particularly grateful to my friends, Professors Louis Stouff and Noël Coulet, who head the important Provençal School of History, now that its founder, Professor Georges Duby, is in Paris. My work on this study, as well as all my past research, has benefited greatly from their wisdom and knowledge as well as from the many kindnesses they have extended to me. As for my colleagues in Toronto, I wish to acknowledge the interest that professors Giulio Silano, Norman Zacour, and Jocelyn Hillgarth always take in my work, saving me from the pitfalls that the manuscripts so often hide. Professors Zacour and Silano kindly read part of the text and offered innumerable corrections and emendations. I am no less indebted to my technical collaborators, Virginia O'Sullivan and Michael Arges, for the effort and enthusiasm they display. My children, Ira and Ron, too young to understand their father's fascination with the microfilm reader when I started this study, will now, I hope, be willing to read it and offer me—as they always do—their sincere criticism. To them and to my wife, Maya Shatzmiller, who knows well what writing is all about, this book is dedicated.

Introduction

With the stage performance of *The Merchant of Venice* in 1605, Shakespeare established for centuries to come the image of the Jewish moneylender as an execrable, pitiless usurer. That this portrait of a Jewish usurer has taken such a hold on the European mind testifies not only to the genius of its creator but also to the fact that Shylock's story and personality genuinely sum up a whole European experience. Feelings of discontent, helplessness, and hatred that tormented people for generations found now, through the genius of Shakespeare, their perfect expression. The argument of the present study is, however, that the image of the Shylockian Jew was not the only one that prevailed among medieval people. Side by side with expressions of resentment and frustration contemporary documents present expressions of recognition and appreciation for a benign and generous Jewish moneylender. Moreover, these references appear in the High and late Middle Ages (twelfth to fifteenth centuries), when the financial activity of medieval society reached its peak.

Through his studies in the archives of Perpignan, the late Professor Richard W. Emery, the eminent American scholar, has contributed more than anyone else to our understanding of Jewish moneylending and its dynamics. More than ten years ago Emery invited historians to entertain "a considerably revised picture of the typical moneylender" of the Middle Ages. "It was a highly competitive business," argued Emery; "there was no monopoly or cartel at work. Under such conditions a moneylender as harsh and strict as the conventional figure of literature would surely have fared badly. The advantage would have lain with the lender whose image and reputation was least disturbing to his Christian clients, particularly since the borrowers in the loan documents were neither poor nor desperate. It must have been almost necessary for a successful moneylender to acquire a reputation for being rather easygoing." Professor Emery therefore calls for a revised picture of the Jewish moneylender "and perhaps even a revision of the traditional view of moneylending in general. It does not appear in the sources very much like the 'degraded and degrading' profession we read about in contemporary history."[1]

While students of Jewish moneylending may thus not be entirely unfamiliar with the argument I intend to pursue, it is my hope that the data I present will be welcomed by laymen and specialists alike. For the most part, this study looks at a long and detailed legal procedure that took place in Marseilles in the first quarter of the fourteenth century, a trial in which a local Jew had to defend his reputation as a moneylender. As part of his defense, the Jew (whose name was Bondavid of Draguignan) brought before the court twenty-four witnesses, all non-Jews, to testify to the high esteem Bondavid enjoyed in the town. The statements made by the witnesses were recorded by a notary and then copied in the first fifty folios of the court register that is today catalogued as III B 7 in the Archives de Provence in Marseilles. From this document we can learn not only about the events leading up to the trial but also about the professional life of a Jewish moneylender as well as, we hope, about what others thought of him.

Admittedly I invite readers to embark on a listing boat leaning heavily toward one side. I would not do so were I not confident that, despite the handicap of unbalanced and imperfect documentation, we have an excellent opportunity to broaden our understanding of medieval attitudes toward moneylenders and the practice of usury. Drawing mostly on the very rich court records of Marseilles and of Manosque, chapter 1 will describe the issue that gave rise to the trial and compare it with similar actions in the Provence of that period. I will try to explain why Bondavid rejected the proposal of his adversary's father-in-law for an out-of-court settlement and why he insisted that a full trial take place. Chapter 2 will reconstruct the life of Bondavid as well as that of a key witness who maintained that the Jew's claim was fraudulent. Chapters 3 and 4 will look beyond the boundaries of

Marseilles and describe the prevailing European attitudes toward Jewish moneylending. Chapter 3 will focus on expressions of hostility toward Jewish moneylenders in England, France, Spain, and Germany, while chapter 4 will present the other face of medieval society: sympathy for and appreciation of Jewish moneylenders. This analysis will provide the necessary background for the last chapter, where I propose to return to Bondavid's trial and to the testimonies given in his favor by the witnesses. We shall have to take care lest we be blinded by the glare of the shining portrait they all draw in court. Though the picture is too good to be true, it nevertheless is my belief that reliable information can be rescued from this portrait—information that will enable us better to understand medieval people and the ambivalence of their attitudes toward money and moneylending.

1

The Trial
of Bondavid —
Marseilles, 1317

The Dispute: Did Bondavid
Claim a Debt Twice?

Between February and July of 1317, the court of the lower city of Marseilles held a trial that involved the Jew Bondavid of Draguignan, a moneylender. A citizen named Laurentius Girardi charged that Bondavid had falsely requested him to pay back a debt of sixty shillings, a debt which he had in fact already paid. The first glimpse we have of the trial proceedings shows us Bondavid's agent presenting to the court a group of citizens of Marseilles, some of high standing in the city, all of them non-Jews, to testify to the moneylender's good reputation. At the same proceeding, Bondavid presents a number of other witnesses who assert that Petrus Guizo, a relation of Laurentius and the only person to testify against Bondavid, is an *infamis* and should not enjoy the trust of the court. These testimonies are all that is preserved for us today in the Archives des Bouches-du-Rhône in Marseilles: there is almost no trace of the documents that must have been submitted by the other side. Nevertheless, from what is preserved of the proceedings we are able to gather some significant information about the background of the affair as well as about the early stages of the court action.

We do know when the affair began and when it ended. The debt itself was contracted on 11 April 1315 and recorded by the notary Guido Burgondionis.[1] The final decision of the court was not delivered until two years later, in July 1317, and was recorded by the notary G. Monernii.[2] Both documents are lost today. While it is not difficult to surmise how the original notarial deed of April 1315 must have read (there are thousands of them preserved in Provence for this period), it is naturally quite disappointing to be left without definite knowledge of the outcome of the trial. Certain clues, however, which will be discussed below, lead us to believe that the decision was favorable to Bondavid. Similarly we cannot ascertain whether Bondavid asked his borrower for a pledge or collateral as security for the loan or whether he wanted to have a guarantor to stand surety. It stands to reason that such was not the case, for nothing of this kind is mentioned in the proceedings of the trial, and because the thousands of promissory notes we have from the period show that in general, for loans of sixty shillings, such securities were not required. A notarial promissory note should have been good enough.

In a typical situation, a sum of sixty shillings (a substantial but not unusually large loan for the fourteenth century, as we shall see below) would be lent for a period of months only; loans lasting more than a year or so were rare in this period. It therefore stands to reason that sometime in the middle of 1316, when Bondavid realized that his client Laurentius was late in paying back the loan, he himself or one of his agents referred this matter to the court. The obligatory note of 11 April 1315, which he had in his possession, was handed over to the judge to serve as a proof of nonpayment. This was a decisive proof, in a way, because had Laurentius paid of his debt, he would have retrieved this document from the moneylender. Neither, in all probability, did Laurentius present the court with a quitclaim. No mention of such a crucial document is made in our records. Laurentius was able to support his defense only with the testimony of a relative of his, Petrus Guizo, who allegedly saw the debtor paying the sixty shillings to the creditor.

Having only a single favorable witness did not in itself unduly harm Laurentius's action. The statutes of Marseilles, as early as the middle of the thirteenth century, included a piece of legislation called "the probation by one witness," which held that the testimony of a single witness could be accepted by the court in cases involving one hundred shillings or less.[3] Indeed, court records from Marseilles in 1321 assure us that recourse to this legislation was made in practice.[4] The statute insisted, however, that the single witness had to be, beyond any doubt, a "notable and worthwhile witness."

As for the fact that Bondavid had in his possession the notarial deed, Laurentius could have claimed that this was due to fraud on the part of the Jewish moneylender. It is not clear from our records whether Laurentius used the testimony of Petrus Guizo to press formally such charges of fraud against Bondavid. Even if such was not the case, we should not be surprised to learn that the moneylender, in order to regain his sixty shillings, set out to destroy the witness's credibility. His move was therefore to offer the court two sets of defense statements (*tituli* or *articuli*, as they were called), each supported by a different group of witnesses. The first group, which was made up of twenty-five citizens, was brought forth to state that the Jew was righteous, respected, and generous, a man who under no circumstances would resort to fraud. The other group, which was composed of eight citizens, was presented to testify to the ill repute of the witness Petrus Guizo, a man whose word should not be considered by any tribunal. Such tactics were not uncommon in litigation in Provence about this time; court records from Manosque dating from 1301, 1311, and 1348 illustrate this very strategy.[5]

As one might expect, the portrait of Bondavid came out unblemished, while that of Petrus was painted completely black. Yet the Marseilles judges, knowing well these legal techniques, saw to it that such testimony was not accepted at its face value alone. First, Laurentius was invited to be present when the witnesses took the oath in court and presumably would have had the right to disqualify some of them (this point is not entirely clear from our documents). Moreover, the judge conveyed a copy of Bondavid's written submission to Laurentius before handing these *tituli* to the court's notary, who recorded them and conducted the actual investigation. The purpose of sharing such submissions with the adversary was to allow the other side to provide the notary with supplementary questions to be addressed to the witnesses. Many such documents (*interrogatoria*) can be found in fourteenth-century court registers of Manosque and of

Marseilles.[6] It is our good fortune to find inserted in register III B 7 a sheet of paper in which the *interrogatoria* addressed to Bondavid's witnesses were recorded. Thus we are able to observe how Laurentius, or his lawyer, intended to counter Bondavid's tactics and provide the court with information in his favor.

But before discussing the trial itself, we must address ourselves in a more detailed way to the background of the dispute: What was the actual value of the sixty shillings in Marseilles in 1316? What choices were available then to moneylenders to recover their debts? Why would the court of Marseilles not immediately rule in favor of Bondavid, since he had the right documents in hand: why, in other words, was this trial necessary at all?

The Value of the Sixty Shillings Involved

What could sixty shillings (*Solidi*) buy in Marseilles in 1317? How hard would a *laborator* like Petrus Guizo have to work to earn that sum? What did sixty shillings mean to Bondavid Draguignan?

Philippe Mabilly, a historian of medieval Marseilles, assembled some data on prices in the city during the first quarter of the fourteenth century, for which he relied mainly on notarial records.[7] He found twenty-seven examples of house prices for the period 1295–1325, which revealed that houses could sell for as much as thirty pounds and as little as two pounds. While the average price in this sample was a bit above the ten-pound level, it is noteworthy that six houses sold at a price of three pounds (sixty shillings) or less. Mabilly was able to find two figures for house rentals, which indicated that the price could be as high as six pounds a year and as low as ten shillings (one-half pound). For prices of rings and other precious objects we can refer to the will of none other than Bondavid's father, Abraham, which is dated 1316.[8] Abraham valued one ring "with a diamond" at four pounds. Another three rings together were valued at twenty pounds, and yet another ring plus a silver goblet was stated to be worth seven pounds. The price of one measure (*canne*) of cloth at Tarascon in 1324 (according to the *Rationnaire général*[9] of Provence) was eighteen shillings—one needed two such cannes for a dress.

The *Rationnaire général*, an official listing of governmental income and expenditure in Provence, reveals details concerning wages in the early fourteenth century. A *vigier*, the highest official in a local administration, would earn one hundred pounds per year (except in Marseilles, where the *viguier* earned the exceptional salary of four hundred pounds). The judge of the *viguerie* would make about seventy pounds. A *clavarius*, who was responsible for keeping the accounts of a locality, would have an annual salary of twenty pounds. Notaries who were attached to local courts were generally given some three to four pounds; for them, though, this may often have been a part-time assignment. Individuals who had a right to an annual pension on account of merit (e.g., for being wounded in military service) got a standard six pence per day, which amounted to a little over nine pound yearly.

Therefore it seems that to the wealthier inhabitants of Marseilles sixty shillings would have been a modest or even a small sum. As a matter of fact, "modest" (*modicus*) was the adjective used to describe such a sum in Marseilles about this time. The council of the city held, for example, that small claims actions (*cause modice*) of sixty shillings or less did not have to be initiated by using the costly written document (*libellus*).[10] For workmen like Petrus Guizo, however, a sum of sixty shillings might have represented something like one-quarter or even one-third of their yearly income. To Bondavid, a person whose fortune was on the order of several hundred pounds (see next chapter), a debt of sixty shillings would not have been very significant. His energetic defense of his claim could not therefore have been motivated by financial considerations alone. It would appear that we must look for other reasons, legal or political, to understand his actions in 1317.

Claiming Unpaid Debts in Medieval Marseilles

Bondavid was probably not particularly concerned when Laurentius did not pay his debt on time (assuming, again, that this was really what happened). Delays in repayments of debts must have been quite common. For the years 1430–1435 Professor Noël Coulet recently has published statistics showing that in Aix-en-Provence during this period more than 38 percent of loans required a delay of between seven and twelve months before being recovered, while 48.2 percent took years (two to twenty) to be resolved. Only 12 percent of the loans studied by Coulet were paid on time or in advance.[11] In Marseilles in Bondavid's time, patterns of nonpayment or of delay in recovering loans are not known to us; they may have been different, but not in a radical way. In any event, such delays would not have put a moneylender in a panicky mood, since legal actions for unpaid debts were well established in Marseilles. The city's statutes delineated a very detailed procedure: when an aggrieved moneylender sought to force the payment of a bad debt, he would submit the required documents to a judge, who in turn would issue an order for the debtor to appear in court.[12] If convinced by the evidence in the moneylender's submission, the judge would issue a judicial *mandamentum* ordering the debtor to pay off his debt within a given period of time.[13] For the first quarter of the fourteenth century, there are many hundreds of such *mandamenta* in Marseilles, a few dozen for each month. Bondavid and his father Abraham (when still alive) figure quite prominently in these documents; indeed, there are not many Jewish moneylenders who appear as often as they do. In the register of the court for 1310, Bondavid appears fourteen times and his father three—a frequency of more than once a month. An analysis of fourteen of seventeen of these *mandamenta* (three are undecipherable) indicates that on average the sum claimed was about one hundred shillings—considerably higher than Laurentius's sixty shillings,[14] as the following table shows.

Table 1
Analysis of 14 Mandamenta Issued in 1310 at the Instance
of Bondavid and His Father

Amount of money involved (in shillings)	No. of *mandamenta*	Total sum (in shillings)	Average
20s.-100s.	8	427s.	53s. 4d.
120s.-240s.	6	972s.	162s.
Totals	14	1399s.	99s. 11d.

For the following year, 1311, an analysis of the *mandamenta* gives basically the same results.[15] Bondavid has eight *mandamenta* to his name, his father four, with the exception that this time the average sum for the son is 63*s.* 8*d.*, for the father 35*s.* For that year (1311) we have over sixty *mandamenta* issued at the request of some twenty Jews of Marseilles. Of the fifty-five decipherable cases (five are illegible or unclear in content), twenty were done for members of the Marvani family, six for members of the Capelli family, four for Isaac de Apta, and the remaining thirteen for various other members of the Jewish community (one or two *mandamenta* each).

Table 2
Analysis of 55 Mandamenta Done in 1311
at the Instance of 19 Jews of Marseilles

Name	No of manda- menta	% of the 55 manda- menta	Sum	% of the sum	Average
Marvanus Marvani	10	18.2	839*s.*	18.73	83*s.* 10*d.*
Ferrerius Marvani	9	16.4	980*s.*	21.87	108*s.* 10*d.*
Ysacus Marvani	1	1.8	60*s.*	1.34	60*s.*
Bondavid de Draguiniano	8	14.5	509*s.*6*d.*	11.37	63*s.* 8*d.*
Abraham de Draguiniano	4	7.3	140*s.*	3.12	35*s.*
Astrugus Capelli	3	5.4	375*s.*	8.37	125*s.*
Isaac de Apta	4	7.3	275*s.*	6.14	68*s.* 9*d.*
11 other persons	13	23.6	1152*s.*	25.71	88*s.* 7*d.*
Totals	52	100	4480*s.* 6*d.*	100	80*s.* 5*d.*

As the table illustrates, only the Marvani family surpassed the "de Draguignanos" in seeking *mandamenta* from the court. It also makes clear that reclaiming an unpaid debt of sixty shillings was not a breathtaking adventure for Bondavid. The number of *mandamenta* he succeeded in obtaining in years previous to 1317 indicates that he may perhaps have been quite confident about a favorable outcome for his legal request.

By virtue of such a *mandamentum*, Bondavid could have asked the court to seize property belonging to the debtor in the event he should fail to produce the sum in question. Lists of such seizure orders by the courts and statements that creditors were "put in possession" of property (real estate in most cases) are to be found in the registers of Manosque by the second half of the thirteenth century.[16] There is little doubt that this practice was followed throughout the region and was quite effective. Failure to satisfy fully the creditor's demands in this way might entail the harsher measures of imprisonment or expulsion from the city. In Manosque, where a more lenient house arrest (*tenere hostagia*) seems to have prevailed, we find from 1243 onward legislation which established that "if someone will not pay his debt in the time given to him by the court . . . and he does not have property to offer, let him 'keep *hostagia*' at the decision of the judge."[17] As for expulsion, this city had an ordinance (quoted in a lawsuit in 1295)[18] that provided for a meeting (*colloquium*) between the court, the creditors, and the relatives of the debtor in question. "If they want [to pay back his debts], he will remain where he is. Otherwise he will be expelled from the city of Manosque and its territory, by the said court, until satisfaction is made to the creditor or creditors." Courts did not hesitate to put such legislation into practice. In Marseilles, in 1310, Isaac de Albanato was put into the royal prison at the instance of a fellow Jew, Isaac de Posqueriis. The reason: failure to repay a debt of sixty shillings.[19] A year before this, in Manosque, the Jew Fossonus was required to "keep *hostagia*" at the request of a Florentine moneylender of the city, Symon de Bayeco.[20] Raymundus de Fonte, a citizen of Manosque, was expelled "perpetually" from the city in 1295,[21] while Ebradus Gibosi, in 1289, who was "indebted to many creditors," was given the choice between keeping *hostagia* and being expelled and answered that "he prefers leaving the city of Manosque to keeping the said *hostagia*."[22]

Finally, Bondavid also could have turned to the court of the bishop of Marseilles. Paradoxical as it may seem, Jewish moneylenders—and other creditors as well—could obtain help from ecclesiastical courts in enforcing their loans. Professor Roger Aubenas discovered in the formulary letters of the courts of Aix and Marseilles of the fifteenth century cases in which Christian debtors were cited before the episcopal court, given a warning, and put under excommunication because of their failure to pay their Jewish creditors on time. In the eyes of the canon law, these debtors had broken their oath, taken before the notary of the court, when undertaking to pay their debt on time and thus became subject to ecclesiastical censure.[23] Thus in 1424 the ecclesiastical court of Arles excommunicated a certain Antoni Carbonells at the demand of his creditors, among whom were two Jews, Vidal Astruc and Salvet Marvani.[24] Evidence for Jewish victories in ecclesiastical courts can be found also in Spanish archives, as the following two examples suggest.[25] In the first, in a document issued in the Catalan city of Vich on 30 July 1321, we find the case of Elisendis de Abada, a Christian lady from the village of Tona, who is brought to the bishop's court by a Jew named Juceff Vitalis. At issue was a debt, probably a loan, but nothing is said about its amount and, naturally, no mention is made about what might have been principal or interest. Instead, the Jew asks that the church authorities compel his antagonist to respect her oath (*compellere ad observationem hujus juramenti*). Vitalis gets satisfaction for his demand: the document specifies that the lady will be properly warned and admonished to respect her oath (*juramentum*) and, if she still fails to come to terms with the Jew within ten days, she will have to appear in the court of the bishop of Vich. A second case comes from Toledo, the capital of Castile, where in 1340 we find a certain Alfonso Gonzalez Cervatos, who was actually excommunicated for not paying off a debt to Yucaf, son of "Rabi Yasaya," an inhabitant of Toledo, and to Alfonso Garcia. The document of the case, done on 24 April, shows him being absolved of the sentence, presumably after coming to terms with Yucaf.

More than thirty years before, this time again in Provence, "while the bells rang and the candles (in the church) were extinguished," an excommunication was pronounced against the heirs of Petrus Ebrari of Manosque for failing to pay a debt of 41s. 4d. to the Jew Mosse Anglicus, acting as administrator of the property of his deceased wife Bella.[26] Another case also recorded in Manosque was that of Raymundus de Fonte and his wife Raymunda, who were excommunicated by the court of the bishop of Sisteron at the request of Mosse of Grassa, a Jewish moneylender of Manosque.[27] The last example of this practice comes from a document issued in 1300, where a cleric named Johannes Floquerius, *rector ecclesiae de Grasauis*, is reported to have been brought to the court of the bishop of Pamiers, in the south of France, near the Spanish border, by the Jew David de Villaforti, inhabitant of Pamiers. At issue was the considerable sum of 37 1/2 pounds, which the Jew was unable to recover. The cleric was solemnly excommunicated and his case was handed to the "secular arm," as was the custom, when it became clear that he persisted in his obduracy.[28]

We are thus tempted to conclude that in the trial of Bondavid of Draguignan in 1317, on the surface, everything seemed to be in his favor: he obviously knew quite well how to make use of the judicial machinery, and he had the necessary documentation at hand. What chances did Laurentius have to convince the tribunal of his uprightness?

Retaining Promissory Notes: Suspicions against Moneylenders

Had the sixty shillings in contention been paid back, it would normally have been Laurentius, not Bondavid (as indicated above), who should have had in his possession the original deed issued on 11 April 1315 by the notary Guido Burgondionis. In this he would have followed a well-established procedure in the south of France, and elsewhere, which entitled the debtor to get back such promissory notes upon reimbursement. This unquestionably would have provided Laurentius with strong, almost undeniable proof for his claim. But the fact that he did not have the document, awkward as it must have been, did not necessarily put him in a desperate position: he still had a fair chance of winning his case. The reason? Moneylenders were notorious then for hanging on to promissory notes, even after repayment. They were suspected of manipulating customers into situations such as that in which, allegedly, Laurentius found himself in 1317.

Provençal legislation became increasingly explicit on the subject precisely at this time. In trying to combat these practices, lawmakers certainly had moneylenders in mind and had established procedures of termination of relationship between creditors and debtors. The *leges municipales* of Arles,[29] to quote legislation going back to the beginning of the thirteenth century, established that "every creditor, once the payment of a debt is made to him, has to return the instrument or letter of the debt immediately after the payment has been made to him—and the debtor, in presence of witnesses, must ask to get back the instrument or the letter." As for a situation where the creditor takes the oath that he cannot provide this instrument or letter, the *leges* would see to it that "he has to make at his own expense an instrument concerning the payment made to him." Similarly, more than a hundred years later, when the prelates of Provence on 3 September 1337 passed legislation regarding the restitution of the instrument of a debt once the debt was paid, they did no more than reiterate the thirteenth-century law: "no creditor, Christian or Jewish, once his debt is fully satisfied, can keep in his possession such an instrument or mandate of debt already paid, against the will of the debtor, unless it may be that the creditor, for some cautionary measure, might wish to keep in his possession the instrument or mandate canceled and torn in the presence of the persons making payment."[30] Then, in a manner similar to the old statutes of Arles, the prelates insisted "that if he wishes to keep in his possession such a canceled and torn instrument or mandate—such as is already stated—he has to make a receipt (*Ypoteca*) for it, if asked to do so." Provençal state legislation of 6 May 1306,[31] entitled "concerning the return of instrument after part of the debt was paid," which attempted to combat "frauds done by usurers," went even further and insisted that a moneylender did not have the right to hold on to the original deed even if only part of the debt was paid off.[32] In practice it meant that the moneylender had to issue a new document: "Whoever will hold on to such an instrument," the legislation of 1306 continued, "will have to pay the court ten shillings (one-half pound) for each pound mentioned in the document."

In Marseilles, less than four years before our trial took place, the city council addressed itself to this problem (23 June 1313). Fraudulent creditors—"not only Jews but also bad Christians," according to the council—were keeping their customers' previous written promises to pay while negotiating new contracts with these same customers—contracts that included the amount of the old debt. These creditors would thus hope to trap their customers into repaying the same debt twice. The council hoped to halt this dishonest practice.[33]

What was deemed by the debtors and their protectors to be fraudulent practice was termed by the moneylenders a precautionary measure. When Mosse Anglicus of Manosque was accused in 1311 *tamquam falsus creditor* of keeping "fraudulently and deceitfully" a deed belonging to a woman named Alasacia Rogerie, he declared that he did so because six shillings were still unpaid out of a total of nine shillings and two and a half measures of wheat.[34] Bontosius Mercerii, inhabitant of the same city, held (in 1304) the deeds given to him by the Jew Leonetus, son of Salomon; although Mercerii was completely reimbursed, he kept the document because, as he said in court, he was not yet indemnified for expenses that arose from the handling of the debt.[35] Matters would become even more complicated when a moneylender died and his heirs, not knowing the state of a particular transaction, would ask debtors to make good an alleged debt paper "twenty or even twenty-five years old" found in the deceased person's archives.[36]

As for debtors, there is little doubt that in southern France they were quite knowledgeable in the ways of recovering their deeds. To quote some examples, in Manosque in June 1296, we find that Beniounus de Sarrato, a poor Jew, confronted his rich relative Rossa, the widow of Abraham of Grasse,[37] regarding some deeds. Beniounus claimed that he had paid back "five or six years ago" all loans received from Abraham. He therefore asked the court to cancel the deeds, provide him with a quitclaim, or order Rossa to return them. In 1309, in Manosque, a villager from the neighboring village of Montfuron sued the Jew Botinus.[38] According to him, the Jew continued to hold a great number of documents after the villager had paid off what he owed. During the litigation a local statute is mentioned to the effect that "no person shall keep in his possession instruments of debt of which he has already been fully satisfied."[39]

About ten years earlier,[40] we find that Petrus Pellegrini of Manosque asked Bella, the wife of Mosse Anglicus, to return an instrument regarding a debt of one hundred shillings. Bella, who insisted that she had not yet been fully repaid, was nevertheless ready to accede to this request. The agreement was recorded in the court of Manosque by the notary Petrus Dalmati. Our fourth example comes from Languedoc in 1302,[41] where the barley merchant (*ordearius*) Johannes Blegerii brought to court in Montpellier one Salomon de Lunello. Johannes claimed that he had repaid this Jewish moneylender a debt of thirteen pounds eleven years ago and now wanted the court to see to it that he got his document back. Although he made this statement under oath, the judge, P. de Tornameira, turned down his claim.

Why did Laurentius not request also the return of his deed, or as an alternative insist that a quitclaim be issued? The many thousands of quitclaims registered with the notaries of Provence or in the roll of the Exchequer in England (in which country they were known as *starra*, from the Hebrew *shetar*,[42]) bear witness to the legal tenacity of debtors.[43] But it did cost money to issue these documents, and in cases where small sums of money were involved, people quite naturally tried to avoid the expense. Instead, and in a way that was quite typical of that period, debtors tended to rely on the good faith of the creditor, occasionally buttressed by the presence of witnesses. "Please come and watch me repay some *denarii* to Bonometus" was the request made by an inhabitant of Manosque to one of his fellow townsmen.[44] Even very large transactions might have no firmer basis than the relationship of trust between the parties. In 1432 the abbot of Saint-Victor in Marseilles obtained a loan of no less than 250 florins from two Jews of Aix "without any public or private document (*scripta*) but by good faith."[45]

But such good-faith agreements had their drawbacks. An agreement reached in Saignon near Apt sometimes before 1290 at the instance of the local bailiff proved to be more fragile than the partners anticipated.[46] According to Jacob Poncii, the debtor, the Jew Bonisac agreed to return all the documents he had concerning this transaction and to see to it that all such documents were declared null and void. Twenty years later, Bonisac's grandson, Segnoretus son of Grayssoni, sued Jacob Poncii at the royal court of Apt, for the sum of four pounds and five shillings. Because no written document (*instrumentum acquitationis*) was taken at the time of the original compromise, the court had to open in February and March of 1308 an inquest inviting the two original *compromisarii*, who were still alive, to attempt to discover the truth by recourse to their memories. As in so many other cases, we do not know what the outcome of this inquest was.

As for the presence of witnesses, they were not always an absolute safeguard. Huga Briona argued in 1322 before the court of Marseilles that she had paid the brothers Isaac and Benivas Corderii the sum of thirty shillings.[47] The first witness for Huga, Beatrix Lombarda—her associate— said that she had been present on all three occasions and was able to quote what she said was the exact speech of Huga when actually handing Vitalis ten shillings paid at that time. The second witness, a maid named Ersmessendis Angelaria, who was sent especially by her master to be present on the occasion, was also very favorable to Huga. Although both witnesses agreed as to the currency in which the money was paid—*oboli* silver—the judge was not satisfied with the evidence. In his decision (which we have in the register in what seems to be his own handwriting) he dismissed Huga's evidence on technical grounds.

Bertrandus Ricardii, according to documents from Marseilles in early 1322, tried yet another cautionary measure.[48] On the occasion of paying forty shillings on account of a larger sum of 15 1/2 pounds to Isaac Corderii (*Isaquus* in the manuscript), he asked one of the witnesses, Hugo Gasgneti, a skinner, to write a statement just for the sake of security. Written in Provençal, this short note indicates a familiarity with legal technique and language on the part of a member of the working class of Marseilles. It translates as follows: "Be it known to all who are present and future, that Isaac Cordier admitted and recognized that he got and received from Sir Bertran Ricart forty 'Royal' shillings which he paid him on account of a debt of £15 10s. that the aforesaid Bertrandus owes the said Isaac Cordier, as it is stated in a *mandamentum* done in presence of Rostaing Blanquier and Pascal

Fabian."[49] Later, when the case came before the court of Marseilles, this man presented the receipt (*apodixa*). It was recorded as part of his testimony, but nothing in the register assures us that the court accepted it as valid evidence.

Another instance in which a debtor found himself without the appropriate document is recorded by the court of Marseilles in January 1328. The representative is quoted as having addressed the creditor in the following solemn manner:[50] "As representative of Raymond Gasqueti, my son-in-law, I ask you, Vinella Marvani, Jew, whether Raymond owes you anything on account of any debts." The document then switches to the indirect account: "The Jew answered on the spot that he was fully satisfied of all the debts of which Raymond was indebted to him up to the present day." Not content with this verbal declaration (if we are to believe the witness), Raymond's agent next saw to it that a written statement was produced: "These being said, Hugo, in the name of Raymond, asked the notary Petrus Geraudi to write down the confession and the acquittal just made by the Jew. Petrus answered, "I will write this, and now hold it as if it were written!" In spite of all these cautionary steps and the formal tone of the proceedings, something must have gone wrong, for when he was sued by Vinellas in the court for the sum of seventy-five shillings, it seems that Raymond did not produce the quitclaim that was allegedly received by the notary (which would have simplified things considerably) but had to make use of the sort of oral testimonies previously described. We know enough about the legal standards employed by the judges of Provence at this time to speculate that they would not have been easily convinced by such evidence.

Returning to the case of Laurentius and Bondavid, it seems that Laurentius would have had a difficult time proving his case without being able to produce a quitclaim or canceled deed. His case was not completely hopeless, however. It was open to him to claim that he had not bothered to obtain a document or that the presence of many witnesses was unnecessary in light of the legislation authorizing "probation through one eyewitness." As we have just seen, the courts were quite used to situations where debtors were lax about obtaining the proper documents or had been misled by dishonest creditors who reassured them that such documents were not needed. Therefore Bondavid, who had the original deed in his hands, was still not free of the menace of being declared a "false creditor" by the court for having requested a double repayment of the same debt.

"Faulty Creditor" and His Punishment

If a moneylender was found guilty *tamquam falsus creditor*,[51] he was in a quite serious situation. As the following five criminal procedures—mostly from Manosque—show, authorities were persistent and severe when dealing with this kind of fraud. When the Jew Sperandeus, acting on behalf of Astes, another member of the Manosque *justaria*, made a claim in mid-1286 for a payment of twenty shillings, the debtor, Guillelmus Furnerus of neighboring Vols, had a quitclaim in his possession.[52] This document—*pactum de non petendo nec ulterius requirendo*—which was given on 8 June 1277 by Bonafos of Manosque (probably Astes's deceased husband) was now presented to the court and recorded in its register. It was Sperandeus who then found himself in deep trouble. The court of Manosque opened an inquest against him, ensuring that Astes was also implicated. That both Jews were probably subjected to heavy fines if found guilty (we do not have the results of this case) can be deduced safely from evidence from similar situations. In Manosque again[53] at the end of 1309, we find that the Jew Fossonos Caracause was accused by another Jew, Leonetus, of asking in a "fraudulent manner" for full repayment of a loan, while in truth Fossonos had received on its account one measure (*sestarius*) of wheat. Fossonus answered in his defense that there had been a misunderstanding. He claimed that his granddaughter, Astrugona, who actually got the wheat, had failed to report this to him. Found guilty by the court, he was fined twenty shillings, which was three to five times the value of the wheat.

Also in 1309, the court of Manosque had to deal with a claim for seven shillings made by a Christian citizen, Vincencius Maurelli.[54] The debtor, Abraham de Castellana, a prominent member of the local Jewish community, refused to pay on grounds that the debt had already been paid. When called to court, Vincencius admitted that such was the case and was presumably punished. Another Manosque Jew, Segnoretus Sartor, refused at the beginning of a trial in 1310 to admit that he had received from a fellow Jew, Botinus, a repayment of five shillings.[55] About two and a half weeks later, when the court returned to the issue, "his memory came back to him" (*rediens ad memoriam*) and he admitted his guilt. One wonders if a threat of torture or a promise of benign treatment helped to trigger his memory. As it was proved that his demand for the five shillings was done *fraudulenter et dolose*, he was fined ten shillings— double the amount of the debt.

In Toulon, ten years alter, we find the Jew Vidalon Barba in a similar situation.[56] A claim that he was owed twenty-four shillings by a citizen of that city named Meillina turned out to be untrue. Though his claim was made by a person who possibly was his agent, Vidalon was now deemed one who had submitted false evidence to the court (*falsa subjectione*) and was fined sixty shillings—two and a half times the amount he had asked for originally. Annoyed by the judgment, Vidalon decided to turn to the Court of Appeal of Provence and asked the judge of the lower court to supply him with the necessary documentation concerning the decision. The judge agreed to this request; the judge's written approval of Vidalon's request is the only record we have of this legal drama.[57]

Bondavid, in 1317, came very close to being declared a "false creditor." Laurentius, in the *interrogatoria* he presented to the witnesses, asked them to inform the court whether Bondavid had ever been accused of being a *falsus creditor* by a court. "Then let them be asked," Laurentius continued, "whether they know of any other occasion when Bondavid asked to be paid a second time for a debt that was already repaid" and "whether an inquiry was carried out against him on that occasion in a court and whether he was found guilty by the court on that occasion." Fortunately for Bondavid, he did not have any previous history of financial wrongdoing—at least none of the witnesses mentioned any previous misdeeds.[58]

But Bondavid must have realized that he might have to face a similar accusation in the future. It was therefore important for him to establish official recognition of his unblemished record, and to obtain this, he had to pass through a tiresome legal procedure. It is little wonder, then, that he rejected an offer by his adversary to settle out of court. We learn about this from the testimony of the last witness, Bonetus Aurioli, Laurentius's father-in-law (III B7 fol. 49r°–v°). Bonetus revealed to the court how he went to see his son-in-law at home and, after admonishing him for creating the legal imbroglio, notified him of his intention to reach an agreement with Bondavid. Laurentius's reaction was that "he does not believe he owes anything to the aforesaid Bondavid" and that he was not ready to compromise. Nevertheless, Bonetus went to Bondavid. In court he told how he would have liked to satisfy Bondavid with a payment of forty shillings— probably the amount of the principal of the loan. Bonetus insisted twice that Bondavid's consent to this offer would be a "very great favor." But Bondavid refused and insisted on full payment. Not only would any other arrangement have blemished his credibility, but also an admission that part of the sixty shillings was due to him as usury would have put him in a worse situation than that of a false creditor—that of "manifestus usurarius."

"Usurers" and "Manifest Usurers" in the Medieval City

Among Laurentius's *interrogatoria* was one that asked whether Bondavid lent money on usurious terms. Although the subject matter of the lawsuit was fraud, not usury, any past condemnation for usury would have harmed considerably the Jew's standing in court. In order to understand this issue, we must first clarify the legal meaning of *usurarius* in that period.

Although at that time hundreds of loans were given out every day in Marseilles, none of the documents explicitly specified the amount of capital or interest. To evade prohibitions against usury—and to enable these documents to be considered in ecclesiastical courts—the parties would pretend that a certain sum was being given out, the same sum to be returned on a specified date. No trace of interest, that is to say usury, could be found on the documents issued by the notaries. If, however, a court could be persuaded absolutely that a rate of interest had been charged, the creditor would be labeled *usurarius*. As an initial punishment, he would not be entitled to that part of the sum which constituted the interest.

Creditors were not allowed carelessness in playing this game. The wise course was never to admit usury—not even orally. Mordacais (Mordechai) Sacerloti, who faced the court of Marseilles in 1322, learned a harsh lesson about carelessness in talking openly.[59] At issue was a loan of fifteen pounds, for which Mordacais provided the judge with the necessary documentation. The representative of the debtor maintained that the actual loan was only for ten pounds—the other five being the usurious interest charge. Then, in what seems to have been a dramatic point in the proceedings, a special witness was brought to testify to the truth of the debtor's defense. This witness, Hugo Michaelis, claimed that he was present when Mordacais admitted orally that the five pounds was usury.[60] This occurred when Mordacais's clients protested the high interest rate that they had to pay. Mordacais reportedly replied, "Do I have to lend my money for nothing?" and continued, "As for these hundred shillings of interest—I have received nothing down to this moment."[61] This outburst put Mordacais in a difficult situation. Threatened with being branded a usurer, he had to find ways to refute his adversary's testimony. In a statement of a defense, he brought a series of procedural claims against Hugo Michaelis rather than trying to argue to the substance of the testimony.

But the authorities did not have to wait for mistakes like Mordacais's to prosecute for usury. About 1309 an edict of Charles II and his son Robert set forth a method by which the status of a *usurarius* could be established.[62] The procedure required the testimony of four honest witnesses and, once declared *usurarius* by the court, the moneylender would be forced to pay back all money acquired usuriously. He would be subject to a heavy fine as well; for each pound (twenty shillings) of usury he would be fined one hundred shillings, that is to say five times the value of the usury.

To be declared a "usurer" was one thing, to be proclaimed a "manifest usurer" quite another. Pope Innocent IV defined a manifest usurer simply as an individual convicted by a court of law.[63] Synodal legislation passed at Cologne in 1280 elaborated upon this definition in holding that manifest usurers were "those of whom it has been clearly established through a decision or a confession in a court of law or through the obviousness of a matter that cannot be concealed by any evasion."[64] This definition was repeated in London in 1287, Aquileia in 1339, and elsewhere.[65] In practical terms, a manifest usurer was in a more difficult legal position than a mere usurer. The famous canon lawyer Bernard of Parma (d. 1266) held that whereas a judicial examination was needed to determine whether one acted as a "mere usurer," no such procedure was needed for a "manifest usurer," and penalties could be applied automatically.[66]

Whether a distinction between "mere" and "manifest" usurers was made in Marseilles in the first quarter of the fourteenth century is difficult to ascertain. What can be established with relative ease is that the procedure for discovering "usurers," as outlined in the edict of Charles II and his son Robert, was indeed put into practice. This is clear, first, from an inquest carried out in October 1328 against Bondavid of Draguignan himself.[67] At this date, Bondavid brought to court a weaver named Johannes Bartholome de Sex Furnis (also called "de Ponte"), suing to collect from him a loan of ten pounds. In his statement of defense, Johannes argued that "it is common knowledge (*fama*) in the city of Marseilles that the aforesaid Bondavid lends his money in usury."[68] A witness, Rostagnus Juliani, "heard some people of Marseilles, whose name he cannot remember himself, saying that the aforesaid Bondavid received and had from them usury." Other witnesses specified amounts of usury: Rostagnus Juliani received from Bondavid four measures (*emine*) of wheat but had to repay six; Johannes de Ponte got a loan of one florin, but in the notarial charter a sum of one and a half florins was recorded; a third witness, Stephanus Giraudi, "laborer," had to pay twenty shillings (one pound) "usury" three years earlier. Obviously, this information, if officially recognized by the court, would have made Bondavid in 1328 subject to the legislation mentioned above.

Another instance in which the legislation of 1309 was applied concerns Mordacais Sacerloti, the Marseilles moneylender mentioned earlier. This time, about 1320, he had to face a charge of being, as the text puts it, "a very wicked usurer or, at all events, a public one" (*usurarius pessimus vel saltim publicus*).[69] The argument was raised in a lawsuit in which the repayment of £4 9s. was in contention. The debtor, Jacoba, the widow of Guillelmus Ymberti, a wheat broker (*corratorius*), promised to bring proof that "the aforesaid Mordechai is a deceitful man, tricky and one of the worst usurers, and at all events a public usurer who has the habit of lending his money for usury, and of demanding usury of usuries, and of committing many frauds, making people admit to him that they owe him more than they actually do. And [that] there is about all this cry and talk (*vox et fama*) in the city of Marseilles among many praiseworthy people who know him." To Mordechai's great relief, it seems that only one of the three witnesses Jacoba brought was ready to subscribe to such a statement, and in fact that witness quoted Jacoba herself as one of her informants concerning Mordechai. The other two witnesses "knew nothing."

Bondavid's Insistence on a Trial

Still, the tactic that Jacoba chose—so similar to that of the previous two cases—could have labeled Mordacais a "usurer." And for Mordacais Sacerloti, as for Bondavid in 1328, to become subject to the legislation of 1309 must have been a very worrisome, perhaps even frightening, possibility. As in the past, therefore, a moneylender first had to ensure that no trace of the real terms of the transaction could be detected. But now this was not enough. Professionals had to see to it that they were not confirmed by any court as "usurers." At stake was not only a particular claim that they might lose in a specific lawsuit: to be declared usurer under the law of 1309 would have marked the beginning of a very uncertain and risky career—or even the end of one. From their point of view, therefore, it was vital to have a clean record.

It is little wonder, then, that when Bondavid was approached with an offer to come to terms with his adversary on amicable terms outside the court, he rejected it. His next step was to go to court. In all probability, the sixty shillings at that point were of secondary importance. It was in Bondavid's best interest to go through the whole procedure in order to be cleared by the court. He would not allow on his record an undecided case of fraudulent practice.

2

The Adversaries: Two Marseilles Portraits

Of the three major participants in the legal proceedings of 1317 in Marseilles—the creditor Bondavid, the debtor Laurentius and the witness Petrus Guizo—it is the personality of Petrus which receives most attention in the record of the trial. While the court documents enable us to piece together significant parts of Petrus Guizo's life story, almost nothing in our sources casts light on the personal background of the debtor Laurentius Girardi. The only one who spoke about him in court was his father-in-law, who simply reported that Laurentius rejected any compromise with Bondavid. We know also that Laurentius shared quarters with Petrus Guizo, his cousin, after Petrus lost his wife. The data concerning Bondavid are more abundant, simply because all twenty-four witnesses knew him and were ready to testify about his good reputation in the community. Yet because their testimony focuses on this single issue, their statements did not reveal much about the less-public aspects of his life, for instance his personal features or his religious concerns. In order to gain a fuller understanding of his life—or that of any other individual involved in this lawsuit—we must turn to other documents in the Provençal archives. Let us first examine whatever can be found about the personal history of the moneylender Bondavid, and then ask what the court documents disclose about the life of his adversary, Petrus.

Bondavid of Draguinian: A Wealthy Jew of Marseilles

We might hope to learn something of Bondavid in contemporary Hebrew writings, but in this respect the record is disappointing. During Bondavid's lifetime the Jews of Provence were in the midst of a Hebrew cultural renaissance, which had begun in the region some 150 years earlier.[1] Jewish intellectuals in Provence, like their colleagues in Spain and Italy, were greatly interested in medicine, mathematics, astronomy, and philosophy in general. Books in these disciplines written by Arabic and Latin authors were translated into Hebrew—which was their language of culture—and then commented on by Jewish scholars. Some of the most famous Jewish Provençal intellectuals, notably Levi ben Gershom (Gersonides), Yedaya ha-Penini Bedresi, and Yosef ibn Kaspi, were all contemporaries of Bondavid—yet his name is not mentioned in their writings. The study of Jewish law (Halakah) was not at all neglected in these regions. Distinguished Talmudic scholars settled in such communities as Marseilles, Manosque, Aix, Avignon, and Tarascon; they attracted students and formed academies (*yeshivot*) where the study of Halakah was cultivated. For the beginning of the fourteenth century we have a list of the rabbinic authorities of southern France compiled by Kalonymos ben Kalonymos of Arles, who later distinguished himself as a translator from the Arabic and who was as well a fine Hebrew writer and sharp satirist.[2] Kalonymos, who in 1305 was seeking on both sides of the Rhône a teacher with whom he could study, noted some thirteen Provençal Talmud scholars under whose guidance a young Provençal Jew could learn the religious law. In Kalonymos's guide to the luminaries of Provence—a private epistle which he called "The Scroll of the Minor Apology"—two authorities in Marseilles are actually mentioned. The first was Aaron ha-Hedri, who appears as "Aaron de Camera" in the archival documents of the years 1305–1323. The other was Avraham of Aix, who, according to Kalonymos, was in 1305 a newcomer in the city and who can be easily identified as Abraham de Aquis. Abraham appears in the documents of Marseilles for the first quarter of the fourteenth century as a neighbor and business associate of Aaron de Camera.[3] Bondavid, a young man in 1305, does not appear in the account of Kalonymos.

Some seventy years later, in 1372, another Provençal scholar, Isaac son of Juda de Lates, compiled a work called *Sha'arei Zion* (Gates of Zion), in which the writings of all the Jewish scholars and sages of the past were presented. The literary history of the Jews of southern France to his own time was covered in the last pages of this book.[4] Again, Bondavid's name does not appear. His absence from both Kalonymos's report and the *Sha'arei Zion* as well as from all other surviving Hebrew literary documents leads one to conclude that in all probability Bondavid did not play a leading role in the Hebrew intellectual life of his time.

When we turn, however, to the *mandamenta* and other court records of Marseilles, and to the city's notarial registers, we are able to learn quite a lot about his position in the business community. The archives of Marseilles have preserved dozens of such notarial registers and court records, and many of these reveal information about Bondavid, who along with his father and his financial agents figures prominently, in fact almost daily. The vast majority of the documents concern his activities as merchant and moneylender. Some, however, deal with other more personal aspects of his life.

By far the most important document concerning the Draguignan family is the will of the father, Abraham, which was drawn up in Marseilles on 10 May 1316.[5] What we have, though, is not the final version of the document but rather a draft of the will hastily written by the notary Petrus Elsiarii in one of his registers. It is, no doubt, Abraham's last will, for in documents of 12 August 1316 he is already referred to as the "deceased Abraham." On that date Bondavid allocated his father's estate to the heirs.[6]

Three generations of the Draguignan family appear in Abraham's will. The first includes the testator, Abraham, his wife Astes, his sister Dulcia, and his brother (possibly half-brother) Moses Artays (or "Artinus") son of Bonjusas. The second generation is that of Bondavid and includes also his sister Bonadona and his first cousin Blanca. The third was the generation of Abraham's grandchildren. Only Bondavid's children are mentioned— these being his daughters Bellaneta and Regina and his son Abramet, who interestingly enough was named after his grandfather when the grandfather was still living. Similarly Bondavid's own grandson carried the name Bondavinus Abrahami, as shown in a document of 1358.[7] Bondavid's daughter Regina was married already to a certain Salomon of Beaucaire when Abraham's will was made, in 1316.

```
Dulcia*** Moses Artinus****Abraham = Astes
filia Davini                      *
de Massilia                       *
     *                            *
     *              ******************
Blanca            *               *
                  *               *
                  *               *
    Dulcia = Bondavid             *
          *           Bonadona = Profachius Deulocrescas
          *
          *
          *
***************************************************************
*                        *                              *
*                        *                              *
*                        *                              *
Abramet                Regina (d. 1321)             Bellaneta
*                      = Salomon Bellicadro         = Davidus
*                                                   Boneti de
*                                                   Avignon
*
Bondavinus Abrahami [?]
```

It is interesting that Profachius Deulocrescas, Bonadona's husband, who since 1302 was designated as *gener* (that is, son-in-law) to Abraham, was given the title "father-in-law" (*socer*) to Bondavid in a document of 1316.[8] If this was really the case (and we do not have simply a mistake on the part of the notary), then we may imagine a rather unusual family relationship—yet still possible in Jewish law—in which Bondavid's brother-in-law was also the father of his wife. This was much more possible, if we consider the young age of marriage in the Jewish communities of the time. That Regineta, Bondavid's daughter, was married already in 1316 may have been, too, the result of such early marriage. We notice at all events that the names of both her and her husband Salamonetus are given in the diminutive "etus" and "eta."[9]

These twelve persons must have been all the close relatives that Abraham had in Marseilles. That we have here a case of a quite narrow family structure is confirmed by closer examination of the two households fully represented in the family genealogy, namely those of Abraham and Bondavid. In the first, we find only two children; in the second, only three.

Such a small family was not exceptional in the Jewish society of the time, as a most interesting document from the city of Aix-en-Provence shows.[10] In the summer of 1341 Aix established a list of Jewish households for the part of the city known as "the city of the count," a list that gives us the number of members of each household. Since 1,199 persons lived in the other 202 Jewish houses, a rather high average of almost six persons per household, close to 30 percent of the Jewish population of Aix lived in extended households, or one might say "clans," of 10 persons or more. The largest of these clans was that of Leo of Moustiers, where 30 persons were counted. Next in size was the household of Isaac de Costello with 23 persons. The Dulcini family, who were very important in the economic life of Aix as well as in community politics, were divided into 3 households. Yet this type of extended family represented less than 13 percent of the households on the list (26 cases out of 202), while another 44 of the households (21 percent) counted 7–9 persons. And in more than half of the households — 107 of 202 (53 percent) — the family size was much smaller: 3–4 persons per household in 28 cases, 5 persons in 35 cases, and 6 persons in 19 cases. In addition, we have 21 instances of 2 persons per household and 4 instances of single-member households. Overall, 5 persons per household was the most common situation.

What was true for Aix in 1341 was in all probability also true for the neighboring Jewish community of fourteenth-century Marseilles. Although we do not have such detailed demographics for the Jews of that city, one might imagine that such Marseillais Jewish families as the Marvani or the Corderii, families who were most likely long established in Marseilles, were equivalent to the clans of the Dulcinis or Costellos of Aix. Equally, we may surmise that in most cases the Jewish households of Marseilles averaged between five and six persons. If such was the case, the Draguignans, with their family of five to nine persons, would fit well into the prevailing pattern. One reason for their small family size may have been a possible recent arrival in Marseilles: Abraham does not appear in notarial documents of the 1280s or the 1290s. We first find him (and his son) in the year 1306.[11] From the "silence" itself of the documents one obviously cannot draw too daring a conclusion; but when coupled with the narrow family structure we have just observed, the "silence" may be of significance.

Bondavid was most likely between thirty and thirty-five years old during the trial of 1316–1317. He may have been younger than thirty but certainly was no more than forty. Not only were both his parents still living in May 1316, but also his children were so young at that date as to oblige the grandfather to take special precautions in the will: Abraham wanted to ensure that Bondavid understood that he was only to administer the inheritance and in no way to consider himself owner of it. To this circumstantial evidence we may add now that a notarial act of October 1311 stated that Bondavid was over twenty-five years old at that time. Although the notary included this piece of information to stress Bondavid's legal competence to sell a vineyard in his possession, we may have here a reference to his exact age.[12]

By today's standards, Bondavid, even if in his mid-thirties, would be considered young or at most middle-aged. Bernard Gordon, the renowned early-fourteenth-century medical professor of Montpellier, also considered a man between fourteen and thirty-five to be middle-aged—to be in his prime. Beyond that came old age.[13] As it happened, Bondavid in 1316 had at least forty-two years of life ahead of him.[14]

From his father's will of 1316 we see that Bondavid was the principal heir of a wealthy man. Abraham bequeathed 500 pounds to his son and assigned another 200 pounds in precious objects and currency to his daughter, grandchildren, and other relatives. We learn also that Abraham possessed a house, a vineyard, and a variety of gold and silver belts—as well as diamond rings and sapphires. He was probably worth more than that. Though not a prodigious sum at that time, 500 pounds should be considered a very respectable estate, in light of the figures for wages and salaries presented in the previous chapter. To compare, the Jews of Marseilles, numbering some 300–400 households, paid to the count of Provence in total an annual tax of some

100 pounds, while the sum of the *tallia judeorum* collected from all of Provençal Jewry—some 4,000 households—was 2,000 pounds.[15]

The Draguignan family's wealth seems to have come, for the most part, from moneylending, but they were also active in the maritime commerce of the city, mostly with the island of Sardinia and the city of Genoa. There is almost no notarial register for the period from 1310 to 1320 in which Abraham or Bondavid does not appear. In fact, the volume of business Abraham and Bondavid did was large enough for them to employ financial agents, or factors. The list of Bondavid's factors between 1307 and 1327 includes seven names: Bonjuzas de Borriano, Mosse Calhi, Bonetus de Perpinhano, Mosse Profaig, Salves de Sancto Egidio, Vidas (also Vidonus) de Alesto, Saomonetus Alibi, and the above-mentioned Profachius Deulocrescas. Crescas Pesat was his agent in 1338.[16] Some of the factors may also have been family relations; others seem to have been salaried professional agents.[17] Mosse Calhi, for instance, was an agent of other moneylenders in Marseilles.[18] In one of the descriptions of Bondavid given in court by Petrus Vitalis (IIIB7, fol. 36v), he is seen walking near the harbor of Marseilles, accompanied by a man "of his house" who was ready to receive orders. His own business register (surely written in Hebrew) has disappeared. To judge from the register of another Jewish moneylender, Heliot of Vesoul, compiled in this period, a businessman of Bondavid's caliber would issue dozens of loans every week and at times every day.[19]

Bondavid and his father were not the only Jews in Marseilles to conduct business on such a large scale. Aaron de Camera, merchant and scholar, and his wife Astes—to cite just one example— also appear prominently in the *mandamenta* and other notarial registers. Astes herself was a very active businesswoman and employed many agents just as Bondavid and his father did. Her staff included Deulosal de Apta, Bonetus de Vivariis, Abraham de Bellicadro, Habramonus de Montepessulano, Astrugus de Nemanso, and Bonafos de Cezerista.[20] As early as 1305, the young Kalonymos noticed the considerable volume of de Camera's family business and claimed that the time needed to administer Aaron's vast fortune prevented him from giving attention to his students.

Whether Bondavid was the richest Jew in Marseilles is impossible to say. In the records of Jewish business activity in Marseilles in our period his name is certainly the most prominent. The late Edouard Baratier, in his history of the commerce of medieval Marseilles, presents Bondavid as the most typical Jewish entrepreneur of the fourteenth century.[21]

One would expect that a man of Bondavid's wealth and standing would, like members of the Marvani family, become heavily involved in Jewish public affairs. In the urban life of the period the wealthy—Jewish and non-Jewish alike—almost always held the positions of power.[22] Surprisingly, neither Abraham nor Bondavid appears on the surviving lists of Marseilles communal leaders. Perhaps this is a consequence of the scarcity of documents; as relative newcomers to the city, however, the two may not yet have made their way into the established ranks of Jewish administration.

From the archives we may glean other pieces of information concerning Bondavid and his family. In May 1322, Bondavid's wife, Dulcia, was involved in a controversy over a silver belt (*zona*) that was allegedly put up as collateral for a loan.[23] Once the claimant, Johannes Montaneys, admitted his mistake, Dulcia insisted on having his statement recorded officially by a notary. Her agent in this affair was Profachius Deulocrescas. Three years later, Dulcia appeared again in court, this time concerning a claim by her to a certain house, "near the Jewish fountain" (*prope fontem judaicum*).[24] Children and grandchildren also appear occasionally. For example, we gather from a document of 1322 that Bondavid's daughter Regina, who had married one Salomonetus son of Crescas de Bellicadro sometimes around 1316, died in 1321. In 1322 Bondavid registered a statement "for the record" (*ad aeternam rei memoriam*) concerning the death of his daughter, apparently in connection with a legal quarrel over property and inheritance.[25] On another occasion, in his later years (1358), Bondavid made a gift of the rent of some houses he owned in the Marseilles *jusataria* to his grandson Bondavinus Abramati, "in recognition of services and favors" done by the young man for his grandfather.[26] Other pieces of information are, in all likelihood, to be found in the archives. These may enlighten us one day as to the exact date of his death, which occurred sometime between 1352 and 1363 (documents of April 1363 and June of that year show that his heirs were already in dispute with the Hopital du Saint-Esprit of Marseilles); they may also help us to determine whether the two Jewish doctors of the 1380s and 1390s, Abraham Bondavin and Bonjudas Bondavin, were descendants of our Bondavid.[27]

We may conclude, then, that by 1317 Bondavid was a man in the prime of his life. Probably he belonged to a family only recently arrived in Marseilles but was surrounded by a growing number of relatives and agents. As heir to a successful moneylender, he was just beginning a career as the head of a prosperous establishment and was already a visible, indeed outstanding, figure in his city. What we do not know is to what extent the lawsuit we are considering was related to any of these facts. Most importantly, is it possible that somebody was trying to undermine his position and, through him, that of all other Jewish moneylenders? Remember that this suit came only three years after the city issued severe regulations against the fraudulent use of documents by moneylenders.[28] Unfortunately, this question will have to remain unanswered.

A "Laborer": Petrus Guizo

Apart from the fact that they were approximately of the same age, Bondavid and his adversary Petrus Guizo (*alias dictus Gernaudi, alias Deven*) could not have been more unlike. While we know little more than the names of most of the Marseilles *laboratores* who appear in the records, and have little understanding of that term,[29] Petrus emerges in the trial of 1316–1317 as a fully visible personality. To demolish Petrus's testimony, Bondavid or his lawyer presented the court with a letter "to disprove the statement or the testimony of Petrus Guizo," which exposed Petrus's allegedly vile behavior and his "illicit life." This tactic was used quite frequently by medieval lawyers, not only in a Mediterranean metropolis like Marseilles but also in a modest inland urban center like Manosque, as the evidence of trial proceedings in the town indicates. Thus, in a letter of defense presented in 1302 by Rostagnus Pandulfi, we have as one of the four articles the following statement: "Firstly, Rostagnus intends to prove in his defense, as in the aforesaid, that Pontius Michaelis, a witness accepted by the court, is a vile man of vile condition, a thief, and that he was condemned last year for theft in the village of Montfuron, as well as in Volx, by the court of Sir Guillelmus de Villemus."[30] In another letter of defense presented by Petrus Arnulfi to the court of Manosque on 30 November 1291, which bears amazing resemblance to what we shall see as Bondavid's strategy, the hostile witness Guillelmus Gaufridus is described as follows: "He is a vile man, staying in taverns, eating and drinking and doing other vile things and playing dice."[31] A special article (*titulus*) insists "that the said Guillelmus is an *infamis* and that he was such at the time he delivered his testimony." In 1327 the court of Manosque acquitted a certain Bernandus Assis in a case of manslaughter, taking into account that while the accused enjoyed good reputation in the city, his accuser was known to be "a man of bad fame . . . who is accustomed to frequent bad society."[32] Bondavid's lawyers were thus deploying a common strategy when trying to destroy the credibility of their opponent.

From the testimonies assembled by the tribunal of Marseilles, we learn quite a lot about Petrus Guizo—his age, his physical traits, and his character. The first of the witnesses, Hugo Bernardi, told the court that Petrus was "a man of big stature around the age of thirty" (III B7, fol. 10v). Another witness, Raymundus Dagulla (fol. 15r), stated that Petrus was only in his twenties (*vicenarius vel circa*) and that he had been married to Laurentius Girardi's cousin, whose name is not given. Most of the witnesses agreed that it was upon the death of Petrus's wife ("six years ago" according to Hugo Bernardi, "four" and "three" according to others) that he entered upon his long decline. However, Johannes Cuponi, the third witness, connected the personal crisis to the death of Petrus's father "five years ago" (fol. 12r). Perhaps this decline was due to the grief of a widowed husband, or perhaps it began when his father-in-law, Betrandus Feda, deprived Petrus of the property brought by the now dead wife into the marriage. In any event, Petrus, like so many other *laboratores* of his time, was once an owner of modest properties: a vineyard, a garden, and shares in two houses. He was on the way to becoming a respected citizen but fell prey to misfortune from which he could not recover.[33] His poverty became a liability in the court, his adversaries proposing to identify him as an impoverished rascal.[34] About the time of his financial debacle, he moved to the house of his cousin Laurentius Girardi.

This close association between the two probably would have made Laurentius's word suspect in court. But Bondavid did not use this fact as a weapon against Laurentius. Instead, he hoped to win the case by describing him, first, as a mischief-making "barfly" (*homo tabernarius*), one who spent most of his evenings in the company of people of ill repute, *cum ribaldis . . . bastaysiis et inhonestis mulieribus* (fol. 17r), to quote the witness Jacob de Sancta Maria. To acquire the name of *homo tabernarius* (fol. 12r), as we have just seen, must have been a severe blow to the reputation of any medieval citizen and would have made him *infamis*. In Boccaccio's *Decameron*, an evil rascal who is doomed to hell is described as a frequenter of taverns and other places of ill repute.[35] Bondavid emphasized this fact in a document submitted to the court: Petrus "spends his time very frequently in taverns and other illicit and dishonest places, drinking with drunkards and other treacherous and suspicious persons . . . playing away his gown in dice . . . indulging often and always in drinking wine . . . drinking and destroying himself."

With only minor variations, all the witnesses whose testimonies were recorded by the court agreed to this description of Petrus. At the request of the notary, they all cited names of the innkeepers (*tabernarii*) at whose establishments Petrus Guizo was seen at one time or another.[36] In these places, it was said, Petrus would devote hours to heavy drinking in the company of suspicious people. Drunk (Raymundus de Alesto was the only one to state this in court), Petrus would mumble incomprehensible words and would not know what he said or did (fol. 11r). Yet Bondavid did not choose the drunkenness itself as the central argument for undermining Petrus's credibility. Instead, he emphasized another of Petrus's addictions: gambling, and especially "playing at dice" (*ludere ad taxillos*), which was considered at that time a criminal offense. Indeed, throughout the High Middle Ages, public authorities attempted to eradicate this vice. In Arles, toward the end of the twelfth century, the commune tried to fight gambling by fining those caught gambling in taverns after the evening ringing of the commune's bell.[37] In Salon, one hundred years later, there was no such time consideration: neither in the daytime nor at night was it permissible to play at dice or "eysagnetos." Those found gambling during the day had to pay a two-and-a-half-shilling fine, while those caught at night would be forced to pay double that.[38] Clearly the repetition of such legislation over the years and in many communities indicated the limited success of attempts to halt gambling. And yet the authorities would not give up. For example, on a register from Arles for the years 1305–1306 where fines and punishments were recorded by the *clavarius* according to categories of crime, we discover a page dedicated to fines received from those guilty of having played *ad taxillos*: "The following persons were discovered playing dice against the regulation."[39] Of the six persons sentenced, five were fined five shillings each and one was fined two and a half shillings. Marking Petrus as a gambler would thus have identified him as a criminal, and surely an *infamis*.

Moreover, Bondavid's witnesses told the court of Marseilles that Petrus was the worst possible sort of gambler, namely a compulsive one. The proverbial expression "to lose one's shirt" (*ludere raubam suam*) when gambling is found in medieval writings, both Christian and Jewish. Thus, to note a Hebrew text, Rabbi Yom Tob ben Abraham Ishbili (c. 1250–1330), a Spanish Talmudist, received petitions from women who were seeking a divorce from their gambling husbands: these husbands had, proverbially, gambled away their shirts.[40] Petrus Guizo—if we can rely on these court proceedings of Marseilles—actually lost his shirt to gambling, and on more than one occasion. While Hugo Bernardi said that he had heard only that Petrus bet on his donkey "last year" (fol. 10v), five other witnesses satisfied the court's curiosity as to the particulars of the gambling. One of them told of a game in which Petrus bet on *quandam tunicam et quandam (uchiam?)* (fol. 12r), while another mentioned *unicam tunicam et calligas* (fol. 15r) that were lost, insisting that this occurred on several occasions and not only once. Jacob de Sancta Maria testified that he had definitely seen Petrus twice gambling away his shirt and that he had heard about many more instances.

Those gamblers, desperate to rid themselves of the habit, would go so far as to register a formal affidavit with a notary which obliged them to put an end to, or at least to limit, their passion for gambling. Several dozen such documents have been found in the notarial registers of southern France. For instance, Richard Emery discovered in Perpignan an act of 1415 in which the Jewish doctor promised his brother not to gamble in any game in which money was involved.[41] However, this doctor limited the time span of his obligation to the period "from now until the coming feast of St. Michael," that is to say, about five months. In 1438 in Tarascon, the Jewish master Jacob de Lunello made a similar undertaking but without a time limit: If he broke his pledge, Jacob was required to pay a fine of thirty-five florins, five of which would go to the *accusator*, the person who would inform on him.[42] Jacob, like all others who recorded deeds with a notary, was obliged to swear an oath, on the Bible, that he would uphold the undertaking. Anyone who broke such an oath was therefore held to be a perjurer.

Petrus Guizo was one of those who made such a contract. In his case we know in great detail under what conditions it was done and what its legal implications were. At a certain point "two or three years ago," as we are told by Raymundus de Alesto (fol. 11r), Petrus was asked by three of his friends to register a commitment with a notary, promising "not to play any more." Perhaps because this was during Lent, as Guillelmus Stephani later told the court, Petrus was persuaded and went on to register with the notary Hugo de Giminis (fol. 19r). In the document he allegedly obligated himself not to play dice "for the rest of his life" (19r). He also agreed to pay a fine of sixty shillings to the three friends who induced him to make the commitment in the event he should break his promise. As might have been expected, he was unable to withstand the temptation and later gambled on several occasions. Guillelmus Stephani testified in the court that Petrus had paid one of them *nomine dicte pene*, handing over to him a trumpet (*unam tubam*).

This was the pivotal point. Bondavid obviously wanted to prove that Petrus, by breaking his oath against gambling, became a perjurer and that consequently his testimony should not be considered. In this, Bondavid was again making use of a quite common tactic in the courts of his day. Thus an identical line was taken in Manosque by a Jewish doctor, Master Isaac son of Resplanda, in the year 1298: accused of botching an abortion, the doctor, in his defense, claimed that one of the witnesses against him, a lady, was a *perjura* at the time she gave her testimony, as she had failed to pay on time a debt owed under contract to an Italian moneylender.[43] In another instance, in April of that same year, Garsendis, the wife of P. Escaforii of Manosque, intended to prove "that Stephanus Ganelli and Raymunda his wife are and were perjurers at the time they brought testimony against her; moreover, that Raymunda and her husband are such persons who in law could not bring testimony against Garsenda."[44] If Petrus had been recognized as *perjurus* by the court, his testimony also would have lost all its value.

It is probably significant that the testimony of a *perjurus* was disqualified not only by Roman law[45] but also—and repeatedly—by contemporary church legislation. During the century that preceded our trial in Marseilles, the church seems to have been particularly concerned with the problem and conceived an elaborate set of rules to combat this form of perjury. The Council of Narbonne of 1227 declared that "whoever will be discovered to have manifestly transgressed his oath will be denounced publicly as *perjurus* in the church." Excommunication was the final sanction for the unrepentant *perjurus*.[46] This legislation was repeated and elaborated upon by successive church assemblies (e.g., Valencia in 1248, Tarragona in 1292).[47] Relevant to Bondavid's defense was the decision promulgated in 1299 by the Synod of Asne,[48] which stated that perjurers, because they had become infamous, should be forbidden to offer testimony or to do any other legal act. This was reiterated four years later, in 1303, by the assembly of Nogaro (France): "All those who will be manifestly shown to have transgressed their oath will be declared not fit for testimony and infamous, and not to be admitted to testimony on any other legal act."[49] What chance would Petrus—*homo tabernarius*, compulsive gambler, *infamis* and now *perjurus*—have to see his word receive credence in any court?

The Credibility of the Depositions concerning the Two Men

Did the judge of Marseilles appreciate the course that Bondavid and his lawyers pursued? How decisive was all this in the eyes of the judge? Petrus was, it must be remembered, the only person who testified against Bondavid. As we have already noticed, the judges knew very well the relative value of the information brought before them and quite understandably looked for supplementary evidence to make their decision: this is the reason for the *interrogatoria* that they authorized the opposite side to initiate. They wanted also to be clear about semantics and to ensure that the witnesses knew, for example, the meaning of *fama*. Their standard question therefore would be *quid est fama?* In 1319, in a case of burglary of a draper's shop in Marseilles,[50] the judge went even further by asking *Quid est fama et quid sit vox, et in quo different, et quot persone faciunt famam ad singulum?* One of the witnesses in the lawsuit of 1319 refused to answer, "as he is a simple layman" (*cum sit simplex laycus*)! Another declined because "he is a layman and does not know such subtleties" (*quod laycus est et nescit talia subtilia*). Only two ventured an answer.

In Bondavid's trial of 1317, the witnesses all took up the challenge and attempted to define *fama*. One of them, Bartholomeo de Geminis, provided the following definition: "When good or evil is said between people about some person or another" (*Illud quando inter gentes dicitur bonum vel malum alicuius persone—*fol. 16v). Three others founded their definition on the alleged conduct of Petrus himself. Thus, the notary was provided with a definition of an *infamis* as "one who devotes himself to drinking and to excessive gambling and does not keep his oath," or "one who drinks, plays in taverns, and swears," *sicut iste Petrus* (fol. 16r). According to Raymundus Alesto, an *infamis* was "one who conducts his life in a bad manner and does not keep his oath."

But the condemnation of Petrus by the witnesses was by no means unanimous. Bartholomeo de Geminis would not agree that what was said about Petrus was enough to make him an *infamis*. In his opinion, and that of Raymundus Dagulla, no one should be stigmatized, unless "a thief and a robber" (*fur, latro, et deraubator—*15v), epithets not attributed to Petrus by any of the witnesses. In 1311, in another legal dispute in Marseilles, an accused, Guillelmus Tortella, was described as "a belligerent man who fights with every person with whom he comes in contact."[51] It is noteworthy that such a statement was not made against Petrus. Nor do we have much insistence on possible sexual misbehavior, although Petrus frequented taverns where pub-

lic women must have been at hand. Likewise Johannes Caponi
—supported by Raymundus Dagulla—went so far as to assert
(fols. 12r–v) that Petrus never hurt a soul nor quarreled with anyone "with the exception of the present strife with Bondavid."
This last statement, a bright spot in an otherwise rather dark and
grim portrait, was underlined in our manuscript by what seems
to have been a medieval hand, possibly the hand of the judge
when reading the notary's report.

The earnestness of the testimonies may be gathered from the
witnesses' frankness about the side they favored in this litigation.
One of the frequent questions put by medieval courts to a witness
sought to discover whom he wanted to see as the victor. In Bondavid's trial, three of the five whose testimonies we have seen in
this chapter answered: "He who is right should win!" which was
perhaps the formulaic response; it occurs, in any event, in many
other trials.[52] The other two replied frankly that it was the Christian they favored. And yet all five exposed the same fundamental
facts about Petrus's misbehavior: they all agreed on his gambling
and staying in taverns. They all knew about incidents when, carried away, he played for his shirt. They were all also aware of
the notarial obligation that he signed and ultimately did not keep.
There is no reason, therefore, for us not to accept these as "hard
facts." Similarly, we may safely accept the other essentials of his
biography brought out in court, namely the story of his marriage,
of the death of his wife, and of the effect it had on his subsequent
decline.

That one may extract solid historical information from such
subjective documents should encourage us when approaching the
data about Bondavid's character and behavior. In his case, the
picture is all too bright, shiny, and rosy; yet we would do a dis-
service to history by automatically rejecting it because of its apparent one-sidedness. Rather, we shall need to search the evidence, using all the lenses and filters available, to get a picture
as focused and reliable as possible.

3

Opposition to Jewish Moneylending: Between Theology and Politics

In the following two chapters I argue that medieval people sometimes found ways to talk about Jewish moneylenders in an appreciative manner. Therefore to describe their attitude toward these moneylenders as one of permanent and unvarying opposition would be, so will run my argument, to oversimplify facts. I do not intend, however, to reverse completely the picture. Like all students of European society in the High Middle Ages, I recognize that in many instances—in most of them, as a matter of fact—we encounter members of these societies expressing harsh reservation toward the profession of moneylenders (Christian or Jewish) as well as sentiments of rejection and even of disgust. In a recent study, *La bourse et la vie* (Paris, 1986) (*Your Money or Your Life: Economy and Religion in the Middle Ages* in the English translation by Patricia Ranum [New York, 1988]), Jacques Le Goff, the famous French historian, reminds us that even if theologians and canon lawyers of the thirteenth century did distinguish between lucrative "usury" and compensatory "interest," and even if some of them found excuses for lenders to make profit on loans on some specific occasion, the overall attitude remained negative, based on a long Christian tradition of condemnation. The study of the short moralistic stories (*exempla*) of this century did not reveal to Le Goff any redeeming feature in the portraits of usurers he was able to discover. Neither were the preachers, who used these moralistic *exempla* for their sermons to their Christian folk, ready to admit any productive role usury might have had in economic life.

Theologians, Lawyers, and Jewish Moneylending

And yet people of the thirteenth century, still enjoying the fruits of a spectacular expansion of the economy, did develop—as we shall see in chapter 4—a very elaborate credit system: there was no way for its members, rich and poor alike, to forgo the services of moneylenders. The real dilemma was therefore how to bridge the gap between the ethics preached by the church and the economic reality displayed daily in the marketplace. An elegant solution, on the surface of it, seemed to be to abandon moneylending to the Jews. For the Jews the biblical injunction "unto foreigner thou mayst lend upon interest but unto thy brother thou shalt not lend" (Deuteronomy 23:20–21) meant a patent permission to lend to Christians, who did not fall, in their eyes, into the category of "brothers."[1] Literate people and well experienced in commerce and in other aspects of monetary economy, Jews seemed to be thus an ideal choice for a society looking for ways to benefit from the advantage of a credit system and at the same time to hang on to the values of economic innocence. Emperor Frederick II of Sicily, taking into account social demand for credit facilities (*necessitas hominum* in his language), put it in very clear terms—unequivocal, as one would expect—in his *Liber Augustalis* of 1231: while usury was forbidden as a "state crime" (*crimen publicum*) to Christians, Jews were exempted and openly permitted to engage in practicing it because, as he put it, "it cannot be maintained that usury is illicit for them. The divine law does not prohibit it. They are not under the law established by the most blessed Fathers."[2]

With the advance of the thirteenth century, however, Jewish moneylenders came more and more under pressure. Restrictive legislation on the part of civil or ecclesiastical authorities—combined with bitter opprobrium on the part of people permanently under the pressure of time to discharge their debts—made the lives of moneylenders intolerable. For influential thinkers like William of Auxerre (1160–1229), Albert the Great (1206–1280), and Albert's disciple Thomas Aquinas (c. 1225–1274), the involvement of Jews in moneylending was unacceptable in principle, not only because they would urge the Jews to extend the notion of fraternity but also, and mostly, because they saw in usury a sin by its very nature (*secundum se*) independent of the question of who was committing it (*secundum quid*).[3] Already in the eleventh century, theologians like Anselm of Canterbury (c. 1033–1109) and his disciples Anselm of Lucca (c. 1036–1086) equated usury with theft and burglary, while others, in the ensuing period, used analogies of perjury, adultery, and homicide.[4] "Usury is the root of all vices" was a maxim quoted to King Edward the Confessor during his stay in France with the royal court.[5] Later medieval rulers and their subjects found new ways to express their reservations, as we shall see shortly. Usurers were insistently and repeatedly declared enemies of the society.

There was also a limit to the ability of Christian thinkers of the High Middle Ages to introduce exceptions to the general interdiction of usury. Admittedly, Gratian's definition of usury as any gain stemming from a loan, no matter how small—"whatever is taken for a loan beyond the principal" (c. 14, 9, 3, c. 4)—was not compatible with reality even when it was pronounced, some time about the year 1140. The need to come to terms with the realities of the market therefore drove Parisian theologians like Robert de Curzon (d. 1219) and his master Peter Cantor (d. 1197) to consider, though not necessarily approve, the possibility of indemnifying a lender for forfeit he was losing (*lucrum cessans*) and for damages he would suffer (*damnum emergens*) when lending money.[6] Even Thomas Aquinas, half a century later, was bound to accept such compensations as legitimate, considering that "human laws leave certain sins unpunished because of the imperfection of man." He was driven to admit the existence of usury, choosing nevertheless very carefully his words: "This is why civil legislation has at times to consider usury: not because usury is thought to be just, but so as not to hinder the advantages that so many derive from it."[7] Yet this was as far as he was ready to go—he or any other medieval canonist or theologian of authority. It is true that the Provençal Franciscan Petrus Joannis Olivi (c. 1248–1298), in his *Treatise about Purchases and Sales, Usuries, and Restitution*, engaged in very sober discussions concerning the commerciability of time and the productivity of money, a very daring inquiry that could have caused a breakthrough in the economic thinking of the Scholastics.[8] But even he, in the final analysis, was far from legitimating usury and was not ready to take away the stigma attached to it. Times were not yet ripe for a divorce between economic thought and moral theology.

Quite the contrary, in fact: the first quarter of the fourteenth century witnessed a reversal of the trend and a more vigorous ecclesiastical opposition to usury. The Council of Vienne (1311–1312) in a famous decree, *Ex gravi*, equated any legitimation of usury with heresy and threatened deviants with appropriate punishment.[9] "If anyone falls into the error of believing and affirming that it is not a sin to practice usury," declared the prelates, "we decree that he be punished as a heretic, and we strictly command the ordinaries of the localities and the inquisitors to proceed against those suspected of such errors in the same way as they would proceed against those accused publicly or suspected of heresy." This injunction, by the way, was aimed not only at Christians but also at Jews: a lawsuit in Manosque in 1342 shows us a Jew named Simon David accused in the court of that city for having maintained publicly that "usury is not a sin."[10] It is quite possible also that Mordacais Sacerloti of Marseilles, mentioned above, got into trouble in 1322 for openly mentioning the interest he was expecting on a loan, precisely because people of Marseilles showed in that year exceptional reverence to the decree of Vienne.

As we are about to see in some detail, Jews' involvement in moneylending made them subject to restrictive legislation and to hostile political actions, not to mention social opprobrium and physical violence. Things went from bad to worse in the thirteenth century. But medieval people were never absolutely clear about what they wanted to do in the matter of usury. The Christian ideology of economic modesty was well and alive, indeed; and the wish to relieve those oppressed by usurers was no doubt genuine. But at the turn of the fourteenth century, individuals probably could not have imagined a world without a widespread and well-entrenched credit system. Governments, as we are about to see, learned how to gain profits from the activity of Jewish moneylenders; this fact added to the confusion. The hesitations, reversals, and changes of mind about to be described in this chapter contributed to a general frustration as well as to actual suffering of both parties: the lenders and the borrowers.

Violent Opposition, Private and Collective

Antagonism toward Jewish moneylenders extended beyond the intellectual world into popular language and even to acts of violence. *Judaizare*, a word used in the early Middle Ages to denote heresies within the church, was now applied in the High Middle Ages to the realm of economic life and was equivalent to *usurare*. Also for such German preachers and poets of the period as Berthold of Regensburg, Walter von der Vogelweide, and Ulrich of Liechtenstein, the word *usurer* was synonymous with *Jew*. Similar statements were made in France by Foulque de Neuilly and Robert de Courçon, for whom the Jew was the archusurer.[11] In 1500 and 1502 in Venice the Senate describes the Jews as "grossly enjoying usury from the blood of our Christian subjects" and "enrich[ing] themselves through Christian blood."[12] Similarly, we are in a position to compile a virtual catalog of expressions to attack Jewish usury that were in use in Marseilles on the eve of the expulsion of the Jews from Provence: "fraud or usury," "the most detestable," "a great malice," "damned usuries," "fraud abuse and malice," and "disturbances and molestations."[13]

As could be expected, at times individuals could not contain themselves and would express their animosity not only verbally but also physically. The court records of Manosque reveal such instances where violence is displayed in connection with moneylending. On 3 January 1276, Joseph de Alesto, one of the leaders of the Jewish community in the city, was wounded in the face after refusing to hand back pledge given to him by a debtor.[14] Simon de Criclada, who came to Manosque after having been forced to leave England during the general expulsion of the Jews in 1290, rejected in 1312 a debtor's offer to satisfy a debt of fifteen shillings with a payment of ten shillings. This customer became violent and called Simon "soyra saguentes," which apparently meant "menstruating pig" ("soyra" could also mean prostitute). At this heated confrontation both parties threatened to use their knives and there was physical violence.[15] In October 1341, the moneylender Jacob de Baherias met in the street one Matheldus Cocellere and asked for a repayment of a debt. Matheldus, who claimed to have paid the money already, struck Jacob with his hand and pulled out his sword. Jacob escaped "as best he could and ran through the streets to the court (of the city)."[16] In another incident, it was the Jew Creisonus, son of Jacob of Chartres, who put his hand to his sword during an argument concerning a loan. A notary present at the time prevented bloodshed.[17]

At times, Jewish moneylenders were also victims of collective violence. On 12 March 1488, in Florence, the famous Bernardino da Feltre preached in Florence a sermon against usury. As a result, an angry mob attacked the Jewish bank named *Vacca* and threatened the life of the owner, Manuele de Bonavito. Only intervention by the authorities prevented a disaster.[18] Three hundred years earlier, in northern England, the Jews of the city of York were not so lucky.[19] According to the chronicler William of Newburgh, the well-known attack of 1 March 1190, which led to the murder and suicide of most members of the community, was planned by members of the nobility who owed money to the Jews. William reported that "many of the province of York plotted against the Jews, not being able to suffer their opulence when they themselves were in need. . . . The leaders of this daring plan were some of the nobles indebted to the impious usurers in large sums, some of whom, having given up their estates to them for the money they had received, were now oppressed by great want. Some bound by their own sureties were pressed by the exactors of the treasury to satisfy the royal usurers."[20] After describing the horrors of that night, the chronicler revealed the motive of the perpetrators: "When the slaughter was over, the conspirators immediately went to the cathedral and caused the terrified guardians, with violent threats, to hand over the records of debts placed there by which the Christians were oppressed by the royal Jewish usurers, and thereupon destroyed these records of profane avarice in the middle of the church with the sacred fire to release both themselves and many others."[21]

Similar scenes repeated themselves in many places in Europe during the Black Death of 1348–1349. Many believed that the Jews had created the pestilence, and as a result Jewish quarters were attacked by fear-stricken crowds. But even in these circumstances the populace was intent on destroying notarial records and other evidence of indebtedness, as Pope Clement IV noted in a bull of 2 October 1348.[22] In the city of Erfurt, the local chronicler had little doubt about the motives of the rioters: "I think that at the root of their [the Jews'] disaster were the huge, infinite sums of money which barons and knights, citizens and peasants owed them."[23]

Debtors Cry For Help: The Role of Public Authorities

The outbreak of collective violence as in Florence, York, and Erfurt was, however, rare in the Middle Ages. As a rule, people would appeal in their distress to the existing institutions, civil or ecclesiastical. Franciscus Ricolf, an inhabitant of Majorca, who found himself in 1312 succumbing to the burden of a huge debt to the Jews, was one of those who appealed for help. In his letter to King Sancho, he revealed that he had by then paid the Jews 8,600 shillings, the end result of usurious interest rates charged on an originally modest sum.[24] Franciscus Ricolf protested that he had "to live out of his work and agriculture" and saw no light at the end of the tunnel. He appealed for help and asked the king to appoint an arbitrator "who will recognize such a fraud and malice on the part of the Jews."

Thirty years later, a document made in the mountainous county of the Dauphiné, reveals more than two dozen such financial horror stories. On 27 November 1342 the inhabitants of the parishes of Rivoire and Epinouze, in the Viennois, crushed under their heavy indebtedness—to Lombards mostly, but also to Jews—put on record the stories of their plight. We learn from the document, published recently by Frédéric Chartrain,[25] that, for example, on a loan of ten shillings *tournois* he had contracted thirty years before with the Lombards of the neighboring Moras (today Moras in Valloire, département of Drôme), Guillelmus Berthelani paid no less than three hundred florins (= 360 shillings), a disastrous burden that reduced him to poverty and put him on charity—him who was one of the better born (*de melioribus*) in the region. At one and the same time, Guillelmus was indebted to several Jews of Moras. To quote another example, Stephanonus Sonnerii of Epinouze started with a loan of six shillings *tournois* from the Lombards: it cost him, during the years, in cash and in grain, three and a half florins (= forty-two shillings) and he was still owing, in 1342, eighteen shillings *tournois*. Johannes Ferlays, Johannes Perrerii, Guillelmus Arpanini, and many other individuals—probably all or most family heads of these communities—were trapped hopelessly in a similar bind. Indeed the communities (*universitates*) themselves, acting as corporate collectivities, were not in a better situation. A loan of four pounds taken by the councillors of Epinouze cost them no less than thirty-three pounds; by the time they recorded their complaints they still owed the Italian moneylender thirty-six pounds. Another loan they took, this time of ten pounds, devoured twenty pounds while twenty-eight others were still outstanding. Squeezed and probably demolished by such a disastrous state of affairs, they negotiated in Grenoble in the autumn of 1342 the following agreement with the dauphin Humbert II: All loans will be handled by the authorities and probably canceled by decree. In return, the inhabitants will pay an annual tax of 5 percent on all their belongings and possessions to the dauphin.

The authors of *Le songe du vergier* (*The Dream of the Shepherd*), a political treatise written in France about the year 1373, knew about similar incidents and even ventured an overall assessment of hopeless indebtedness in France in their generation. "I know a person who borrowed fourteen francs from a Jew," declared a cleric in chapter 163 of the work.[26] The narrator continued to note that the unfortunate debtor had "paid back for it in terms of principal and interest (*usures*) fourteen hundred francs and is not yet acquitted!" The anonymous writer was certain that "if somebody will care to inquire diligently, he will surely find in the kingdom of France fifty thousand persons who were disinherited or brought to poverty because of the damned (*feault*) Jews." These figures were presented to illustrate the author's contention that the Jewish moneylenders "bring such a poverty upon Christians and that once a Christian is in their hands, he can hardly escape them and, as a matter of fact, would never be able to acquit himself."[27] People certainly were looking for help.

It was no doubt to such situations that the famous Canon 67 *Quanto amplius* of the Fourth Lateran Council (CorpIurCan X.5.19.18) of November 1215 must have referred, when it mourned the fact that "the more Christian religion is restrained in the exaction of interest, so much more does the knavery of the Jews in this matter increase, so that in a short time they exhaust the wealth of Christians."[28] The prelates assembled in the Lateran Palace showed themselves therefore resolved to go beyond complaints and see to it that excessive usury be eliminated so as "to provide for Christians in this matter, lest they be burdened excessively by the Jews." But by the very mentioning of "immoderate usury" (and not simply "usury") they recognized implicitly that they could not stand any more behind the canon-law definition given by Gratian. At the same time, their commitment to the *Decretum* prevented them from stating explicitly what would have been considered by them as a "moderate" or acceptable rate of interest. Would it have been 20 percent, or more, or less? This evasion contributed, as we shall see, to the ineffectiveness of this decree.

The legislation of the Lateran Council was reiterated and elaborated upon by ensuing provincial synods and councils throughout the thirteenth century. The assemblies of Narbonne (1227) and Béziers (1246)[29] included *Quanto amplius* in their ordinances and succeeded even in simplifying its wording and in sharpening its formulation. As for sanctions, it was made clear that any collaboration (*participatio*) with Jewish moneylenders should be forbidden and that such Christians who overlooked the interdict would be excommunicated. Two other church assemblies, that of Albi in 1254 and that of Montpellier in 1258, although not restating *Quanto amplius*, went to further extremes.[30] Albi decreed that no judge would compel Christians to pay back interest, while

Montpellier wanted the Jewish moneylender to declare under oath which part of his claim represented the principal and which the interest. It goes without saying that he could then only claim the principal.

However, all of this conciliar legislation suffered from the same weakness as the original Lateran decree. They would not, and could not, spell out exactly what moderate usury was. This might be also the reason for the brief life-span of *Quanto amplius*. The Council of Vienna in 1267 seems to be the last one to refer to *grave et immoderate usure* taken by Jews.[31] Not that preoccupation with it was very extensive even then: Vienna and Poitiers, along with Narbonne in 1227 and Béziers in 1246, were the only synods to include *Quanto amplius* among their ordinances. Although enactments concerning the Jews from the Lateran Council in 1215, such as the wearing of a special badge, the exclusion from public office, and the confinement to their homes during Holy Week, were repeated time and again by councils like those of Oxford (1222), Castres (1231), Arles (1235), Valencia (1248), and Mainz, the usury provision was not mentioned.[32] This was not from negligence. Usurers and usury received ample attention throughout that period, as can be seen from the legislation of both councils of Lyon in 1245 and 1274, or—to refer at random to two fourteenth-century assemblies—in Padua and Aquileia, both held in 1339.[33] But this legislation had Christian usurers in mind. The legislation threatened them with excommunication, deprived them of the sacraments, embarrassed them with public denunciations in churches, and so forth. It had nothing to do with *Quanto amplius*.[34]

In surveying the legislation assembled by Mansi in volumes 23–25 of his *Sacrorum Conciliorum Nova et Amplissima Collectio*, one gathers that at some point the church took its hands off the question of Jews and moneylending. It might have been as a result of the vagueness of *Quanto amplius* itself, as mentioned previously. However, far more important, in my view, is the fact that the withdrawal of the church coincides with the arrival on the scene of the civil authorities. Saint Louis of France—according to the testimony of William Carnot—made it clear that while Christian usurers fell under the jurisdiction of the church, it belonged to him to deal with the Jewish moneylenders, because "they are subjugated to me under the yoke of servitude."[35] And in fact there is marked evidence that, with the advance of the thirteenth century, it is the civil authorities who lead the fight against Jewish moneylending.

Civil authorities could do a great deal more in the way of restricting Jewish moneylending. They could set a moderate rate of interest and enforce it by threatening usurers with confiscation of their property, incarceration, or even straightforward expulsion. Aggrieved individuals and indeed entire communities were aware of this, and at times—as we have just seen—would apply what we would today call political pressure to persuade the authorities to intervene in their favor. On some occasions, communities would specify which rate of interest was acceptable to them. Thus the syndics of the city of Saint-Symphorien-d'Ozon submitted to the council of the Dauphiné, on 13 December 1408, a petition wherein they bitterly complained that the Jewish moneylenders, in charging compound interest and engaging in other illicit practices, were bringing financial ruin to the region: "Many citizens (*homines*) and subjects of the Dauphiné have already become destitute because of the usurious practices, and many are about to become so if nothing is provided by your excellency."[36] They demanded therefore that an official rate of interest be established, "four to five (= 25 percent) and this for the whole year"—a rate lower than that charged by the Jews. They also insisted that Jews should not receive "usury on usury."

Medieval authorities would indeed establish an official "moderate" rate of interest, either in response to such demands or on their own initiative. This rate varied from place to place and depended on local conditions. In Provence a rate of "five pennies per month per pound" (= 25 percent) was established by legislation in 1245. This rate still held there in 1453, while in Marseilles the rate was even lower, three pennies per month per pound.[37] In Aragon, a document issued by King James I in 1228 fixed it at a level of 20 percent, and this rate was insisted upon in ensuing legislation of 1229, 1240, and 1251.[38] Indeed, the Jews of Montpellier were assured in 1262 that so long as their profit did not exceed four pennies per month per pound (20 percent), they could not be accused of usury.[39] In England in the twelfth century, by contrast, where economic conditions must have been different, the rate was much higher: two pennies per week per pound (= 43 ⅓ percent) was legal.[40] The same rate was decreed in Konstanz in Germany in 1383.[41] Also in Germany, Bishop Otto of Minden, in 1270, considered a rate of four pennies per week as perfectly "moderate,"[42] and such was also the case in Burgundy in the late fourteenth century, where a rate of 86⅓ percent was charged.[43] In remote eastern parts of Europe, the going rates were reported to have been even higher.[44]

Establishing an official rate of interest was just one of the measures taken by civil authorities. To avoid exponential growth of debts, compound interest was universally prohibited and a time limit was set beyond which a loan would automatically cease to carry interest or even cease to be valid.[45] In 1234 and again in 1245, Prince Raymond Bérenger of Provence established that once three years had passed from the first repayment of an installment on a debt, it would become void, unless the creditor had entered a claim in court within a year and a half after this first repayment.[46] In Majorca, King Pedro IV simply decreed in February 1356, at the request of the inhabitants of the island, a time limit of five years for Jews to claim their loans.[47] Aiming at a possible uncontrolled growth of interest, King Alfonso X of Castile, Bérenger's younger contemporary, decreed that "no further interest be charged on a debt after the interest amounts to as much as the capital." A similar law—almost identical in wording—was enacted about the same time in Montpellier and in the neighboring city of Alais.[48]

Another common device to reduce some of the citizens' ire was an occasional or partial reduction of debts. The case of the inhabitants of Rivoire and Epinouze, quoted above, was certainly not an isolated one. In France such monarchs as Philip Augustus and Saint Louis occasionally reduced debts by a third, following a pattern established by Popes Eugenius III and Innocent III, who, in order to encourage people to take the cross, promised to reduce their debts.[49] Saint Louis, presumably, offered these reductions out of piety, while Philip insisted that part of the confiscated moneys be channeled into royal coffers.[50] The legality of such action was based on the emergence of the concept of "Jewish serfdom" and the designation of Jews (since the 1230s at least) as "serfs of the royal chamber" (servi camere nostre), a status that meant (to quote Emperor Louis of Bavaria in 1343) that "you, the Jews, your bodies—as well as all your property—belong to us and to the empire, and we can do, to you, treat you, and handle you the way we want and consider proper."[51]

Scaling down of debts was a way to gain popularity, as is seen from the detailed agreements struck in 1385 and again in 1390 in Germany between King Wenzel and the representatives of thirty-seven German cities.[52] The monarchy, while struggling with the nobility, was trying to win over the support of the Burghers. Rebels like Simon de Montfort in England in the 1260s[53] and Enrique of Trastamara in Castille a hundred years later would have recourse to the same ploy. Trastamara, who became King Enrique II, canceled in 1377 one-third of the debts owed to Jews at the request of the Cortes of Burgos. The reason for the request was the devastating effects of recent weather on the region's economy.[54]

With such measures at their disposal, it seems that civil authorities were most effective in attacking usury on a case-by-case basis. Not only did many leading medieval statesmen realize, as we shall see in the next chapter, that a country's economy could not develop without the availability of a credit system, but some of the rulers discovered, perhaps to their amazement, that legal campaigns against usurers generated an unexpected source of income. As monarchs of the High and later Middle Ages were chronically short of income, some of them found themselves thus caught in a trap of their own making. The following discussion of Aragon and France will, it is hoped, demonstrate this point.

Aragon: The Government's Commitment to the Official Rate of Interest

Many of the Aragonese documents of the High Middle Ages indicate how and by what means the monarchy originally tried to defend the official rate of interest of 20 percent it established. Restatements of the law of 1228 were issued periodically, and Jewish communities of the kingdom were expected to pronounce an excommunication (*Altama vel Nigduy*) against all possible transgressors. The ceremony took place—as a royal writ of

October 1313 mentions—every year about the first of October in the presence of all the members of the community. The Jews stood up, holding the Torah scrolls in their hands, while the royal ordinance was read out.[55] There even exists a notarial confirmation in Latin that such a ceremony took place on 10 October 1383, when a group of nine Jews from Tarragona took such an oath, while in Vich, in 1335, it took place for some reason on 3 August. Also, five court documents from Valencia, done between 1354 and 1390, have the names of dozens of Jews, probably the whole community, who took such an oath annually. The lowest Valentian number, 110, appears in a list of the year 1390, while the highest, 156, appears in 1381.[56] At times, particular individuals were singled out and compelled to swear an oath. Thus Vidal Baron, a Jew of Cardona who perhaps was accused beforehand of malpractice, had to take the oath on 20 February 1299; his hand on the "ten precepts of Moses," he promised to observe the laws of King James I faithfully. This was done in the presence of the subvicar of Manresa and three other Christian witnesses.[57]

These Aragonese laws were at times strictly upheld. We know in fact that several thirteenth-century Jews, accused of having charged excessive rates of interest, were brought before the courts and punished quite severely. Thus on 27 August 1283, the infante don Alfonso initiated an inquiry against two Jews, Ismael Aborrabe and Jucef the son of Bices. A Christian lady, Sibilia Guillelmo, complained that they had extorted from her an exorbitant usurious sum.[58] On another occasion a few years later Rabbi Halayme, a Jew of Huesca, was denounced by Abdelan, a Moslem, over a debt of fifty shillings. Alfonso I, now king of Aragon, gave an order on 26 October 1287 to initiate an inquiry to determine whether excessive usury had taken place.[59] Another document indicates that the allegedly usurious practices of Bonfos Vidal and Habraam Maymo, Jews of Barcelona, were investigated on 19 November 1289 at the request of some inhabitants of Cervera.[60]

The registers of the Crown of Aragon also disclose what happened when such allegations were discovered to be true. On 17 April 1309, for instance, Josef Benveniste of Barcelona was fined 1,600 shillings.[61] Three other Jews of Huesca, Muca Abnalcavit, Vidal Abulbaca, and Abrahim Arapinaz, were fined 1,500 shil-

lings on 3 August 1321: this penalty was accompanied by the confiscation of another sum of 5,000 shillings on similar charges.[62]
A day earlier, two Jews of Montculus, Bonafos Juceff and Vidal
Gallipapa, were fined 3,300 shillings.[63] These were not isolated
cases: the registers of the Crown of Aragon carry the names of
other Jews from Tortosa, Teruel, Majorca, and many other
places—all were brought to court in connection with alleged usurious activity.[64] So we are safe in concluding that the government
of Aragon, committed to the defense of its official rate of interest,
was ready in principle to extend help to the humble members of
society and to display justice when required to do so.

But what was conceived as a campaign to enforce notions of
social and religious responsibility sometimes degenerated in Aragon into yet another tactic for the monarchy to extract money
from the Jews. The king of Aragon periodically would promise
Jewish communities, after due payment, not to sue them inad-
vertently for usurious activities, or not to sue them at all. It became, in fact, a tax. (This development is similar to the insistence
of the rulers of Catalonia and France on periodic payments in return for promises to secure the stability of coinage.)[65] Thus in
1254, in a privilege granted to the Jews of Majorca, King James
conceded that only individuals guilty of usurious practices would
be held responsible for their actions, not the Jewish community
as a whole.[66] Some thirty years later, similar promises were extended to the "Jews of Calatayad,"[67] "the Jews of the kingdom
of Valencia,"[68] and to many other communities accused of usurious transgressions. Toward the end of the thirteenth century a
more general arrangement was conceived in that entire Jewish
communities had to negotiate with the monarchs (*compositio* was
the term in the documents) and redeem themselves collectively,
and at times ahead of time, by paying large sums of money. Thus
documents of 29 May and 6 June 1290 indicate that the Jewish
community of Barcelona "composed" with the monarch for
95,000 shillings after accusations of usurious activities were
raised against its members.[69] Eight years later the same community "composed" for 100,000 shillings.[70] According to a document of 22 June 1290, the Jews in Majorca were burdened with
paying a sum of 37,000 shillings.[71] In the case of Lérida the penalty was 12,000, and for Teruel, only 500. The capital of Aragon,

Zaragoza, "composed" for 20,000 shillings.[72] In the catalog of
Aragonese registers published by Jean Régné, there is information on more than two dozen such "compositions." In the unpublished archives themselves, one would surely encounter many
more cases.

Once the sum of money was paid, the Jewish community was
promised, "for the coming five years," freedom from legal attack. "Given the poverty of the Jews of Lérida," a royal privilege
promised on 15 March 1298 that "no process concerning usury
will be instigated against them in the coming five years."[73] They
"composed" for 12,000 shillings that very day. Huesca received
such an assurance on 5 April of the same year.[74] Then, on 15 May
1326, all Jewish communities of the kingdom applied, no doubt
after "composing" collectivity, for such a five-year exemption.
Indeed, a promise to this effect was issued by James II.[75]

The Aragonese monarchy of the thirteenth century found itself thus caught between two desires. On the one hand, it wished
to defend its inhabitants by making the Jews observe the official
rate of interest. On the other hand, the prospect of payments
from Jewish communities tempted monarchs to issue collective
exonerations as well as exemptions for considerable lengths of
time in the future. Not surprisingly, the rulers could not resist the
temptation, and made out of their commitment to supervise and
police the Jews' "usurious" activities yet another source of income for their treasury.

France: Campaigns against Usury
and Capetian Propaganda

In France of the thirteenth century, things were not
much different. There also the monarchy made it its task to extend help to suffering debtors. There too it is readily apparent
how this act of responsibility declined into yet another source of
income and into a vehicle for royal propaganda.

In accordance with the analysis of theologians and canonists
who considered the taking of usury to be theft or robbery, Christian moneylenders had to make restitution for usury.[76] As for
Jewish moneylenders, there are some indications in southern

France that they too were required by the courts to make restitution.[77] Events were much more dramatic in northern France. There, at the time of Saint Louis and his brother Alphonse of Poitiers, the Jews were forced by the monarchy to make restitution. *Enquêteurs* were sent to the provinces to collect complaints from individuals about usury extracted from them. In the center of the village or city, the herald would proclaim that "all who might claim for usury" should appear before the *enquêteurs* accompanied by their witnesses. People would indeed come forward to register their *querimoniae*. Once satisfactory proof was presented, claimants would be indemnified.[78] The money for this indemnification was that previously confiscated from the Jews in campaigns that were called "general captures (*captiones*) of the goods of the Jews." We know about *captiones* in the years 1234, 1247–1248, 1256, and 1269.[79] It is not at all certain that these four were the only anti-usury campaigns conducted by the Capetians in the thirteenth century.[80]

In the Archives Nationales and in the Bibliothèque Nationale in Paris, one can see today excerpts of rolls written down on such occasions where hundreds of *querimoniae* brought against Jewish usurers are recorded (file J 943). The lost registers of the bailiwicks of Orléans, Gisors, Bourges, Touraine, Reims, Estamps, and so forth, mostly for 1256–1260 but also from the year 1269, would have recorded how restitution was actually made by the royal bailiff.[81] Some of the rolls of *querimoniae* preserved at the Bibliothèque Nationale were published by L. Delisle in the last century,[82] and some others were published, more recently, by the American scholar William Chester Jordan, who connects them with the *captiones* of 1247–1248.[83] In quantitative terms, we have in print some 250 such *querimoniae*. A similar number, in the above-mentioned file J 943 at the Archives Nationales, still await publication.

The following is a typical claim: "Maria the wife of Peter de Vadis complains that Daniel Ysac together with Bienvenus extorted from her, seven years ago, (usury of) thirty shillings *parisis* for a principal of one hundred shillings. Witnesses are Douce de Camac, Simon de Novavilla, John de Vadis, and Martin Louis."[84] Another claim concerned the Jew Ayoliot Josse, who "extorted usury of fourteen shillings for a loan of four pounds."[85]

A certain Gode li Purie "took the oath, not having witnesses though, and said she truly believes that her father and mother paid H (a Jewess) twenty shillings in usury. This she believes because she often went with her mother when she got money as loans, and when she paid usury to the said Jews."[86]

The formulas registered in the rolls J 943 at the Archives Nationales are even shorter. They are given not in Latin but in the vernacular and read, for example: "Perret Harmez testifies and says that Mensier took from him for two years of thirty shillings. Witness Perrier de Warno le Dames."[87] Other rolls of file J 943 record the names of claimants and the sums demanded back. They are arranged, however, according to the names of the Jewish creditor. Thus we have in the case of "debita Moxei Judei" the names of ten claimants, together with the sums of money that each of them requested. In the case of "Sons of Bonfil" only three names of claimants figure, while for Samuel the number is six.

As for actual restitutions, it seems that the king was quite cautious and thrifty, indeed tightfisted, in redistributing the money he confiscated from Jewish usurers. In a document issued by Saint Louis possibly as early as 1248—and copied in June 1270, virtually word for word, by his brother Alphonse of Poitiers, on the eve of the ill-fated crusade to Tunisia—a very detailed *modus probandi* was written down for the use of the *enquêteurs*.[88] The amount of money an individual could claim was limited; depending on the individual's circumstances, he could claim sums only on the order of ten, fifty, or, at most, one hundred shillings. Larger claims had to go before the royal court. A most telling proviso comes toward the end of the instruction, where it was stated that it was not the intention of the monarch to restore to individuals harmed by one Jewish usurer money confiscated from yet another Jew. It was not, in other words, a common chest that the *captio bonorum* created from the money confiscated from the Jews. The royal mandate made it crystal clear that payments to his claimants should end once the money confiscated from a given Jew was exhausted: "It is not our intention to restore usuries as extracted by one Jew with the confiscated property of another Jew, but only inasmuch as the property of him from whom usury is claimed will suffice to make such a restitution."[89] This then must be the reason why the rolls in file J 943 are arranged according to the names of the Jewish usurers and not according to places where claims were made or according to the chronological order of presentation. It is no wonder also that the monarchy found itself with a surplus of money after the confiscations and restitutions of 1234 or 1259. The aim of the legislation quoted above might have been, precisely, to create such a surplus: a very welcome by-product of the whole exercise of *captio-inquisitio-restitutio*.

To clear his conscience, King Louis wrote Pope Gregory IX in 1237 for instructions as to what to do with the surplus money "that bears the stigma of usury."[90] The following year a similar question was directed by Theobald, count of Champagne, also to the pope.[91] In the same vein, Countess Adelaide of Brabant called upon St. Thomas Aquinas sometime between 1261 and 1267 to instruct her on the issue.[92] Could she use moneys confiscated from Jewish usurers? Aquinas answered, as did the pope previously, that "if you can find with certainty those from whom usury was extorted, you must make restitution to them; otherwise, such money must be put to pious use according to the advice of diocesan bishops and other upright men."[93]

As for Saint Louis, he seems to have been quite experienced in handling this problem by the 1250s, if not earlier. File J 367 in the Archives Nationales, compiled in 1259, reveals a monarch apparently embarrassed by the "surplus moneys" left in his hands after the *captio bonorum Judeorum* (presumably of 1256).[94] Since it was impossible to ascertain to whom this money should rightfully go, Louis asked the bishops of France for help. But now it was no spiritual guidance that he sought. Rather, the bishops were sent a formulary letter, exonerating Louis, which they were asked to sign. It was no more than a bureaucratic routine. And indeed, the prelates extended their "indulgence" to Louis as requested, expressing at the same time admiration for his sincere religiosity in this matter. They allowed him to spend the remaining moneys for "pious work" as he pleased. Few of the bishops, from the evidence of file J 367, introduced any alteration to the royal letter sent to them.

If this reconstruction is correct, it gives us good reason to believe that in France, as in Aragon, the pious intentions of the monarchy were ultimately tainted by pecuniary considerations.

Even though William of Chartres, the king's biographer, tells us that Louis became involved in these confiscations "not indeed with the intention of retaining them," it appears that the monarch would be left holding a large sum of unclaimed money after a confiscation. This might have led to criticism of the monarchy, but none of it is known to us today. On the other hand, it is not difficult to imagine the effect such campaigns must have had upon society. They not only showed the inhabitants of France how sensitive the pious monarch was to their welfare but also—although occurring only infrequently—reminded everyone that the dream of a society free of moneylenders might still come true one day.

"Ameliorating the Jews": A Prelude to Their Expulsion

During the thirteenth century, efforts were made to do away with Jewish usury once and for all. Political thinkers, such as the author of *Le songe du vergier*, insisted that Jewish moneylending harmed not only individuals in society but the state itself.[95] "I know that the king gets much taxation out of the Jews," this author began, going on to argue that what the king "gains on one side he certainly loses ten times and more on the other." The reason: "because his subjects thus impoverished by the Jews cannot extend help to him nor pay their ordinary and extraordinary taxes." This was also the thinking of King Alfonso XI of Castile in 1348. Not only, stated the monarch, "is usury . . . a great sin, forbidden both by the laws of nature and by Scripture and grace, a thing that weighs heavy with God," but it also "brings trouble and misfortunes in the country where it is practiced . . . and . . . brings destruction and ruin on the properties of all persons and the inhabitants of the country where it is allowed."[96] Alfonso therefore urged the Jews to abandon usury and find other "useful" occupations.

Similar demands for more "productive" Jewish economic activity were raised with increasing frequency as the Middle Ages wore on.[97] In the letter of Peter the Venerable to King Louis VII of France, on the eve of the second Crusade, the famous abbot of Cluny reminded the monarch that "it is not by honest agriculture, by military service, or by any kind of honest and useful office that they [the Jews] fill their barns with produce and their cellars with wine."[98] Thomas Aquinas, in his above-mentioned *responsum* to Countess Adelaide of Brabant, maintained that rulers should see that Jews be "compelled to work" and not "live in idleness and grow rich by usury." Robert Grosseteste, when still archdeacon of Leicester, counseled the countess of Winchester (in 1231) to admit Jewish refugees to her territories on condition they abandon usury and gain their living by working with their hands.[99] In a much friendlier tone, yet in the same vein, the archbishop of Narbonne, Guillaume de la Brue (reigned 1245–1257), is reported by the Hebrew polemicist Meir ben Simeon to have addressed the issue in the following manner: "You know well that my proper advice is that you lend money no more at interest from this day forth. . . . Behold, the land lies before you, inhabit it, trade throughout it, and remove the stigma of usury from your souls."[100] About a hundred years later, Alfonso XI of Castile offered an incentive to the Jews to abandon usury: as part of the great reform laws enacted at Alcalá de Hénares in February 1348, the Spanish monarchy allowed the Jews to acquire, if they had the means, considerable tracts of land in his kingdom. North of the Duero River they might buy to the value of twenty thousand maravedis, while to the south of the river they were allowed up to thirty thousand maravedis.[101] Alfonso's effort was the most extensive and the most concrete made by a medieval ruler to facilitate the "amelioration" of the Jews. Nothing on such a large scale was attempted again until the end of the eighteenth century, when the "amelioration" of the Jews once more became a major issue, and enlightened rulers such as Joseph II of Austria ventured—with some success—to bring Jews back to agriculture.[102]

"Ameliorating" the Jews was an uncertain and probably not very serious option for medieval rulers to consider, while expelling them was a much more immediate possibility. Already in the first half of the thirteenth century, several medieval rulers held out expulsion as a threat to Jews who did not "ameliorate." "All Jews who wish to remain henceforth in my land must live by their own labor and by honest business, abstaining completely from usurious exactions," Count Archambaud of Bourbon ordered in

1234. Archambaud intimated that he reached the decision after consultation with King Louis.[103] Saint Louis himself decreed in the following year that "henceforward all Jews shall live by their own labor or let them leave the country." This was repeated in legislation of 1253.[104] William of Chartres, Louis's chronicler, attributes the following statement to the monarch: "Let them abandon usury or they shall have to leave my land completely in order that it may no longer be polluted with their filth."[105] Louis reached this conclusion after years of unsuccessful legislation against Jewish usury, legislation begun as early as 1223 by his father, and strengthened in a *stabilimentum* of 1230 which repeated the royal refusal to enforce Jewish loans. After 1230 Louis gave up all hope of changing the Jews' economic behavior and, motivated by his hostility to their religion, issued at least three decrees of expulsion against the Jews. We have today almost no information about these decrees and thus are unable to say how universal or effective they really were.[106]

In England, Edward I ordained in his *Statutum de Judaismo* "for the honor of God and common benefit of the people that no Jew hereafter shall in any manner practice usury."[107] The young monarch came to this decision, in 1275, after "having observed that in the time past many honest men have lost their inheritance by the usury of the Jews and that many sins have from thence arisen." When Edward realized, fifteen years later, that such a change in Jewish activity had not occurred, he decreed their expulsion from the kingdom. Not surprisingly, the blame was placed on the Jews who (according to the decree of expulsion) refused after 1275 to "live by their own commerce and labor" and "did thereafter wickedly conspire to and continue to a new species of usury more pernicious than the old."[108]

English Jewry, against whom those decrees of 1275 and 1290 were issued, was financially exhausted by ruinous taxation and pushed out of the mainstream of the money market by vigorous Italian banking firms. It was impractical to expect them to change the patterns of their economic behavior in such a short term.[109] Impoverished and no longer needed by Christian England, they could be safely removed.[110] Similar observations about the economic uselessness of the Jews of Nuremberg, in Germany, on the eve of their expulsion in 1519, were made recently by Markus J.

Wenninger.[111] In England, clearly, the royal demand in 1275 for a transformation of Jewish life can be considered a prelude to their expulsion. In France of the thirteenth century, as well, such calls for "amelioration" should have served the Jews as a warning. Once they failed to transform themselves from moneylenders to "productive" subjects, rulers could decree their banishment with good conscience. They did not do it, as we now are about to see, without engaging also in pious rhetoric imbued with self-righteousness.

The Politics of Expulsion

A decree of expulsion of Jews almost always had as a major justification an unwillingness to continue the toleration of moneylending. Not only were rulers of the High Middle Ages certain that the argument would be appreciated: they presented the expulsion of the Jews as a sacrifice on their part, a loss they incurred in order to render a service to the community. The monarchs claimed that they were losing valuable revenue by sending away the "serfs of the royal treasury." We have seen already that the author of *Le songe du vergier* would agree with them. But nowhere was this reasoning expressed more clearly than in Anjou.[112] "Although we enjoy extensive temporal benefits from the aforesaid Jews," declared Count Charles II in late 1288, "we should provide for our aforesaid counties and for their inhabitants through the expulsion of the Jews." The count then evoked religious motives and talked about his duty to care for the happiness of his subjects "rather than fill our coffers with the mammon of iniquity." Despite this contempt for "mammon," Charles took great care at the close of the document to specify how the inhabitants of Anjou had to indemnify him for the losses he incurred in banishing the Jews: "We ought to receive from each hearth three shillings once only, and from each wage earner six pence once only, as some recompense for the profit we lose through the expulsion of the aforesaid."

The inhabitants of other places also were taxed to recompense the authorities for the expulsion of the Jews. In particular, cities that requested expulsion of Jews (as well as Lombards, Cahorsins, and other undesirables) from their territory were made to pay for it. Thus English cities like Newcastle-on-Tyne (1234), Derby (1260 or 1261), and many others collected revenue for the purchase of such a "liberty," while in France the citizens of Angy, Saint-Pierre-sur-Dives, and Villefranche did the same.[113] Alphonse of Poitiers, in preparation for the Crusade of 1248, proposed to impose in his county a tax of four shillings on a household in return for expelling the Jews of La Rochelle, Saint-Jean-d'Angély, Saintes, Poitiers, Niort, and Saint-Maixent. But in this instance the Jews offered a higher sum and managed to stay.[114] The chroniclers of Augsburg in the fifteenth and sixteenth centuries knew very well that the city had to offer monetary remuneration to King Albrecht in the late 1430s to expel the Jews. They were unsure only as to the exact sum involved: was it two thousand florins or twelve thousand or even thirteen thousand florins?[115]

Once agreed upon, expulsion was almost invariably presented as an act of benevolence for the suffering Christians. The chronicle of Saint-Denis shows King Philip Augustus (who expelled the Jews in 1182) "moved by pity and by compassion" when learning about his people's indebtedness to Jewish usurers.[116] Rigord, the famous biographer of Philip, explains the reasons for the monarch's compassion: "The Jews so heavily burdened in this way the citizens and soldiers and peasants in the suburbs and in the various towns and villages, that many of them were constrained to part with their possessions. Others were bound under oath in the houses of the Jews in Paris, held as captives in prison."[117] Philip's decree of expulsion thus became justifiable. Some three hundred years later, in Marseilles, the representative of the council of the city, Honnorat Forbin, one of the most powerful men of his time, tried to gain the consent of King Charles VIII for an eventual expulsion of the Jews, by claiming similarly that they "molest, tire out, and wear out said Christian debtors by imprisonment, they excommunicate them and do other things which the debtors fear and which for the most part destroy them."[118] This complaint was made on 7 November 1485; about a month later Honnorat Forbin asked openly that the Jews be expelled from Marseilles, insisting again that "most of these Jews live only from the usury and the larceny that they are always committing and taking from Christian men and women."[119] Nevertheless, on both occasions his efforts failed. But when, some eleven years later, Charles VIII finally brought himself to decree the expulsion of the Jews, at first from Arles and then from Tarascon, he came back to the argument and mentioned, as one of the reasons for his decision, "the great abuse, usury, depredation, and other tricks that the Jews commit."[120] In Nuremberg also, in 1498, when Emperor Maximilian consented to the expulsion of the Jews, mention was made as a matter of routine that "various wicked, frightening, and clever usurious transactions were carried out against fishermen, townsmen, and others."[121]

Indecisiveness: The Usages of *Usura*

We thus see that, before an expulsion of Jews, rulers at the last minute were still trying to generate some income for themselves. At the same time, they deployed anti-usury rhetoric to play on the prevailing sentiment of hostility against moneylenders. Clearly, they were mixing utilitarian considerations with social and religious righteousness, as did the monarchs of Aragon and France—as we have seen—when combating usurers in their countries. To some contemporary observers, this must have seemed an intolerable duplicity, a cynical talking out of both sides of the mouth. But it is also possible that people in medieval urban centers were not as resentful about such practices as some modern critics may be, especially since such "duplicity" corresponded to a profound ambivalence toward moneylenders and moneylending prevalent at the time. Side by side with social opprobrium and religious hostility toward usurers and their evil ways, some people at least recognized the contribution of these "usurers" to the economy. On more than one occasion, as we shall see in some detail in the next chapter, public personalities found words to express their recognition that credit facilities were necessary and beneficial to their society. At the point of the discussion where we now find ourselves, it will be useful to observe this duality of attitude, these hesitations and uncertainties, by following the employment of the word *usura* in documents of the period and by tracing the rhythm of its appearance and disappearance in them.

To be sure, the canon-law definition of *usura* as given by Gratian was not forgotten in the ensuing centuries. "We understand usury to be anything that is beyond the principal," declared King Louis and his barons in 1230; a similar clarification was made by the prelates assembled in the Synod of Béziers in 1245, who certainly did not forget their *decretum*.[122] And as the word *usura* was fraught with prohibitive connotations, it was commonly avoided in notarial documents. In records from Manosque, Orange, Arles, Aix, and Marseilles, notaries as a rule do not distinguish between interest and principal, and do not mention even the term *usura* or *lucrum*. Instead, the loan (*mutuum*) is declared as a lump sum of money handed out from one person to the other as an act of friendship and affection.

But there were exceptions to the rule. For the small Catalan city Castello d'Empuries, the notarial records of the first quarter of the fourteenth century reveal hundreds of instances where an open distinction is made between capital and interest (*sors* and *lucrum*). At times the notaries insisted that the rate of interest was the official one in Catalonia.[123] Professor Richard Emery did not discover any reluctance in the neighboring city of Perpignan to use the term *usura*.[124] Similarly, in documents from the Catalan city of Vich, recorded between 1277 and 1345, there is open mention of the profit (*lucrum*) that the loans were expected to generate.[125]

Most remarkable is the open usage of the noun *usura* and the verb *usurare* in the Italy of the High and later Middle Ages. In 1288, for example, the council of the city of San Gimignano talks about "legitimate usuries" (*pro usuris legitimis*) when deciding an official rate of interest permitted in the city.[126] An Italian Jewish banker like Sabatuccio of Recanati, who together with his brother Gaio wished to start business in the city of Urbino, stated simply in his application (dated 28 March 1433) that "he intends to run a bank in your city Urbino and lend on interest (*sub usuris*) . . . to all who wish to borrow money on interest (*mutuo sub usuris accipere*)."[127] In the official constitution given him by the city, we read that Sabatuccio and his associates will indeed hand out loans *sub usuris* and *ad lucrum*.[128] This was not peculiar to Urbino: documents from the duchy of Milan or the republic of Florence reveal the same open acknowledgment of usury.[129] And, as is shown by the following incident in Piacenza on 5 March 1449, the councillors of these cities had no doubts about the semantics of the word *usura*.[130] Guillelmo Rubro, one of Piacenza's councillors, refused to take part in a vote concerning an application of a Jewish moneylender "because he refused to get involved in usuries or in usurious matters," and he stated this in the meeting. The other members of the board listened to his speech but obviously did not feel so strongly about it. In any event, they did vote eight to one in favor of a motion to introduce the "usurers" into the city.

However, the open usage of the term *usura* by some led others to rail against the practice and to suppress it. An example of such a suppression is recorded in Toulouse at the beginning of the thirteenth century.[131] While at the end of the twelfth century the loan contracts of the city openly indicated the amount of principal and of the interest, now, after the anti-usury campaign of Bishop Foulques during the Albigensian War, the documents ceased to make such a distinction. A similar change occurred in England.[132] From the accounts of the Canterbury priory from 1215 to 1295, we are able to establish, following a study by Professor Mavis Mate, that the term *usura* was used by the administration of the priory down to the year 1240. In 1221, for example, when recording a loan of 420 *marcae* received from Roman and Sienese merchants, the treasurer had no compunction about recording that eighty marks were owed as *usura*. Then the term disappears from the records. This disappearance after 1240 was in all probability due to the order of Henry III, issued in June of that year, which required all usurers to leave the country.

An abrupt decline in the fortunes of *usura* is observed in Marseilles, in the times of Bondavid of Draguignan. To be sure, in Provence, we discover the word *usura* in an ordinance issued in 1243 where Raymond Bérenger, count of Provence, decrees that Jews can get *usura* of four *denarii* on the pound each month.[133] It is repeated more than two hundred years later, when the Jews are allowed to charge the same rate of interest (25 percent). King Rene of Provence on 26 June 1453 mentions a rate of *usura* of "twenty-five florins for a hundred."[134] But nothing compares with the free and open usage of the term in an ordinance of the municipal council of Marseilles issued toward the middle of the thirteenth century.[135] The statute, entitled "For What Amount of Usury One Should Be Brought to Court," stated that judges of the city should not compel individuals to pay "usury" beyond the level of three pennies per pound per month. *Usura* is mentioned eight times in that fairly short clause of 180 words, each time in a businesslike manner and without animosity or reservation, in flagrant contradiction of church ethics and law.

Already about the year 1250, when it was enacted, the paragraph must have irritated some pious souls in Marseilles: some sixty years later, in February 1318, in a dramatic move the council of the city decided simply to obliterate it from its books. In the concluding pages of chapter 5 of this study, I will try to trace the reasons, religious and political, that induced the leaders of Marseilles to come to such a decision. At this stage it suffices to point out that this was done in order to comply with the decree *Ex gravi* of the Council of Vienne, because, as the Council of Marseilles itself states, the citizens wanted to live henceforth in compliance with the basics of Christian ethics and according to the teaching of the holy canons. Be that as it may, the sudden change in *usura*'s fortunes in Marseilles does epitomize the experience of the medieval West as a whole.

When the pendulum swung to one extreme, people talked about usury in an open and frank, even approving, manner. When it reached the opposite extreme, we witness outbursts of piety and of nervous campaigns against *usura*. Under the blue skies of Marseilles a statute, "For What Amount of Usury One Should Be Brought to Court," was formulated in the middle of the thirteenth century; under the same skies, seventy years later, moneylenders had to see to it that no traces of profit or increment could be detected in their transactions. Bondavid's witnesses in 1317, although time was running out, were still allowed to talk about moneylenders with a certain sympathy. They could still talk about the business of moneylending with equanimity.

4

Indebtedness in Medieval Society: Need, Habit, and Equanimity

While some readers of *The Merchant of Venice* may discern redeeming features in the personality and life story of Shylock, it is difficult to find any sympathy in the play for the profession of moneylending. In view of the medieval expressions of antagonism toward moneylending previously examined, it is justifiable to observe that *The Merchant of Venice* fits comfortably within a long European anti-usury tradition. How then can one explain why, in 1317, during a real trial, so many persons were ready to testify in favor of Bondavid, even to his good reputation as a moneylender? In this chapter I shall venture to highlight another attitude existing in medieval society which envisioned the Jewish moneylender as a benign and even benevolent practitioner of his profession. In order to explain how this positive image could exist, I propose to present first the results of research on the history of moneylenders done over the last twenty-five years in the notarial registers of the cities of southern France for the thirteenth, fourteenth, and fifteenth centuries. They convey a picture of a society in which virtually everyone was permanently in debt. Rather than viewing the act of borrowing money as an extraordinary experience, people seem to have been quite at ease in their contacts with the world of credit. In addition, this easy attitude was often accompanied by a good-natured appreciation of the services provided by Jewish moneylenders.

The Universality of Indebtedness: Some Quantitative Assessments

At this point, one should be forewarned about what one can expect from quantitative analysis of notarial documents. The tens of thousands of financial records preserved in the archives of southern France represent only a minuscule portion of the actual transactions. In addition, as no city has preserved a complete series of notarial records for even one year, it is difficult to ascertain how much of the reality we are observing and analyzing. As for registers written by Provençal Jewish moneylenders, not one has survived.[1] Moreover, we are dealing with three centuries for which only certain aspects have been surveyed by historians. Conditions in Perpignan in the 1280s were probably very different from those of the small city Trets, or Salon or Carpentras a hundred years later, if only because those three cities, by 1380, had undergone traumatic social and demographic changes caused by the Black Death of 1348 and the ensuing years of epidemics and crises. Where scholars have conducted research on different places in the same era, as with Arles and Aix in the 1430s, or Salon and Carpentras around 1400, they do not always find similar answers to identical questions. This is no doubt due to differences in local conditions or perhaps to the nature of the documentation preserved in each locality. But it is important that these difficulties do not discourage us from trying to discover general patterns and trends despite the fact that only isolated case studies are available.

The seventeen notarial registers of Perpignan extant from the second half of the thirteenth century, which Richard W. Emery studied in a 1959 monograph, tell us in great detail how moneylending reached virtually every segment of society in southwestern France, in both cities and villages. Working on a sample of loans from 1312, Emery was able to put together a revealing picture of the social distribution of loans made between 1261 and 1286.[2]

Table 3
1,321 New Loans by Jews to Christians
in Perpignan, 1261–1286

Debtors	No. of Loans	Percent of all loans	Total sums payable	Percent of sums payable	Median
Villagers	862	65	84,469s.	43	60s.
Townsmen	399	30	80,156s. 7d.	41	75s.
Knights & Nobles	32	2	17,107s.	9	225s.
Clergy	12	1	10,930s.	5	500s.
Royal Officers	5	1	2,068s.	1	250s.
Unidentified	11	1	862s.	1	60s.
Totals	1,321		195,5983s. 8½d.		65s.

Not surprisingly, the most substantial borrowers were royal officials and clergy, as well as members of the feudal aristocracy. Yet it would seem that members of the governing elite did not generally give their business to Jews but rather sought most of their loans from Christians. To quote one example, when his estate was confiscated by the king of Majorca on grounds of treason, Viscount Gillelmus de Castronovo had several Christian creditors but only one Jew.[3] The Jewish business community of Perpignan was geared primarily toward dealing with the lower end of the social ladder. An overwhelming 95 percent of all the loans made by Perpignan Jewry, (84 percent of the volume of money involved), were contracted either with the townspeople of Perpignan (30 percent), or with the villagers of the surrounding area (65 percent).

Of 308 loans to the townsmen of Perpignan, more than half (159) were made to craftsmen, with merchants and agricultural workers representing 20 percent of this group.[4] Among the craftsmen were skinners, shoemakers, tailors, and wagoners. As for the villagers, the majority were peasants, generally poor and seeking loans out of distress. It is also possible that the poorest peasants and impoverished townsmen borrowed money on pawned goods—thus leaving no records.[5]

Emery stated that "If we ask who borrowed money from the Jews of Perpignan . . . the answer is very simple: everybody."[6] That is also true, according to his analysis, for the villages near the city. Thus one is entitled to speak of a "universality of indebtedness to the Jews." To quote just two examples: in Saint-Laurent-de-la-Salanque, a village of forty-seven hearths in 1355, there were forty principal debtors and fourteen who stood surety in the same period; the corresponding figures for the village of Pia in 1384 are thirty-six hearths, with thirty-seven principal debtors and twelve standing surety.[7] The small city of Puigcerda, not far from Perpignan, served in its turn, too, as a headquarters for Jewish moneylenders and hence as a borrowing center for the surrounding villages. From the *Liber Judeorum* of that city, covering eighteen months in 1286–1287, which contains records of hundreds of loan operations transacted by the Jews, Mathias Delcore was able to establish a list of more than 160 villages and hamlets whose inhabitants were indebted to the Jews of Puigcerda.[8]

What was true for the small villages of the Pyrénées-Orientales, for Perpignan and Puigcerda, was also true for the city of Arles in the late Middle Ages. "At one moment or another of his life every inhabitant of the city of Arles had recourse to loans," according to Professor Louis Stouff.[9] To reach this undoubtedly conservative conclusion, he compared data obtained from notarial deeds extant for 1432–1441 (perhaps only 25 percent of the original number) with the list of family heads and proprietors in the city for 1437–1438 which he drew up. He discovered that no fewer than 456 of the 1,223 persons on his list contracted at least one debt during these ten years. The loans were short-term, generally for a few months or a year at most. Very rarely did people contract a debt for longer than twelve months. They had, therefore, to see their moneylenders quite frequently, several times a year perhaps, either to renew a loan or to take another one.[10]

Table 4
Duration of Debts in Arles, 1432–1441

3 months or less	25.12%
3–6 months	34.10%
6–12 months	36.80%
More than a year	2.10%
At first requisition	1.24%
	99.27%

Not all scholars, however, reached results similar to those of Emery and Stouff. With regard to Salon in Provence, Monique Wernham was able to determine with certainty the occupational background of only 236 of the borrowers from a total of 3,423 loans she found for the years 1391–1405.[11] According to her, sixty-two loans (26 percent) were to craftsmen while an almost equal number, sixty, were to members of the nobility, and twenty (8 percent) to lawyers. For the peasantry, Wernham found only eighteen loans. Do these results reflect limitations in the documents in Salon or are we dealing with social conditions different from the ones we encountered in the Pyrénées-Orientales?

Limited documentation becomes a stronger possibility when one compares the results Professor Noël Coulet obtained from an analysis of records for Aix-en-Provence in the 1430s with those obtained by Emery for Perpignan.[12] Coulet established for the area around Aix (1430–1435) a geographical pattern of Jewish lending similar to that for the Pyrénées-Orientales at the end of the thirteenth century. In Aix, Jews were heavily involved in loans to the neighboring villages. In fact, more than 80 percent of loans to villagers were contracted with Jews. Aix townsmen, in contrast, tended to do business with Christian moneylenders. To be more precise, 84.5 percent of loans to villagers came from Jewish sources, while 61.7 percent to citizens of Aix were from Christian lenders.[13]

Arles offers historians the opportunity to examine more closely the various groups that had recourse to the services of Jewish moneylenders. Professor Louis Stouff was able to calculate the degree of probability of various Arles professionals borrowing from Jews during the ten years from 1432 to 1441.[14]

Table 5
Probability of Indebtedness, Professionals in Arles, 1432–1441

Manual farm laborers	91%	Butchers	83%
Fishmongers	81%	Millers	73%
Herdsmen—animal			
Breeders	69%	Woodcutters	69%
Plowmen	66%	Cowherds	62%
Blacksmiths	55%	Weavers	54%
Fishermen	53%	Sheepmen	47%
Shepherds	43%	Manual	
Bakers	40%	laborers	42%
Carpenters	22%	Cobblers	26%
Notaries	20%	Masons	22%

Still, it is important to remember that the notarial archives cover neither the entire class structure nor the totality of lending and borrowing activity. Thus we might lack information about loans that were given on security of pledges, since pawnbroking was a casual business and did not require the presence of a notary. That most pawnbrokers' loans were for small sums can be gathered from the legislation of cities such as Manosque,[15] in which Jews were forbidden to take certain categories of pledges, such as tools or other instruments which borrowers might need to make their living. Thus, information is missing about the borrowing habits of a whole segment of society: the poorest and possibly the most numerous. It is evident from Provençal lists of fines (latae) imposed on delinquent debtors that such humble people were borrowers. Professor Rodrigue Lavoie, who examined such lists for the bailiwick of Castellanne, in Provence, in the first quarter of the fourteenth century, discovered that 90 percent of the fines were imposed by the court upon people who could not afford credit of more than sixty shillings.[16] His analysis is based on a sample of 398 cases:In fact, in 62 percent of these cases the sums did not exceed twenty shillings, while more than a third were less than ten shillings.[17]

Table 6
Sums Borrowed in Castellanne
according to Amount of Money Involved

Years	1s to 92s	10s to 19s	20s to 59s	and +	Totals
1302–1305	80 (36%)	50 (23%)	61 (28%)	29 (13%)	220
1312–1316	63 (36%)	52 (29%)	52 (29%)	11 (6%)	178
Totals	143 (36%)	102 (26%)	113 (28%)	40 (10%)	398

Lavoie also discovered that people in Castellanne were indebted to several creditors simultaneously.[18] About 60 of the 250 individuals who were fined by the court of the bailiwick of Castellanne were condemned on more than one occasion. Twenty-two of these were cited twice, and 19 were cited three or four times. In Castellanne there were also 13 individuals who were fined on five, six, or seven occasions; while in two instances individuals were fined twelve and fourteen times, respectively. For these people, then, in the first quarter of the fourteenth century, indebtedness was—to quote Lavoie—"a chronic" state of affairs. "Chronic" was also the term used by Christian Castellani when commenting on the fact that in Carpentras, capital of the Vaucluse, individuals indebted to several creditors often paid off one debt by contracting another.[19] Castellani's conclusions—in a study yet to be published in full—are based on an analysis of thirty-five hundred credit transactions found in the notarial registers of the city between 1396 and 1418.

Just how heavily indebted some individuals became is apparent in the court registers of Manosque. On the occasion of bankruptcy or execution of a will, creditors would be invited by the court to present their claims. The lists of indebtedness thus established specified the sums of money requested and the date of the contract between the claimants and individual in question, and gave in most cases the cause of the indebtedness: for example, a loan (*mutuum*), a purchase on credit (*emptio*), a partnership (*societas*), or repayment of a dowry. The lists give us some idea of the extent of credit transactions in the last decades of the thirteenth century. In April 1294, no fewer than seven people (one of them Jewish, the others Florentine moneylenders) figured as creditors of one Johannes Nigri, who had died some time earlier.[20] In the case of R. Astrugi, seven of his eight loans were contracted in the year 1286.[21] They amounted to at least £16 7s. (the final entry is illegible). He used the money to pay for cereals, wheat, and textiles. Astrugi invested in a partnership with Petrus Devilla and borrowed thirty-three shillings from the Jew Mosse de Grassa. The progress of his indebtedness in 1286 is striking. He borrowed money on 4 March, 20 April, 12 June, 10 and 13 September, and 4 and 15 October. According to a list made on 29 June 1289, another citizen of Manosque, Ebrard Gibosi, who may have been in financial trouble in 1289, became indebted three times in 1286 and twice in each of the years 1287 and 1288.[22] The sums involved were 246 shillings in the first year, 42 in the second, and 39 in the third. Of the more than fifty-one pounds he owed, 30 percent was owed to three Jews in the city. Similar information can be drawn from this register for a profile of the indebtedness of R. Sartoris (five claims between 1283 and 1286)[23] and Bertrandus Malipili (twelve claims between 1282 and 1287 plus one loan that went back to 1270).[24]

It is difficult, in most cases, to learn much about the reasons for this indebtedness. An exception is the famous yet curious record made by Richard of Anesty, an English knight of the time of Henry II, of his descent into indebtedness.[25] During the period 1158–1163, Richard contracted no fewer than twenty-one loans with nine Jews, mostly from Cambridge, Newport, and London. In all, he borrowed ninety-two pounds from them to cover legal expenses connected with establishing a claim to succeed his uncle William de Sackville. It is not clear why Richard, who won his case, bothered to record his experience with moneylenders with such precision. He may have had the documentation at hand or have been endowed with a very remarkable memory, for the task does not seem to have been very difficult for him. He recorded the names of the creditors, the sums he received, and—what is most rare in medieval documents—the interest he paid (up to 87 percent in eight of the twenty-one cases). He also remembered very clearly the occasions that led him to turn to moneylenders: for example, "when I first pleaded in the court of the bishop of Chichester," or "when I sent my clerks to Rome." Eight of these loans were given by a single Jew, Hackelot, and three others by

Jacob of Newport, while from the other moneylenders Richard **had only one** or two loans. It is readily apparent from his report that **Richard** contracted for new loans while others were not yet paid. For instance:

> In the feast of St. Martin, when I pleaded again in the court of the same judges (the bishop of Chichester and the abbot of Westminster), then Jacob the Jew of Newport lent me seventy shillings . . . and at the same time Benedict the Jew of London lent me ten shillings at [two pence] a week, which I kept three years and for which I rendered for usury twenty-six shillings.[26]

While Richard does not state explicitly whether he paid off **some of his** old debts with the new loans, in their business register **the clerics** of the priory of Canterbury cathedral made no secret **of this practice.** For example, in 1255 they received a loan of 235 **marks from** a Florentine society to pay off a debt to a Sienese **company.**[27] What was true for a religious institution must certainly have been true for private persons. Castellani's findings for Carpentras support this supposition.[28]

That this widespread and often permanent indebtedness did not legitimate the practice of usury is apparent from the findings presented in the previous chapter. But from information we have gathered up to this point, we may conclude, simply, that by 1300, becoming indebted to a usurer was not as appalling as Shakespeare's treatment implies.

Can Society Function without "Usury"?

Turning now from economic realities to the realm of popular attitudes, the main question is to what extent people were ready to challenge the prevailing ideology of usury. Was there any degree of economic realism or a readiness to express a more positive view of the role of banking, loans, and interest in society? From the vehemence of the Council of Vienne and its readiness to bring before the tribunal of the Inquisition those who maintained that "it is not a sin to practice usury," one can conclude that such opinions were actually circulating and that the danger was real. Indeed, in one case recorded by the court of

Manosque in 1342, a Jew named Simon Davit was accused of expressing such a heresy.[29] Originally brought to court for the unrelated but serious accusation of desecrating the holy cross, he supposedly said on another occasion that it was not a sin to practice usury. Unfortunately, the witness who testified against Simon Davit did not address this accusation, so there is no further information about the position of the accused on this issue.

That such opinions might not have been confined to Jews or found only in isolated individual cases—but may sometimes have been common wisdom—is apparent from the preachings of Saint Bernardino of Siena. In Assisi in 1425 he addressed himself to the prevalence of such notions and set out to destroy them. Bernardino recorded a common saying that "a city cannot exist without a manifest usurer"[30] and held that it was the opinion of Jews and non-Jews alike.

Meir ben Simeon of Narbonne, a scholar who flourished in southern France in the thirteenth century, was very outspoken in his opinions on the positive role of loans and banking in society. *Milhemeth Mitsvah* assembled pieces of his polemical writings from about 1245 to the 1270s. In the late 1240s, Meir, a spokesman for his people, commented on the usury laws introduced by Saint Louis.[31] On at least five occasions in his book, Meir expressed himself in terms very similar to the maxims recorded by Saint Bernardino. Instead of *civitas*, Meir used the Hebrew word *olam*, meaning "world" or in this instance "society."[32] For "usury" he substituted "loans" (*halva'a*). Yet the maxim recorded by Saint Bernardino is clear in Meir's statements that "society could not do without loans" and "who can imagine the existence of society without loans?" In his rhetorical argument Meir set forth the proposition: "given that society cannot do without loans."[33] Indeed, Meir treated this statement as if it were a biblical or Talmudic maxim requiring exegesis.

Meir ben Simeon also urged his Christian listeners (presumably he expressed his opinions in public debate) to observe and recognize the contribution of moneylending to society, especially to those less privileged:

> Since your wealthy [Christians] refrain from lending free of interest, how will the common people [*Beinonim*] and the needy make

a living? Or isn't it true that many [of these less privileged] bring livelihood to their households through [the help of] a loan of money [to purchase] one single [cow] for plowing or a bit of cereal or wheat for sowing and [also] for the protection of their families?[34]

In the ensuing paragraph Meir again evoked the hardships of daily life and mentioned the need for bread, meat, clothing, and medical care which these poor families had to meet.

His insistence on the role of the Jewish loan as a relief to the humble and the poor must have sounded very convincing to his contemporaries. In Pavia, in Siena, and in Florence of the fifteenth century, the argument was repeated nearly word for word—not by preachers or polemicists but by responsible public authorities. Thus when Pavia's podesta, in a letter to the duke of Milan on 14 August 1482, repeated a rumor that the Jews had decided to stop lending money to both rich and poor, he was alarmed that this would harm the poor, "who do not have other means of purchasing food if not through placing as collateral an object with the Jews," and he feared that many of them "might starve to death." Similar language was employed by the city council of Siena on 25 May 1457 to justify a charter they awarded to a Jewish moneylender, Jacob di Consiglio, who wished to establish himself there. For its part the Florentine "Council of the Hundred" referred on 25 December 1476 to the poor people whose subsistence depended on getting loans from the Jews. Deprived of this source of credit, these humble people would be dependent on Christian lenders—which would bring ruin upon them.[35]

Despite all this, ben Simeon did not limit his argument to the poor and needy. Instead he directed the attention of his audience to the fact that the king of France, during the "War of the Great Count," turned to Jewish moneylenders. This could be a reference—as suggested by Robert Chazan—either to the uprising of Raymond VIII of Toulouse in 1242 or to the rebellion of Raymond Trancéval of Béziers, "the enemy of the king," in 1247. Special reference was made by polemicists to services offered to Saint Louis on that occasion by a faithful Jewish official (unnamed), who brought Jewish moneylenders together to raise money needed for war in southern France:[36]

> Even the officer and kings must borrow—indeed, even the great king, the king of France. His officers have not been able to pass two consecutive years without large loans. In fact he almost lost some of his fortified cities during his war with the great baron until his faithful Jewish official of Narbonne found him loans at high rates of interest.[37]

This gave him an "all the more so" argument in conclusion: why do the dignitaries of the land not realize that if they have to borrow at interest, there is even more need for it among the common people?

A younger contemporary of Meir, the polemicist Jacob ben Elijah, also knew how to use in his arguments the fact that the highest dignitaries of society were forced to secure loans from Jews. Jacob was born and raised in Montpellier, but he lived and wrote in Venice.[38] In a polemical letter written in the 1260s or 1270s in reaction to propaganda of the former Jew Paulus Christiani, he pointed to the activities of the *mercatores domini pape*,[39] the pope's financial servants, whom he called "the people of Tuscany."

The way that the quest for money and greed for profit made the huge papal machinery work was expressed by Jacob in the following manner:

> Look at and consider this court of Rome, to which all Christians are subject, and which extends its dominion from one ocean to the other; everyone is greedy for profit and sends out collectors to extort money from the people (Judges 8:2). In truth, it is thus that they establish their preeminence, carry out their decisions, bring their projects to successful conclusions, fulfill their plans and foil those of their adversaries, ravage towns and erect fortresses!

Then, in a manner quite similar to that of Meir ben Simeon, he argued, through a series of rhetorical questions, for the unavoidable necessity of recourse to the credit services of those "people of Tuscany" to enable church and state to conduct their various projects.

> How do they gather armies for great massacres and vast attacks? How do they dethrone kings and set up others in their place? How do they contrive their alliances and unite dynasties? How do they

arrange princely marriages? How do they humiliate their adversaries and reduce them to their will? How did they break the pride of the people of Ishmael, who aroused the wrath of the Almighty? How did they overthrow the arrogance of the despicable Greek kingdom? How did they conquer the execrable heretics and their crowd of followers? How did they exterminate them, overthrowing their fortresses, laying waste their towns, burning them and their children?

Is not all this the work of prelates who came from every country to hear the decrees [of the pope] and to bow down [before him]? Now, when they are short of money, when they can no longer offer gifts, what is left for them to do?

Certainly, the people of Tuscany are at the bottom of it all.

Similar opinions were expressed in previously mentioned Italian texts of the fifteenth century. Other Italian documents used even stronger terms, but before presenting them it is important to note that recognition of these facts was not limited either in time or in space to that peninsula in the later Middle Ages. Even around Saint Louis, similar assessments were expressed. William of Chartres, the king's biographer, reported about 1270 that when the royal council was discussing expulsion of the Jews, some of the monarch's councillors advanced arguments against such a project, arguments that closely resembled those of Meir ben Simeon: "Without lending, the populace could not exist nor the land be cultivated nor labor or commerce be pursued."[40]

Records of discussions by several Italian city councils concerning the admittance of Jewish moneylenders inside their walls reveal the economic thinking displayed on such occasions. On 5 March 1449, for example, the council of Piacenza discussed the case of Magier, a moneylender, who proposed to come with his family and establish himself in the city where there was already another Jewish incumbent. Those who supported the application said that it would be very beneficial for as many Jews as possible to come to live in the city and urged that "for the benefit of public life of that city, let be admitted to it whoever wants to come . . . for the more Jews there will be, the more help will the citizens and people of the city get in their need."[41] No less strong is the wording of a document of 23 December 1310 which expresses the attitudes of the priory of the city of Perugia:

... These Jews are of much benefit [and indeed] are necessary to the city, to the *comune* as well as to individuals ... especially in providing them the opportunity to get and receive money from them in loans, [loans needed] for carrying on the war and for other needs that present themselves.[42]

The documents concerning San Gimignano assembled by Robert Davidsohn show the amount of effort Italian cities would make at the beginning of the fourteenth century in order to attract Jewish moneylenders.[43] The Jews Mosse, son of Diodato, and his associate were living in neighboring Siena and signified their willingness to transfer to San Gimignano. "Let the syndic himself come over to us with a legal mandate and, on our side, we shall have everything carried out in the name of God," they wrote to the council on 16 July 1309. The council, two days later, decided to send a syndic as requested. When the Jews failed to show up, the council sent on 14 August a messenger "to induce the Jew to come to San Gimignano as promised." Apparently this did not happen, for in October 1311 the city sent a messenger to Pisa to see what could be achieved there. On 27 February, according to evidence from Davidsohn's *Dossier*, a messenger was dispatched by the San Gemignanesi to Rome to persuade the Jew Moisetus to make good his promise to settle in their city.

Jewish and Non-Jewish Moneylenders

Jews, in Bondavid's lifetime, were not the only moneylenders in the medieval city or countryside. There were, first and foremost, places where there were no Jews resident, and yet loans and other credit facilities were available. The countryside around Bologna in the 1230s is a case in point. Professor Francesca Bocchi discovered in those small villages quite a heavy rate of indebtedness among the peasantry (221 debts are recorded). Of eighty-three families, at least seventy-one were in debt that year, many of them on several occasions simultaneously.[44] The records inform us who the creditors were: notaries, craftsmen, and also members of the local clergy. There were monks, *conversi*, and even an archpriest lending money to parishioners. From the fact that some of these creditors appear more often than others, we can even label them as "semiprofessional" moneylenders.

A similar situation in the English countryside of the late fourteenth century was revealed by Elain Clark. Her study of debt litigation in the court of Writtle, a royal manor in Essex, between 1382 and 1400, did not produce any professional moneylenders. Jews, in any event, had been banished from England a hundred years earlier. Since, however, there was need at Writtle for loans and for credit, society organized itself so that these were available. Neighbor relied upon neighbor. Peasants would turn to craftsmen (weavers, spinners, dyers, or smiths) or to village officials (the constable or the reeve) for loans. Clerics and chaplains were approached as well, not to mention wealthy landowners who were called upon more frequently than the others.[45] Also in England, but in the first half of the fourteenth century this time, scholars have long noticed the activities, as moneylenders, of two dignitaries, Walter Langton (d. 1321), bishop of Coventry, Lichfield, and Chester, and William Melton (d. 1340), archbishop of York, both immensely wealthy men who served, each in his turn, as treasurers of the realm. Melton, as his register shows, lent money on hundreds of occasions to knights and barons, to priories and fellow bishops, as well as to simple parishioners. Such was also the case of Langton: the proceedings of his trial, between 1307 and 1311, leave no doubt about his motives, which—as Ralph B. Pugh puts it—"seem to have been nakedly usuries." A similar impression is gained by observing the evidence of three other clerks of the monarchy (under Edward III): Wooler, Ravendale, and Ingelby, whose deeds were described by Professor Pugh. In the 1300s and through the 1360s, jointly or separately, they advanced dozens of loans to their clients—be they religious houses, prelates, or parishioners. At times such loans would reach the level of 200 and 300 pounds (in the case of the two bishops, the sums were even higher), but in most cases the sums corresponded to the modest status of the clients. Obviously, each of the trio was thus supplementing handsomely his income as a chancery official. We can be sure that close scrutiny of British historical material will bring up evidence about dozens of such moneylenders active after the expulsion of the Jews from the island in 1290.[46]

Even where a Jewish colony did exist, its members were not the only moneylenders. In his recent study of the activity of the fifty-two Jewish moneylenders of Santa Coloma de Querlat in the last years of the thirteenth century, Professor Yom Tov Assis discovered, for the three years 1293–1295, traces of the activities of twenty, possibly over twenty-one, Christians who lent money to Jews. One of them, the nobleman Arnaldo de Benivre, recorded with the notaries significant loans of 140, 280, and even 840 shillings. And since his Jewish borrowers were moneylenders themselves—and among the most prominent ones—we have to agree with Professor Assis's conclusion that these loans were taken by the Jews "in order to be used as part of a lending capital."[47] They had thus to compete with Christian inhabitants of the city, some of whom were operating openly, while others were carrying on their profession in a clandestine or semiclandestine manner.

It is this Christian group of moneylenders that scholars have generally found difficult to find in the documents. They are brought to light only when a campaign has been waged against them. Such an occasion occurred in 1285, during the episcopal visitation of Simon de Beaulieu, archbishop of Bourges, in his capacity as primate of Aquitaine in the priory of Vigan, diocese of Cahors.[48] No fewer than thirty-seven inhabitants of the parish of Goudron, all "defamed" as usurers, were convicted before the prelate on 4 April and confessed to various amounts of interest they received. Bertrand de Faviers, the first convicted, "promised to do restitution for one hundred shillings." Gérard de la Omieda, the second on the list, did not have on his conscience more than fifteen shillings, while Gerard du Moulin declared interest of one hundred shillings. The list goes on to record schematically sums as low as five shillings and as high as two hundred. To judge from the modest sums which twenty-three of them declared, these "usurers" must have been involved in the illicit activity only occasionally. Of the remaining fourteen individuals, nine mentioned sums between fifty and one hundred shillings, and five went much higher, quoting numbers of 160 and even 200 shillings. These five, and probably all fourteen, most likely may be designated as professionals. Cahors, as is well known, gave its name to professional usurers practicing all over Europe.[49] One wonders whether the parishioners of Goudron had anything to do with these *Cahorsins*. The document is not of much help in this respect, since it gives just names and sums of money. On the frequency of their involvement in the profession, their clients, and their legal support, we are left in the dark.

Pistoia between 1291 and 1300 and Toulouse in 1255 offer much better observation posts. A study by Armando Sapori of the court records of Pistoria revealed the existence of at least fifteen usurers. They placed a *tabula* in front of their houses and openly carried on business. Some admitted at court that they had been involved in the activity for twenty years.[50] In Toulouse in 1255, a campaign against Christian usurers was waged by Archbishop Guillaume de la Brue, who was, incidentally, the disputant against Meir ben Simeon.[51] Four individuals were targeted, and more than twenty-five inhabitants of the city were called to testify about their activities.

This was not the first time such a campaign took place in Toulouse: In 1205 and again in 1215, Foulques, the bishop of Toulouse, waged a fierce battle against usurers in his city.[52] He established a special tribunal, and he himself headed a confraternity ("the whites") with banners bearing the slogan, "war against usurers." The houses of notorious usurers were attacked and destroyed. Yet, as if nothing had ever happened, in 1255 Christian usurers seem to have become quite firmly established in the city. Presumably, after the convulsion of anti-usury sentiment was over, society became tolerant again toward Christian usurers in the 1230s and the 1240s.

In May 1255 all twenty-six Toulousains who were invited as witnesses to the investigation knew about the activities of the usurers under examination. "It is well known [*fama*] in Toulouse that they are usurers," stated the first of the witnesses, and this was repeated by the others. Fifteen of the twenty-six witnesses were notaries, two were judges, and two were messengers of the court. They all reported that the four accused frequently used the judicial institutions of Toulouse not only to record loans with the notaries but also to enforce them. Also, some of the witnesses had been present when transactions were concluded or had been parties to the business. Thus they were in a position to report that the value of repayment on one of the loans had begun at 60 shillings and had reached 260 because of compound interest, while another grew from 140 to 470. They asserted also that by 1255 some of the usurers had been active in the city for five, ten, or even fifteen years. There could not have been much doubt about their activities, yet two of the four suspects were discharged because of insufficient evidence. There is no hint whether the other two were convicted. One of them, Tholomeus de Portali, only nine years later, served as a councillor to the commune—which might suggest that the campaign of Bishop Guillaume de la Brue did not harm his reputation.

While these Christian usurers in Toulouse or Goudron were clandestine or semiclandestine professionals, tolerated by authorities but by no means considered legitimate, people in the medieval city, in the period that interests us, were exposed to a more important group of Christian moneylenders who acted openly and lent money in a legitimate way—the Italians. Arriving from Florence, Siena, Pisa, and many other flourishing city-republics of the peninsula, these Italian businessmen, like the Jews, had to pay special taxes in order to practice their activities openly, but in return were covered by charters of rights which they obtained from civil authorities. At the beginning of the fourteenth century, before their most important companies failed and went into bankruptcy, the volume of their activity far exceeded that of the Jews. Florentine companies like the Bardi, the Peruzzi, or the Acciaiuoli (failed in 1325) dealt in France and Flanders with monarchs, prelates, and nobility and handled sums of money that were on the order of magnitude of budgets of counties and even whole realms. In England, the Riccardi of Lucca, bankers to Edward I (1272–1307), were involved in the high finance of England. Their story was told recently by Professor Richard W. Kaeuper.[53] In service to the English government for most of the last quarter of the thirteenth century—they collapsed in 1294—the *Societas Riccardorum* was expected to finance the military campaigns of the monarch, to provide money for the building of castles, to control customs, and to handle the state's income from the wool trade. The Riccardi were thus handling sums of money that amounted to thousands and tens of thousands of pounds. There is no comparison at all to the sums handled by the impoverished Jews of England on the eve of their expulsion in 1290.

Yet these Italian bankers were not engaged exclusively in high finance. Kaeuper noted that the Riccardi, despite all their involvement with the monarchy, extended their interests. They were, in his words, "creditors to a broad section of society ranging from earls and archbishops to simple knights and townsmen."[54] Evidence from France shows this popular aspect of Italian moneylending in an even clearer light. For the principality of Savoy in the first half of the fourteenth century, Anna Maria Patrone, an Italian historian, was able to discover thousands of credit operations transacted in the region by moneylenders of the city of Asti.[55] There is virtually no city and no agricultural center of importance in this mountainous region where a banking house (*casana*) did not operate, as shown by documents she found. Their presence in Chambéry, Aix, or Montmélian is not surprising, but they were also established in dozens of other, much smaller localities like Vugine, Conflans, or Talloires, to cite just a few names. Similar evidence of the extent of Italian moneylending in Burgundy for that period can be found in Léon Gauthier's study done at the beginning of our century.[56] The career of one Italian banker—a mediocre and unsuccessful one—was tracked in a special study by the French historian Charles de La Roncière.[57] The man, Lippo di Feda del Sega (c. 1285–1363)—a contemporary of Bondavid—was not involved in high finance and was not active, at the beginning of his career in France, in the capital city but rather in the provincial center, Pontoise. Many other Florentines settled in northern France, in cities like Verneuil, Andelys, Beauvais, Provinse, Doutilly, and Meaux. When Lippo moved to Paris, after ten years, it was not success but rather disaster that awaited him in that city.

Provençals, at the time of Bondavid, were exposed to these Italian moneylenders, not only in Avignon—around the papal court their services were considered indispensable—or in the port city of Marseilles[58] but also in less important centers: Carpentras, Pernes, Valréas, Mormoiron, Mazan, and Corombe in the Comtat Venaissin; Manosque, Pertuis, and Forcalquier in the upper Provence.[59] To date, no systematic study has been made of their presence and their activities in the region. Consequently, the question must remain open whether there was a possible division of labor between them and the Jews, or among Italians, Jews, and the other, clandestine usurers. There is no way to quantify which part of the market was handled by each of these three groups. Still, from the evidence of one notarial register in Manosque, we can get an idea about such a functional division.

That register comes from a study of the Manosque notary, Petrus Gibosi; it records contracts made in the city between April and December 1313. It is particularly interesting since 89 of the 290 acts it records concern the activities of Florentines in the city.[60] "Florentines" meant—according to the Gibosi evidence—one family headed by Laurentius Daunazati who was aided by two nephews, Pera Baldoyneti and Robertus Ugolini, as well as by Jacob Nigri, a Manosque native, hired as their agent. This Florentine establishment was very small compared with the thirty-five or so Jewish households in Manosque.[61]

Moneylending emerges as the most prominent occupation of Daunazati and his associates. To be sure, they were also, in four cases, involved in the commerce of textiles, but this seems to have been just a sideline for them. Their involvement in the commerce of wheat and other cereals was, as with the Jews of Manosque, a result of their "usurious" activity. Part of the interest on their loans, and at times all of it, would be paid by the peasants in kind, not money. The Florentines' clientele—like that of the Jews—was not limited to Manosque. Some came from neighboring villages like Vols, Sainte-Tulle, Pierrevert, and Reillane, while other customers traveled from relatively distant places like Digne and Cadarche. No fewer than thirty-five places of origin are indicated in the corpus of eighty-nine documents.

While there does not seem to be much difference between Jews and Florentines in the geographical spread of their activities, it would seem that those who borrowed from the Florentines were, on average, of a higher social status. In the document for 1313, sixteen financial transactions involved individuals who carried the title *nobilis* while ten others were *domicelli* (*demoiseaux*). As well, there were two priests, two notaries, and one medical doctor. To be sure, there were representatives of those groups among the customers of the Jews, but seldom in such proportions.[62] The Florentines of Manosque extended their services to humbler people as well. Inhabitants of Manosque and peasants of the neighboring villages did appear in their contracts, but—while for the Jews they seem to have constituted the vast majority of the clientele—these humble people, according to Petrus Gibosi's register, did not represent more than 40 percent of the total. It is not surprising, therefore, that the volume of business of the Florentines differed markedly from that observed by Emery in Perpignan (there, Emery found they were more than 90 percent of the customers). It is true that some of their loans did not exceed 25 shillings, but on average the amounts were much higher. Forty of the seventy-nine identifiable sums—53 percent—were greater than 120 shillings, twice as much as the average Jewish loan in Perpignan. A considerable number of Florentine loans exceeded 500, 1,000, and even 2,000 shillings. We have nine loans of such order of magnitude in our corpus, more than 10 percent.

Of course only a more comprehensive study on a much wider scale will be able to establish how universal these findings are, and whether there was such a division of labor in which the Jews had, for the most part, the poor customers while the Lombards made loans to the rich. Then we may be in a position to appreciate Meir ben Simeon's insistence on the social role of Jewish moneylending in offering relief to the poor—and to them especially.

What can be ascertained at this stage is that the division of labor was not a simple one—in that individuals and institutions would not choose one of the agencies over the others but rather would turn simultaneously to Jews, Lombards, and indigenous Christian moneylenders in the quest for money. The information gathered by Rodrigue Lavoie, based on analysis of lists of fines (*latae*) imposed on tardy debtors in upper Provence, reveals such a pattern. It is repeated in the analysis I did on four indebtedness lists for Manosque, and this pattern is confirmed by observations made by Mavis Mate on the history of the indebtedness of the Canterbury cathedral priory in the thirteenth century.

The priory of Canterbury seems to have had dealings with Jews only down to 1244. In the subsequent fifty years the clerics turned for credit to Christian moneylenders, mostly to Lombards.[63] In 1254, when the debt of the priory was 3253 marks, 83 percent of the sum was owed to the Lombards. Four years later the debt amounted to 4,623 marks and almost 66 percent was owed to the Lombards, one group from Siena and another from Florence. But even during the years when the priory transacted business with Jews, the Jews were far from holding a monopoly. Figures for the years 1240–1244 reveal that Jews never commanded more than 25 percent of the priory's indebtedness:

Table 7

Year	Total indebtedness	Part owed to Jews	Part owed to Jews in %
1240	#518 6s. 8d.	#20 5d.	3.85
1242	#590 13s. 4d.	#66 8d.	11.28
1244	#417 6s. 8d.	#103 4s.	24.76

For Castellane, in the first quarter of the fourteenth century, Lavoie found information concerning 226 claims made in court by creditors against borrowers in the three registers of *latae*. Ninety-six of these, 43 percent, were presented by Jews.[64] The Jews' claims amounted to £603 7s. out of a total of £1,101 1s., or 55 percent. Castellane, a rural center of some importance in upper Provence, probably did not harbor more than half a dozen Jewish families. Although they had a major part in providing credit to the people of Castellane, it is clear that credit was easily available from non-Jews.

For Manosque, the four lists of indebtedness in register 56H 904, discussed previously in this chapter,[65] reveal a very similar pattern. Indebtedness recorded in this register arose not only from loans given *causa mutui* but also for other operations such as partnership or purchase on credit. The Jews, however, appear in these four lists as moneylenders only. The following table illustrates how much of an individual's total indebtedness stemmed from Jewish transactions, and the extent to which loans (as opposed to other sorts of transactions) made up the indebtedness.

Table 8

Name of indebted person	Total indebted- ness	Indebted- ness due to loan	Indebted- ness to Jews	Part of Jews	
				Total	Loans
R. Sartoris	890s.	290s.	160s.	17.97%	55.17%
B. Malipili	497s.	284s.	55s.	11.06%	19.36%
R. Astrugui	327s.	61s.	33s.	10.09%	54.09%
E. Gibosi	1033s. 8d.	661s.	311s.	30.10%	47.04%

In three of these four cases, indebtedness to Jews does not represent even a fifth of the total. Although in debts resulting from loans the place of Jews in two cases passes the level of 50 percent, they have no exclusivity. Each of these four Manosquins applied to Christians when in need for money. Since, however, this is a mere sampling from the archives of Manosque, these findings can by no means claim universality. There is still much work to be done before it will be possible to measure the percentage of loans owed to Jews in the general indebtedness of medieval society.[66] Supported, however, by research from Castellane and Canterbury, the Manosque findings make it very clear that Jews were just one of the groups of moneylenders medieval people had to deal with, and not necessarily the predominant one.

Choosing among Moneylenders

Jews were, of course, very much aware of the existence of Lombards and indigenous moneylenders around them. As much as they may have resented the competition, in their polemics they did not fail to refer to their presence in order to deflect some of the criticism aimed at them. "On what ground do you accuse us of [practicing] usury when the gentiles themselves lend money on interest to Jews as well as to their own brethren, the Christians?" proclaimed a Hebrew writer (probably in the 1260s) who, like Jacob ben Elijah, was writing a polemic against Paulus Christiani.[67] A century earlier, when Italian moneylending was not as widespread as it became in the thirteenth century, the Hebrew intellectual of Narbonne, Joseph Kimhi (1105?–1170?), presented the same argument with no less determination:

> The Jews are indeed scrupulous about usury and the taking of interest from their brethren as the Torah forbade. . . . A Jew will not lend his brother wheat, wine, or any commodity on a term basis in order to increase his profit, while you [Christians] who have disdained usury sell all commodities to your brethren on a term basis at twice the price. You should be ashamed to say that you do not lend them with usury, for this is enormous usury.[68]

In the thirteenth century Jacob ben Elijah's polemics were largely shaped by the great extent of the Italians' business. Jacob wrote: "They are legion; some of them possess a hundred thousand or fifty thousand [pounds?]. . . . Their houses are filled with silver, gold, and precious stones." He was particularly gleeful in pointing out that churchmen were among the Italians' best customers. According to Jacob, prelates needed loans to bribe superiors, hold religious celebrations, and discharge their obligation of almsgiving to the poor. Ecclesiastics were always afraid of not being able to pay off their loans, which would expose them to the threat of excommunication (as we have seen in chapter 1). Always searching for loans, they panicked at the thought of the arrival of the date of repayment:

> The unfortunates [i.e., the prelates] are reduced to seeking the services of these usurers. With tears and supplications, they must borrow the sums they need, "so as not to appear empty-handed before the lord" [i.e., the pope]. They promise interest, a hundred on a thousand and a thousand on ten thousand; they obtain postponements, but "the new moon [shall] devour them with their portions" (Hos. 5:7), for they must celebrate their festivals, offer gifts to the lords, and distribute them also to the poor. If they do not keep their promise, they will be "cursed with the curse" [i.e., excommunication] (Mal. 3:9).[69]

Repeating the arguments made by Christian opponents of moneylending,[70] Jacob could not refrain from insisting on the unlawfulness of these loans made by Christians to other Christians:

"They demand usury from their own brothers, who yet worship the same God, observe the same law, and follow the same faith. . . ."

Christian opinion was quite sensitive to such arguments. In fact, legal and polemical literature of the epoch reveals three kinds of arguments raised in non-Jewish society which, regarding Christian usurers critically, saw many advantages in Jewish moneylending and even came to its defense. One of the three is founded on religious considerations while the other two rest on simple, secular observation of reality.

First, there were Christian thinkers and statesmen who maintained—unlike Thomas Aquinas—that religious law prohibited Christians, but not Jews, from lending money. I have quoted already Frederick II, who asserted that Jews were exempted from the anti-usury laws of his realm, because "they are not under the law established by the most blessed Fathers."[71] By letting Jews practice usury, no religious law was broken. Moreover, so the argument went, banning Jews from a country meant that an open invitation was handed to Christians to engage in the profession. Thus the councillors of Saint Louis (according to the report of William of Chartres) suggested to their monarch "that it was better and more tolerable that the Jews, who are already condemned (according to traditional Christian theology), exercise this function of damnation rather than the Christians."[72] Precisely the same argument appeared in Meir ben Simeon's polemics, without the assumption that Jews were condemned. Meir argued:

> Given that society cannot function without a credit system (loans), it would have been preferable [that the king] for the sake of his own salvation, rather than make Christians transgress their law, should tolerate the practice of moneylending by Jews. They do not belong to his religion, and it is not his duty to make them practice it. The Christians [in contrast] belong to his religion, and sins they commit because of his fault will be imputed to him.[73]

The second argument turned on the alleged rigidity of feudal law and the institutional framework of professions in the medieval city. It stated that Jews were forced by social and economic circumstances into moneylending. This theme was fully developed at the very end of our period by the German jurist Johannes Purgoldt, writing in 1503 or in 1504, as Professor Guido Kisch suggests. According to Purgoldt, the Jews may engage in money-lending

> because they may not own real property in this country, nor own hereditable possessions, from which they are excluded. And if they had such property, people would damage it; if they work in handicrafts, the guilds and master artisans would not tolerate it, and they would not be received into their associations, and the people would not let them work; if they then engage in trading, no one would like to buy from them. And therefore must they thus engage in usury, and this is their excuse.

He then added a punchline: "But the Christian usurers have no such excuse, since they do it from their greed and their abandoned malice."[74]

Purgoldt was not the first to offer a materialistic explanation in defense of Jewish moneylenders. Guido Kisch noticed that the explanation appears in the *Meissener Rechtsbuch*, composed between 1357 and 1387.[75] In fact, more than three hundred years earlier it was promulgated, in a less-developed form, in the *Dialogue between a Philosopher, a Jew, and a Christian* (written in 1136) by Peter Abelard. Abelard had his Jewish protagonist complain that

> we are allowed to possess neither fields nor vineyards nor any landed estates, because there is no one who can protect them for us from open or devious attack. Consequently, the principal gain that is left for us is that we sustain our miserable lives here by lending money at interest to strangers.[76]

Abelard and Purgoldt thus came very close to a fully secular line of argument. Purgoldt took into account the nature of feudal institutions, the rigidity of guilds and crafts, and the social opprobrium people reserved for the Jews. Abelard focused on the military aspects of the seigneurial system, since Jews lacked the means to defend themselves. As some modern historians argue today, these medieval thinkers tried to explain that Jews had no choice but to engage in moneylending.

The third line of argument in defense of Jewish moneylenders was apparently much more widespread, relying as it did on simpler observations. Christian usurers, so the argument ran, charged more than their Jewish counterparts and were harsher toward their customers. This belief became a commonplace among Christians and Jews alike, almost a maxim, and inevitably surfaced whenever a defense of Jewish moneylending was criticized. "I will not mention those Christian moneylenders, if they can be called Christians, who, where there are no Jews, act, I grieve to say, in a manner worse than any Jew,"[77] claimed Bernard of Clairvaux in 1145, on the eve of the second Crusade. At the end of the Middle Ages, the German poet Sebastian Brant, in his *Ship of Fools*, written in 1493, described the pressures of usury on society in similar terms, referring to Christian usurers as "Christian Jews" practicing the art of "the Jewish cut-throat. . . . Really tolerable was what the Jews had asked. The Christian-Jews drove them out. They practice [now] the art of the Jewish cut-throat. And all justice and laws are silent over it."[78]

There was more to these claims than merely better rates of interest charged by Jews. According to a report of Matthew Paris in the *Chronica Majora*, Robert Grosseteste, bishop of Lincoln, had a kind word to say about Jewish moneylenders, as he lay dying in 1253 and delivered a diatribe against Pope Innocent IV, the protector of the Cahorsins.[79] The Cahorsins, Grosseteste said, would force a man who borrowed 100 marks (about 67 pounds) to repay 100 pounds. Even if the borrower offered to pay back his loan ahead of time, the Cahorsins would not take less than 100 pounds. The Jews, in contrast, would ask only for interest on the hundred marks in relation to the time the borrower actually kept the money. In the words of Matthew Paris: "This is worse than a Jew's condition, for the Jew will receive the principal courteously whensoever you shall return to it, with only so much interest as is proportionate to the time for which you had it in hand."

In the Jewish side, Meir ben Simeon of Narbonne did not let this common belief elude his arsenal of arguments: "Were the king to order an investigation all over his realm, he would discover that ever since moneylending was forbidden to Jews, a fair number of his own coreligionists have engaged [in the profession] and have proliferated [and that] they lend on a higher rate of interest, that is, higher than used to be charged by the Jews."[80]

After the expulsion of the Jews in 1306, the mood in France became almost nostalgic. The Jewish usurer, once hated and resented by so many, was now missed by all. A Norman chronicler wrote of the Christian suffering that resulted from the expulsion: "After the expulsion of the Jews they [the Christians] could not find any money except by borrowing it through agents from certain Christians, both clerics and laymen, who lent at such an enormous rate of interest that it was double what was charged by the Jews."[81] These transactions were clandestine, hence "it was done in such a way that the debtors did not know who was in possession of their pledges. This was a dangerous situation, for if the agent died or gave up the business they did not know where to recover [the pledges]." A passage from a rhyming chronicle attributed to Geoffrey of Paris bemoaned the departure of the Jews and described the suffering of the poor, now completely at the mercy of the usurers:

> All the poor complain, for the Jews were much milder
> In the conduct of their business than the Christians
>   are now;
> These demand guarantees and mortgages, pledges, too,
>   and take everything
> Until they have stripped men quite bare . . . but had the
>   Jews remained
> In the kingdom of France, Christians would have had
> Much succor that is theirs no longer.[82]

Indeed, when the Jews were readmitted to France, Louis X indicated that this was due to public pressure ("à la commune clameur de peuple").[83] The document granting their readmission, issued on 28 June 1315, first stated Louis's pious intention to see them engaged in productive occupations but then went immediately to the heart of the matter, that is, the organization of their lending operations.

The ensuing history of Jewish-Christian relations in France is not known in such detail. It is safe to presume, however, that once the euphoria of 1315 passed, moneylenders and borrowers did not live happily ever after. Only two years after the readmission of the Jews, inhabitants of the city of Beaucaire in Languedoc recorded complaints against the excessive usury that Jews charged.[84] In 1360, the royal administration of the *sénéchaussée* of Beaucaire was called upon to "offer remedy" against the excesses of Jewish usurers. Beaucaire's inhabitants, represented by the legal counsel of several cities and villages, claimed that the usury was so high that "it exceeds the principal in one year."[85] *Le songe du vergier*, which as we saw in the previous chapter was strongly critical of Jewish usury, was published about this time. It is safe to conclude that antagonism toward Jewish usury soon reestablished itself in France.

It is worthwhile, nevertheless, to indicate that condemnation of Jews was neither permanent nor universal. People learned to differentiate between the various usurers, and, what is more, they found ways to express their appreciation of some moneylenders. But did Jewish moneylenders really offer a better deal to their customers? To explore this point, we must turn to medieval Jewish documents.

Ma'arufia: Preferred Customers

One result of the state of permanent indebtedness in medieval society, described at the beginning of this chapter, was that moneylenders established a regular clientele. Many borrowers gave their business to the same usurer repeatedly. Louis Stouff observed this phenomenon in Arles in the 1430s and cited the example of Andreas Bellot, who took out four loans from the same Jew, Pons Bone.[86] In England we have already noted how Richard of Anesty, in the middle of the twelfth century, transacted much business with Hackelot the Jew. Was this because he was offered better terms by Hackelot? That this might have been the case is supported by the fact that, while some Jews of London and Cambridge charged Richard a rate of interest of four pence a week (= 87 percent), Hackelot was satisfied with three pence. In fact, on two of his eight loans to Richard, he demanded just two pence a week.[87] A practice of charging a different rate of interest to clients is noticed also in another corner of the world, in Catalonia. Professor Manuel Grau's study of the *Instrumenta Judeorum* of the city of Bessalu for the years 1327–1328 and Immaculoda Ollich i Castanyers's explorations in the *Libri Judeo-*

rum of Vich for the years 1266–1278, leave no doubt about it.[88] There is of course nothing surprising in this. Dynamics of economic life, then as today, tend to favor such special arrangements businessmen have with permanent clients.

Most significantly, Jewish documents of the High Middle Ages (from Germany, in particular) indicate not only that moneylenders often gave favored customers preferential terms but also that such arrangements were often institutionalized and formalized by law. To designate such a preferred customer, medieval Hebrew jurisprudence used a term apparently of Arabic origin— *ma'arufia* or *ma'arif*. Scholars today dispute the exact etymology of *ma'arufia*[89] as well as the way this word reached northern Europe.[90] They all agree, however, that *ma'arufia* appears in German Hebrew documents quite early, around the year 1000, and it can be found throughout the High Middle Ages.

The rabbis of the High Middle Ages were asked to discuss the issue of *ma'arufia*, mostly, when a question was raised of economic monopoly. A Jewish moneylender who wished to cultivate a relationship with a Christian customer would naturally strive to prevent intrusion by others. To safeguard his relationship, he would even ask that rabbinic and community authorities officially and legally sanction his monopoly. For instance, the German rabbi Gershom ben Judah of Mainz, the "luminary of the Diaspora" (c. 960–1028), dealt with the problem of a Jew who "approached the community with the request that a ban be pronounced restraining all persons from doing business with his *ma'arufia*, since he assiduously cultivated the friendship of the latter, often lent him money at no interest and countless times served him in various capacities."[91] In some Jewish communities such arrangements were indeed supported by local customs and ordinances, and the beneficiaries were expected to purchase this privilege from the community. In others, no such legislation existed. "The law of *ma'arufia* depends on local custom," declared Gershom.[92] In one of his *responsa* Gershom observed that "the law of *ma'arufia* is not accepted in your community," and in another he inferred from the community's letter "that the law of *ma'arufia* is not accepted in your community." Even as late as the twelfth century no standard law of *ma'arufia* existed among Jews of Europe,[93] but there is ample evidence that these special relationships persisted between Jews and their "preferred customers" throughout the High Middle Ages and even down to early modern times.[94]

Along with the rabbinic writings on *ma'arufia*, there are half a dozen or so short Hebrew *exempla* from about the year 1200, assembled in Germany, principally by Jehuda Hasid, his son, and his disciples, in a collection of some two thousand *exempla* known today as *Sefer hasidim*.[95] From these *exempla* it is possible to learn about the services performed by the Jewish moneylender in favor of his customer and also to share some of his thoughts and anxieties.

The first thing apparent from this evidence is that the "preferred customer" expected to receive a reduced rate of interest on his loans. *Exemplum* number 1205 of *Sefer hasidim* refers to a Jew who "lent money . . . to a gentile whom he used to favor, his *ma'arif*. If he [the gentile] had been another, he [the moneylender] would have claimed from him thirty pennies. But from him he only takes twenty."[96] To this straightforward explanation one might juxtapose a situation described in a *responsum* of Eliezer ben Nathan of Mainz (c. 1090–1170), in which a moneylender turned to a colleague for a favor.[97] Eliezer quoted the moneylender as asking that his colleague "please lend money to my *ma'arufia* at a certain rate of interest per week." Obviously, he sought cheap credit for his customer. At any event he assured his colleague: "All losses that you may incur on that account, I take it upon myself to cover them." A hundred years later, also in Germany, a similar exchange of services in the profession is recorded. This time the pledges which the Christian *ma'arufia* offered were not good enough and would not cover the principal or the interest. The moneylender, eager to get a loan for his *ma'arufia* from another, agreed to become guarantor for the loan.[98]

It seems also that Jewish moneylenders would be expected to desist from asking the *ma'arufia* for a pledge. *Sefer hasidim* does not list this as one of the favors a *ma'arufia* might receive. However, some fragments from a Jewish moneylender's notebook from Konstanz in southern Germany, written sometime in the second half of the fourteenth century[99]—summer 1372 was recently suggested for its composition—support this supposition. For each loan this unknown moneylender recorded the sort of security he received from the customer: a ring, a chalice, a girdle, a written instrument, an oath. Once he even admitted that he had forgotten what the pledge was. On two occasions he stated that loans were given "without pledge." One of the loans was issued without the security of a "pledge or a written instrument." Although in neither of these instances was the customer identified as a *ma'arufia*, it is obvious that only the most trusted clients would not be asked for a pledge.

For moneylenders, being short of liquid capital must have been fairly common nightmare. In *exemplum* number 1211 of *Sefer hasidim*, the concern of a Jew who was about to hire a scribe to copy a book is described.[100] Would he be able to pay the scribe on time? The Jew reflected: "I will surely have them [i.e., the sums of money] available then, but I will not be able to give them to him," because "perhaps my *ma'arufia* will come and I will have to lend him money."

Shortage of money was not the only problem. No less embarrassing a situation could occur when clients urgently needed money on a Sabbath or Jewish holiday, when Jews were not permitted to do business—nor even to touch money. Rabbinic authorities were certain not to offer any leniency in this matter. The Jews of Lérida in Catalonia, in order not to be confronted with such a complication, obtained on 3 July 1265 a special privilege from James I in which Christians were forbidden to disturb Jews with business requests on the Jewish Sabbath and holidays.[101] However, in the case of a Jewish "lesser feast" (*Hol ha-Moed*)— that is, the days between the first and the last days of the feast of Tabernacles, or the feast of Passover—there was a firm tradition which permitted Jews to advance money to the *ma'arufia* but not to charge interest for those days.[102] The authority for this was the illustrious Meir of Rothenburg (c. 1219–1293). His younger contemporary, Asher ben Yehiel (c. 1250–1327), would even allow interest to be charged on the lesser holidays.[103] Both showed leniency for the same reason: "so that he [the Jewish moneylender] does not lose his *ma'arufia*."

In their efforts to keep business, Jews would bestow upon customers favors not necessarily related to moneylending. Eliezer ben Nathan of Mainz recorded a situation in which a Jew asked a colleague of his: "Let me have your coat [on an advance payment of] one mark. It is my wish to offer it [as a present] to my *ma'arufia* and I will send it to him. If he likes it, I will pay you its full price—if not, you will get your coat back."[104] The *ma'arufia*, whom our text document described as an important lay dignitary (*ha-Sar* in Hebrew), did not want the present. On the Jew's return from the castle, he was assaulted by bandits who stole the coat. Eliezer ben Nathan was called upon to decide whether the Jew should reimburse the original owner for its full value. The promotional intent of such gestures surely did not escape the attention of medieval people. They may have regarded such acts, nevertheless, as an essential aspect of commerce, which emphasized trust and compliance in the business of moneylending.[105]

Marseilles 1317: Clients in Defense of Their Moneylender

All this is relevant to the question of the sincerity of the twenty-four people who testified in Marseilles in 1317 in defense of a Jewish moneylender. By now we have enough evidence to realize that medieval people, accustomed to loans and indebtedness, generally considered moneylending a necessary part of life. If "society could not function without loans," the question was, Who was the best moneylender? People in Marseilles in the 1300s, as in so many other places, could readily make comparisons between Christian and Jewish moneylenders. While no toleration could be given to Christian usurers, Jewish practitioners could be accepted on grounds of Christian religious law as well as social and institutional considerations.

Experience may have persuaded many people that they got a better deal from the Jewish moneylender. Evidence about *ma'arufia* indicates that Jews did indeed make special efforts to serve their Christian clients. In many cases, there was a relaxed, cordial relationship between the moneylender and his client. It is in this framework that we should understand the depositions heard in favor of Bondavid at the court of Marseilles in February and March of 1317. Because over twenty of these depositions were recorded and because some of the witnesses were so outspoken, the documents preserved at the archives of Marseilles are exceptionally valuable. They are the only records we have in which we can hear the *ma'arufia* speaking.

5

Shylock Reconsidered: Bondavid Seen by His Friends

The Document, Once Again

In order to evaluate better the documents that relate to Bondavid's trial in 1317, let us briefly review the chronology of the case. Bondavid made the contended loan to Laurentius on 11 April 1315. Two years and three months later, on 11 July 1317, a decision was issued by the court. While we do not know when Bondavid first asked, in court, for repayment of the loan of sixty shillings, it is certain that his witnesses in the second stage of the procedure were sworn in, a few at a time, through the month of February 1317. Laurentius had the legal right to designate some of them as unacceptable, which he apparently did. Then, in the period between 11 and 15 February, the notary recorded testimony from all persons who were called as witnesses to the character of Petrus Guizo, the only witness Laurentius had. Afterward, between 18 February and 2 March, a second group of individuals testified about Bondavid's probity. All this testimony was taken by the notary without the presence of Bondavid and Laurentius so that the witnesses could testify freely. On 6 April— more than a month after the last witness was questioned— Bonetus Aurioli, Laurentius's father-in-law, testified and confirmed Bondavid's version of their conversation. From 11 April,

Bondavid, eager to know what the witnesses had said, sought publication of the evidence. Since Laurentius was not in town, and in general did not seem eager to cooperate, this was not done until two days later. On 4 May, the judge handed the controversial obligatory deed for the loan to Bondavid, who, for his part, must have interpreted this gesture as a very favorable omen. Therefore, from 10 June he once again pressed the court to invite both sides to attend and to give the final decision in their presence. Laurentius was still not cooperating, so there was further delay. Finally, on 11 July the decision was issued.

In register III B37 at the Archives des Bouches-du-Rhône, Provence, in Marseilles, documents describing the proceedings are not presented according to this chronological sequence. The first page (folio 5r) contains the oaths taken between 9 and 14 February by the first group of witnesses, but a log or résumé of the whole trial down to the final act on 11 July takes up subsequent pages (to 9r). Folios 10r–19r revert to the testimony of that first group of witnesses, but not in chronological order. First there is Hugo Bernardi's deposition taken on 15 February, and then that of Raymundus de Alesto, which was given four days earlier. This chronological disorder characterizes not only registration of the testimony of the first group of witnesses but also that of the second group, whose depositions were taken between 18 February and 2 March (28r–49r). Folio 27r, in a way similar to 5r, records the selection of witnesses who belonged to the second group, a procedure that took place between 18 and 24 February.

Thus register III B7 is not a spontaneous and continuous record of the procedure but rather an edited version of it. The notary surely took preliminary notes in his draft book and only later, in his *bodega* (44v), wrote up a good copy in the court register. As Bondavid's was not the only lawsuit the notary handled, he had to estimate how many folios in the register should be left free for the final version, and then had to go on immediately to the other pending cases. This is why we have in this register the common occurrence of so many blank pages (e.g., fols. 19v–23v, 25r–26v, 38r, etc.) and such apparent disorder. In addition, when the notary discovered that he had indeed miscalculated, he had to record documents that belonged to one lawsuit in a section that originally was intended for another. For instance, folios 13r–14r and 24v do not belong to Bondavid's trial. In order to find his way through this disarray, the notary used different symbols to indicate where in the register the various entries could be found: "Seek above for such a sign" (*Quere supra ad tale signum*) in 5r, and in 12v "Seek below for such a sign in the third folio" (*Quere infra ad tale signum in tertio folio*).

As mentioned in chapter 1, folio 49Ar–v contains the *interrogatoria*, that is, questions the other side asked the notary to present to the witnesses for each of Bondavid's "titles" or "articles." Although there is no record of these titles or articles, it is not particularly difficult to reconstruct their major thrust and even their possible wording. Of the three *articuli* in Bondavid's letter, the first dealt with the proposal Bondavid received from Laurentius's father-in-law: accept a partial payment of forty of the sixty shillings in dispute. This first article must have read something like this: "First Bondavid intends to prove that he was asked by several individuals [*per aliquas personas*] to reach an agreement [*facere compositionem*] with Laurentius but that he refused to do so."[1] Petrus Bonifilii, one of the first witnesses, and probably the very first, did give testimony on this article on 18 February, the first day of the hearings (44v). When Bondavid or his lawyer decided to withdraw the article, all other witnesses in February and March referred to articles 2 and 3 only. There is no written explanation for this withdrawal. Was it omitted because the plural "individuals" was used in the article, while the proposition came from one person, or because most of the witnesses could not have known anything about it? Only a month after the hearings were finished, when Bonetus Aurioli, the key witness, had a change of heart and appeared in court, was the content of the title read again. This must have been a turning point in the drama, for less than a week later (11 April), Bondavid started to apply pressure on the court to publish all testimony.

As for articles 2 and 3 in Bondavid's letter, they both seem to have been of a much more general nature. Article 3 apparently referred to favors Bondavid was known to have extended, stating "that Bondavid usually grants favors [*gratiae*] to many individuals concerning their loans." It is not impossible that the article described these favors, which may have been "prolonging the time of repayments of these loans, restoring part of the loan to the debtors, and rendering freely [*gratiose*] instruments [*mandamenta*] to these individuals, without the loan being completely paid off."[2]

For this study, the heart of the matter was article 2, which stated Bondavid's virtues and qualities as a *homo legalis*. It contained the claim that he had never been known to ask for payment of the same loan twice and concluded with a statement that these facts were well known all over the city. The article that can be reconstructed from the depositions of at least three witnesses employed a style and terminology very common in practice then (we find similar language in Bologna, Manosque, and elsewhere) and must have read something like this: "That the said Bondavid is a good man, pacific and of good standing [*legalis*], of good reputation [*bone opinionis*], and that he has never defrauded anybody or committed deceit by word, deed, or machination. Neither would he ask a second time for a loan that had been paid to him. In regard to these things he has a reputation [*fama*] in the city of Marseilles among neighbors and people of eminence."[3]

Analysis of testimony in register III B7 clarifies the repetition in the text, since witnesses simply restated the contents of the articles. Fortunately, there were also statements which went beyond the article and contributed unexpected information. Thus when Bernardus Gardii (45v) stated that Bondavid was known as one who was always engaged in *bona facta bonas conversationes cum bonis gentibus perseverantem et conversantem*, he probably added, on his own initiative, an assessment which his contemporaries may have particularly appreciated. Saint Louis, king of France, also surrounded himself with "faithful and discreet men of good conversation and repute,"[4] and this ideal of conduct was still held in Marseilles in the time of Bondavid. When Guillelmus Gasqueti (41v) exclaimed, approvingly, that there was in the whole world no one of better standing (*legalior*) than Bondavid, this, too, went beyond the linguistic confines of article 2.

Bondavid's Witnesses

The individuals Bondavid requested to appear in court were, obviously, people on whom he could rely to testify in his favor. His adversary Laurentius had the right to bar the testimony of certain witnesses. From the list of witnesses in folio 27r, which contains names of persons who did not later appear in court, one may conclude that he exercised this prerogative.

All of the witnesses knew Bondavid through his moneylending. Ricavus Ricavi knew him (28v) "from the time he was born," a statement that implies he was a client of Bondavid's father, Abraham. The nobleman Arnaud de Baux and the *mercator* Hugo Mercerii, also designated *apothecarius*, had appeared as witnesses to the last will of Abraham, Bondavid's father. Girardus Monteolivus (40r) met Bondavid when the Jew came to Girardus's house to do business with his brother Monteolivus de Monteolivo and with their mother Maria. Master Pascal, a notary, had known Bondavid for twenty-five years or more (33r), while others mentioned acquaintances of ten, fifteen, or eighteen years.

The exact volume of business which Bondavid or his father engaged in with these witnesses is impossible to determine. Ricavus Ricavi, however, told the court that in his case it was extensive. As for the other witnesses, documents found in the notarial archives indicate that they had vital economic dealings with the Jewish community. Thus a list of the holdings of Maria de Monteolivo, the mother of two witnesses, reveals she owned at least eight houses in the *jusataria* of Marseilles in 1321.[5] In 1301 the nobleman Petrus Bermundi of Saint-Félix—another of Bondavid's witnesses—was the owner of at least two houses in the Jewish quarter.[6] In 1319 the Jewish doctor Vitalis de Neumaso had to pay Petrus Bermundi a tax called *directum* or *dominium* for a house previously inhabited by Aaron de Camera.[7] Another Jew, Salves Corderii, also paid to Petrus Bermundi, about this time, the *dominium* for a house located *in quadam carreria jusaterie, dicta de Viridario*.[8] These, of course, are just glimpses of what were no doubt extensive business relationships.

On the question of the social status of these witnesses, there is more information available. Did Bondavid succeed in bringing to court only individuals who were on the margins of society, or did they belong to the mainstream of the social, economic, and political establishment of their time? Taking into account formal and professional criteria, eight of the twenty-four carried the title *nobilis, domicellus,* or *miles* and therefore ostensibly did belong to the upper echelons of society. In addition, one was a clergyman, three were public notaries, one was a merchant (*mercator*), and two were designated *civis Massilie.* Less is known about the other witnesses, but some actually seem to have been poor people. They were brought to court because some of them had much to say about Bondavid's generosity. It is not impossible that Bondavid also wanted to have in his list representatives from all walks of life, so it would be a true reflection of the society in which he was carrying on his activities. In canonization processes of the period, André Vauchez noticed recently a similar tendency to have witnesses representing all classes and professions testify before the commissions.[9]

When trying to sketch the career and status of Bondavid's witnesses, we must concentrate our attention on the noble and affluent because of the nature of the extant documents. Very rarely do the other individuals surface in the documents. Even with the wealthy, there is more information about their families than about the individuals themselves. Thus the noblemen Arnaud de Baux and Andreas Bonvini remain almost anonymous despite extensive searches in the archives; but the status of their families can be described in some detail.[10]

Arnaud de Baux carried the name of one of Provence's most ancient and ambitious feudal families, prominent in Provence's struggles for independence.[11] Barral de Baux was a key figure in the 1250s, when he headed a Provençal coalition against the Angevins, who were then about to impose their rule over the region. This very old family, which appears in our documents in the second half of the tenth century and had its origins in Arles, by 1300 possessed holdings all over the southern part of the country, especially in the area of Berre and Aix. Among the titles held by members of the Baux family were Prince of Orange and, since the beginning of the thirteenth century, Viscount of Marseilles. Like other aristocratic families, the Baux too had to admit defeat and come to terms with the victorious Angevins. In 1310 one of them, Raymond de Baux, held the position of Seneschal of the county. Another, Hugues de Baux, held the title in 1343.

As for Andreas Bonvini,[12] his ancestors in the 1220s had participated in the attempt to create an independent republic in Marseilles. Not as distinguished as the Baux family, the Bonvinis by the 1280s became part of the new regime created by the Angevins. Andreas's father, Barthelmus, served in the last quarter of the century in the highest naval position in Provence, with the title *admirallus regius in Provincia*. Among Barthelmus's descendants, we know the names of Nicholas, Girardus, and Barthelmus, as well as Andreas, who seems to have been the first of his family to be ennobled. They all held very distinguished positions in the municipal institutions of Marseilles during Bondavid's lifetime.

A similar profile could be drawn for the Ricavis or the Sardis or the Bermundis.[13] These, too, are families that appear in our documents at the beginning of the twelfth century in connection with efforts for independence for Marseilles. By 1300, they were already ennobled and were part of what is generally designated as the governing urban oligarchy. Of special interest is the Monteolivus family, with which Bondavid had a close relationship. Girardus de Monteolivo expressly mentioned this fact, and the name Monteolivus de Monteolivo was referred to constantly when witnesses enumerated Bondavid's friends at the request of the court.[14] The Monteolivi had acquired considerable wealth in the previous centuries, chiefly by participating in the maritime commerce of the city. Although by 1300 they had a noble title and possessed considerable real estate, they continued their involvement in the city's commerce through the century.

Other members of the family, such as Guillaume, Foulque, Blanquier, and Maria, appear in the documents, although how they were related to one another is not always indicated. However, Monteolivus de Monteolivo is one person for whom the archives reveal much information. His involvement in the political life of the city is reflected in the records of municipal deliberations from at least the 1320s, when these documents form a continuous series. After that date, there is hardly a year when he is not mentioned in one capacity or another. In 1323 he participated in military operations in Italy, and a year later he was in Naples as *consul Massilhiensis*,[15] a vitally important position reserved in

Date Due _____   Item No. _____

Place on hold _____

Recalled _____

Shelves checked _____

Verification:

OCLC _____

NUC _____

Other _____

Trying locs _____

_____

Shipped _____

Due _____

Rec'd _____

Ret'd _____

Lib _____

BOOK REQUEST FORM
STATE LIBRARY OF FLORIDA

Date _____

Patron _____

Card Number: _____

Agency: _____ Bldg. _____ Rm. _____

Mailing Address _____ Phone _____

Author _____

Title _____

Publisher _____ Date of Pub. _____

State Library Call Number _____

Marseilles for the most powerful and influential families. Ten years later, back in Marseilles, he was a member of a committee of four elected to collect a very unpopular tax of five hundred-pounds. As an ambassador for the city, he negotiated with the highest dignitaries of his time. In March 1348, when Queen Joan of Naples entered the city with the usual solemnity and pomp, it was he who headed the group of local dignitaries who received her. In 1357, a year of war, he served as one of the syndics of Marseilles and displayed much energy in the effort to save the city from collapse. It was not the first time he served in this capacity: in 1332 he was elected syndic and held this position for a year. He survived the Black Death and continued his involvement in politics in the following years. To judge from the municipal documents, after the year 1348 his activity did not diminish at all. Rather it seems that nothing was done in city politics without his knowledge and consent.

One of the features of municipal government of the time, in Provence as elsewhere, was that the urban oligarchy, in coalition with the nobles, kept a very strong grip on the political institutions of the city. This was also the situation in Marseilles.[16] It is not astonishing, then, to discover that most of the other witnesses for Bondavid, whose lives are not as well documented as Monteolivus's, also participated actively in the politics of Marseilles. Andreas Bonvini served as a syndic in Marseilles in 1323. His brothers were members of the city council.[17] Ricavus Ricavi represented the quarter (*sixaine* or *seysene*) of Saint-Jacques in the municipal council. Since the city had six such districts and each generally sent only one representative, the prominence of Ricavus becomes a bit clearer.[18] Arnaud de Baux, who certainly is not well represented in the documents, was a member of the city council in 1320.[19] Petrus Bermundi of Saint-Félix participated in a delegation that Marseilles sent to the papal court in 1295, on the occasion of a dispute with the city's archbishop.[20] When, in 1307, the council of Marseilles decided to lobby for the beatification of Louis of Toulouse, son of Prince Charles, Petrus Bermundi was one of the four proctors entrusted with this important mission.[21] In January 1318 he and Vivandus de Jerusalem, member of another aristocratic family, served as *ambaxiatores pro civ-*

itate Massilie pro magnis et arduis negotiis civitatis predicte, and were sent to meet the court.[22] Three years later Petrus Bermundi was made *familiaris* and *magister hostiarum* by King Robert in return for his services, an honor that was bestowed previously on another member of the urban aristocracy, Augier de Mar.[23]

It is true that not all the families of Marseilles's oligarchy were represented at the lawsuit of Bondavid. Members of such great families as Conge, Cornat, Jerusalem, Tempte, and Mar did not appear. Nonetheless, the testimony of members of the Baux, Bonvini, Monteolivi, Ricavi, and Bremundi families reveals that it was certainly not to the fringes of society that Bondavid looked for help. Additional support for their mainstream status can be gathered from the fact that among Bondavid's witnesses were four of the five members of the committee appointed ten years earlier (1307) by the council of Marseilles to promote the canonization of Louis of Anjou—the most important religious and political project of the time. These four were Master Raymundus Egidii and Raymundus Viridis, as well as the nobleman Petrus Bermundi of Saint-Félix and the "citizen of Marseilles" Hugo de Fonte. The fifth member of the committee, "Dominus Gufridus Ricavi Miles," must have been related to Ricavus Ricavi, Bondavid's friend.[24]

Praise for Bondavid

It is remarkable that none of the elite witnesses for Bondavid—or indeed any of the other witnesses—contradicted in any way the content of either of the "articles," but rather endorsed them enthusiastically. Even Bonetus Aurioli, once he was brought before the court, had only praise for the Jewish moneylender. As for the others, one gets the impression that they regarded the statements of both articles as understatements of Bondavid's virtues and hence made a special effort to elaborate on them.

Four statements in particular merit our special attention because of their content and also because of the way in which they were told. Historians of medieval literature might find it profitable to analyze the structure of these statements, in order to determine whether they are stylized renditions by a notary or examples of popular medieval narrative. For the purposes of social history, these statements are valuable in that they remove us from the realm of generalities and show us in concrete terms the relationship between a moneylender and his favored customers.

One account about Bondavid was told by two different witnesses, probably because it was the most remarkable of the incidents reported. In folio 29v, the reporter was Petrus Ferreri, *domicellus*, while in folio 46v it was Dominus Raymundus Viridis, cleric. The story revolved around a sum of two thousand *tournois* (two hundred pounds in Marseilles' currency, according to the historian Philippe Mabilly)[25] which Canon Raymundus Egidii had deposited *ad custodiam* with Bondavid, "without witnesses or any written document." When the canon died, Bondavid went to see Hugo Guacelini, executor of the deceased man's will. Hugo told the story to Petrus Ferrerini:

> [Bondavid asked,] "Sir Hugo, did my Sir Raymundus Egidii—may his soul rest in peace—before his death hand over to you any obligatory note, that is, a receipt, or a public and private act in which I Bondavid am obligated to him? . . . " The said Sir Hugo answered Bondavid that he did not discover any document in which he was obligated to the said Sir Raymundus. And without delay Bondavid told the said Sir Hugo, in his capacity as executor [*gazarius*] of the will of the said Sir Raymundus, that he [Bondavid] has two thousand silver *tournois* "which the said Sir Raymundus handed over to me so that I might guard them for him." And immediately he gave them to me.

The narrator, Petrus Ferrerini, assured the court that he had heard the story from Hugo in his chamber. Hugo introduced the story with the phrase: "Do you want to hear about the excellent standing [*legalitas*] of this Jew?" In the version of Raymundus Viridis, himself a cleric, the story ran along similar lines. He too insisted that—although Bondavid could have taken all the money, there being no document extant—he in fact returned it.

A witness at the other end of the social scale told the tale of a workman's wife who went to Bondavid to return a loan or part of a loan. Petrus de Trella, *civis Massilie*, was at Bondavid's house on that occasion, and it was he who reported the incident to the court (38v–39r). After the woman (*quadam bona mulier*) handed over the money, Bondavid asked her: "Tell me, mother, how do you live and what profession do you have?" She answered: "Know, Sir, that I have nothing to live from if not the labor and the toil of my husband." According to the report, "When Bondavid heard it, and considering her poverty, he gave back to the woman a great quantity of money, as the witness himself saw."

Petrus Vitalis, fisherman, provided the court [36v] with yet another illustration of *gratia* which Bondavid displayed without being asked to do so:

> One day when the witness was on the bank of the Saint John [of the port of Marseilles] and wanted to purchase a certain quantity of fish, but did not have [money] to pay for them, he was murmuring to himself and saying to some others that he does not have anything with which to pay for these fishes. Bondavid, while walking on the same bank, heard it and ordered one of his household to hand him twenty florins without any deed, without [any written] mandate or [the presence of] witnesses . . . and without charging him interest, if he will give it back.

The fourth account, that of Bonetus Aurioli (49v), has as its origin a Jew's inability to do business on the Sabbath. It is also reminiscent of the services a *maarufia* could receive according to *Sefer hasidim*. Aurioli, who found himself in urgent need of cash, turned to Bondavid on the Sabbath for help. He "immediately opened his case and the witness took as much as he needed, and that is forty silver *tournois*." Bondavid did not then touch the money nor establish any conditions for the loan.

These four accounts are the most detailed and, in a sense, the most dramatic in these documents. What other people said was no less significant and involved larger sums of money. The notaries Pascal de Mayranicis and Petrus Columbi, who worked very closely with Bondavid in recording deeds for him and filing his claims, reported on the generosity and said that it was a feature of his business life. Pascal (32r–v), who knew Bondavid for sixteen years, related the case of "the son of Johannes Drago," who was later hanged, to whom Bondavid returned some silver *tournois* despite Johannes's admission in court that he owed it to Bondavid on a loan. "The witness [Pascal] also saw some *mandamenta* involving significant quantities of silver *tournois* being torn up by the said Jew." The text continued, "the notary [who was reading the content of these *mandamenta* to the Jew] saying to the witness, that the *mandamenta* were of friends who passed away."

The other notary, Petrus Columbi (42v), saw and heard many of Bondavid's debtors turn to the Jew for favors, both in and out of court. "Some asked to prolong the term of payment, while others asked that he forgo part of the debt. Never did he see him denying a favor to anybody, but rather did he always extend to them favors; so that the said debtors were thankful to the said Bondavid for the favors which he did." Petrus continued: "Bondavid said to almost all his debtors, 'How much time do you want or how much do you want me to discount for you?'"

Several of the witnesses were people who had actually enjoyed Bondavid's largesse, while others knew about favors he bestowed on a third party. Petrus Ferreri, *domicellus* (29v), was given a discharge of a debt, "and it seems to him that it was a sum of six or seven pounds." Guillelmus Stephani (39v), who stated "that he had much to do with Bondavid in what concerns money and other business," testified that the Jew "extended him a lot of favors," lending him money *gratis*, without any profit of gain. Bondavid also "prolonged [the date of payment] of loans he contracted with him according to his [Guillelmus's] wish." Another preferred client, or *ma'arufia*, of Bondavid, Guillelmus Gasqueti (41v), got his money back from Bondavid on several occasions. "Also he lent him money on many occasions without any deed or mandate or witnesses."

Bondavid also extended favors at the request of persons who interceded on behalf of others. Petrus Bartholi (35v) was instrumental in a great favor Bondavid extended to Johannes Girando. "At his [Bartholi's] request," Bondavid postponed the date of payment on a loan of sixty-four pounds, "twice and thrice and in intervals of one month and more." Similarly, Petrus Bartholi obtained deferrals for Petrus Bollimeni. The nobleman Arnaud de Baux (48r) knew of "Dominus Jacob Angelicus," who benefited from Bondavid's generosity in "prolonging" his debt, after de Baux requested Bondavid to do so. A similar request by de Baux on behalf of Hugo Langeriirus also met with success. Petrus Bonifilii (44v–45r) saw how "Bondavid discharged part of the debt of a certain man while he, the witness, was present in the house of Bondavid." To another, Raymundus Payrolerii, a kinsman of the same witness, Bondavid extended a similar favor.[26] Other beneficiaries of Bondavid's generosity mentioned by various witnesses were Jacob Petri, *mulaterius* (29r), Guillelmus Brindin, and Rostang Pugani.

All in all, it seems that there were three major ways in which a moneylender could benefit his client. The first was postponement of repayment; the second, remittance of part of the interest; and the third, not asking for documents or any security in connection with the loan. Of the three, it would seem that most requested and most appreciated was the *prolongatio* or *prorogatio*, also labeled in Spanish documents of the time as *elongamentum*, *elongatio debiti*, or *provisio*. Jacob ben Elijah of Venice referred—as we have seen in chapter 4—to prelates who trembled at the thought of an approaching repayment date. In Aragon, and in Provence as well, people expected help from the monarchy in this respect, and indeed we hear that James I and his successors forcibly imposed such *elongamenta* on Jewish loans. Jews in Aragon had to obtain special privileges (presumably against payments or in return for special services) which for a year, or even several years, would grant them protection against such intervention in their business practice. "From now on and for the coming three complete years we shall not prolong to any of your debtors or to their guarantors [*fidejussores*] any of the debts they owe you," promised James I of Aragon to the community of Perpignan.[27] In the previous decade they had obtained from him a similar promise at least twice, as did the communities of Saragossa, Barcelona, and many others.[28] In 1333, the doctor Eliezer Aben Ardut obtained protection against enforced prolongation for himself and his immediate relatives, as did another doctor, Astrug, in 1350.[29] However, Bondavid was ready to

award such *prolongationes* on his own. We may better understand the appreciative tone of the witnesses in describing his generosity in this respect, now that we know how much effort and
money people invested in the issue of *prolongationes*.

Partial remittance of interest was not considered a rare act on
the part of moneylenders, judging from what people said about
Bondavid. He would do this either by returning some quantity
of money or by making void, tearing up, or handing over the documents before the debt was fully paid. Was this perhaps related,
consciously or unconsciously, to the restitution that Christian
moneylenders were forced to make, and which Jews, under Saint
Louis, were forced into? From what the witnesses had to say
about the frequency with which Bondavid offered remittances,
one has the distinct impression that moneylenders were expected, as a matter of course, to remit part of their gain.

The third manifestation of Bondavid's probity was his ap-
proach to documents for pledges and the presence of witnesses.
An easygoing attitude to security for loans was also a quality one
would expect to find in an ideal moneylender. It was due, no
doubt, to the embarrassment and discomfort, indeed hostility,
that so many felt when dealing with legal formalities.[30] Medieval
men still wanted to believe that a man's word was his bond. In
his almost nonchalant attitude toward legal documents and written formalities, Bondavid shared this value of his society. Although a Jew and a merchant, he acted according to a code of
behavior that was appreciated by all: ideals of largesse, generosity, openhandedness, loyalty, and compliance. These ideals were
possessed by men of distinction, such as William Marshall, the
famous English baron of the twelfth and the thirteenth century
described recently by Georges Duby,[31] and they found their way
into the city and were adopted by the world of commerce and
moneylending as well. Bondavid, in his day-to-day life, displayed
such attributes and was careful to cultivate them. He knew how
society expected him to behave. When asked by Bonetus Aurioli
(reported by Petrus Bonifilii, 44v) to agree to forty shillings, he
refused. "Let Laurentius pay back the whole sum," was his decree, and then "he [Bondavid] was ready to do what an honest
man [*bonus homo*] has to do."

We may safely state therefore that moneylending was not isolated from the mentality and from the ethics that governed society. People very much appreciated moneylenders who displayed
qualities that made one an honest and righteous man. The degree
of appreciation some of them had for Bondavid can be measured
by the superlatives they used. Hugo Mercerii (31v) did not believe "that in the whole world can be found a Jew more righteous
in his law, or according to his law, or more just" than Bondavid.
In the judgment of the noble Andreas Bonvini (43r–44r), one
could not consider anyone more righteous than Bondavid, "and
he does not believe that there is a more righteous man in the city
or elsewhere." Petrus Bermundi of Saint-Félix (37v) did not find
"among those who belong to his law anybody more righteous,
and this is well known among Jews of the city." The insistence
of Hugo Mercerii and the two others just quoted on Bondavid's
"law," that is, his religion, should not, in my opinion, lead us to
conclude that they were insinuating that he was acceptable for
a Jew—but no more than that. On the contrary, so long as he remained within his religion, Bondavid or any other Jew was expected to behave as "a good and legal Jew living according to his
law" (*bonus et legalis judeas vivens secundum legem suam*).[32]

That the use of superlatives was to express absolute appreciation can be seen in the remarks of Guillelmus Gasqueti, a clergyman, as well as those of two other laymen, Petrus Columbi and
Arnaud de Baux. Gasqueti (41v) knew that in the *jusataria* of
Marseilles Bondavid was considered the most righteous Jew in
the city. Then, in order to prevent any misunderstanding,
Gasqueti added the following clarification: "And actually [Bon-
david is] more righteous than anybody he ever met in his life. He
does not believe that there is [one] more righteous than he in the
whole world. For, if one may say so, he never met or saw a Christian more righteous than he." Petrus Columbi (43r) assured the
court that Bondavid would not change his righteous behavior
even if there were a "thousand pounds or infinite sums of money
to be gained," while the nobleman Arnaud de Baux (48r–v)
stated that as far as moneylending was concerned, he would
count on Bondavid as on himself and would trust him as he would
his own brother.

The Shadows of the Council of Vienne

The excesses of enthusiasm are, beyond doubt, a tribute to the personality of Bondavid. Rarely, if anywhere, can we find in medieval literature so much praise bestowed upon a Jew, especially a moneylender. It is a tribute also to the civic spirit of Marseilles that leading citizens could display so much tolerance and humanity. Bondavid's opponents, in the *interrogatoria* which they handed over to the notary, must have foreseen the praise he would receive and therefore inserted a question to dampen their enthusiasm: Did the witness "know that the said Bondavid lends money on usury, that he is a *fenerator*, and that he publicly lends money on usury?" The two witnesses whose answers to this particular question were recorded knew that very well but did not mind it. Monteolivus de Monteolivo answered he believed that such was the case, "like all other Jews." Hugo Mercerii answered in the same vein (31v). Neither saw anything unusual in the fact. In the spirit of equanimity which we have noticed in Italian city-republics and which inspired the legislation of Marseilles, they might have even been surprised that the question was raised.

This exchange took place in March 1317. A year later, it would have been impossible to talk about *usura* in such a neutral tone in Marseilles: On 24 February 1318, in a dramatic move, the council of the city decided to remove from its *statuts* the paragraph "for which amount of money one should be brought to court"—which legitimated usury, as we have seen, and to make the canon "Ex gravi" part of their municipal legislation. They did not explain what caused this change of heart, yet it is possible to figure it out, even though the records of the municipal council for 1317 or 1318 are not extant.

The canon *Ex gravi* promulgated by the Council of Vienne (in 1311–1312) labeled as heretics those who held that "usury is not a sin" and threatened them with the Inquisition; the prelates in Vienne went however beyond generalities and proposed a precise and practical plan for extirpating evil. Civic authorities were commanded to remove from their written statutes any item that legitimated usury. "Reliable sources inform us," declared the council, "that certain communities, in violation of the law both human and divine, approve the practice of usury. By their statutes, confirmed by oath, they not only permit the exaction and payment of usury but deliberately compel debtors to pay it. They also try by heavy statutory penalties and various other means and threats to prevent recovery by individuals who demand repayment of excessive interest."[33] The prelates announced that a sentence of excommunication would follow "if within three months they do not remove such statutes from the books of those communities, . . . or if they presume in any way to observe the said statutes or customs to the same effect."

The leaders of Marseilles gathered that their city was meant by this decretal. Brussels in Brabant was another city that showed (in 1319) some concern in this respect.[34] For Marseilles this obviously meant the removal of the paragraph *pro qua quantitate usure adjudicentur*, and this was done on 24 February 1318. In its new legislation, the council acknowledged that in this particular statute there was a recognition of usury (*tacite vel expresse*) and decided to remove it from their laws. In a special decree entitled "revocation of statutes concerning usuries"—which expressly mentioned Pope Clement, the Council of Vienne, and the threat of excommunication, and where some phrases of *Ex gravi* are quoted verbatim—the city council expressed the wish of its members to obey the conciliar legislation as "faithful Christians should." This was not a minor event in the city's political life. Once the decision was made, it was publicized with the usual pomp and ceremony. "This *statutum*, which was recently decided upon," wrote the notary, "was read by me, Bartholomeus de Salinis, notary public of Marseilles, and publicized in the General Council of the vicomital city of Marseilles, summoned to the hall of the royal palace by the voice of the herald and the sound of the bells as is the custom, and was confirmed by the aforesaid council in the presence of the *vicarius* of this city, Sir Raymond of Villanova."

Why did this reversal happen on 24 February 1318 and not before? What is the reason for this gap of five or six years? This is not a difficult question to answer as a review of the chronology of the publication of the Canons of Vienne indicates. For while the Council of Vienne took place in 1311–1312, its canons were published only five years later.[35] Pope Clement V intended to edit them himself but took his time in doing so. On 21 March 1314 he assembled a consistory in Monteux, near Carpentras, where he apparently read his edition. He then wanted, before publishing it, to send it to various universities in Europe, but he died four weeks later. It was left to his successor, John XXII, elected to the Holy See only on 7 August 1316, to publish the "Clementines." John did so within a year or so; they became public on 25 October 1317. We can thus conclude that Marseilles was actually quite quick in adopting the legislation only four months after the content of *Ex gravi* came to their knowledge.

But why did the Marseillais feel at all compelled to react and implement the decretal *Ex gravi* in their city? No document that I know of provides an answer to this question; the most one can do, therefore, is to provide a hypothesis that takes into account the fact that 1317 was an exceptionally eventful year in the political and religious history of Marseilles. Louis of Anjou—the local saint—was finally canonized in April of that year.[36] Brother of King Robert, Louis was appointed—as is well known—to the see of Toulouse, but abandoned it and died at a very young age in August 1297. He was buried in the House of the Franciscans in Marseilles. The council of the city, supported by popular demand and led mostly by King Robert's ambition to have his brother declared a saint, promoted Louis's canonization for years.[37] Although the Angevin house pressed hard for this canonization, it was only in 1307 that Pope Clement created a committee to inquire "about the habits, the merits, and the miracles" of Louis, and it was another ten years before the papacy approved the canonization in April 1317. The transfer of Louis's relics to the main altar of the House of the Franciscans of Marseilles was expected to take place with much ceremony in the presence of the pope, King Robert, the kings of Aragon and Majorca, and of thousands of other guests. The city was thus taken over by sentiments of piety and righteousness; the papacy had sanctioned the local saint. But would not the municipality have wished to reciprocate by obliterating the irritating "pro-usury" paragraph? The hypothesis I offer links thus the promulgation of the *Ex gravi* and

the canonization of Saint Louis of Anjou. I am the first to recognize that nothing in the documents we possess today tells us
that there existed such a connection between the two events; yet
the fact that both happened at the same time must not have been
entirely coincidental. One can, in any event, imagine that, had
the trial of Bondavid taken place just a few months or a year later,
many of the witnesses, or even all of them, would not have expressed themselves with as much frankness and sympathy as they
did in February and March of 1317.

Conclusion

My aim in this inquiry into the trial of Bondavid in 1317 has been to explore the image of the moneylender in medieval society and the changes this image underwent. The praises for Bondavid, as recorded in register III B7, were a source of concern to me, because I was not sure how much credence they should be given. Having compared the twenty-four depositions with other expressions of popular attitudes to moneylending and moneylenders, I became convinced that these favorable declarations, even though solicited by the Jew, can be considered spontaneous expressions of the attitudes of the time. Thus, the twenty-four depositions recorded in this register provide us with a new and reliable document: a source for the understanding of the history of the Jews in one of the most important periods of their existence. And although the evidence they bring to light does not allow us to deny that the image of Shylock was haunting the minds of medieval people, it compels us to make place, next to him, for the sympathetic personality of Bondavid. The document also provides us with yet another argument (to the extent that we needed one at all) to cast aside the perception of an unbroken history of hatred and misunderstanding between Jews and Christians in the Middle Ages, and to acknowledge the existence of friendship, consideration, magnanimity, and mutual recognition in the relations between members of the two societies.

Viewed from the perspective of the history of economic thought in the medieval West, the evidence recorded in register III B7 has obvious advantages over most documents available to scholars today. It gives us an opportunity to listen to opinions and feelings expressed by common people instead of theologians or canon lawyers: to merchants, lawyers, and laborers involved in the daily life of Marseilles. Surely there is much that can be rescued from the testimony of these individuals—much more than I am capable of doing—to help us to understand the frame of mind of those who participated in the activities of a thriving commercial city like Marseilles, to see their optimism and their confidence in themselves. We have here an occasion to explore their attitudes toward credit and profit, toward fairness and honesty, as well as toward the economic teaching of the church—not only by analyzing what they dared to put on record but also by considering what they did not say and what they preferred to overlook. For once we are not obliged to reconstruct the minds of people of the past by analyzing short and isolated phrases they uttered or by interpreting mute monuments they left behind them. In the archives of Marseilles—exceptionally ample for these years—we listen to them talking, answering questions, and telling their stories.

As for optimism and confidence, 1317 seems to be one of the last years of the High Middle Ages in which people saw their economic world in such bright terms. The decree against usury of the Council of Vienne was more realistic. It announced that a new, more somber era was arriving, though it was not the prelates' legislation that had brought about the decline of the economic system. More crucial were the profound mutations European society was experiencing at this time. Today we know that by 1317 the trend of economic growth had already passed its peak in most regions of the medieval West. Beginning a staggering "boom" in the twelfth century and continuing less dramatic growth in the following century, the European economy reached its highest point in the 1280s and 1290s. At the turn of the century the economic system found itself in a decline from which it would begin to recover only 150 years later.[1]

Just as today, in the fourteenth century even the most brilliant minds needed some perspective in order to realize what was happening around them. In Marseilles, we see some of them attempting to gain an overview as early as 1342. In November of that year a document was produced in which some members of the city's mercantile elite offered explanation of its lamentable situation, that is, that "the city of Marseilles is not in as good shape as it used to be."[2] Most outspoken was Monteolivus, still as prominent in 1342 in the city's public life as he had been a generation before. He singled out two reasons. The less important one pointed to the exhausting effects of the wars in which the city had been involved. The other, more pointed, reason concerned the fall of Acre ("Akon") in 1291, the last stronghold of the Crusaders in the Holy Land. Most historians today would endorse Monteolivus's remarks about the fall of Acre—given the dependence of Marseilles's prosperity on the commerce with the Levant. Unlike Honnorat Forbin, 150 years later, neither Monteolivus nor any of his colleagues in November 1342 seized upon Jews or usury to explain Marseilles's bad fortunes: they all looked for reasons outside the city.

Already in 1317 some people in Marseilles may have realized that times were becoming harder and harder—especially since along with the rest of the West they had experienced devastating harvest failures in the previous two years.[3] But this does not imply that they saw reason either to be alarmed or to question the major tenets of their economic attitudes. Rather, they might have regarded the difficulties in agriculture as owing to chance, and they might have interpreted any slacking in the economy as temporary. Better times could have been still ahead for them. It is true that the fall of Acre in 1291 was fresh in their minds. But projects to reconquer Palestine were contemplated seriously, and the recovery of the Holy Land was deemed imminent by many. All in all, the people of Marseilles in 1317 could still have clung to the economic values and attitudes that had brought so much prosperity to their forefathers. Even when they finally realized the kind of crisis which they were experiencing and when their mood presumably changed for the worse, it is not at all certain that their attitudes toward Jews or moneylending—or indeed their whole economic thinking—changed automatically. The dynamics of social life and of social attitudes cannot be conceived as simply following a hydraulic system in which the level of liquid in one pipe depends on the pressure exercised on the other. Then as today, economic attitudes were guided by many variables, many of them spontaneous and unexpected. And yet if there is something that the study of the documents from the medieval West can teach us, it is that such attitudes are neither permanent nor static. They are subject to change and depend on conditions of time and of space. Social historians are among the happy few who can aspire to follow their movements properly.

Appendix 1
Minutes of the Trial
of Bondavid

Minutes of the trial of Bondavid de Draguignano in the court
of the lower city of Marseilles (*Curia Palatii*) February-July 1317.
Though the minutes are incomplete and essential parts of them are missing (e.g., the letter of accusation against Bondavid, the decision), an effort was made by the notary to record the minutes in a systematic way
(see discussion in chap. 5). We can distinguish easily between (a) the
court's calendar, (b) depositions of witnesses concerning Petrus Guizo,
and (c) depositions with the same aim concerning Bondavid. We also
possess, by chance, (d) the *Interrogatoria* (i.e., additional questions)
proposed by Bondavid's adversary, Laurentius Girardi (Archives départementales des Bouches-du-Rhône, III B 7, fol. 5r–53r). *Sigilla*: ⟨ ⟩-
added by the editor; [1 word]-one or several words not deciphered;
hos[tagiu]m-word completed; (Petiit?)- reading uncertain.

A

Calendar of the court of the lower city of Marseilles dealing
with the case against Bondavid from 9 February 1317 down to 11 July of
the year, when a decision was issued. It starts with the presentation of
a letter of defense by Bondavid's representative, Boniuzas de Borriano,
and includes also fragments of the oath taken by the witness in the presence of Laurentius Girardi. Registered also is an invitation to Laurentius
to present his *interrogatoria* to the said letter of defense. While these
steps are taken in February, the calendar records in April Bondavid's requests to the court to make public the content of the inquest of witness
done by the notary. After repeated citations of Laurentius by the messenger of the court, Bondavid is handed back, on 4 May, the original
promissory note, which was held by the court. In July, demands are

made by Bondavid for a pronouncement of a judgment in the case. After more efforts to assure Laurentius's presence at the event, a judgment is given on 11 July. (Fols. 5r–9r).

[5r]   Tituli oblati pro parte Boniuzas de Borriano judei procuratoris Bondavini de Draguignano judei.[1]

Anno domini millesimo cccxvi die ix feboarii. Infra scripti tituli sunt oblati per Boniuzas de Borriano judeum, procuratorio nomine Bondavini de Draguignano judei, et consimiles traditi Laurentio Girardi eidemque ad faciendum interrogatoria sua cras per totum diem, et dicto judeo ad probandum hinc ad quinque dies. Quorum titulorum tenor talis est, ut sequitur.

Adversus quandam depositionem seu testimonium quam seu quod fecit seu tulit Petrus Guizo coram discreto et sapienti viro domino Johanne de Revesto judice palatii Massilie contra Bondavinum de Draguignano judeum, civem Massilie, et pro Laurentio Girardi. Et Boniuzas de Borriano judeus, ut procurator et procuratorio nomine dicti Bondavini, volens predictum Petrum Guizo a suo testimonio seu depositione quam seu quod dicitur fecisse seu tulisse reprobare, et animum dicti domini judicis de iure dicti Bondavini informare, cuius est procurator, eumdem Petrum reprobando, probare intendit ut infra sequitur.

In primis reprobando probare intendit dictus Boniuzas, nomine procuratorio quo supra, quod predictus Petrus Guizo, qui dicitur tulisse testimonium coram dicto domino judice ut supra, est homo vilis vite et.[2]

X die feboarii. Et Petrus Asa laborator in presentia dicti Laurentii Girardi, dicente et protestante quod possit dicere et obicere dictis et persona dicti testis et testium producendorum per dictum judeum, juravit etc. Martinus Petri juravit presente dicto Laurentio et protestante ut supra die predicta. Die xi feboarii juraverunt testes infrascripti, Jacobus de Sancta Maria et Bartholomeus de Geminis et Raymundus de Alesto et Johannes Caponi et Petrus Bonifilii laborator et Hugo Bernardi presente supra dicto Laurentio, dicente et protestante ut supra. Guillelmus Stephani die xi feboarii, presente dicto Laurentio et protestante [etc.] Item die xiiii feboarii Raymundus Dagulla, dicto Laurentio presente protestante ut supra. Item Guillelmus de Curia juravit xiiii die feboarii, presente dicto Laurentio et protestante ut supra.

[5v]   Anno quo supra, comparuit dictus Boniuzas procuratorio nomine quo supra coram discreto viro domino Johanne de Revesto judice curie palatii Massilie, presente dicto Laurentio, et obtulit eidem domino judici titulos infrascriptos de novo (petiit?) consimiles tradi dicto Laurentio per dictum dominum judicem et diem sibi assignari ad probandum, et dicto Laurentio ad sua interrogatoria facienda, si que facere voluerit.

Ex adverso comparuit dictus Laurentius coram dicto domino judice et dixit dictos titulos non esse admitendos, nec dictum procuratorem non debere admiti ad probandum super eis, cum habuerit dilationem v dierum in executione ad probandum et predictam petat dilatorie, et propter subterfugias cum dictam dilationem [dedisse?] potuisset dictos titulos et probasse super eis si voluisset.

Et dictus Boniuzas nomine quo supra non obstantibus dictis propositis frivolis et [. . 1 word . .] per dictum Laurentium, dicit se fore admitendum ad predicta per eumdem petita, potissime cum infra primam dilationem v dierum ipse Boniuzas aliquos testes produxit super causis productis per eumdem et nunc novos ipse offerat dictis causis et rationibus supradictis ipsum admiti debere ad probandum per eumdem.

Et dictus dominus judex admisit dictos titulos, si et in quantum de iure sunt admittendi, assignans eidem judeo ad probandum super dictis titulis et precedentibus dilationem v dierum, et dicto Laurentio ad faciendum interrogatoria si que facere voluerit cras per totam diem.

Et in continenti dictus Boniuzas ad probandum secundum titulum super periurio et infamia super titulo oblato supra per eumdem, produxit quoddam judiciarium mandamentum cum executione in dorso ipsius, quod mandamentum scriptum est manu Johannis de Maris notarii publici sub anno domini mccexiii, pridie nonas martii. Et executio scripta manu G. Raynaudi notarii publici sub anno domini millesimo cccxvi, ydus julii, quorum mandamenti et executionis tenorum secuntur.

Anno domini millesimo cccxiii [6r] pridie nonas martii, Dominus Raymundus Rostagni judex curie Massilie iniunxit de partium voluntate Petro de Evena filio Hugonis de Evena civi Massilie moranti in carreria de Pilis presente confitente et postulanti et volenti, et omnia bona sua creditori suo infrascripto obliganti, et omni juri renuntianti et ad sancta dei evangelia sponte juranti, quatinus hinc ad unum annum proxime venturum sic statuto termino de partium voluntate, det et solvat Habrahe de Draguignano judeo civi Massilie presenti et petenti, quindecim solidos regalium seu Massiliensium minutorum quos confitebat se eidem Habrahe debere ex causa mutui gratis et amore. Ego Johannes de Maris notarius etc.

Anno domini mcccxvi iiiº ydus julii. In executione quod [. . 4–5 words . .] Boniuzas de Borriano procuratorio Bondavini de [6v] Draguignano filii et heredis creditoris retroscripti condam, et jubente domino Raymundo Rostagni judice curie Massilie, juravit debitor solvere debitum retroscriptum hinc ad v dies proximos aut bona sua in scriptis dicte curie consignare. Ego Guillelmus Raynaudi notarius etc.

[6r]   Et dictus Laurentius petiit sibi dari transcriptum dicti mandamenti et executionis.

Et dictus dominus judex concessit copiam dicti mandamenti et executionis dicto petenti.

Anno domini millesimo cccxvi die ultima febroarii, Bartholomeus Lique nuntius juratus et preco curie retulit mihi Johanni de Spinatiis notario citasse Laurentium Girardi ad instantiam Boniuzas de Borriano procuratorio nomine Bondavini de Draguinano judei, cum ipse Boniuzas velit aliquos testes producere, et cum dilatione prima lapsa sit, intendatque aliam dilationem petere ipsi Laurentio invento personaliter precepit ut veniat coram dicto domino judice ad videndum et audiendum ea que supra dicta sunt et ut supra petitum est.

Qui dictus nuntius yens et deinde rediens, dixit et retulit se predicta dixisse dicto Laurentio eri, qui respondit, ut retulit nuntius, quod nesciebat ad quid veniret.

Postquam anno quo supra die ultima febroarii comparuit dictus Boniuzas coram domino Pontio de Sancto Martino juris perito, locum tenente domini Johannis de Revesto judicis curie palatii Massilie petens sibi aliam dilationem dare ad probandum, in contumaciam dicti Laurentii.

Et dictus dominus locumtenens visa citatione predicta et dicto Laurentio minime comparente et citato ut supra propter dictam contumaciam dicti Laurentii, dilationem v dierum ad probandum concessit dicto judeo.

[6v] Anno domini millesimo ccc xvii die xi aprilis. Comparuit predictus Bonus David coram predicto domino judice, non revocando propter presentem comparitionem predictum procuratorem suum neque acta per eum, set ad cautelum confirmando petit testes pro parte (sua?) productos vocato Laurentio Girardi parte adversa aperiri legi et publicari.

Et dictus dominus judex precepit Bartholomeo Lique preconi publico et nuntio curie Massilie, jurato, presenti, quatinus statim vadit ad dictum Laurentium et ipsum citet ut die crastina compareat coram predicto domino judice occasione premissa, alias dicti testes producerentur eius absentia non obstante.

Anno domini quo supra die xii aprilis dictus Bartholomeus nuntius retulit dictam citationem fecisse in domo dicti Laurentii ipso non invento. Cui fuit responsum, ut retulit, quod non erat in Massilia nec veniret usque diem dominicum.

Ad quas diem et horam supra proxime assignatas comparuit dictus Bondavin coram predicto domino judice pro tribunali sedente, et cum dictus Laurentius Girardi citatus ad videndum publicationem testium per dictum Bondavinum productorum et non comparuit, Idcirco accusans ipsius Laurentii contumaciam petiit testes suos productos aperiri legi et publicari.

Et dictus dominus judex voluit quod iterum citatur, precipiens Martino Petri, nuncio, presenti, quatinus in continenti citet dictum Laurentium ut cras in mane compareat coram eo ad audiendam publicationem dictorum et faciendam.

[7r]   Qui nuntius yens et rediens retulit mihi notario infrascripto, se mandato dictum Laurentium personaliter inventum ad id quod supra et die et hora citasse, qui respondit ut retulit quod veniet libenter.

Ego G. Monernii notarius hoc scripsi.

Anno quo supra die xiii aprilis hora tertie die et hora supra proxime assignatis, comparuit dictus Bondavin judeus coram predicto domino judice et accusendo contumaciam dicti Laurentii citati legitime ut supra per acta aparet, absentis et comparere nolentis, petit testes suos aperiri legi et publicari.

Et dictus dominus judex precepit Blanchono nuntio curie Massilie jurato, presenti, quatinus vadat ad domum dicti Laurentii Girardi et eum citet precise et peremtorie ut hodie in vesperis compareat coram predicto domino judice pro publicatione dictorum testium facienda, alias dicti testes publicarent ut eius absentia non obstante.

Qui dictus nuntius iens et deinde reddiens retulit dictum Laurentium citasse in domo sua, licet eum non invenit. Cui responsum fuit per stantes in domo quod non erat in villa. Ego Bartholomeus de Salinis notarius hec scripsi.

[7v]   Anno quo supra die xiii aprilis hora vesperorum die et hora supra proxime assignatis, comparuit dictus Bondavi judeus coram predicto domino judice pro tribunali sedente, absente dicto Laurentio et citato perhemptorie et contumaciter comparere nolente et accusando eius contumaciam, petiit cum summa instantia testes suos aperiri legi et publicari.

Et dictus dominus judex in contumaciam dicti Laurentii citati et comparere nolentis, jussit dictos testes aperiri legi et publicari, salvo tamen jure dicto Laurentio quod possit dicere et obicere in dictis et personis testium superius productorum.

Et fuerunt lecta et publicata dicta dictorum testium videlicet dictis trium testium pro omnibus.

Anno domini quo supra die iiii madii. Fuit restitutum mandato dicti domini judicis dicto Bono David judeo, presenti et humiliter postulanti, quoddam instrumentum quod sequestratum fuerat in posse curie ad instantiam dicti Laurentii, asserentis debitum contentum in eo solutum fuisse, non obstante assertione predicta cum dictus Bonus David plures testes produxerit ad sui intentionem fundandam adversus aserta per Laurentium supradictum.

Ego Bartholomeus de Salinis notarius hec scripsi presentia et testimonio G. Molnerii notarii, Petri Raymundi et plurium aliorum.

[8r]   Anno quo supra die x junii hora tertie. Cum Bonus Davinus de Draguinhano judeus civis Massilie peteret a Laurentio Girardi laboratore, solidos regalium sexaginta coram domino Johanne de Revesto judice maiore curie palatii Massilie, ex tenore cuiusdam publici intrumenti scripti manu Guidonis Borgondionis notarii sub anno domini mccccxv indictione xiii, iii ydus aprilis hora vesperis, dictusque Laurentius super solutione dicti debiti testem unicum, ut dicitur, produxisse, dictusque Bonus Davinus judeus ad reprobandum ipsum testem, testes quamplurimos produxisset, idem dominus judex volens finem in ponere questioni, assignavit diem dictis partibus ad congnitionem suam super predictus audiendam, die mercurii proximi in terciis.

Anno quo supra die nona junii. Pontius Raymundi nuntius retulit mihi notario infrascripto se heri vesperis mandato dicto domini judicis et ad instantiam dicti Boni Davini de Draguinhano citasse et personaliter invenisse dictum Laurentium Girardi ut hodie in tertiis coram ipso domino judice compareret dicto judeo de justicia respondendo. Qui respondit, ut retulit, quod veniret libenter.

Ad quam horam comparuit dictus Bonus Davinus coram predicto domino judice et petiit procedi contra dictum Laurentium tanquam contra contumacem. Et dictus dominus judex jussit iterum dictum Andream citari, precipiens Pontio Raymundi nuntio, presenti, quatinus in continenti citet dictum Andream ut hodie in vesperis
[8v]   compareat coram dicto domino judice dicto judeo de iusticia responsurus, alias idem dominus judex procederet contra eum tamquam contra contumacem.

Qui nuntius retulit se dictam citationem ad domum dicti Laurentii fecisse et ipsum non invenisse. Et fuisse sibi responsum per stantes in domo quod ipse erat apud Sanctum Vincentium et dum veniret, sibi predicta dicerent.

Anno quo supra die x junii Pontius Raymundi nuntius retulit mihi subscripto notario se mandato dicti domini judicis et ad instantiam dicti Boni Davini judei heri vesperis dictum Laurentium Girardi personaliter inventum citasse ad id quod supra. Qui respondit quod libenter veniret.

Ego G. Monernii notarius hec scripsi.

Anno quo supra die viii julii hora tercie. Comparuit dictus Bondavinus coram predicto domino judice, pro tribunali sedente, et petiit citari dictum Laurentium Girardi ad audiendum cognitionem dicti domini judicis super predictis.

Et dictus dominus judex voluit quod dictus Laurentius citetur, precipiens Bartholomeo Lique nuntio et preconi Massilie, jurato, presenti, quatinus incontinenti citet dictum Laurentium ut die lune in terciis compareat coram eo ad procedendum in dicta causa debito modo.

Qui nuncius yens et reddiens retulit mihi notario infrascripto se dictum Laurentium personaliter inventum citasse, et in modum predictum ad id quod supra. Qui respondit, ut retulit, quod libenter veniret.

[9r]   Anno quo supra die xi julii hora tercie, die et hora supra proxime assignatis, comparuit dictus Bonus Davinus judeus coram predicto domino judice pro tribunali sedente, absente dicto Laurentio Girardi contumaciter et citato ut supra et minime comparenti et accusando eius contumacia, petiit procedi contra eum tanquam contra contumacem.

Et dictus dominus judex voluit quod dictus Laurentius perhemptorie et precise citetur ad cras in terciis, precipiens Bertrando de Tritis, nuntio presenti quatinus in continenti citet dictum Laurentium ad domum suam ut cras in terciis compareat coram eo, perhemptorie et precise, ad audiendum cognitionem domini judicis antedicti, alias idem dominus judex procederet ad eius cognitionem proferentem, eius absentia non obstante. Quam horam dictis partibus assignavit ad eius sententiam audiendam super predictis.

Qui nuncius yens et reddiens retulit mihi notario infrascripto se dictum Laurentium personaliter citasse ad id quod supra. Qui respondit, ut retulit, quod veniret.

Ad quam horam supra proxime assignatam comparuit dictus Bonum Davinus de Draguinhano judeus coram predicto domino judice pro tribunali sedente, absente dicto Laurentio et citato ut supra et personaliter invento et comparere nolente, et accusando eius contumaciam, petiit in eius contumacia exigente, procedi contra eum, videlicet dictum dominum judicem ad suam cognitionem proferendam procedi super predictis. Et ad cautelam exhabundanti rectifficavit et confirmavit [9v] omnia acta et gesta per dictum Boniuzas procuratorem suum, et que fient in presenti causa eius nomine et pro ea et ad faciendum fidem de procuratorio dicti Boniuzas produxit quoddam instrumentum pro vero et publico scriptum manu Pascalis de Maranicis notarii publici, quod incipit in secunda linea "peris" et finit in eadem "civis."

Item ad faciendam fidem de procuratione dicti Vidoni de Alesto produxit quoddam instrumentum pro vero et publico scriptum manu dicti Pascalis notarii quod incipit in secunda linea "de" et finit in tertia "indictione."

Item ad docendum de debito dictorum LX solidorum producit quoddam instrumentum scriptum manu Guidonis Borgondionis notarii publici, quod incipit in secunda linea "Massilia" et finit in eadem "judei." Quibus productionibus factis, petiit ut supra.

Postquam comparuit dictus Laurentius Girardi citatus, dicens se dicto Bono Davino judeo satisfecisse de debito LX solidorum predictorum, et hoc probasse. Et dictus Bonus Davinus, non concentiens ymo contradicens, predictis petiit ut supra.

Et dictus dominus judex assignavit diem dictis partibus ad audiendum cognitionem suam super predictis, diem hodie in vesperis.

Ad quam horam supra proxime assignata comparuit dictus Bonus Davinus coram predicto domino judice pro tribunali sedente, presente ibidem dicto Laurentio, paratus audire dicti domini judicis cognitionem, ad quam proferendum presens hora extiterat assignata.

Et dictus Laurentius petiit idem.

Et dictus dominus judex processit ad suam sententiam proferendam prout in cartulario G. Monernii notarii continetur.

B

11–15 February 1316: Testimonies of eight citizens of Marseilles, in reference to three statements (*tituli*) presented by Bondavid. These statements concern the personality of Petrus Guizo, the witness who confirmed Laurentius Girardi's version in the conflict with Bondavid. The witnesses talk about the vile life Petrus led, thus helping Bondavid in his claim that since Petrus is an *infamis* and *perjurus*, his testimony should not count in court. (Fols. 10r–19r)

[10r] Anno domini millesimo cccxvi, xv die febroarii. Hugo Bernardi civis Massilie testis productus per dictum Boniuzas procuratorio nomine dicti Boni Davini ad reprobandum dictum seu testimonium Petri Guizonis, qui deposuerat pro dicto Laurentio Girardi, qui juravit dicta die, presente dicto Laurentio dicente et protestante ut supra, et deposuit dictum suum eadem die. Qui juramento suo requisitus dicere veritatem super dictis titulis ipsi lectis et expositis de verbo ad verbum in vulgari, et primo super primo titulo dixit ita esse verum ut in ipso primo titulo continentur, et predicta dixit se scire visu et audito. Interrogatus quid inde vidit et audivit, dixit se vidisse dictum Petrum in titulo nominatum et cognovisse a xv annis citra vel idcirca, quorum a sex citra vidit ipsum frequenter et frequentius perseverantem in tabernis et aliis locis illicitis et inonestis, bibentem ibi cum potatoribus et hominibus trichatoribus et suspectis, et ludentem quandoque raubam suam ad taxillos, et bona sua et raubam suam vendendo ibidem et inpignorando et se expoliando ad ludum palam absque aliqua verecundia tamquam vilis persona et inhonesta, se vino sepe et sepius inebriantem et pro tali testis ipsum habet hodie, et habuit a dicto tempore citra, et pro tali habetur inter notos et vicinos ac cognoscentes eum.

Super secundo titulo dixit quod nichil aliud scit nisi quod per vitam illicitam assuetam per dictum Petrum ut supra testificatus est, habet ipse testis et habent plures alii de civitate dictum Petrum pro homine vili et infame. Item requisitus testis super tertio titulo, dixit se nescire quod dictus Petrus habeat vel possideat aliqua bona mobilia seu immobilia in civitate Massilie seu eius territorio, licet aliqua habuerit suo tempore. Interrogatus testis si bene cognoscit dictum Petrum in titulo nominatum, dixit quod sic quia multo tempore citra notitiam de eo habuit et suorum factorum veram experientiam, et est homo [10v] magne stature, circa xxx annorum, qui morari consuevit cum dicto Laurentio Girardi et qui habuit neptem ipsius Laurentii in uxorem. Item requisitus testis cuius modi vilitates fieri vidit dicto Petro, respondit ut supra. Item requisitus in quibus tabernis vidit dictum Petrum bibentem et potantem et se spoliantem ad ludum, et cum quibus personis, et quibus anno septimana et die, et quando ipsum vidit ebrium, dixit quod anno preterito nam vidit eum et audivit quod lusit asinum suum in foro, ignorat tamen nomen illius cum quo lusit, dixit in diversis tabernis specialiter in taberna Chalaman Droni vidit ipsum ebrium et raubam suam inpignorantem post modum ludentem ipsum frequenter in campo Cabroli. Et cognoscebat ipsum Petrum ebrium, quia quando loquebatur nesciebat quid dicebat, et in eodem campo ipsum spoliantem et ludentem peccuniam quam mutuabat super rauba sua. Item interrogatus testis inter quas personas est fama de predictis et que cognoscunt dictum Petrum, respondit quod inter ipsum testem et Chalamam Dronum tabernarium, Guillelmum de Curia et Raymundum de Alesto et plures alios de quibus non recordatur. Interrogatus quid est infamia in homine, respondit quando quis bibit, ludit in tabernis et vitam illicitam ducti sicut iste.

Interrogatus quam partem vellet potius obtinere in hac causa, dixit quod partem jus habentem in causa. Tamen dixit quod magis diligit suum fratrem christianum.

Item interrogatus generaliter si prece pretio gratia odio amore vel timore fert hoc testimonium, dixit et respondit, diversis aliis interrogationibus sibi factis, quod non, set quia veritas sic se habet prout supra per eum testificatum est.

[11r]   Anno quo supra et die xi febroarii. Raymundus de Alesto testis productus per dictum judeum, dicto Laurentio dicente et protestante ut supra, et deposuit dictum suum dicta die. Qui juramento suo requisitus super dictis titulis ipsi testi bene et diligenter lectis et expositis de verbo ad verbum in vulgari. Et primo super primo titulo dixit ita verum esse ut in ipso titulo continetur. Interrogatus qualiter scit, dixit se hoc scire visu et auditu. Item interrogatus quid inde vidit ne audivit, dixit et respondit se vidisse dictum Petrum bibentem et spoliantem in tabernis et ludentem raubam suam, et ebrium, et qui cognoscit dictum Petrum

Guiso. Interrogatus de loco et in quo loco vidit eum ludentem, dixit quod in quodam stabulo Hugue Giraude quadam nocte. Interrogatus qua die et quo mense et quo anno, dixit se non recordari, nisi tantum quod bene sunt tres anni lapsi ut sibi videtur, de nocte circa tintinabulum vel circa. Interrogatus in quibus tabernis vidit ipsum ludentem et bibentem et ebrium, dixit quod in taberna Chalaman Droni et Andree Suan et in pluribus locis aliis de quibus non recordatur. Interrogatus qualiter cognoscebat dictum Petrum esse ebrium, respondit quod eo quia quando loquebatur balbutiebat ac neciebat quid faciebat nec dicebat. Interrogatus cum quibus personis vidit ipsum ludentem et bibentem, dixit quod cum diversis personis et diversis lusoribus quorum nomina ignorat. Interrogatus inter quos est fama de predictis, dixit inter deponentem et Lo Boyre del Cascelet et Petrum Foresterii, et Raymundum Dagulla et plures alios de quibus longum esset enerrare. Interrogatus si scit dictum Petrum esse infamem et periurum. Super secundo titulo, dixit se tantum inde scire super eo videlicet quod duo anni vel tres lapsi sunt quod cum dictus Petrus Guizo in [11v] titulo nominatus lusisset cum quibusdam, et raubam suam inpignorasse, juravit ad sancta dei evangelia quod nunquam aliquo tempore luderet in manibus Hugonis de Geminis notarii, et inde debuit facere instrumentum, ut audivit dici Guillelmo Stephani, Fulconi de Torrenes et Raymundo Lo Gran, et imposuit sibi penam LX solidorum, quos LX solidos promisit dare predictis Guillelmo, Fulconi, et Raymundo, et quod ipsi possent sibit deponere vestes pro dictis LX solidis vel accipere pignus in ospitio suo. Et post dictum prestitum juramentum vidit ipsum pluries ludentem, et ideo dixit ut sibi videtur quod dictus Petrus est periurus et infamis. Interrogatus quid est infamia et ex quibus causis homo est infamis, dixit et respondit quod quando quis deierat vel turpem vitam ducit sicut dictus Petrus fecit. Interrogatus de loco et ex quibus causis et coram quibus personis et an in judicio vel extra iudicium et si ferendo testimonium vel aliter, dixit ad singula et respondit quod in presentia predictorum, et extra judicium, et ex causa predicta. Interrogatus de anno mense die et septimana, dixit quod ignorat et nescit.

Item super tertio titulo diligenter interrogatus si scit quod dictus Petrus possideat bona aliqua mobilia vel immobilia, dixit et respondit se nescire. Interrogatus a quo tempore citra cognoscit dictum Petrum Guizo, dixit et respondit quod a xviii annis citra et plus, et a quatuor annis citra vidit dictum Petrum predicta facientem, videlicet ludentem bibentem in tabernis cum diversis personis licitis et illicitis. Interrogatus si dictus Petrus atinet dicto Laurentio, dixit quod nescit, tamen neptem ipsius habuit in uxorem, et a tempore quo decessit uxor sua vidit ipsum conversatem cum dicto Laurentio.

[12r]   Anno quo supra xiii die (!) Johannes Caponi existens in carreria pilarum deposuit suum testimonium, et juravit dicere veritatem xi die febroarii. Qui juramento suo requisitus super dictis titulis sibi diligenter lectis et expositis de verbo ad verbum in vulgari, et primo super primo titulo sibi exposito dixit se tamen inde scire super eo, non visu set auditu, tantum dixit enim se audivisse quod dictus Petrus, in dicto titulo nominatus, est homo tabernarius et qui indiferenter consuevit ire in tabernis, et est homo qui immoderate consuevit bibere vinum, et homo qui lusit raubam suam, et ita audivit a quodam qui nominatur Raymundus Dagulla qui moratur in carreria Monacorum, et etiam hoc audivit a Marquesio Bernardi qui moratur in dicta carreria in traversia Jarreti. Et audivit a dicto Raymundo et Marquesio qui quodam die de quo non testis recolit, a festo Sancti Michaelis citra, quod ipsi luserant cum dicto Petro in titulo nominato, et ab eo lucrati fuerant raubam suam, videlicet quandam tunicam et quandam (uchiam?) dicto deponente existente et laborante, fodiendo in vineis, cum adinvicem loquebantur eundo vel redeundo, dixerunt dicto deponenti, et per intervalla diversorum dierum. De die mense nec septimana non recordatur se a dicto tempore citra audivit predicta. Interrogatus testis inter quos est fama de predictis, dixit quod ab aliis non audivit nisi a duobus hominibus predictis, nam conversationem nec familiaritatem ipse deponens non habet nec habuit cum dicto Petro in titulo nominato.

Super secundo titulo respondit auditu dici quod dictus Petrus in titulo nominatus juravit non ludere aliquo tempore, et hoc audivit a Jacobo de Sancta Maria et a Guillelmo Stephani, et est bene annus lapsus ut ipsi deponenti videtur.

Super tertio titulo dixit se scire quod dictus Petrus non tenet nec possidet bona aliqua mobilia nec inmobilia nec nomina debitorum set dicit eum esse obligatum, et scit in sex libris regalium. Interrogatus qualiter hoc scit, respondit de quatuor libris quod ipse fuit testis quando ipsas mutuavit ab Astes de Camera judea et quod tanto erat resta inter eos, de quadraginta solidis audivit a matre dicti Petri Guiso in titulo nominato, et istos dicit mutuasse a Maruano Maruani. Interrogatus deponens si aliquo tempore infra domum dicti Petri Guiso fuit, dixit quod sic, et si tunc temporis [12v] tenebat aliqua bona mobilia nec immobilia, dixit quod sic videlicet suppellectilia domus situs Las Yarcas et alia supellectilia domus situs Ligores Podaoyras et pluria alia, dicit tamen quod in presente simul bona mobilia nec immobilia possidet, et hoc dicit scire visu et auditu, nam scit quod unum vas vendidit cuidam vicino suo nomen cuius est Raymundus Alsanti. Alia bona dilapidavit, ignorat tamen cum quibus et quibus. Interrogatus testis a quanto tempore citra cognoscit dictum Petrum, dixit quod a xviii annis citra.

Interrogatus a quo tempore citra audivit et vidit dictum Petrum male facientem facta sua et administrantem, respondit se non vidisse set tamen audivisse quod a v annis citra, mortuo patre suo, dictus Petrus inchoavit male facere facta sua, et hodie facit prout audivit. Dicit tamen quod non audivit quod dictus Petrus malum alii faciat nisi sibi ipsi, nec audivit aliquem querentem de eo *nisi istum Bon Davinum seu Boniuzas eius procuratorem*.[3] Interrogatus testis a quo tempore citra dicit se scire quod dictus Petrus nulla possideat bona mobilia vel immobilia, respondit et dixit quod a festo omnium sanctorum vel circa, et pro tanto quia Bertrandus Feda fecit sibi extimari medietatem unius carteriate et medie[tat]em cuiusdam horti quem habebat dictus Petrus apud Jarretum ratione legitime patris sui ut socer dicti Petri, et pro dote cuiusdam filie sue que obiit, et quartam partem ospitii paterni. Quare dixit quod dictus Petrus nulla bona possidet, eo sciente, set penitus ignorante.

Interrogatus quam partem vellet potius obtinere in causa, dixit quod ius habentem, nisi quod si christianus habet jus in causa in iure suo magis eum diligit quam iudeum.

Et generaliter si prece, pretio, gratia, hodio, amore vel timore ad singula respondit quod non set quia verum dicit esse ut testis deponens testificatus aliqua visu aliqua auditu ut predictum est.[4]

[15r]   Anno domini millesimo cccxvi die xiiii febroarii. Raymundus Dagulla civis Massilie, testis productus per dictum Boniuzas procuratorio nomine quo supra, juravit dicere veritatem super titulis predictis, presente dicto Laurentio dicente et protestante ut supra, et deposuit dictum suum die predicta. Qui diligenter interrogatus super dictis titulis sibi lectis et expositis de verbo ad verbum in vulgari, et primo super primo titulo dixit ita esse verum ut in titulo continetur, et predicta dixit se scire visu et auditu. Interrogatus quid inde vidit et audivit, dixit ipse Petrus in titulo nominatus est homo vicenarius vel circa et a viginti annis citra cognoscit eum et vidit eum post quam eum cognovit sequentem et perseverantem in tabernis et ludentem raubam suam eam deponendo et ludendo tam in tabernis quam alibi, et predictas vilitates vidit fieri per eundem Petrum. Interrogatus cum quibus personis vidit dictum Petrum ludentem bibentem et spoliantem ad ludum, dixit quod cum ipso deponente, Petro Fabri, Bertrando Mana et cum [. . 1 word . .] Gilardi et cum ribaudis et bastaysiis et cum personis cuiuscumque conditionis. Interrogatus quotiens vidit eum spoliantem et ludentem raubam suam, dixit quod ter vel quater, dixit quod cum ipso deponente et Rostagno de Costa et pluribus aliis de quorum nominibus non recordatur. Interrogatus de loco, dixit quod in domo Guillelmi Petri et Raymundi de Aquis. Interrogatus quam et qualem raubam vidit eum ludentem, dixit quod uchiam tunicam et caligas, pluribus vicibus. Tamen

dixit ipse testis quod aliquo tempore non vidit eum ebrium tali ebrietate quod malum faceret alicui, nec quod vilitates diceret nec faceret. Et predicta deposuit super ebrietate. Interrogatus inter quas personas est fama de predictis, dixit et respondit quod inter deponentem [15v] et predictos superius nominatos et viciniam suam.

Super secundo titulo dixit se nichil aliud inde scire, nisi quod dictus Petrus est homo lusor et qui consuevit esse in tabernis et morari, non avertens cum quibus personis conversatur. Dixit tamen quod secundum suam opinionem non habet eum propterea infamem, nam dixit tamen ipse deponens quod non credit esse hominem infamem qui predicta facit nisi sit fur et latro et deraubator.

Super tertio titulo dixit ita esse verum ut in eo continetur, et predicta dicit se scire visu et auditu. Interrogatus quid inde vidit et audivit, dixit quod vidit eum possidentem quemdam ortum in valle Jarreti quem non possidet quia extimatus fuit, ut audivit, a dicto P. Guizo socero suo pro dote cuiusdam filie sue, uxoris condam ipsius Petri. Et predicta dicit se scire a festo omnium sanctorum citra, nam a dicto festo citra non vidit eum bona mobilia nec inmobilia possidentem.

Interrogatus quam partem vellet potius obtinere in causa, dixit quod ius habentem in ea et non aliam. Et generaliter ⟨etc.⟩

[16r]   Anno domini millesimo cccxvi die xi februarii. Bartholomeus de Geminis testis productus per dictum Boniuzas judeum procuratorio nomine quo supra, juravit dicere veritatem super titulis predictis oblatis per dictum judeum lectis sibi de verbo ad verbum in vulgari, et primo super primo titulo ipsi testi bene et diligenter lecto et exposito, deposuit dictum suum xiiii die dicti mensis. Qui requisitus super primo titulo, dixit ita esse verum ut in ipso titulo continetur, et predicta dixit se scire visu et auditu. Interrogatus quid inde vidit et audivit, dixit quod vidit et cognovit dictum Petrum in titulo nominatum a xvi annis citra, et vidit eum bibentem et ludentem in tabernis, et ludentem raubam suam, et inebriantem. Interrogatus de loco, dixit quod in domo Andree Sua et Jacobi de Sancta Maria et in Campo-Cabroli vidit eum ludentem raubam suam nam eam deponentem et ponentem in pignore. Interrogatus de tempore quando vidit testis dictum Petrum ludentem et deponentem raubam, dixit quod anno preterito in vindemis preteritis proximis est annus lapsus. Interrogatus quando vidit eum conversari et bibere in tabernis et cum quibus personis, dixit quod indifferenter cum quibuscumque personis et eum vidit ebrium, ita quod sibi videbatur quod immo biberat immoderate, nam sua facta et verba erant inordinata et sine ratione et ea faciebat et dicebat ut ebrius. Interrogatus a quo tempore citra consuevit facere et dicere dictus Petrus predicta, dixit quod a sex annis citra et plus. Interrogatus si propter ebrietatem vidit

eum prostratum in terram se cadentem seu vomitum emitentem, dixit
quod non. Interrogatus inter quos est fama de predictis, dixit testis quod
inter eum et G. de Sancta Maria et Bertrandum Pallans et Germanum
Hugo et inter eos qui eum cognoscunt et eius viciniam. Interrogatus quid
est fama, dixit et respondit quod fama est illud quando inter gentes
dicitur bonum vel malum alicuius persone. Interrogatus quot homines
faciunt famam, dixit se nescire.

Super secundo titulo testis interrogatus dixit se nichil aliud inde scire
super eo nisi quod audivit a Guillelmo Stephani et Fulconi de Torrenes
et Andrea Suan, quod, cum quadam die dictus Petrus in titulo nominatus
lusiset, ipsi eum fecerunt iurare quod non luderet aliquo tempore vite
sue et hec Petrus juravit [16v] in manibus predictorum ut audivit ab eis,
tamen non vidit nec erat presens. Et de hiis dicitur fecisse instrumentum
Hugo de Geminis notarius. Interrogatus ex quibus causis sit homo infamis, dixit quod homo infamis sit et est quando se exponit factis illicitis,
sicut immoderate bibendo, ludendo, sicut iste Petrus, et deierando prout
audivit quod ipse Petrus fecit. Interrogatus si in iudicio vel extra
iudicium dicitur fecisse dictum juramentum et inferendo testimonium
vel aliter, dixit se nescire nisi in modum predictum.

Super tertio titulo testis interrogatus dixit ita esse verum ut in eo
continetur et hoc dicit scire visu et auditu. Interrogatus quid inde vidit
et audivit, dixit quod vidit quod ipse Petrus in titulo nominatus tempore
dudum lapso habebat plura bona sicut vineam, ortum et partem habentem in quodam ospicio. Nam dixit ipse deponens quod ipsa bona fuerunt
extimata Bertrando Feda socero suo ratione dotis cuiusdam filie sue
condam, uxoris dicti Petri Guiso, alias dicti Garnant alias Devena.
Interrogatus si in domo quam inhabitabat dictus Petrus in primo titulo
nominatus fuit aliquo tempore, dixit quod sic, et pluribus vicibus. Item
interrogatus a quo tempore citra scit ipsum Petrum esse absque eo quod
bona mobilia nec immobilia possidat, dixit quod annus lapsus est.

Interrogatus quam partem vellet potius obtinere in causa, dixit quod
ius habente in ea et non aliam.

[17r]   Anno quo supra die xi febroarii. Jacobus de Sancta Maria testis
productus per dictum Boniuzas, procuratorio nomine dicti Bondavi
judei, juravit dicere veritatem et deposuit dictum suum xiiii febroarii.
Qui juramento suo requisitus super dictis titulis ipsi testi diligenter lectis
ac expositis de verbo ad verbum in vulgari, et primo super primo titulo
ipsi testi exposito, dixit ita esse verum ut in eo continetur, et predicta
dixit se scire visu et auditu. Interrogatus quid inde vidit et audivit, dixit
quod vidit dictum Petrum in ipso titulo nominatum existentem in
tabernis et ludentem et deponentem raubam suam et ipsam ludendo ad
taxillos, et ebrium, et inter gentes tam viles quam alterius conditionis,

videlicet cum ribaldis et cum bastaysiis et inhonestis mulieribus. Et in
taberna Petri Asam ubi vendebat vinum Lo Boyres del Castelet, et in
pluribus aliis locis et tabernis, ipsum ludentem inebriantem et raubam
suam ludentem. Similiter in tabulis carrerie recte predicatorum de nocte
et hora suspecta, circa tintinabulum et mediam noctem, ignorat tamen
cum quibus personis. Interrogatus quotiens vidit eum exponentem
raubam suam et eam ludentem, dixit se vidisse semel tantum, tamen
pluries audivit, et a diversis personis de quorum nominibus non
recordatur, qui dicebant quod viderant eum lusisse raubam suam.
Interrogatus de loco in quo vidit dictum Petrum semel ludentem, dixit
quod in Campo Cabroli videlicet unam uchiam et illam posuit in pignore
pro peccunia quam lusit. Interrogatus quo anno, dixit quod anno
preterito tempore cadragesimali, de mense septimana die, non
recordatur. Interrogatus quando ipsum vidit ebrium et quo tempore,
dixit quod anno isto bis vel ter, et alio tempore pluries. De mense
septimana die non recordatur. Et vix vidit eum diebus festivis, quin ipse
esset ebrius et aliis diebus multotiens. Interrogatus qua ebrietate, dixit
quod ebrietate tali quod verba sua dicebat eo modo quod videbantur
verba [17v] fatui, et ut ebrius sicut homo demens loquebatur, et qui non
dicebat nec faciebat dicta nec facta hominis sapientis, set hominis
dementis. Interrogatus inter quos est fama de predictis, dixit quod inter
eum et Andream Suan et Bartholomeum de Geminis et viciniam.
[18r]   Anno domini millesimo cccxvi die xi febroarii. Guillelmus de
Curia testis productus per dictum Boniusas judeum procuratorio
nomine quo supra, presente dicto Laurentio et protestante ut supra,
juravit dicere veritatem super titulis productis ⟨per⟩ supradictum
judeum, lectis sibi de verbo ad verbum et expositis in vulgari, et deposuit
xv die dicti mensis. Et primo super primo titulo dixit se tantum inde scire
super eo videlicet quod vidit dictum Petrum Guizo in titulo nominatum
bibentem in tabernis et ludentem raubam suam, ipsam deponendo tam
in tabernis quam extra, ludentem raubam suam, et hoc dicit se scire visu
et auditu. Vidit tamen ipsum potantem in tabernis, non ideo tantum vidit
eum ebrium ut hoc cognosceret. Interrogatus quid inde vidit et audivit,
dixit quod in taberna ipsius deponentis et in taberna Hugoni Fosii et
in taberna de Miramas, et universaliter et indifferenter, et cum[5]
quibuscumque personis. Interrogatus testis quotiens vidit dictum
Petrum spoliantem et ludentem raubam suam, dixit quod semel tantum,
tamen audivit a quibusdam, scilicet a Miramas et a Rostagno de [C]osta
et a Francisco de Piscaria tabernariis quod quilibet eorum luserat cum
dicto Petro in titulo nominato, et ab eo ter [vicibus?] lucrati fuerant
raubam suam, et in tabernis ubi vendebant vinum. Interrogatus testis de
anno die et mense quod ipse vidit dictum Petrum ludentem et

deponentem raubam suam, respondit quod duo anni lapsi sunt, de mense die septimana non recordatur. Interrogatus inter quos est fama de predictis, dixit quod inter predictos et ipsum deponentem et plures alios.

Super secundo titulo dixit se nichil scire.

Super tertio titulo dixit et respondit quod ignorat ipsum Petrum in titulo nominatum bona aliqua possidere. Et dicit se scire quod vidit (eum?) aliquo tempore dudum lapso bona aliqua mobilia et immobilia [18v] possidere, que nunc ut audivit non tenet nec possidet nam pars que sibi contingebat cuiusdam orti apud Jarretum fecit sibi extimari socer suus qui nominatur Bertrandus Feda pro dote cuiusdam filie sue uxoris condam dicti Petri in titulo nominati. Alia dixit se nescire super ipso titulo in bonis precedentibus nisi prout supra testificatus est. Interrogatus quam partem vellet potius obtinere in causa, dixit quod ius habentem in causa et non aliud.

Et generaliter, interrogatus si prece, precio, gratia, odio, amore vel timore instructus, seu [?] ad singula, respondit non.

(VIII)   Anno quo supra die xi febroarii. Guillelmus Stephani, laborator, civis Massilie, testis productus per dictum Boniuzas judeum juravit dicere veritatem, presente dicto Laurentio et protestante quod possit dicere et obicere in dictis et personis ipsius testis et productorumque producendarum. Qui deposuit dictum suum die xvii mensis febroarii, juramento suo requisitus super dictis titulis sibi expositis in vulgari, et primo super primo titulo dixit se tantum inde scire super eo videlicet quod vidit eum sepe et sepius existentem in tabernis, et bibentem et ludentem tam in tabernis quam extra, tamen non vidit eum ludentem raubam suam nec eam spoliantem ad hoc ut eam luderet, tamen bene vidit eum pluries prostratum, et tunc temporis audivit dici quod luserat raubam suam. Interrogatus testis inter quos est fama de predictis, dixit inter ipsum deponentem, et Boyre de Castellet et Chamam Dronum, et plures alios de quibus nominibus non recordatur.

Super secundo titulo interrogatus testis sibi lecto et exposito in vulgari [19r] dixit se tantum inde scire super eo videlicet quod quadam die de qua non recolit, sunt duo anni lapsi vel circa, tempore cadragesimali ut sibi deponenti videtur, cum dictus Petrus Guizol, alias dictus Garnaudi, alias de Evena, lusiset ad taxillos, dictus' deponens et Raymundus Logran et Fulco de Torrenes corripientes et corripiendo dicentes dicto Petro Guiso quod male faciebat quia se exponebat totiens ludo, et qua devastabat bona sua. Qui Petrus respondit quod non luderet amodo aut aliquo tempore vite sue, et ita juravit ad sancta dei evangelia in manibus Hugonis de Geminis notarii, et inde fuit facta nota publica, tamen dixit dictus Petrus quod si contrarium faceret, penam sibit imposuit LX solidorum. Interrogatus testis si post ipsum juramentum

vidit ludentem dictum Petrum Guizol, dixit quod ut audivit a Fulcone
Torrenes et a pluribus alliis de quorum nominibus non recordatur dictus
Petrus lusit postea. Interrogatus testis si dictus Petrus solvit penam
supradictam, dixit quod nescit, tamen dictus deponens audivit a dicto
Fulcone quod ab ipso Petro nomine dicte pene habuit unam tubam. Et
factis sibi pluribus aliis interrogationibus, dixit se nichil aliud inde scire
super dicto titulo quam supra testificatus est.

Super tertio titulo dixit testis esse verum ut in eo continetur, et hoc
dicit se scire visu et auditu, nam vidit dictum Petrum tempore preterito
cum bonis mobilibus et immobilibus videlicet habentem froyre de scal,
et vineam quandam inter se et fratrem suum, ignorat tamen ubi est vinea
nunc. Interrogatus testis, dicit esse dictum Petrum absque eo quod bona
aliqua habeat mobilia nec immobilia. Interrogatus testis si umquam fuit
in ospitio dicti Petri, dixit quod sic, et tunc vidit et sciebat predicta. Aliud
dixit se nescire, factis sibi diversis interrogationibus, nisi quod supra dictum est. Interrogatus testis si prece, pretio, gratia fert hoc testimonium
et si doctus, instructus esset, dixit quod non est doctus.

C

9 February–14 April 1316. A second set of depositions made in
the court of Marseilles at the initiative of Bondavid of Draguignan.
Twenty-four citizens relate this time to three statements (*tituli*) in
Bondavid's letter of defense, describing his excellent reputation in town,
his generosity, and his kindness. It starts (fol. 27r) with the swearing of
the witnesses in the presence of Laurentius (Fols. 27r–49r).

[27r] Tituli et testes oblati de novo per Boniuzas de Borriano
procuratorio nomine Bondavini de Draguignano judei.

Anno domini mcccxvi die xvii februarii. Constitutus Boniuzas de
Borriano judeus procuratorio nomine dicti Bondavini judei, presente
dicto Laurentio, et obtulit titulos infrascriptos.

Die xviii februarii, juraverunt testes infrascripti presente dicto
Laurentio, dicente et protestante quod possit dicere et obicere in dictis
et personis testium producendorum in hac causa super titulis predictis.

Et primo Petrus de Trella. P. Bertholi, pro curia. Item Petrus
Columboni notarius, Guillelmus Raynaudi notarius, Pascalis Roch
notarius, et dominus Bertrandus Montolivi, Petrus Bonifilii. Juraverunt
etc. domini Ricavus et Petrus Bermundi de Sancto Felicio et dominus
Raymundus Viridis. Item magister Pascalis de Marraneguetis, Petrus
Vitalis piscator, Laurentius de Revesto filius Boneti de Revesto quondam, Raymundus de Rupe Fort, Giraudus de Monte Olivo domicellus

filius domini G. [27v] de Monte Olivo militis quondam, Bonetus Aurioli, Magister Guillelmus Johannis notarius, jurati. Et predicti juraverunt in presentia dicti Laurentii Girardi, dicentis et protestantis quod posit dicere et obicere in dictis et personis testium producendorum et que juraverunt et sunt in futurum parati in contentis fidem curie, etc. Et in Johanni de Spanatiis notario receptionem iamdictorum testium producendorum per dictum Boniuzas in hac causa. Item xxii die dicti mensis, juraverunt Guillelmus Ronelli, dominus Arnaudus de Baucio [et] Hugo Mercerii. Item Nicholas Bonivini. Item Petrus Fereri, Guillelmus Gasqueti, Petrus de Trella, Guillelmus Stefani. Item xxiii die mensis februarii, juravit Raymundus Logran. Item die xxiiii februarii, juravit magister Bartholomeus Salinis notarius. Item Bernardis Gardii juravit prima die martii.

[28r]   Anno domini millesimo cccxvi die xxi mensis februarii. Dominus Montolivus de Montolivo, testis productus per dictum Bondavi judeum, juravit dicere veritatem presente dicto Laurentio et protestante ut supra, et deposuit dictum suum xxi die mensis februarii. Qui requisitus super secundo titulo titulorum noviter oblatorum, aliisque titulis jam omissis de voluntate producentis, dixit suo juramento quod ipse testis habet et reputat dictum Bondavid in sui lege bonum, legalem, pacificum et quietum, boneque fame et bone opinionis, et qui numquam, quod testis sciverit vel dici audiverit consuevit aliquem defraudare nec decipere, nec debita sibi soluta repetere. Et de hiis supra per ipsum testem testificatis dixit testis famam esse in civitate Massilie inter notos et vicinnos eiusdem. Etiam dixit testis quod ipse veram experientiam habuit de premissis in suo facto propter quorumdam suorum amicorum, et quod pluribus et diversis personis gratias multas et magnas fecit suo tempore. Interrogatus inter quas personas est fama de supra per eum testificatis, dixit quod inter eum deponentem et Raymundum de Rupe Forti et Ricavum Ricavi domicellos et plures alios. Item requisitus testis si scit dictum Bondavid mutuare ad usuras, dixit quod credit quod sic, sicuti faciunt alii judei. Item requisitus si scit, vel dici audivit, quod dictus Bondavit ab aliquo petierit debita sibi soluta, dixit quod non, nec habet ipsum talem quod peteret, propter multas gratias quas vidit quod dictus Bondavit fecit de [28v] debitis propriis suis dicti Bondavit de debitis et incartamentis suis et quod vidit et presens fuit quod multis dimisit et gratiam fecit deminuendo eis quantitatem et partem debitorum que dicto Bondavid debebant. Interrogatus testis a quanto tempore citra habet notitiam dicti Bondavid, dixit quod ab origine sua et pro tali ipsum habet usque nunc ut supra testificatus est. Et generaliter, interrogatus.

Anno domini mcccxvi die xviii februarii. Dominus Ricavus Ricavi, domicellus, testis productus per dictum Boniuzas procuratorio nomine dicti Bondavidini, juravit dicere veritatem, presente dicto Laurentio et protestante ut supra, et deposuit dictum suum xxi die mensis febroarii. Qui juramento suo requisitus super secundo titulo et tertio, ipsi testi bene et diligenter lecto et exposito in vulgari, dixit se tantum inde scire super eo quod dictus Bondavit [29r] est homo bonus, pacificus et quietus, et est homo legalis et bone fame et bone opinionis, et qui consuevit suo tempore et ese sine[6] eo quod defraudaret nec deciperet nec debita sibi soluta ab aliquo repeteret, et eum pro tali habet juxta legem et opinionem vivens. Et quod ipse sciat nec audivit de eo nemo audivit dici et pro tali habetur inter omnes illos qui eum cognoscunt. Interrogatus testis inter quos est fama de predictis, dixit quod in civitate Massilie communiter inter personas eum cognoscentes, videlicet inter ipsum deponentem et Hugonem [de Rupe Forti?] et dominos P. Bermundi de Sancto Felicio et Flavium de Sancto Felicio et Montolivum Montolivi et Raymundum de Rupe Forti. Et ultra dixit testis quod non credit esse in lege sua in mundo judeum legaliorem eo. Et de predictis dixit testis bonam experientiam habere tam in sociis suis quam quorundan amicorum suorum.

Super tertio titulo dixit se tantum inde scire super eo quod vidit et audivit quod dictus Bondavid pluribus hominibus fecit gratiam de debitis suis, et specialiter sibi. Et fecit (frequenter?) gratiam Jacob Petri mulaterio, juxta vocem dicti debitoris. Interrogatus si aliquo tempore audivit nec vidit quod dictus Bondavid repetierit debita sibi soluta, dixit et respondit quod nunquam audivit.

Interrogatus a quo tempore citra cognovit dictum Bondavit, dixit quod ab origine sua, et a tempore quo eum cognovit usque nunc habet ipsum pro tali ut supra testificatus est.

[29v]   Anno domini mcccxvi xxi die mensis febroarii. Petrus Ferreri domicellus juravit dicere veritatem, absente dicto Laurentio, sacramentum seu juramentum ipsius testis commitente mihi notario et curie et aliorum testium producendorum prout supra patet, dicente et protestante ut supra. Et lecto sibi secundo et tertio titulis, alio omisso de voluntate producentis, et expositis de verbo ad verbum in vulgari, dictum suum die xxiii dicti mensis deposuit super eis. Et primo super secundo tituto dixit se tantum inde scire super eo quod dictus Bondavid est bone fame, bonus, pacificus et quietus ac bone opinionis, et de eo non audivit nec scit quod consueveret esse defraudator nec deceptor nec debita soluta repetierit aliquo tempore. Et de predictis dicit esse famam inter omnes illos qui eum cognoscunt. Et veram experientiam habuit et audivit de predictis, propterque dicit testis quod eum pro tali habet, ut predictum est. Nam dixit quod quodam tempore post obitum domini Raymundi Egidii canonici ecclesie sedis Massiliensis audivit a domino

Hugone Gantelini operario dicte ecclesie sedis Massiliensis, quod quodam die cum esset in ospitio dicti domini Hugonis audivit deponens ista verba, pluribus aliis hic existentibus ut sibi videtur de quorum nominibus dicit testis se non recordari, quod dictus dominus Hugo dixit hec verba: "Vultis audire magnam legalitatem judei? Dominus Raymundus Egidii condam eo vivente tradiderat Bondavino judeo filio Habrahe de Draguiniano duo milia turonenses argenti. Et dicto domino [30r] Raymundo ab humanis ablato, dictus Bondavid venit ad me." "Domine Hugo, dominus meus meus dominus Raymundus Egidii "decessit, cuius anima in pace requiescat, dimisit vobis aliquam "scripturam continentem obligationem aliquam, sicut apodixam vel "scripturam publicam vel privatam, in qua sibi essem obligatus ego "Bondavid"? Qui dictus dominus Hugo respondit dicto Bondavid quod non inveniebat aliquam scripturam in qua ipse esset dicto domino Raymundo obligatus. Et confestim ipse Bondavid dixit dicto domino Hugoni ut gazario dicti domini Raymundi, quod ipse habebat in posse suo duo milia turonenses argenti "quos mihi tradidit dictus dominus "Raymundus animans ut eos sibi custodirem. Et ego tradam eos vobis, "nam adhuc sunt sigillati in caxia mea. Et confestim eos mihi restituit." Et hec audivit deponens a dicto domino Hugone in sua camera existente.

Super secundo titulo dixit se tantum inde scire super eo videlicet quod experientiam habet de se ipso, nam sibi deponenti magnam gratiam de quodam[7] debito, nam partem ipsius debiti sibi deponenti dimisit gratiose. Et fuerunt vi vel vii libre ut deponenti videtur, et cuidam operario suo, et idem audivit a pluribus aliis. Interrogatus testis si audivit ab aliquo quod ipse repetierit debita sibi persoluta, dixit quod numquam audivit nec credit quod ipse hoc faceret propter bonam famam suam que fuit et est de eo in civitate Massillie. Interrogatus testis inter quos est fama de predictis, dixit.

[30v]   Anno domini m̃cccxvi die xxiii mensis febroarii Raymundus Logran civis Massilie, testis productus per dictum Boniuzas, absente dicto Laurentio, et protestante ut supra commitente tamen sacramentum ipsius testis et aliorum curie et mihi Johanni de Spinaciis notario, lectis sibi et expositis in vulgari titulis de novo.

[31v]   Anno domini m̃ccxvi die xxii febroarii Hugo Mercerii apothecarius, testis productus per dictum Boniuzas procuratorio nomine dicti Bondavid, juravit dicere veritatem absente dicto Laurentio protestante et commitente ut supra, super titulis supradictis de novo oblatis, et eis lectis videlicet primo omisso de voluntate producentis, super secundo et tertio dictum suum deposuit die xxiii dicti mensis, et eis sibi lectis et expositis in vulgari primo super secundo titulo dixit se tantum inde scire super eo quod dictus Bondavid est homo bonus,

pacificus, et quietus, et legalis, bone fame et bone opinionis, et qui numquam quod ipse testis sciat nec audiverit, consuevit aliquem defraudare nec decipere nec debita persoluta repetere. Interrogatus qualiter scit predicta, respondit testis, causam redens sui dicti, quod eo quia numquam audivit de eo contrarium, et quia experientiam habet et habuit pluries de predictis, quia cum eo multa negotia gessit cum eo mercando, emendo, vendendo, et tam in peccunia quam in rebus, quod numquam invenit in eo deceptionem nec corruptelam set summariam legalitatem. Et non credit quod in lege sua, vel secundum legem suam judeus eo legalior sit, nec magis iustus in lege sua poset in mundo reperiri. Et de predictis dicit famam esse inter eum deponentem et Ricavum Ricavi domicellum et Raymundum de Trella et Guillelmum de Jherusalem et omnes personas que eum cognoscunt quas et essent longissime enarrare.

Super secundo titulo dixit ita esse verum ut in eo continetur, et hoc dixit se scire testis visu et auditu. Nam vidit quod dictus Bondavid gratiam magnam fecit Guillelmo Benedicti de quodam debito, ignorantem tamen quantum, quod ipse ipsum debitum diu est sunt duo anni et plus, prolongavit, ab eo non petendo nisi sortem, interesse dimitente vel lucram. Et adhuc sibi debet. Et certificatus postea dixit quod debitum est vi librarum vel circa. Et pluribus aliis [32r] idem fecit, prout testis vidit et audivit. Interrogatus testis si dictus Bondavid mutuat peccuniam sub usuris, credit quod sic sicut alii judei. Interrogatus testis si scit nec audivit aliquo tempore quod dictus Bondavid debita sibi soluta repetierit, dixit suo juramento quod non credit nec audivit nec credit quod ipse hoc atemptaret facere secundum legem suam quod [. . 2–3 words . .] ipse deponens faceret. Et generaliter.

Anno domini m̃cccxvi xviii die febroarii magister Pascalis de Mayraneguetis testis productus per dictum Boniuzas procuratorio nomine antedicto, juravit dicere veritatem. Et ostensis sibi duobus capitulis, videlicet secundo et tertio, alio omisso de voluntate producentis, dixit tantum inde scire super eis, et primo super secundo titulo dixit se scire et semper dici audivisse, a sexdecim annis citra et plus, qui fuit notarius civitatis ville superioris, in qua de ipso Bonus Davinus et eius pater condam multa habebat facere cum personis dicte civitatis ipsum Bonum Davinum fuisse et esse hominem quietem, legalem, pacificum, bone fame bone opinionis et bone conditionis. Et multas gratias et largas facientem de debitis [32v] que sibi debebantur a debitoribus suis, et numquam vidit nec dici audivit dictum Bonumdavinum aliquam baratariam sive fraudem facientem nec [. . 1 word . .] contra veritatem, potissime ymo vidit quod dictus Bonus Davinus aliquam quantitatem turonensium argenti, de qua testis non recolit, remisit filio et heredi Johannis Drago qui suspensus fuit, quam dictus Johannes coram judice ipsius civitatis superioris in presentia ipsius deponentis et aliorum, confessus fuerat se de puro mutuo dicto Bono Davino debere, quam quantitatem ipse testis scripsit in cartulario, et quam idem judeus jussit per dictum testem notarium cancellari. Vidit etiam aliqua mandamenta plures quantitates turonensium argenti continentia, per ipsum judeum lacerari, dicentem ipsi testi notario, qui dicta mandamenta ipsi judeo legerat, quod ipsa mandamenta erant defunctorum amicorum suorum. Et numquam ea peteret ab heredibus eorumdem ne exeredaret eos, et de hiis est vox et fama in civitate predicta. Et ipsum deponentem et cognoscentem dictum Bonum Davinum. Et hoc dixit et testificatus est quia veram et certam experientiam habet et habuit de predictis supra per eum testificatis prout supra testificatus est.

Super tertio titulo dixit ut supra in secundo dixit.

[33r] Anno domini millesimo cccxvi, xviii die febroarii magister Pascalis notarius juravit dicere veritatem super secundo et tertio titulis, omisso primo de voluntate producentis, dixit se tantum inde scire super eis et deposuit dictum suum xxiiii die dicti mensis, et dixit se tantum inde scire super secundo titulo videlicet quod xxv anni sunt et plus quod ipse testis habet notitiam dicti Boni Davini a quo tempore citra non vidit fieri nec audivit dici ab aliquo contrarium de contentis in titulo, ymo ipse testis habet ipsum judeum unum de melioribus judeis civitatis Massilie et legaliorem in lege sua, bone fame inter omnes qui eum cognoscunt, et specialiter inter curiales Massilie videlicet inter ipsum deponentem, Johannem de Matis, Guillelmum Serandum, Bartholomeum de Salinis et ceteros alios qui notitiam habunt de dicto Bono Davino. Interrogatus qualiter scit predicta, dixit et respondit quia veram experientam habet de hiis que testificatus est.

Item super tertio titulo dixit quod nichil aliud scit nisi quod frequenter pluribus vicibus audivit dici a pluribus debitoribus dicto Boni Davini de quorum nominibus non recordatur testis, quod dictus Bonus Davinus erat eisdem in debitis que sibi debebant valde gratiosus et diu gratias eis fecerat. Et de hiis est fama inter predictos ut supra.

[33v] Anno quo supra die xxiiii mensis febroarii. Dominus Raymundus de Rupe Forti juravit dicere veritatem super secundo et tertio titulis, primo omisso de voluntate producentis, deposuit dictum suum xxiiii die mensis febroarii. Qui testis juramento suo requisitus super predictis titulis, et primo super secundo titulo, dixit se tantum inde scire super eo quod a sex annis citra et plus nam alio tempore non habuit conversationem nec notitiam ipsius, et ab illo tempore quo novit eum numquam audivit nec scit quod ipse Bondavinus contrarium fecerit de eis que in ipso titulo continentur. Interrogatus qualiter scit, dixit quod eo quia

multotiens habuit negotia secum, et numquam invenit in eo nisi legalitatem et facta vidit fieri propter que habet eum bone fame et legale[m] et bone opinionis. Interrogatus si audivit de eo dici, nec vidit fieri, propter que posset de eo dici signum aliquod mali sicut fraudis vel deceptionis, dixit quod non set semper summam legalitatem secundum legem suam in eo invenit, nec audivit nec scit quod aliquo tempore consueverit debita aliqua sibi soluta repetere. Interrogatus inter quos est fama de predictis, dixit deponens quod inter eum et dominos Ricavum Ricavi et Montolivum de Montolivo domicellos, et Hugonem Mercerii et Raynaudum de Sirella mercatores, et multos alios quod esset longissimum enarrare. Et ea dixit quia veram experientiam habet et habuit in factis suis [34r] propriis et plurium amicorum suorum et aliorum hominum.

Super tertio titulo dixit tantum inde scire super eo quod scit quod dictus Bondavinus fecit gratiam de debitis suis, et sibi specialiter, prolungando sibi ea que sibi debebat et Petro Ferrerii et quibusdam aliis prout audivit ab eis, neminem nominando set dixit quod nescit aliquem cui ipse sciens daret fidem in negotiis suis quam faceret dicto Bondavino. Et sine instrumento et sine testibus daret fidem mille librarum, et omnium que ipse deponens habet tam mobilium quam immobilium. Et non est doctus. Et generaliter etc.

[34v] Anno domini m̅cccxvi die xxii febroarii. Guillelmus Novelli testis productis super secundo et tertio titulis, omisso primo de voluntate producentis, juravit dicere veritatem super dictis titulis et deposuit dictum suum xxiiii die dicti mensis, et primo super secundo titulo ipsi testi diligenter exposito in vulgari, dixit se tantum inde scire super eo quod nunquam audivit nec scit quod dictus Bonus Davinus fecerit contrarium, nisi si et prout in ipso titulo continetur. Et scit eum bonum, pacificum et legalem, bone fame, et bone opinionis, et qui non consuevit aliquem decipere verbo nec facto nec defraudare verbo, facto vel opere, nec debita sibi soluta alias repetere, set multas gratias facere tam deponenti quam pluribus aliis ut vidit et audivit, et sine eo quod aliquod emolumentum seu lucrum haberet ex eo, et cotidie facit et non cessat facere. Interrogatus testis a quo tempore citra habet notitiam dicti Bondavini, dixit quod a xv annis citra, et ab illo tempore citra nunquam audivit dici contrarium de eo nisi bonum et bonam famam et summam legalitatem tam inter populares mercatores quam alios. Interrogatus testis qualiter scit predicta dixit quod eo quia omni tempore, a tempore quo ipse habuit notitiam de eo, veram experientiam habuit tam propter negotia sua, et prout audivit ab aliis pluribus et diversis personis, et quia in eo nullam fraudem deceptionem aliquo tempore invenit. Et ultra dixit quod non credit quod ipse fraudem comite ret [35r°] nec sustineret. Interrogatus

testis inter quos est fama de predictis, dixit quod inter ipsum deponentem et magistros Petrum Elsiarii, Johannem de Maris, Paris Calenvoe notarium, Petrum Bertholi [procuratorem?] et plures de quibus esset sermo prolixus.

Super tertio titulo dixit se tantum inde scire super eo quod scit et vidit quod dictus Bondavinus magnam gratiam fecit sibi deponenti de debitis suis omni tempore post quam novit eum, et scit et audivit quod Rostagno Pagani de sorte dimisit sibi v solidos vel circa, et pluribus gentibus de quorum nominibus non recordatur. Et non est doctus etc.

[35v°] Anno domini millesimo cccxvi die xviii febroarii. Petrus Bertholi testis productus per dictum Boniuzas procuratorio nomine dicti Bondavini juravit dicere veritatem super secundo et tertio titulis, primo omisso de voluntate producentis, qui deposuit dictum suum super dictis titulis xxiiii die dicti mensis, et primo super secundo titulo dixit se tantum inde scire super eo quod dictus Bonus Davinus est homo bonus pacificus bone fame et bone opinionis, et sine eo quod consueverit nec atemptaverit aliquem defraudare seu decipere, nec facta facere, verbo, [dicto?], vel opere, propterque fraus aliqua posset comitti, et predicta dicit se scire causam reddens sui dicti, eo quia veram experientiam et manifestam habet de predictis, visu et auditu. Nam vidit et audivit quod ad preces dicti deponentis dictus Bonus Davinus magnam gratiam fecit Johanni Giraudo qui moratur in burgo predicatorum, prorogando sibi debitum quoddam Lxiiii librarum regalium ad preces dicti deponentis, semel, secundo et tertio, et per diversa intervalla quolibet intervallo per unum mensem et plus. Et cuidam alii nominato Petro Bollimoni qui sibi debebat magnam quantitatem peccunie, cui similiter debitum prorogavit per longum tempus ad preces similiter deponentis, et pluribus aliis de quorum nominibus testis dicit se non recordari, et etiam in factis suis propriis. Interrogatus testis a quo tempore citra habet notitiam dicti Boni Davini, dixit quod a decem octo annis citra vel id circa, et ab illo tempore citra de eo non audivit contrarium, nisi prout supra testifi [36r] catus est. Et quia veritas sic se habet ut dicit testis prout supra testificatus, et hoc dicit quia de eo nunqum vidit ne audivit de eo dici contrarium.

Super tertio titulo dixit idem in omnibus et per omnia ut supra testificatus est.

Et non est doctus etc.

[36v]   xx florenos sine lucro

Anno domini mcccxvi, xviii die mensis febroarii. Petrus Vitalis piscator testis productus per dictum Boniuzas de Borriano procuratorio nomine dicti Bondavini juravit dicere veritatem, presente dicto Laurentio, dicente et protestante ut supra, et deposuit dictum suum xxiiii die dicti mensis super secundo et tertio titulis, primo omisso de voluntate producentis. Qui deposuit dictum suum super secundo titulo, ipsi testi diligenter exposito in vulgari, dixit se tantum inde scire super eo videlicet quod ab octo annis citra habet notitiam et experientiam dicti Boni Davini et in factis suis ipsius deponentis quod ab illo tempore citra quo eum cognovit usque nunc, vidit et cognovit dictum Bonum Davinum, et hodie habet eum ut hominem bonum pacificum et quietum et legalem, bone fame et bone opinionis, et qui non consuevit aliquem decipere nec defraudare, nec decepit post quam de eo habuit notitiam quod ipse sciat nec sciverit nec debita sibi soluta repetere. Ymo quadam die cum ipse depponens esset in ripa Sancti Johannis, cum vellet emere quandam quantitatem picium et non haberet unde solveret, murmurando inter se et loquendo cum aliis quod non habebat unde solveret ipsos pisces, ipse Bonus Davinus hec audiens cum faceret transitum per ripam. ipsam mandavit sibi per quemdam de domo sua xx florenos, sine eo quod instrumentum, mandamentum seu teste ipse Bonus Davinus haberet ab ipso deponenti, et sine aliquo lucro sibi dictos florenos tradit et tenuit. Et multas gratias eidem deponenti alias fecit. Et non est doctus.

[37v]   Anno quo supra die xviii febroarii. Dominus Petrus Bermundi de Sancto Felicio juravit dicere veritatem super secundo et tertio titulis, primo omisso de voluntate producentis, qui deposuit dictum suum die xxiiii febroarii. Et primo super dicto titulo secundo dixit se tantum inde scire super eo videlicet quod a decem annis citra cognovit, et adhuc cognoscit, dictum Bondavinum et ab illo tempore citra dicit et cognoscit ipsum Bondavinum ut hominem bonum, pacificum, bone fame et bone opinionis et legalem, et sine eo quod aliquo tempore viderit nec audiverit dictum Bondavinum aliquem decipere nec defraudare verbo facto vel opere, nec debita soluta sibi alias repetere. Et predicta dixit se scire dictus deponens ex eo quia experientiam et notitiam de eo habuit, tam in factis suis propriis quam etiam ut audivit a personis fide dignis et quibus est veritas adhibenda. Interrogatus dictus dominus Petrus, testis ut supra, inter quos est fama de predictis, dixit quod inter ipsum deponentem et dominos Ricavum Ricavi et Raymundum de Rupe Forti et Montolivum de Montolivo domicellum et plures alios. Et ultra dixit testis quod inter illos qui sunt de lege sua nunquam audivit nec vidit legaliorem eo, et etiam est fama de predictis inter judeos istius civitatis.

[38v]   Anno domini millesimo cccxvi xxii die febroarii. Petrus de Trella civis Massilie mercator, juravit dicere veritatem, absente dicto Laurentio et comitente et protestante ut supra, super secundo et tertio titulis, primo omisso de voluntate producentis, et deposuit dictum suum xxv die dicti mensis. Qui juramento requisitus super secundo titulo ipsi testi bene et diligenter lecto et exposito in vulgari, dixit se tantum inde

scire super eo videlicet, quod ea que continentur in ipso titulo sunt vera ut in eo continentur. Et predicta dixit se scire visu et auditu. Interrogatus quid inde vidit et audivit, dixit ⟨quod⟩ vidit et experientiam habuit in factis suis quod dictus Bonus Davinus sepe et sepius mutuavit sibi deponenti peccuniam gratis, et prolungando sibi terminum et terminos juxta eius beneplacitum et voluntatem suam. Et quod numquam sibi gravamen aliquod intulit, sed vidit multotiens, ipso deponente existente in domo sua, quod dictus Bonus Davinus cum gentes alterutre conditionis venirent in domos [sic] sua restituebat et restituit diversis personis indigentibus, ut sibi deponenti videbatur, quando solverant debita que debebant dicto Bondavino, quod ipse Bonus Davinus restituebat eis sorte deducta totum lucrum, inspiciendo paupertatem et querendo si indigebant persone quibus restituebat. Et etiam audivit et vidit quod ipse Bonus Davinus querebat ab ipsis debitoribus qualiter et unde vivebant. Et vidit inter alios quandam bonam mulierem que venit [39r] quadam die ad domum ipsius Boni Davini pro solvendo quoddam debitum in quo dicto judeo erat obligata, ignorat tamen testis quantitatem debiti, et vidit quod ipsa mulier solvit debitum. Quo facto, ipse Bonus Davinus quesivit ab ea de vita sua per hec verba: "Dicatis mater, et quomodo vivitis vos nec quam artem habetis". Que respondit: "Sciatis domine quod non habeo unde vivam nisi de labore et sudore mariti mei". Et hoc audito, respiciens ipse Bonus Davinus paupertatem ipsius mulieris, magnam quantitatem peccunie vidit deponens quod ipse judeus ipsi mulieri restituit. Et pluribus aliis hoc idem fecit. Et ob predicta dicit eum et habet bonum, suavem, legalem, bone fame, bone opinionis, et sine eo quod consueverit decipere nec defraudare aliquem quod ipse testis viderit, nec aliquo tempore audivit. Interrogatus testis si scit quod ipse Bonus Davinus debita aliqua sibi soluta repetierit, dixit quod numquam vidit nec aliquo tempore audivit, cum sepe et sepius viderit quod ipse gratias multas et largas pluribus fecerit. Et plus dixit similiter vera esse quia veram experientiam habuit de predictis. Et quia veritas sic se habet ut supra testificatus est.

Super tertio dixit se nichil aliud scire quam supra deposuit ut supra deposuit.

[39v]   Anno domini mcccxvi die xxii febroarii Guillelmus Stephani testis productus per dictum Boniuzas super titulis per eum oblatis, absente dicto Laurentio, et comitente sacramentum ut supra, et protestante ut supra, et deposuit dictum suum die ultima dicti mensis. Qui requisitus super secundo et tertio titulo, primo omisso de voluntate producentis, dixit ita esse verum ut in ipso secundo titulo continetur, et ea dixit se scire visu et auditu. Nam ipse deponens multa habuit facere cum dicto Bondavino sicut in peccunia et aliis negotiis, et dixit quod multas gratias

sibi fecit, mutuando sibi peccuniam gratis et absque lucro aliquo seu emolumento, et aliquando cum emolumento. Et etiam debita que contraxit cum eo ad voluntatem suam sibi prolungavit et quod nunquam invenit in eo nec de eo nisi legalitatem bonitatem et omnem modestiam. Et quod nunquam vidit nec audivit quod ipse aliquem deceperit nec defraudaverit, nec debita sibi soluta repetierit, propter que dicit quod ipsum habet in lege sua bonum, legalem, pacificum, bone fame, bone opinionis, et in lege sua non credit esse legaliorem in mundo. Et predicta dixit testis quia veram experientiam habuit, tam in factis suis quam etiam in alienis. Nam sibi deponenti pluries dimisit de debitis partem in quibus erant (sic!) sibi obligatus, et idem vidit de pluribus aliis personis. Et etiam dicit quod pluribus amicis suis sine instrumento et pignore vidit mutuari, et adhuc debent debita sine eo quod ⟨non⟩ habeat dictus Bondavinus instrumenta nec mandamenta, ut dixit deponens.

[40r] Super secundo titulo dixit se nichil aliud scire inde quam supra in secundo titulo testificatus est.

Et non est doctus. Et generaliter.

Anno domini millesimo cccxvi, xviii die febroarii. Girardus de Montolivo domicellus, filius domini Guillelmi de Montolivo militis condam testis productus per dictum Boniuzas procuratorio nomine dicti Bondavini, presente dicto Laurentio, dicente et protestante ut supra. Qui deposuit dictum suum ultima die dicti mensis super dictis titulis videlicet super secundo et tertio, primo omisso de voluntate producentis, et ipsis expositis dixit se tantum inde scire super secundo videlicet quod dixit vera esse ut in ipso titulo continetur, et predicta dixit se scire visu et auditu. Interrogatus quid inde vidit et audivit, dixit quod ab illo tempore quo habet notitiam [40v] dictus deponens dicti Boni Davini, dixit quod a tribus annis citra et ab illo tempore citra cognoscit eum et de eo audivit et vidit omnia gesta bona que potest facere et dicere, bonus homo et bonus judeus, propterque habet et dicit eum bonum, justum pacificum, legalem, bone fame bone opinionis. Interrogatus testis si vidit aliquem de dicto Bono Davino conquerentem et decipientem seu defraudantem, dixit et respondit testis suo juramento quod aliquo tempore non vidit nec audivit aliquam personam que diceret de eo fraudem nec deceptionem, nec quod eam deceperit nec defraudaverit, set semper de eo audivit bonam famam. Interrogatus testis qualiter scit predicta, dixit et respondit quia nunquam audivit contrarium, et quia experientiam habet de predictis tam in factis domus paterne, quam aliis, nam sibi et fratri suo et domine sue multas gratias fecit tam mutuando peccuniam et prolungando eam et gratiam faciendo de ea. Et non tantum sibi, set pluribus amicis suis. Interrogatus testis inter quos est fama de predictis, dixit quod inter ipsum deponentem et

Ricavum Ricavi et Montolivum de Montolivo et Raymundum de Rupe Forti et plures alios. Dixit etiam juramento suo quod secundum facta que vidit de eo non credit legaliorem esse in civitate nec in mundo.

[41r]   Super tertio titulo dixit ita esse verum ut in eo continetur et predicta dixit se scire visu et auditu. Nam vidit et scit quod sibi et Raymundo de Rupe Forti socero suo, multas et largas ⟨gratias⟩ de debitis in quibus sibi erant obligati. Alia dixit se nescire nisi prout supra testificatus est.

[41v]   Anno domini millesimo cccxvi die xxii febroarii. Guillelmus Gasqueti testis productus per dictum Boniusas, absente dicto Laurentio,, comitente et protestante ut supra, juravit dicere veritatem super secundo et tertio titulis, primo omisso de voluntate producentis, et deposuit dictum suum die prima martii. Et lectis sibi et expositis invulgari, super secundo titulo dixit se tantum scire videlicet quod inter alios judeos totius juzatarie ipse Bonus Davinus est et eum habet pro legali et legaliorem inter omnes judeos totius civitatis. Et etiam legaliorem quem ipse[8] viderit et audiverit aliquo tempore vite sue, nec credit hodie in mundo legaliorem. Nam si posset dici chrisianum numquam invenit legaliorem eo, nec vidit. Et ea propter ipsum dicit et habet hominem bone fame, bone opinionis, bonum et legalem et qui non consuevit aliquem decipere nec defraudare quod ipse testis sciat nec audiverit. Interrogatus testis si aliquo unquam tempore vidit nec audivit quod dictus Bonus Davinus debita sibi soluta alias repetierit, dixit juramento suo quod non, nec credit quod ipse hoc faceret. Nam multotiens vidit specialiter de se quod ipse Bonus Davinus solutione sibi facta de quibusdam debitis reddebat sibi peccuniam. Et hoc idem fecit de pluribus aliis ut vidit, et etiam peccuniam multotiens sibi mutuavit sine mandamento et instrumento et testibus, et etiam gratis. Interrogatus testis si aliquo tempore vidit nec audivit de eo dici aliqua per que fraus nec deceptio in dicto Bono Davino nec de eo posset excogitari, dixit quod non, ymo omni tempore de eo audivit et vidit summam [42r] legalitatem, et conversantem semper cum bonis personis et honorabilibus et fide dignis. Interrogatus testis qualiter scit predicta, dixit quod rationibus antedictis, et quia de eo veram experientiam habet et habuit in factis suis quam etiam alienis, ut vidit et audivit, nec de eo non posset dici secundum presentiam contrarium nisi bonum. Interrogatus testis a quo tempore citra cognoscit dictum Bonum Davinum, dixit quod a xiiii annis citra, et ab illo tempore de eo non audivit contrarium de hiis que supra testificatus est, set semper vidit eum bonum et legalem, et facta legalia facientem, et inter bonos et legales perseverantem.

Super secundo titulo dixit nichil aliud scire quod supra testificatus, nisi quod vidit et audivit quod sibi deponenti et pluribus aliis bonis personis gratias magnas fecit, debita prolungando, partem debiti debitoribus restituendo, et specialiter sibi, et instrumenta seu mandamenta vidit omni tempore gratiose reddere debitoribus suis sine aliqua conditione.

Et non est doctus etc.

[42v]   Anno domini mcccxv [sic!] die xxii febroarii. Magister Petrus Columboni testis productus per dictum Boniuzas procuratorio nomine dicti Bondavini, presente dicto Laurentio et protestante ut supra, et deposuit dictum suum super secundo et tertio titulis, dixit se tantum inde scire super eos, et primo super secundo dixit juramento suo ita esse verum ut in eo continetur, et predicta dicit se scire visu et auditu. Interrogatus quid inde vidit et audivit ⟨dixit se vidisse⟩ dictum Bonum Davinum rogari per plures suos debitores in diversis curiis et etiam extra curias quod faceret eis gratias de eorum debitis, scilicet aliquis querebat sibi prolungari terminum solutionum, et aliqui sibi dicebant et requirebant ut partem aliquam de debito sibi dimiteret. Et nunquam vidit ⟨eum⟩ denegari gratiam alicui, ymo semper faciebat eis gratias, ita quod dicti debitores regratiabantur eidem Bono Davino gratias quas eis fecit idem Bonus Davinus, et quasi omnibus dicebat idem Bonus Davinus eisdem suis debitoribus: "Quantum vultis de tempore" vel "Quantum vultis quod vobis dimitam". Et ipsi debitores dicebant suum velle. Et ipse Bonus Davinus eisdem consentiebat ut petebant, imo videbatur ipsi testi prout vidit ab ipso BonoDavino quod in faciem[9] gratiam et gratias ipse locabatur dicit etiam ipse deponens quod ipse habet eum ut legalem bonum et bone fame et bone opinionis et sine eo quod unquam vidit nec audivit de eo aliqua [43r] signa, verbo facto vel opere propter que deceptio nec fraus in eo sive de eo posset dici nec excogitari, nec si mille libras vel infinitam peccuniam lucreretur quod aliud diceret nec faceret nisi ut interest facere homines boni et legales. Et predicta dixit et testificatus est ex eo quia nunquam vidit contrarium de eo, ymo dixit suo juramento quod non credit esse legaliorem eo in lege sua in civitate nec in mundo. Nam de predictis experientam veram in factis suis quam aliis habet.

[43v]   Anno domini mcccxvi die prima martii. Dominus Andreas Bonivini testis productus per dictum Bonum Davinum, absente dicto Laurentio, citato et contumaciter absente, juravit dicere veritatem super secundo et tertio titulis, primo omisso de voluntate producentis, dixit se tantum inde scire super secundo titulo, sibit exposito in vulgari, et dixit dictum suum die predicta, videlicet vera esse que in titulo continentur, et ea dixit se scire visu et auditu. Interrogatus quid inde vidit et audivit, dixit quod vidit de eo semper bona facta, bona verba, bonos gestus, et perseverantem cum bonis hominibus et melioribus huius ville, et qui nunquam consuevit aliquem decipere nec defraudare, set bona facta

facere et legalia, propter que ipsum dicit et habet, suo judicio, bonum, legalem, bone fame, bone opinionis, et qui semper ab illo tempore quo congnovit eum, bona facta et legalia, ut homo bonus et ut legalis fuit et est, et pro tali ipsum habet hodie, et habetur inter omnes gentes qui eum congnoscunt prout vidit et audivit. Interrogatus inter quos est fama de predictis, dixit quod inter ipsum deponentem et dominos Ricavum Ricavi et Raymundum de Rupe Forti et Montolivum de Montolivo et P. Bermundi de Sancto Felicio, et plures homines quod esset longissimum enarrare. Nam audivit pluries de eo loquentem et inter bonas personas quod nunquam de eo audivit nisi bonum et summam legalitatem, [44r] suo judicio, quod legalitas maior de aliquo suo respectu non posset dici, nec credit esse legaliorem hominem in lege sua in civitate ista nec alibi. Et predicta dixit et testificatus est quia veram experientiam habet de eo Bono Davino, nec credit quod contrarium posset dici per aliquem viventem.

Super secundo titulo dixit se nichil aliud inde scire quam supra testificatus est.

Et non est doctus. Et generaliter interrogatus.

[44v]   Anno domini millesimo cccxvi, xviii die februarii. Petrus Bonifilii fusterius testis productus per dictum Boniuzas procuratorio nomine dicti Boni Davini, juravit dicere veritatem super[10] dictis titulis sibi testi bene et diligenter lectis et expositis in vulgari, dixit se tantum inde scire super eis, et primo super primo titulo dixit se audivisse ad botigam magistri P. Elsiarii ab Stephano de Vians, quibusdam aliis presentibus, videlicet dicto P. Elsiarii et dicto Laurentio et Stephano de Vians predicto, quod dictus Stephanus fuit allocutus cum dicto Laurentio dicendo sibi verba ista: "Laurens! Bonum esset quod dimiteretis causam istam quam habetis cum Bono Davino, nam vobis non est sanum causidicare". Et tunc dictus Stephanus sibi dixit quod audiverat dici a Boneto Auriolo socero dicti Laurentii quod ipse socer voluit sibi Bono Davino dare XL solidos de illis LX solidis unde est causa. Interrogatus testis si audivit nec vidit quod dictus Bonus Davinus esset presens in predictis, dixit quod non; set tantum audivit a dicto Bono Davino in suo ospitio quod nunquam sibi dimiteret aliquid de dicto debito, tractatu habito cum eo quod conveniret dictus Bonus Davinus cum dicto Laurentio. Qui respondit, ut testis audivit, quod solveret sibi debitum suum ipse Laurentius, et erat presto facere sicut bonus homo debet facere. Alias non.

Super secundo titulo dixit ita esse verum ut in eo continetur, et hoc dixit se scire visu et auditu. Interrogatus testis quid inde vidit et audivit, dixit quod scit et vidit ipsum facientem bona facta et gratiam facientem et curialiter [45r] et suaviter facta sua faciente, et petentem sua debita et recuperantem sine briga sive contentione, cuilibet gratiam faciendo de hiis que vidit. Nam vidit in ospicio dicti Boni Davini quod ipse partem debiti cuiusdam dimisit cuidam homini cum ipse testis erat presens in ospicio ipsius Boni Davini. Et cuidam cognato ipsius deponentis prolungavit debitum quoddam quod sibi debebat dictus cognatus suus nominatus Raymundus Payrolerii. Et plures gratias alias, ut audivit deponens, fecit aliis gentibus. Et sibi deponenti fecit etiam pluries gratiam de debitis suis. Quare dicit testis suo judicio quod dictus Bonus Davinus est bonus, mitis, suavis, legalis, bone fame, bone opinionis et qui[11] consuevit semper cum bonis gentibus conversari, et facta legalia facere, et quod nunquam audivit nec vidit quod ipse Bonus Davinus consuevit, quod ipse vidit, debita sibi soluta alias repetere, set vidit de se ipso quod sibi mutuavit peccuniam diversis vicibus et gratiam sibi fecit de debito, partem aliquam sibi dimitendo, et sibi pluries debita sua prolungando. Et predicta dixit se scire quia experientiam habuit de predicitis veram de dicto Bono Davino.

Super tertio titulo dixit testis, factis sibi pluribus interrogationibus, verum esse ut in eo continetur. Et hoc dixit se scire quoniam ita vidit de pluribus personis de quorum nominibus non recordatur, nisi quam de hiis que nominate sunt supra in secundo titulo, et de se ipso deponente, plura dixit se nescire.

Et non est doctus. Et generaliter interrogatus.

[45v]   Anno domini m̊cccxvi die prima martii. Dominus Bernardus Gardii testis productus per dictum Boniuzas procuratorem dicti Boni Davini, absente dicto Laurentio, citato et in eius contumacia, juravit dicere veritatem super secundo et tertio titulis, primo omisso de voluntate producentis, et deposuit dictum suum secunda die dicti mensis, et primo super secundo titulo ipsi testi exposito in vulgari. Qui dixit se tantum inde scire super eo videlicet quod a sex annis citra vel circa cognoscit et cognovit dictum Bonum Davinum, et fuit conversatus et conversatur cum eo. Et ab illo tempore citra et postquam ipsum cognovit dicit eum bonum justum et legalem, bone fame et bone opinionis, et hoc dixit et dicit testis quia de eo nunquam vidit contrarium, nec hodie est de eo contrarium, nec vidit aliquo tempore dictum Bonum Davinum aliquem decipere nec defraudare nec audivit dici set semper suo judicio vidit in eo et de eo semper bona facta, bona verba, bonas conversationes cum bonis gentibus et legalibus, perseverantem et conversantem.

[46v]   Anno domini millesimo cccxvi die secunda martii. Discretus vir dominus Raymundus Viridis testis productus per dictum Boniuzas procuratorio nomine dicti Boni Davini, dixit in veritate sacerdotii[12] sui, sibi lecto secundo et tertio titulo, primo omisso de voluntate producentis, ita esse verum ut in ipso secundo titulo continetur, et

predicta dixit se scire visu et auditu. Interrogatus quid inde vidit et audivit, dixit se hoc scire quod a x annis citra, ut sibi videtur de tempore, cognovit dictum Bonum Davinum cum quo notitiam habuit testis pro amicis suis amicorum ipsorum negotia peragendo. A quo tempore citra invenit ipsum bonum, pacificum, rationabilem, quietum et legalem et gratiosum, verum et integrum secundum legem suam, bone opinionis et bone fame et qui nunquam, quod testis sciverit, credidit, vel dici audiverit, consuevit aliquem defraudare nec decipere, nec debita sibi soluta repetere. Et de hiis est vox et fama inter personas dictum Bonum David cognoscentes. Interrogatus testis inter quos est fama de predictis, ⟨. . . . .⟩[13] videlicet inter ipsum deponentem et dominum Raymundum de Montiliis precentorem et cannonicum ecclesie sedis Massilie et dominum Gantelmum Columbi et Raymundum de Ulmo et Johannem de Fagiis et Johannem de Casausono et plures alios. Interrogatus testis si scit vel dici audivit quod dictus Bonus Davit peterit debita sibi soluta alias, dixit quod non.

Item super secundo titulo sibi testi lecto, dixit ita esse verum [47r] ut in titulo continetur. Et predicta dixit se scire quia veram experientiam habuit de eo in factis quorundam amicorum suorum.

Item in secundo titulo testis addens quod ad legalitatem ipsius Boni Davini. Dictus Bonus Davinus familiaris existens domini Raymundi Egidii canonici ecclesie Massilie Avinione, sibi tradidit duo milia turonenses argenti in custodia sine testibus et aliqua scriptura, quod testis sciret, cuius quidem domini Raymundi ipse deponens fuit executor cum operario ecclesie Massiliensis, qui quidem operarius nominatur dominus Hugo Gantelmi. Post eius obitum quiquidem Bonus Davinus audivit quod dictus dominus Raymundus obierat ut retulit deponenti et deponens ita dixit, et sine eo quod ipse deponens quereret ab ipso Bono Davino aliquid, ipse Bonus Davinus dixit sibi deponenti, sine questione aliqua per eum deponentem sibi facta: "Domine Raymunde! Ego intellexi vos esse executorem domini Raymundi Egidii predicti. Sciatis quod ipse tradidit michi in custodia duo milia turonenses argenti. Et ego tradam eos vobis", Prius investigato ab ipso deponente per ipsum Bonum Davinum si dictus dominus Raymundus aliquod sibi deponenti dixisset de predictis. Et, ut dixit testis, ipsos duo milia turonenses argenti restituit ipsi deponenti et suo socio, videlicet dicto domino Hugoni Gantelmi. Addens etiam quod suo judicio in lege sua non credit esse legaliorem eo.

[47v]   Anno domini millesimo cccxvi die secunda martii. Magister Bartholomeus de Salinis notarius testis productus per dictum Boniuzas procuratorio nomine dicti Boni Davini juravit dicere veritatem super titulis supradictis, videlicet super secundo et tertio titulis, et deposuit

dictum suum die quarta dicti mensis, absente dicto Laurentio, citato et contumaciter absente. Et dixit se tantum inde scire super eis, et primo super secundo et tertio titulis, dixit quod ipse testis habet et habuit a decem annis citra quibus notitiam habuit de eo Bono David, ipsum bonum, favorabilem, benignum, pacificum, quietum et legalem, et qui nunquam, quod testis sciverit vel dici audiverit, recipere, petere, vel exhigere consuevit credita sibi soluta, potius ipsa credita et debita remitere, et favorabiliter contribuere suis debitoribus et aliis amicis suis pro eis postulantibus sepe et sepius ac largiflue consuevit, ut de predictis omnibus et singulis supra per ipsum testem depositis, dicit idem testis famam publicam esse in civitate Massilie, inter bonos et graves, potissime inter eumdem Bonum David cognoscentes Ricavetum Ricavi, Petrum Ferrarii, Montolivum de Montolivo, dominum Raymundum Viridis, Fulquetem de Montolivo et Girardum, et multos alios. Et predicta dixit se scire quia veram experientiam habet de supra testificatis per eum, relatu predicto.

[48r]   Anno quo supra xxii die febroarii. Dominus Arnaudus de Baucio testis productus per dictum Boniuzas procuratorio nomine dicti Boni Davini juravit dicere veritatem super secundo et tertio titulis, primo omisso de voluntate producentis, absente dicto Laurentio, comitente et protestante ut supra, et deposuit dictum suum die quarta mensis martii. Et primo super secundo titulo dixit se tantum inde scire super eo videlicet quod a decem octo annis citra habet notitiam dicti Boni Davini et ab illo tempore citra, suo judicio, nec propter facta, dicta seu aliqua que ipse perpendere valuerit et potuerit, non vidit de eo nisi legalitatem equitatem patientiam et [quietem?] veram, et ea propter dicit et habet eum, suo judicio, bonum, pacificum, legalem, bone fame, et bone opinionis et qui nunquam, quod ipse testis audiverit nec viderit, consuevit aliquem decipere nec defraudare, nec debita sibi soluta repetere,[48v] set semper legalitatem et facta boni hominis et boni judei facere. Et predicta dicit vera esse quia veram experientiam de eo habuit, tam in factis suis quam etiam in alienis ut audivit, videlicet dominus Jacobus Anglici et Hugoni Laugerio, prout audivit ab eis dici, prolungando debita eis juxta eorum voluntatem. Et nunquam ipse deponens fuit deceptus per ipsum Bonum Davinum nec aliquam maculam in eo invenit. Set dixit testis quod que ad fidem in mutuando peccuniam et in contractibus quibuscumque sicut ipse posset de se ipso confidere vel de fratre suo, sic ipse quod ad legem suam confidit et confideret de dicto Bono Davino. Et quod aliquo tempore ipse non habuit peccuniam ab ipso Bono Davino quod ipse de aliquo mutuo dedit usuram nec lucrum aliquem, cum sepe ipse testis ab eo mutuaverit pluries peccuniam, et quod erat maior legalitas aliquando. Et pluries

mutuavit sibi peccuniam sine testibus et aliqua scriptura, publica seu privata, nec unquam invenit errorem solutionis nec contradictionem aliquam in eo nec de eo, set semper legalitatem sicut in bono homine et legale potest inveniri, et predicta dixit testis se scire quia veram experientiam habuit de eisdem. Interrogatus inter quos est fama de predictis, dixit quod inter ipsum deponentem et Ricavum Ricavi et Petrum Ferrerii, Bartholomeum Juvenis, Bartholomeum de Salinis, nec Hugonem Mercerii, Hugonem Laugerii, et plures alios, et communiter inter omnes de civitate Massilie. Et ultra addens suo dicto, quod semper vidit dictum Bonum Davinum conversantem semper cum bonis gentibus bone fame et vite laudabilis et honeste. Et nunquam cavit de eo testis solutiones facere clam vel in aperto, qui testis, ut dicit, habuit facta secum in magnis quantitatibus peccunie, quod nunquam invenit in eo nec cum eo errorem calculi nec alii solutiones qui posset, si vellet, derrogare solutiones quod nunquam faceret.

[49r]   Super tertio titulo dixit se nichil aliud inde scire quam in secundo

Anno domini quo supra. Bonetus Aurioli testis productus per dictum Boniuzas judeus procuratorio nomine dicti Boni Davini judei, presente dicto Laurentio dicente et protestante ut supra. Qui juravit dicere veritatem super dictis titulis de novo productis per dictum Boniuzas, et deposuit dictum suum mcccxvii die sexta aprilis. Et primo super primo titulo dixit se tantum inde scire videlicet, quod isto anno ante festum nativitatis Domini, ut ipsi deponenti videtur, ipse deponens venit ad domum dicti Laurentii Girardi generis sui et dixit sibi ista verba: "Laurenti, quare habes tu questionem cum Bono Davino, male facis."[14] Qui Laurentius respondit quod ipse non credebat debere aliquid dicto Bono Davino. Et [49v] tunc ipse deponens dixit dicto Laurentio: "Male velle (tuo?) ego conveniam de isto debito cum Bono Davino." Qui Laurentius respondit quod non daret de suo aliquid ipsi Bono Davino. Et tunc ipse deponens accessit ad domum dicti Boni Davini et dixit sibi ista verba: "En Bon Davin, Daquella question ques aves am mon genre da qu[el]s LX sols que li demandas. Ego vellem ut gratiam faceretis mihi. Et ego haberem pro maxima gratia ut de illo debito Lx solidorum quod petitis a Laurentio genero meo, faceretis mihi gratiam pro XL, et ego solvam eos vobis." Qui dictus Bonus Davinus respondit ut testis dixit quod hoc non faceret, nisi ex toto solveret ipsos LX solidos. Et tunc ipse deponens, cum ipse Bonus Davinus non vellet consentire verbis suis, recessit. Interrogatus testis si potest perpendere nec credit quod ipse Bonus Davinus peteret dictos LX solidos nisi eos sibi deberet dictus Laurentius gener ipsius deponentis, dixit, de credulitate loquendo, quod non credit quod ipse Bonus Davinus eos peteret nisi sibi deberentur.

Nam nunquam audivit aliquem conqueri de ipso Bono Davino. Et dolet
quia gener suus conqueritur. Nam ipse deponens si potuisset libenter
convenisset et fecisset concordiam inter ipsos Laurentium et dictum
Bonum Davinum.

Super secundo titulo dixit ita esse verum ut in eo continetur. Et ideo
quia nunquam audivit de dicto Bono Davino dici nisi summam
legalitatem, et hoc dixit se scire visu et auditu, visu, quoque dixit se scire
ideo quia experientiam habet de eo et habuit postquam ipsum cognovit
in factis suis, nam sibi mutuavit peccuniam et sine instrumentis et
mandamentis aliquando. Et quodam die Sabati ipse venit ad eum ut sibi
mutuaret de peccunia et incontinenti ipse Bonus Davinus aperuit caxiam
suam, et ipse deponens accepti quantum fuit sibi neccesarium, videlicet
xL Turonenses argenti ut sibi deponenti videtur. Et multotiens cum
instrumentis et mandamentis (et?) Qui deponens dixit quod nunquam
invenit in eo deceptionem nec aliquid mali nec audivit aliquem de eo
conqueri, set semper bonum [53r] audivit de eo, nec aliquo tempore
audivit, postquam eum cognoscit, quod ipse debitum nec debita sibi
soluta repetierit, set sibi deponenti multas gratias fecit, sibi sua debita
prolungando et multotiens, et juxta voluntatem ipsius deponentis. Et
nunquam invenit in eo errorem calculi nec quod ipse Bonus Davinus
repeterit nec negaverit aliquod debitum sibi solutum, set semper invenit
in eo legalitatem et integritatem persone, et ut integer homo in lege sua
regnavit, et adhuc regnat inter illos qui habent secum negotia. Nam
aliquo tempore neminem audivit conquerentem de eo, quapropter dicit
eum legalem, bonum, pacificum, bone fame, bone opinionis, et sine eo
quod aliquo tempore ipse consueverit aliquem decipere nec defraudare,
set, suo judicio, dixit ipse deponens quod non credit legaliorem in lege
sua quam sit ipse Bonus Davinus.

Super tertio titulo dixit quod multas gratias sibi deponenti fecit in
prolungando sibi debita ut supra in secundo titulo dixit.

Et predicta dixit et testificatus est ipse deponens quia ita verititas se
habet, ut supra testificatus est.

D

The additional questions—*interrogatoria*—Laurentius wanted
the court notary to ask the witnesses when registering their depositions
about the *tituli* of Bondavid's letter of defense. Dozens of similar
interrogatoria are inserted in the court registers of Marseilles and of
Manosque. This one is between the folios 49 and 50 of the register III
B 7 and given by me the number 49A.

Si testes quos Boniacus de Borriano judeus procurator et procuratorio nomine Bonidavini judei dixit ut fore vera que in primo titulo titulorum per ipsum oblatorum continetur, interrogentur quomodo et qualiter ea sciant que testificantur.

Item interrogentur per quas personas fuit rogatus dictus Bondavin et per que verba etc.

Item et si dicte persone rogate fuerunt per dictum Laurentium, et per que verba fuerunt rogati, et de quo fuerunt rogati, et quando, et quibus presentibus et de quo debito fuerunt rogati quod facerent compositionem, et cuiusmodi compositionem debebant facere, et si dictus Laurentius concessit eis dictam compositionem. Item quid respondit dictus Bondavin dictis personis de compositione predicta. Item interrogentur per quem dicte persone fuerunt rogate et ad cuius instantiam et requisitionem, et per que verba requisivit dictus Laurentius dictas personas quod facerent dictam compositionem. Item de anno, mense, septimana, die et hora, et quibus presentibus.

Item super secundo titulo, si dixerunt fore vera que in dicto titulo continentur, interrogentur si sciant dictum Bondavin mutuare sub usuris et ipsum esse feneratorem et mutuantem publice sub usuris.

Item interrogentur si sciunt vel dici audiverunt quod dictus Bondavin alias peterit ab aliquo debita aliqua sibi persoluta, iterum sibi solvi, et si fuit propter hoc contra ipsum in curia inquisitum, et si occasione predicta alias fuit per curiam condempnatus.

Appendix 2
Abraham of
Draguignan's
Last Will

Abraham of Draguignan's will, 10 May 1316. What is preserved in the register of the notary Bernard Blancard is in fact a draft,
written probably at Abraham's deathbed. Some of the notes, especially
those scribbled at the margins, are difficult to decipher. The document
is interesting for the changes introduced by the testator while dictating
his last will. They may possibly indicate some tension in the family.
Archives de la Ville de Marseille, Notaires II 19 between folios 61 and 62

[In nomine] domini nostri Jhesu Christi [amen]. Anno incarnationis
eiusdem millesimo cccxvi indictione xiiii, vi ydus madii hora diei circa
primam.

Notum sit etc. quod ego Abraham de Draguignano judeus civis
Massilie sanus[1] mente per dei gratiam [. . 2 words . .] et in mea bona
et sana existens memoria, facio condo et ordino testamentum meum
nuncupativum et meam ultimam voluntatem et bonorum meorum
dispositionem et ordinationem ultimam in hunc modum:

In primis lego jure institutionis Bonodavino de Draguignano judeo,
civi Massilie, filio meo, quingentas libras regalium seu Massiliensium
minutorum in quibus quidem quingentis libris dicte monete dictum
Bonum Davinum filium meum mihi heredem instituo et ex eis ipsum
volo esse tacitum et contentum, ita quod nichil amplius petere valeat in
ceteris bonis meis.

163

Item lego Astes uxori mee filie Davini de Massilia judei condam, quod sit domina et segnoressa omnium et singulorum bonorum meorum et quod dicta bona teneat et possideat et fructus gauziat et [. . 2–3 words . .]. Item lego dicte Astes vi cacias argenti.[2] Item lego jure institutionis Bone Done judee filie mee, uxori Profachi Dieu lo Cresca judei, C. Libras[3] regalium seu Massiliensium minutorum, in quibus quidem C. Libris et in dote quam dedi cum ea dicto Profacho dictam Bonam Donam in heredem instituo, et ex eis eam volo esse tacitam et contentam, ita quod nichil amplius petere valeat in ceteris bonis meis. Et volo et jubeo quod dicta Bona Dona filia mea aquictet et aquictare debeat cum instrumento publico omnia et singula alia bona mea. Et si dicta bona mea aquictare recusaverit, in illo casu adhunc deminuo[4] et substraho sibi dictum legatum dictarum C. Librarum.[5] Et eo casu lego dicte Bone Done jure institutionis quinque solidos regalium seu Massiliensium minutorum, et in dictis quinque solidis in dicto casu et in dicta dote eam mihi [heredem] instituo, ita quod nichil amplius petere valeat in aliis bonis meis.

Item lego jure institutionis Abrameto felezeno meo, filio dicti Boni Davini, filii mei, quandam vineam meam francham et liberam ab omni jugo servitutis, et census prestatione, sitam in territorio Massilie loco qui dicitur "Rocha Cancha" confrontatam ab una parte cum vinea Manulsse et ab alia cum vinea Hugonis Laugerii et cum vinea Jacobi Vaquerii ab alia, et a parte alia cum vinea Guillelmi Guigonis et ab alia cum via publica.

Item lego dicto Abrameto duas zonas argenteas quarum una habet singulum lividum [verulatam?] cum filo argenti fini, et alia habet singulum rubeum cece, que valent x libras dicte monete ambe. Et unum annulum auri cum lapide maracdinis et unum annulum auri cum parvo diamant, et unum annulum cum saphilo, qui iii annuli valent xx Libras dicte monete. Quas zonas et quos annulos habeo. Et veto et prohibeo quod dictus Bonus Davinus filius meus, pater dicti Abrameti, non habeat nec habere possit nec accipere fructus dicte vinee, ymo volo et ordino quod fructus dicte vinee sint et esse debeant dicti Abrameti, tantum non obstante quod dictus Abrametus esset post mortem meam in potestate dicti Boni Davini patris sui.

Item lego jure institutionis Bellenete felezene mee filie dicti Boni Davini filii mei, unam zonam argenti deauratam cum singulo de argento que valet xiiii libras dicte monete, et decem libras dicte monete pro emenda un nescla auri, et lx solidos dicte monete pro emendis unum parcacellorum argenti, et unum annulum auri cum lapide vocato diamant, valentem iiii libras dicte monete de illis que ego habeo, et xxv libras, in peccunia, et unam caciam argenti quam habeo, valentem iiii libras dicte monete, dum tamen predicta non habuerit in vita.

Item lego Mosse Artin fratri mei x libras dicte monete.

Item lego jure institutionis Reginete felezene mee filie dicti Boni Davini filii mei, uxori Salamoneti filii Crescas de Bellicadro judei condam, unum gobellum argenti cum quo bibo, et unum annulum auri cum lapide vocato diamant, valentem vi libras dicte monete, de illis que habeo in caciam meam, et cloquaria argenti,[6] et quandam domum sitam in juzataria Massilie confrontata ab una parte cum scola meridiana, et ab alia cum domo Profach, et servit xii denarios heredibus [. . .][7]

Item lego jure institutionis Blanquete nepoti mee, filie Dulcie sororis mee xxv libras regalium seu Massiliensium minutorum.

In omnibus vero aliis bonis meis mobilibus et immobilibus, juribus et actionibus meis ubicumque sint quecumque qualiacumque quantacumque et quocumque nomine censeantur, instituo et facio heredem meum universalem et in solidum[8] Bonum Davinum de Draguignano judeo filium meum.

Notes

The following two journal titles are abbreviated in these notes:

Annales: ESC = Annales: Economies, sociétés, civilisations
*REJ = Revue des études juives. (A.D.) = Archives départementales
des Bouches-du-Rhône (Marseilles). (A.M.) = Archives municipales
de la ville de Marseille.*

Acknowledgments

1. Paris, 1968–1974. For a list of documents, see especially vol. 2.
pp. 989, 1213–1216.

Introduction

1. See R. W. Emery, "Le prêt d'argent juif en Languedoc et Roussillon," in *Juifs et judaïsme de Languedoc*, Cahiers de Fanjeaux, vol. 12
(Toulouse, 1977), pp. 85–96, esp. p. 93. Professor Emery's article appears in this book in a French translation by Gilbert Dahan; Emery has
very kindly allowed me to quote from the original English version which
he read in the colloquium "Juifs et judaïsme du Languedoc" held at Fanjeaux in the summer of 1976.

1. The Trial of Bondavid—Marseilles, 1317

1. See fol. 8r in register (A.D.) III B 7.
2. See fol. 9v.
3. See Régine Pernoud, *Les statuts municipaux de Marseille* (Monaco and Paris, 1949), pp. 89–90,: *Statuimus ut si quis per unum et ydo-
neum testem probavit vel probabit in causa pecuniaria rerum mobilium
vel immobilium aut se moventium, que, vel ejus extimatio, 100 s. non ex-
cedat, tunc cum sacramento veritatis aperte illum testem, producente*

167

facto, si veritatem inde sciat, si pars illa producens bone opinionis est vel esset, audiatur, et per hoc plene probasse intelligatur, unde in eo casu causa per judicem vel arbitrum decidatur, a quo tunc judicatur pro dicto producente, ita tamen si plures testes ad illam causam probandam se non posse habere ille producens assereret vel affirmaverit suo sacramento, vel si pars adversa ante illius sacramenti delationem in contrarium non probaret sive probaverit. An example of the application of this paragraph in July 1321 could be seen in (A.D.) III B14, fol. 47r and esp. fol. 47A, where a notary by the name of Johannes de Areis, in his lawsuit against the Jew Isaac de Areis, declares that he has only one witness.

4. For procedural aspects, see E. Esmein, *A History of Continental Criminal Procedure,* trans. John Simpson (New York, 1968), pp. 79–144.

5. (A.D.)   56H958–16A–26.2.1301;   56H963–134A–9.3.1311; 56H988–28r–v–23.9.1348. These documents will be discussed later on in this chapter.

6. An example in which the judge hands the *tituli* submitted by one party to the other party in order that the latter may prepare his *interrogatoria* is spelled out in (A.D.) III B14 fol. 40r, where we read: *Et dictus dominus judex ipsorum titulorum dicto Arnaudo Maurelli presenti concessa copia pro suis interrogationibus faciendis, quas faciat et tradat die Lune proxima per totam diem.* See also (A.M.) F.F.511 13A: *Hec sunt interrogatoria Mordacasii Sussurlot judei super titulis oblatis contra eum . . . judice curie Massilie per Jacobam uxorem Guillelmi Lamberti,* or in fol. 37A of the same register: *subscripta interrogatoria fieri vult et requirit Bertrandus Durandi tabernarius testibus quos asserit se velle producere Hugo Bonafos.* For the same procedure in the court of Manosque see, for example, (A.D.) 56H923 fol. 49v or (A.D.) 56H918–45v–46v, where the title reads: *Interrogatoria infrascripta petit fieri Raymundus Descautii testibus productis per Mateldam Martinam super titulis oblatis per eam in causa quam habet cum dicto Raymundo.* Matelda, incidentally, submitted her *tituli* on 8 November 1317.

7. Philippe Mabilly, *Les villes de Marseille au moyen âge: Ville supérieure et ville de la prévôté, 1257–1348* (Marseilles, 1905), pp. 169–174. Mabilly has prices of some commodities at the same epoch (pp. 174–175). See also Georges Lesage, *Marseille angevine* (Paris, 1950), esp. pp. 163 ff. For thousands of examples of prices and of different commodities and services, see Bernard Guillemain, *Les recettes et les dépenses de le Chambre apostolique pour la quatrième année du pontificat de Clément V (1308–1309)* (Rome, 1978), passim, and esp. in Karl Heinrich Schäfer, *Die Ausgaben der apostolischen Kammer unter Johann XXII* (Paderborn, 1911), passim.

8. See appendix 1.

9. Louis Blancard, *Inventaire sommaire des Archives départementales antérieures à 1790, Bouches-du-Rhône, Archives civiles, Série B*, 2 vol. ((Paris 1865–1879), pp. 8–48, where a detailed analysis of register B 1519 is given. For the pension of Hughes Mirendole of Nice, mentioned above, see ibid., p. 34.

10. See R. Pernoud, *Les statuts municipaux de Marseille*, p. 81: *ab hac constitutione excipimus causas modicas in quibus non erit necesse libellum offeri quamvis fuerit postulatus; causas autem modicas dicimus 60. s. reg. [solidorum regalium] vel infra.* See also pp. 44 and 170.

11. See Noël Coulet, *Aix-en-Provence: Espace et relations d'une capitale (milieu XIVe s.–milieu XVe s.)*, vol. 1 (Aix-en-Provence, 1988), pp. 516–518.

12. *Qualiter debitores cogendi sunt in debitis liquidis ad solvendum*, in Pernoud, *Les statuts municipaux de Marseille*, pp. 73–80. For an analysis of this procedure see R. Aubenas, *Cours d'histoire du droit privé*, vol. 7 (Aix-en-Provence, 1961), pp. 47–51, 68–110. For a similar procedure in Montpellier, see P. de Saint-Paul, ed., *Thalamus Parvus: Le petit Thalamus de Montpellier* (Montpellier, 1840), pp. 80–86. See also Kathryn L. Reyerson, *Business, Banking and Finance in Medieval Montpellier* (Toronto, 1985), pp. 95–106. For the kingdom of Navarra, see Eloísa Ramírez Vaquero, "Cartas tornadas y quenaces," *Sefarad* 44 (1984): 75–141. See (A.M.) 504, fol. 115r–176r, for a list of such citations *de citationibus et sazimentis* in 1311. See also (A.P.) III B 802, fols. 1r–25v, 61r–65v for citations for the year 1289.

13. For a list of thirty-eight *mandamenta* done in Manosque in the 1260s, see my *Recherches sur la communauté juive de Manosque au moyen âge, 1241–1329* (Paris, 1973), pp. 83–84, where four of them are presented. For Marseilles of the first half of the fourteenth century, we have several registers, where thousands of such *mandamenta* are recorded. See, for example, (A.D.) III B6, for the years 1316–1317, or (A.D.) III B373 (1310), (A.D.) III B374, etc.

14. (A.M.) FF 503, fols. 77r–148v.

15. (A.M.) FF 504, fols. 74v–113r.

16. See (A.D.) 56H 904, fols. 113r–117r for the year 1287 and 56 H 906, fols. 87v–88v for 1294. In (A.D.) 56H 908, 80v, 30.8.1301, we have the case of the Jew Ferrerius, son of Mucipus Tauros, indebted heavily to Bertrandus Felicii and Raymundus Stephani. The judge orders a seizure of his property, which will include also his clothes, *precepit dicto judeo quod reddat dictis creditoribus vestimenta sua que ipse portat et scalares et caligas.*

17. Camille Arnaud, *Histoire de la viguerie de Forcalquier*, vol. 1 (Marseilles, 1874), pp. 239-240: *Si quis non solverit debitum in termino sibi dato in curia . . . [et] bona non habet que offerant, teneat hostagia*

ad cognitionem judicis. House arrests of course were not limited to Manosque or to Provence. In a notarial agreement done in Vich, Catalonia, on 11 March 1334 concerning a debt of eighty-five shillings owed to the Jew Astruch Vitalis by Raymundus de Sabassona, the borrower, a knight, promises the Jew that in case he will fail to pay in time, *Promitto intrare in civitate Vicen(se) et ibi tenere vobis hostagium ita quod mei pedibus vel alienis aut alio quolibet ingenio sive fraude non exibo terminos dictae civitatis quousque de debito praedicto et ejus lucro fuistis plenarie satisfacti, sub pena C. solidorum barchinonensium*. See Ramón Corbella i Llobet, *L'aljama de jueus de Vic*, 2d ed. (Vich, 1984), pp. 177–178 (document no. 15).

18. (A.D.) 56H 906, 31r–v, 9.2.1295: *Si quis pro debitis suis qui dicat se non posse solvere et propter hoc dicat se velle cedere bonis suis, citentur omnes consanguini vel amici per curiam, et habito coloquio cum eisdem queratur et sciatur ab eis si volunt debita sua solvere. Quod si facere volunt, remaneat dictus debitor in statu suo. Alioquin per dictam curiam de predicta villa Manuasce et eius territorio perpetuo expellatur quousque de dicto debito creditori seu creditoribus fuerit satisfactum.*

19. (A.M.) FF 503, 85r, 23.10.1310. In a writ to his administration in Gerona, issued on 26 September 1358, Peire, king of Aragon, reenacted an order given by his father on 26 April 1330 which exempted Christians from going to jail on account of nonpayment to Jews: *Cum intellexerimus quod vos pluries capitis et captos tenetis christianos aliquos pro debitis in quibus tenentur judeis, dictique judei eisdem christianis suas peccunias mutuant aliquociens sub usuris*. The concern of the city council of Gerona, the need to issue the writ and reenact it, all show that imprisonment at the request of moneylenders was quite common. See Enrique Claudio Gíbral, *Los judios en Gerona* (Gerona, 1870), p. 72 (document no. 6).

20. (A.D.) 56H 913, 44v, 28.1.1309. In our document the bailiff orders the release of the Jew. On 1 June 1306 (A.D. 56H 960, 31r) the Jew Ferrerius Taurosi is ordered by the court to "keep *hostagia*" for a debt his father owed to a Christian.

21. (A.D.) 56H 907 31v–32r, 14.12.1295.

22. (A.D.) 56H 904, 91r, 12.8.1289. *Et pocius voluerit exire de villa Manuasca quam tenere dicta hostagia.*

23. Roger Aubenas, *Recueil des lettres des officialités de Marseille et d'Aix*, 2 vols. (Paris, 1938), 1:78–79, 87–89 (and n. 5), 103–104; 2:38, 40–42 (a Jew cites a fellow Jew!), 64, 66, 68–69, 102–104, 115, 133–134. Aubenas (1:88 at the footnote) quotes a document of 1468 according to which Jews bring their cases to ecclesiastical courts very often (*sepissime*). See more evidence in Paul-Louis Malaussena, *La vie en Provence orientale aux XIVe et XVe siècles* (Paris, 1969), pp. 229–230.

24. Louis Stouff, *Arles à la fin du moyen âge*, 2 vols. (Aix-en-Provence and Lille, 1986), 1:315.

25. Corbella i Llobet, *L'aljama de jueus de Vic*, p. 197 (document no. 43). For Toledo, see Pilar León Tello, *Judíos de Toledo*, vol. 2 (Madrid, 1979), p. 114 (no. 397).

26. (A.D.) 56 H 961, fol. 28v and esp. fol. 28A. (9.3.1308): *dictos heredes . . . excommunicationis vinculo innodamus . . . in vestra ecclesia singulis diebus dominicis et festivis, pulsatis campanis et candelis extinctis . . . excommunicatos publice. . . .*

27. (A.D.) 56 H 907, 34v–35r, 15.3.1296. The seigneurial court of Manosque would not look with equanimity to such turnings to an ecclesiastical court. Jealous of its jurisdiction and income, the seigneurial court would dissuade people from bringing cases to its rival. Thus on 1 December 1302, (A.D.) 56H 908, 59v, the judge warned Guillelmus Fromenti not to bring a group of Jews to the court of the bishop, threatening him with a fine of fifty pounds. See also Raymond Collier, "Excommunications à Moustiers Sainte-Marie (Basses-Alpes) au début du XVe siècle," *Bulletin philologique et historique (jusqu'à 1610) du Comité des travaux historiques et scientifiques* (Paris), 1962:565–579, esp. p. 572.

28. The text was published by Bernhard Blumenkranz and Genéviève Chazelas, "Un dossier sur les juifs en Languedoc médiéval dans la collection Doat," *Archives juives* 5 (1968–1969): 47–48. It was mentioned already in Ulysse Robert, "Catalogue d'actes relatifs aux juifs pendant le moyen âge," *REJ* 3 (1981): 224 (document no. 96). On papal interventions in 1220 on behalf of Roman citizens to enforce debts owed to them, and on sentences of excommunication pronounced on these occasions, see the recent publication of Shlomo Simonsohn, *The Apostolic See and the Jews: Documents, 492–1404* (Toronto, 1988), documents nos. 116, 120, 128.

29. Charles Giraud, *Essai sur l'histoire du droit français au moyen âge*, vol. 2 (Paris, 1846), pp. 201–202: *quilibet creditor, facta sibi solutione debiti, teneatur restituere instrumentum seu libellum illius debiti incontinenti postquam fuerit solutio sibi facta, et debitor petierit sibi restitui instrumentum vel libellum coram testibus. Si vero dictus creditor juraverit se non posse habere illud instrumentum vel libellum, quod ipse teneatur facere instrumentum expensis propriis suis de solutione sibi facta. Et qui contra fecerit, puniatur in duobus solidis pro qualibet libra quantitatis debiti illius.*

30. Ibid., pp. 107–108: *De instrumentis debitorum soluto debito restituendis et si apud creditores remaneant cancellandis. Item, cum nulla juris patiatur ratio, quod bis debitum exigatur, nos volentes materiam exigendi bis idem debitum et vexationes indebitas quantum possemus amputare statuimus quod nullus creditor christianus vel judeus postquam*

sibi fuerit integre de debito satisfactum possit contra voluntatem debitoris instrumentum vel mandamentum soluti jam debiti retinere; nisi forsitan creditor, ad aliqualem cautelam, vellet instrumentum praedictum vel mandamentum in presentia solventis cancellare et ruptum apud se conservare. Quod si instrumentum vel mandamentum ut praemittitur cancellatum et ruptum penes se conservare voluerit, ypotecam si petatur, teneatur facere de soluto creditor; autem postquam per debitorem soluto debito requisitus, restituere vel rumpere et cancellare non curaverit instrumentum vel mandamentum praedictum si christianus fuerit, ea propria auctoritate presentis concilii, excommunicationis incurrat sententiam ipso facto. Si vero Judeus fuerit, a participatione fidelium sit exclusus.

31. Ibid., pp. 80–81: *De instrumentis reddendis parte debiti soluta. Creditorum et usurariorum fraudibus obviare volentes, statuimus ut quaecumque debita vel pars debiti soluta eisdem, ipsum instrumentum originale, in qua tota debiti quantitas continetur debitori solventi restituere teneantur, licet etiam instanter debitor hoc non petat. Si tamen pars debiti remanet, fiat pro ipso debiti residuo per debitorem sufficiens creditori cautela. Creditor vero qui contra hujus statuti tenorem instrumentum tenuerit pro qualibet libra in intrumento contenta, curiae solidos decem nomine solvat poenae, in quam poenam incidat ipso facto.*

32. This is also expressed clearly in a privilege given by Jaime I of Aragon on 23 May 1268 to the monastery of Cornellia: *Intelleximus quod judei aliquociens denegant soluciones eis factas per aliquos christianos de debitis que eis debent. Volumus et statuimus quod quocienscumque aliquis judeus solucionem aliquam receperit a Monasterio de Corneliano et hominibus suis vel de aliquo de debito vel debitis in quibus dictum Monasterium vel homines sui sibi sint obligati, teneatur inde facere cartam publicam recognitionis dicto Monasterio vel illi qui in dicto debito vel debitis obligatus fuerit eidem et aliter solutionem aliquam inde recipere non audeat et si quis judeus confecerit penam, C. morabatinorum incurrat quotienscumque hec fecerit.* Francisco de Bofarull y Sans, *Los judíos en el territorio de Barcelona (siglos X al XIII)* (Barcelona, 1910), p. 74.

33. Pernoud, *Les statuts municipaux de Marseille*, p. 228: *Ad evitandas perniciosas fraudes que cotidie fiunt non solum per Judeos sed etiam per aliquos malos christianos exercentes usurariam pravitatem, qui renovando et reformari sibi faciendo semel, secundo et pluries debita que debentur eisdem retinent penes se incartamenta et mandamenta vetera nullam mansionem ab ipsis faciendo in ultimo incartamento seu judiciario mandamento, licet dicta vetera incartamenta seu mandamenta sint in dicto ultimo incartamento seu mandamento inter creditorem et debitorem verbo tenus computata, et postquam tractu temporis et temporum ex ipsis omnibus incartamentis et mandamentis exigunt a predictis debitoribus seu ab eorum heredibus, qui predictam fraudem et falsitatem ignorant, omnes*

quantitates pecuniarum in ipsis incartamentis et mandamentis contentas; propterea presenti statuto duximus ordinandum quod nullus Judeus aut etiam Christianus audeat hujusmodi renovationes et refirmationes debitorum facere et incontinenti satisfacto prius sibi de debito in quo aliquis sibi obligatus erit teneatur incartamentum seu mandamentum dicti debiti suo reddere debitori; et quod simul non possit habere in diversis incartamentis seu mandamentis aliquod obligatum, nisi expresse fiat mentio de precedentibus debitis seu debito in ultimo incartamento seu judiciario mandamento.

34. (A.D.) 56H 963, 133v, 2.3.1311. See the letter of accusation in n. 51 below.

35. (A.D.) 56H 959, 96v, 2.4.1304: *Confessus fuit quod ipse . . . de quo debito sibi est satisfactum. Tamen non est satisfactum sibi de sumptibus et expensis quas fecit pro dicto debito.*

36. Such a possibility was raised by the syndics of Saint-Symphorien-d'Ozon at the end of 1408. They asked the authorities to take measures *sub penis formidabilibus* to prevent such occurrences. In their language, *Item supplicant, ut supra dicti syndici, quod dicti Judei litteras ad se retinent, et debitoribus ipsorum, licet eisdem sit satifactum, reddere contradicunt, ita quod, quando Judei decedunt, eorum liberi seu heredes dictas litteras obligatorias reperiunt et de viginti annis, aliquotiens de viginti octo, ab heredibus obligatorum, qui ignorant dictas obligatorias litteras, debita fraudulenter ipsi Judei infideles recuperant, licet alias fuerint soluti, attento quod non est verisimile quod Judei ipsi, tanto tempore, eorum debita creditoribus dimississent; vobis placeat super premissis providere, injungendo eisdem sub penis formidabilibus ut instrumenta obligatoria de debito eisdem satisfacto non retineant nec debita Judeorum mortuorum recuperent a debitoribus de tanto tempore, nisi saltem de decem annis ante eorum mortem, et alias provideatur, prout Dominationi Vestre videbitur pro bono justicie et dalphinalium subditorum generaliter faciendum. Et ulterius quod Judei culpabiles de premissis, qui sunt plures, puniantur taliter quod ceteris cedat in exemplum.* See A. Prudhomme, "Notes et documents sur les juifs du Dauphiné," *REJ* 9 (1884): 231–263. For the quotation, see esp. p. 260.

37. (A.D.) 56H 907, 64v, 13.6.1296: *requisivit dictum dominum judicem quatinus dictas cartas sibi restitui faciat per Rosam judeam uxorem condam dicti Abrae . . . seu eas cancellari faciat seu cartam aquitationis eum faciat, aut, si aliquid intendunt petere ab eodem paratus est respondere eis juri coram dicto domino judice, et de predictis petiit sibi fieri publicum instrumentum.* See also ibid., fol. 98v–99r.

38. (A.D.) 56H 961, 16r, 22.4.1309: *denunciavit Petrus Martini de Montefurono quod Botinus judeus filius Caracause judei condam maliciose et dolose et fraudulenter, eundo contra preconizationes factas per*

villam Manuasce quod nulla persona detineat penes se instrumenta debitorum de quibus ei fuerit plenarie satisfactum sub certis penis, penes se detinet plura instrumenta in quibus est dicto judeo ut dictus petrus judeo obligatus et de quibus est dicto judeo ut dictus Petrus asserit, plenarie satisfactum.

39. See also (A.D.) 56H 961, 86v, 7.11.1309: *veniens contra preconizationem factam in villa Manuasce ne aliqua persona petat debitum solutum sub pena XXV librarum.* For similar legislation, in 1315, see Dumas Arbaud, *Etude historique sur la ville de Manosque au moyen âge* (Digne, 1864), p. 100.

40. (A.D.) 56H 908, 66v, 2.12.1300.

41. Salomon Kahn, "Documents inédits sur les juifs de Montpellier au moyen âge," *REJ* 28 (1894): 131–132. *Johannes . . . petiit et cum instancia requisivit dictum judeum per dictum dominum judicem compelli ad reddendum sibi dictum instrumentum juxta formam et tenorem consuetudinis Montipessulani que incipit, "Si quis habens aliquem obligatum." Et dictus dominus judex dictum juramentum dicti Johannis Blegerii non admissit, potissime cum dictus judeus coram dicto domino judice sicut idem dominus judex asseruit, proposuerit justas causas, que petitis per dictum Johannem obstare dicuntur, prout in actis dicte curie continetur.* In Manosque in 1307, the bailiff did satisfy a similar demand made by Hugo Augerius: *Precepti Ysacono Judeo quod hinc ad diem jovis et sub pena x solidorum restituat Hugone Augerio instrumenta et mandamenta que habet contra eum* (A.D.) 56H 885–19r–26.10.1307.

42. Cecil Roth, *A History of the Jews in England.* 2d ed. (Oxford, 1964), pp. 110–111; Israel Abrahams, H. P. Stokes, and Herbert Lowe, *Starrs and Jewish Charters Preserved in the British Museum,* vol. 1 (London, 1930), XIII–XXVIII; Hilary Jenkinson, *Calendar of the Plea Rolls of the Exchequer of the Jews,* vol. 3 (London, 1929), pp. xxi–xxiv.

43. See, for example, the roll of starrs published by H. G. Richardson, *Calendar of the Plea Rolls of the Exchequer of the Jews,* vol. 4 (London, 1972), pp. 37–39 and 53. Also see D'Blossiers Tovey, *Anglia Judaica* (Oxford, 1738), pp. 41–42. See also n. 52 below.

44. (A.D.) 56H 907, 155r, 30 (?).1.1297. The debtor, Peyronetus, addresses a certain Giraudus Rogerius, *Domine Giraut! veniatis, quia nos solvimus Bonomento aliquos denarios. Veniatis et videatis.* Not willing to get involved, *ipse respondit quod non iret.*

45. See Noël Coulet, "Autour d'un quinzain des métiers de la communauté juive d'Aix en 1437," in *Minorités, techniques et métiers: Actes de la Table ronde du Groupement d'intérêt scientifique Sciences humaines sur l'aire méditerranéenne, Abbaye de Sénanque, octobre 1978* (Aix-en-Provence, [1980]), pp. 79–104, and for the citation, p. 92. Bondavid will be hailed by many for such bonafide actions.

46. (A.D.) 381 E63, fol. 31r–35v and 35A, 28.2.1308. The testimony of Raymundus Thibaudi of Apt is the most pertinent: (fol. 32v) *Dixit . . . se vidisse et audivisse et presens fuisse quando Bonisac Judeus pater Creyssoni judei et avus dicti Segnoreti generaliter de omnibus hiis quibus dictus Jacobus tenebatur eidem verbo eius quitium et absolutum clamavit bona fide et propria voluntate prout ab ipso Isaac audivit. Interrogatus si exinde compromissum seu instrumentum aquitationis factum fuit, dixit quod non, quod ipse sciat, ymo dictus judeus Bonisac dicto Jacobo restituere debuit omnia mandamenta et instrumenta que ab eo habuit, tractante domino Dalmassio de Sagnono milite.*

47. (A.D.) III B12, fol. 64A and 65r–66r, 14.8.1322–11.9.1322: . . . *intendit probare dicta Huga quod predictus Ysacus corderii judeus habuit et recepit a dica Huga de dictis xxx solidorum per tres annos proxime preteritos scilicet quolibet anno dictorum trium annorum proxime preteritorum x solidos. Item, Benivas judeus frater dicti Ysaqui habuit et recepit ex alia parte occasione predicta a dicta Huga per duos annos . . . x solidos.*

The judge, Jacobus Bermundi, disqualified Beatrix Lombardas's testimony on the ground that as an associate to Huga she was a *debetrix principalis*. As for the second testimony, he did not find anything certain in it (*nichil dicit certum*) and added that he would not have accepted it in any event, relying on the principle that *vox unius vox nullius*. He must have also noticed some discrepancies between the testimonies of the two. While Beatrix claimed to have been present on all three occasions, Ersmessendis did not see her on the one occasion she (Ersmessendis) was present. Also, they disagreed as to which of the brothers Corderii was present then.

48. (A.M.) FF 511, 7A, 7B 8r–11r, 27.1.1322. It might be compared with the document of 1277 copied in n. 52 below. See the following note.

49. Ibid., fol. 9r: *Coneguda cauza sia a totz presens ezesdevemdor con Isac Cordier confessa e reconoys quez el aut et receuput den Bertram Ricart XL sol rials lascals li paga per lo deute de XV lib, X sol quel dig Bertran deu aldig Ysac Cordier, aysi con si conten per 1 mandament en presencia denn Rostagn Blanquier et de Pascal Fabian.*

50. (A.D.) III B23, fol. 10r, 13.1.1328–28.4.1328: *Hugo Bannerii testis . . . audivit et vidit . . . quod idem Hugo Michael dixit dicto judeo hec verba vel similia: "Ego ut procurator Raymundi Gasqueti generis mei peto a te Vinella Marvani judeo si ipse Raymundus tibi in aliquo seu aliquibus debitis tenetur." Qui judeus incontinenti respondit quod sibi erat plenarie satifactum de omnibus debitis in quibus ipse Raymundus sibi judeo extiterat obligatus usque ad illam diem quo ipse judeus fecit dictam confessionem etc., ipse judeus tunc dictum Hugonem dicto nomine aquitiavit de omnibus que petere posset dicto Raymundo quacumque occasione usque ad illam diem. Quo dicto, ipse Hugo petiit dicto nomine a*

dicto Petro Garnaudi notario quondam ut dictam confessionem dicti judei et aquitationem per eum tunc factam scriberet. Qui Petrus respondit: "Ego hoc scribam et habeo pro scripto."

51. As a typical letter of accusation against a *falsus creditor* where the standard terminology figures, one may quote the following document, dated 2 March 1311, addressed against Mosse Anglicus: (A.D.) 56H 963, 132r, 2.3.1311. *Anno quo supra et die secunda martii . . . quod Mosse Anglicus judeus fraudulenter et dolose tamquam falsus creditor petiit quodd am debitum de IX solidorum et duorum sestariorum annone Alastie Rogerii pro quo debito dicta Alasatia receperat mandamentum x et v dierum in curia predicta, quodquidem debitum dicta Alasatia dixit solvisse eidem judeo et quod dictum mandamentum ei in signum solutionis fuit per dictum judeum redditum et traditum.* For similar procedure against *falsi creditores* see: (A.D.) 56H 907, 119v–120v, 20.8.1296; (A.D.) 56H 959, 12r, 11.6.1303; (A.D.) 56H 962, 48v, 26.2.1310; (A.D.) 56H 965, 26v–28r, 9.11.1312; (A.D.) 56H 978, 44r–v, 3.12.1324; (A.D.) 56H 982, 132r–133r, 12.8.1337 and (A.D.) 56H 955, 106v, 20.11.1298, where an agent of a Florentine moneylender is charged *de petendo bis debita.*

52. (A.D.) 56H 952 37v, 18.5.1286. The document which Guillelmus Fornerius presented reads as follows: *In nomine domini anno incarnationis eiusdem MCCLXXVII, VI idus junii noverint universi presentes pariter et futuri quod Bonafossius judeus de Manuasca fecit finem et plenam refutationem et pactum de non petendo nec ulterius requirendo per perpetuum Guillelmo Furnero de Vols presenti et recipienti de omni debito sive debitis que eidem debuerat usque ad istam diem presentem, cum cartis et sine cartis, et de omnibus tenuit se pro pagato et contento et si aliquod instrumentum seu carta reperiretur in qua esset ei obligatus pro se tamquam nulla cassavit et irritavit et de cetero voluit quod nullius esset valoris, quam finem et plenam refutationem et pactum de non petendo nec ulterius requirendo per inperpetuum dictus judeus etc. Quod instrumentum factum est per Pontium Aicardum notarium.*

53. (A.D.) 56H 961, 98v, 3.12.1309. A case that involved Christians on both sides was brought before the court on 11 June 1303. Giraudus Rochi of the nearby village of Dauphin accused Hugona Arnea and her son of having actually succeeded (*furtive fraudulose et maliciose*) in getting from him part of a loan that his deceased father got, *ex causa mutui,* a loan for which he was in time fully satisfied. See (A.P.) 56H 959, 12r.

54. (A.D.) 56H 73r°, 30.9.1309. *Vincencius Maurelli habitator Manuasce maliciose et fraudulenter petiit VII solidos Habramono de Castellana judeo quod debitum fuerat ei solutum per dictum judeum.*

55. (A.D.) 56H 963, 104v, 20.11.1310. The formal accusation reads: *Segnoretus judeus sartor filius Vitalis judei sartoris fraudulenter et dolose*

quoddam debitum v solidorum quos dictus Botinus judeus dicto Se-
gnoreto debebat et quos dictos v solidos a dicto Botino recuperaverat ab
eidem Botino iterato exegit et petiit . . . , dolum et fraudem commitendo.
. . . At the end of the interrogation, we have the following admissions:
postquam rediens ad memoriam dixit quod dictos v solidos post solu-
tionem factam eidem a dicto Botino exigit, cum dictus Botinus sibi aliqua
denegaret. For similar cases where litigants recover their memory see
(A.D.) 56H 963, 35r, 25.6.1310 and (A.D.) 56H 971, 66v and 68v–69r.

    56. *(A.M.) II 37, fol. 27v, 17.7.1320:   Vidaloni Barbe judei. In*
nomine domini amen, anno incarnationis eiusdem millesimo cccxx die
xvii julii tertie indictionis. Noverint universi presentes pariter et futuri,
quod cum discretus et sapiens vir dominus Ceranus de Gosalengo judex
Arearum et Tholoni in curia Tholoni hodie in secundo parlamento per
ipsum facto in dicta civitate Tholoni pro tribunali sedens, quandam tulisse
sententiam condempnatoriam cuius tenor per omnia talis est ut ecce.

    Item quia constat nobis dicto judici quod Vidalonus Barba judeus
quoddam debitum solutum Rindelo Simonis per Meillinam de Tholono
viginti quatuor solidorum, falsa subiestione repeti faciebat in curia per Jo-
hannem Royay, familiarem dicti Rindelli, idcirco dictum Vidalonum con-
dempnamus in sexaginta solidis. Quaquidem sententia condempnatoria
lecta et recitata in dicto parlamento ut supra, predictus Vidalonus Barba,
presens ibidem, sentiens se gravatum a dicta sententia, ad nobilem et cir-
cumspectum virum dominum judicem primarum appellationum commi-
tatuum Provincie et Forchalquerii, publice et viva voce appelavit, petens
apostolos seu litteras dismissorias sibi concedi et tradi cum toto processu
habito super predictis. Et de predictis petiit sibi fieri publicum instrumen-
tum. Quam appellationem dictus dominus judex non admisit, nisi si et
quantum de jure esset admitenda, concedens dicto appelator apostolos seu
litteras dismissorias cum toto processu habito super predictis, presigans
sibi terminum x dierum ad presentandum se coram dicto domino judice
ad quem appellavit.

    Actum Tholoni in curia regia in presentia testium domini Gauterii de
Ulmeto jurisperiti, Raymundi Calasari, Sinhoni Sinoni, [G. Nas.?], no-
tariorum, testium vocatorum et regatorum. Factum est instrumentum.

    57. I limited the inquiry to what I found in Provençal archives only;
such lawsuits, however, were carried on in other countries as well. For
England, see the case recorded by H. G. Richardson, *The English Jewry*
under Angevin Kings (London, 1960), p. 113 n. 7, or J. M. Rigg, *Calen-*
dar of the Plea Rolls of the Exchequer of the Jews, vol. 1, 2d ed. (London,
1971), p. 121. For Germany, see Guido Kisch, *Jewry Law in Medieval*
Germany (New York, 1949), pp. 201–202, 164–167, 169, 175, 183. For
Aragon, see Jean Régné, *History of the Jews in Aragon: Regesta and*
Documents, 1213–1327 (Jerusalem, 1978), no. 1316 (also pp. 428–

430) and no. 2077. For the county of Savoy, see Renata Segre, "Testimonianze documentarie sugli ebrei negli stati Sabaudi (1297–1398)," *Michael: On the History of the Jews in the Diaspora* (Tel Aviv) 4 (1976): 273–413, document 105 (p. 316). See also Roger Kohn. "Les juifs de la France du Nord à travers les archives du parlement de Paris (1359?–1394)" REJ 141 (1982); 5–139, document 102 (p. 90).

58. Raymundus Aymerici of Manosque sued one of the court's clerks of the city for just suggesting that he might be a *falsus creditor*. It happened when Raymundus requested the court to execute some of his debts and Stephan Florii, the clerk, mentioned, on that occasion, that one of the debts was already paid off. Raymundus saw in this a defamation and reason to sue Stephan in court. See (A.D.) 56H 974, 88r, 7.11.1321: *Cum Raymundus Aymerici existeret in judicio in curia dicti Hospitalis in presentia domini Petri de Valle judicis dicte curie et peteret ab Stephano Florii facere quandam executionem aliquorum mandamentorum, dictus Stephanus dixit quod predictum debitum solvetur bis, diffamandum dictum Raymundum.* For a similar case in 1298 see (A.D.) 56H 955, 106v, 20.11.1298: *Isnardus Raynerii . . . (dixit Johanni Nigri) . . . quod ipse Johannes bis fuit repers* [for *repertus*] *de petendo bis debita sua.*

59. (A.M.) FF 511 fol. 21r–30v, 6.2.1322–11.5.1322 and n. 61 below. Mordacais's name is spelled in our documents in different ways: "Mordacaysius," "Mordacays," "Sacerloti," "Sacerlot," "Sacerllot," "Sussurlot," etc. For an Abrahim Churcrixulot in Saragossa in 1264, who may have borne the same or a similar name, see Fritz Baer, *Die Juden im christlichen Spanien*, vol. 1 (Berlin, 1929), p. 105.

60. Hugo Michaelis must have been a professional lawyer or court official. As n. 50 above shows, he represented in 1328 Raymundus Gasqueti in his lawsuit against Vinellas Marvani. For other evidence of his activity, see for example (A.D.) III B14, 5v–11r, 30r–32r (for the year 1321) and (A.D.) III B 804, 20r–v (for 1319), or (A.M.) FF 504, 67v–68r: *causa facta per Hugonem Michaelem procuratorem, domini Gaufridi Ricavi militis* (the year is 1311).

61. (A.M.) FF 511, fol. 24v, 5.5.1322: *Anno domini millesimo trecentesimo vicesimo secundo die quarto madii Hugo Michael. . . , testis productus super dicto ultimo titulo . . . dixit . . . quod cum ipse testis tractaret de compositione facienda inter dictum Mordacaysium et dictos Bertrandum Sermin et eius filium Jacobum de debito supradicto XV librarum, scilicet quod per terminos solveretur, prefatus Jacobus et ipse testis dixerunt ipsi judeo quod bene debebat eisdem . . . gratiam ipsam facere et, cum debitores ab judeo non habuissent de ipso debito nisi tantumodo decem libras. Qui Mordacaysius respondit et confessus fuit ac*

dixit "et debeo ego in vanum ipsam pecuniam prestare et de ipsis c. solidos de lucro adhuc nichil habui a vobis." Qui Jacobus respondit: "Certe verum et est quod de ipsis c. solidis quod vobis de lucro ipsarum x librarum dare promissimus ad huc nichil habuistis." Dicens dictus testis quod dictus judeus dictam confessionem in modum predictum ter facit tam in platea curie quam in carreria ante ecclesiam beate Marie de Acuis. Hugo Michaelis had already raised this point about April 20, in all likelihood (it is recorded with acts of this date, on fol. 23v), almost three months after the procedure began.

62. See Giraud, *Essai*, pp. 37–39: *Quod si quis de caetero attemptaverit, et inde legitime convictus fuerit ad tollendum sibi hujus probationis difficultatis fiduciam, si publice contra eum fama praecedenter, quatuor saltem testibus fide dignis et omni exceptione majoribus, usurarius sit inventus, quamvis idem testes inscii sint, quoad loca et quantitates et tempora, singulares, dum tamen ad id concordent, quod principaliter agitur, scilicet ut infamatus deinceps usurariam exerceat pravitatem, habeatur idem usurarius pro convicto, et pro qualibet libra cujuslibet monetae quam dicto utroque (judicio) convictionis, vel eorum altero, habuisse inventus fuerit, pro usuris, in centum solidos ejusdem monetae multetur, nostrae curiae applicandis, et usuras hiis a quibus receperit, eas restituere teneatur. De quarum utique usurarum quantitate, ubi legitima probatio forte defuerit, dictorum quatuor testium, cujuslibet de quantitate de qua testificatur, stare volumus juramento.*

63. I rely on T. P. McLaughlin, "The Teaching of the Canonists on Usury," *Mediaeval Studies* 2 (1940): 12, who refers in n. 130 to Innocent's *Commentaria* on X 5.19.3 *manifesti.*

64. *Sacrorum Conciliorum Nova et Amplissima Collectio*, ed. G. D. Mansi (hereafter cited "Mansi, *Concilia*"), 24:359: *Manifestos autem usurarios esse dicimus et vocamus qui per sententiam vel confessionem factam in jure vel evidentiam rei quae tergiversatione celari non poterit, comprobantur.* See also Max Neumann, *Geschichte des Wuchers in Deutschland* (Halle, 1865), p. 22.

65. See Mansi, *Concilia* 24:936–937 (Leodiensis, 1287): *Manifestos autem usurarios dicimus de quibus per sententiam vel confessionem factam in jure, aut evidentiam rei quae aliqua tergiversatione non potest celari, constituerit evidenter, et illos etiam qui per usuras diffamati infra tempus statuendum ab eo qui super hoc habet potestatem se non purgaverint reputamus pro manifestis usurariis puniendos.* And ibid., 25:1120 (Aquilegensis, 1339): *Manifestum autem usurarium eum declaramus de cujus crimine constat per notorium facti scelus, per rei evidentiam, ut puta si mensam ad foenerandum tenuerit paratam, vel per notorium juris, si per sententiam vel confessionem factam in judicio vel coram parochiali*

sacerdote vel notario publico recipiente cautionem ab ipso de restituendis usuris, vel contra quem probatum fuerit in judicio eum esse talem per legisperitos testes, vel per alias probationes legis peritatis, Idem dicimus si per duos testes idoneos etiam si sint in suis testimoniis singulares, maxime contra eum fama publica laborante.

66. See McLaughlin, "The Teaching of the Canonists on Usury," *Mediaeval Studies* 2:12–13.

67. III B23, 53A 54r–56r, 10.6.1328. The same accusation is found in the lawsuits against Mordacais Sacerloti, nn. 59 above and 69 below, and Isaac Corderii, n. 47, above, referred to in this chapter. This is (possibly) also a major contention of Huga Briona in her action against Vitalis Corderii (n. 47 above). Indeed, as one of her witnesses testified: *et dixit dictus testis quod quando dicta Huga recepit dictum debitum, . . . tunc petit, et recepit tantum XX solidos, et incartavit dicto judeo tradenti dictum debitum XXX solidos. Et per alios duos annos sequentes habuit dictus judeus pro lucro dicti debiti anno quolibet X solidos.* The deciphering of the number XX in "*XX solidos*" is, however, not absolutely certain.

68. (A.D.) B23, fol. 54r: *Jacobus de Sex Furnis de Massilia . . . (dixit) . . . quod . . . dictus Bondavid est usurarius et exercet usuras (mentionem) facienti. Et requisitus testis juramento suo dixit . . . quod audivit dici a personis de quorum nominibus non recordatur, ut dicit, quod dictus Bondavinus recepit usuras.* Also fol. 55r: *Rostagnus Juliani laborator . . . dixit quod . . . audivit ab aliquibus de Massilia quorum nominibus non recolit dicentibus quod dictus Bondavinus ab eis usuras habuit et recepit.* And also fol. 55v: *Johannes de Ponte . . . dixit quod fama est in civitate Massilie quod dictus Bondavinus pecuniam mutuat sub usuris.*

69. (A.M.) FF 511, fols. 5r–7r; 12r–13r and some documents inserted between these folios. Especially folio 5r: *quod dictus Mordacquayssius est homo dolosus falsus et usurarius pessimus vel saltim publicus et qui suas consuevit tradere pecunias ad usuras, et usuras exigere usurarum, et multas fraudes comitere, faciendo sibi recognossi a personis pluribus plus sibi deberi quam sibi debeatur re vera de hiis est in civitate Massilie inter personas plurimas, laudibiles, eum cognoscentes, vox et fama.*

2. The Adversaries: Two Marseilles Portraits

1. See I. Twersky, "Aspects of the Social and Cultural History of Provençal Jewry," *Journal of World History* 11 (1968): 185–207. On the

Provençal scholars mentioned below, see the still useful chapters in Ernest Renan, *Les écrivains juifs français du XIVe siècle* (extract of *L'histoire littéraire de la France*, vol. 31) (Paris, 1893). For the translations into the Hebrew, see Moritz Steinschneider, *Die hebräischen Übersetzungen des Mittelalters und die Juden als Dolmetscher* (Berlin, 1893) as well as his *Gesammelte Schriften* (Berlin, 1925), passim. For recent scholarship, see Bernard Blumenkranz, *Bibliographie des juifs en France* (Toulouse, 1974).

2. See my publication of "Meguilat ha-Hitnatslut ha-Katan," "Scroll of the Minor Apology" (Hebrew, wrongly translated as "Petite épître de l' excuse"), in *Sefunot* 10 (1966): 9–52. There, in Renan's *Les écrivains juifs français du XIVe siècle*, pp. 417–60, and in Steinschneider's *Gesammelte Schriften*, pp. 194–215, the reader may look for more information about Kalonymos.

3. Abraham of Aix still appears in a document of 1326, (A.D.) 381 E32, 116r–119v, 21.8.1326, which is a quitclaim he and his associate Vitalis de Nemauso, *physicus*, give to Astes, the wife and heir of Aaron de Camera. Aaron, who was their business associate, passed away some time in or before 1319. Abraham and Vitalis continued their association after Aaron's death, as witnessed by another document of 23.4.1326, in (A.D.) 381 E66 13r. Interestingly, all three associates—whom we might also imagine to be intellectual friends—lived as neighbors in a row of houses in *carreria viridaria jusatarie*, as shown by a series of notarial documents: (A.D.) 381 E30, 89v–90r, 20.12.1329; (A.D.) III B19, 31r–37r, 29.1.1326; (A.D.) 381 E14, 82r–83v, 23.10.1319; (A.D.) 381 E68, 12v–13v, 2.9.1329. The houses owed the tax *dominum* to Petrus Bermundi de Sancto Felicio, himself incidentally a witness in Bondavid's trial.

4. See Salomon Buber, ed, *Schaare Zion: Beitrag zur Geschichte des Judentums bis zum Jahre 1372 von Rab. Isaac de Lattes* (Jaroslaw, 1885) (Hebrew), esp. pp. 39–48.

5. (A.M.) II 19, a folio inserted between folios 62 and 63. Edouard Baratier, in his *Histoire du commerce de Marseille*, vol. 2 (Paris, 1951), p. 95 n. 2, mentions this will of Abraham, which when he examined it was placed in another place in the same registers. Jews do not seem to have done their wills very frequently with the common notaries, possibly because they were recognized by court even if done by a communal scribe in Hebrew. See Antonio Pons, *Los judíos del reíno de Mallorca durante los siglos XIII y XIV*, vol. 1 (Palma de Mallorca, 1984), pp. 207–208: *Quod judei possint facere per scriptorem judeum cum littera hebraica et cum testibus judeis inter eos testamenta, et instrumenta nuptiale rata et firma, ac si per notarium publicum christianum essent facta.* This is cited from a document issued by James II of Aragon on 25 May 1278.

6. (A.M.) II 19, 74v–75v, 12.8.1316: *Mosse Artinus judeus civis Massilie filius Bonjudas judei condam civis Massilie fratris dicti Mosse . . recepisse illas decem libras . . . quas dictus Abraham dicto Mosse legavit in suo ultimo testamento scripto manu mei Petri Elsiarii notarii.*

7. (A.D.) 381 E81, 14r, 6.5.1358. Bondavid rewards his grandson with *ususfructum . . . domorum quas idem Bondavidius habet in jusataria Massilie.* I should like to thank my friend Professor Diane Hugues for calling my attention to this document.

8. See (A.D.) III B6, 31r, 13.4.1316, where Bondavid figures as *procurator Profachi Dieulocresca judei soceris sui.* The two words *soceris sui* were added between the lines. Notice also (A.M.) II 56, 37r, 21.12.1321, where he is called *Profachius Dieulocresca judeus de Massilia alias cognominatus de Na Mayrona.*

9. On marriage of minors in Germany and France, see I. Agus, *The Heroic Age of Franco-German Jewry* (New York, 1969), pp. 277–289. For early age of engagement in Provence, see Isidore Loeb, "Le procès de Samuel ibn Tibbon, Marseille 1255," *REJ* 15 (1887): 70–98; 16 (1888): 124–137. For marriage within the very narrow family see the statement of Judah son of Asher ben Yehiel of Toledo (mid-fourteenth century): "One of the good methods which I desired for maintaining the family record was the marriage of my sons to members of my father's house. I had many reasons for this. First, it is a fair and fit thing to join fruit of vine to fruit of vine. . . . Furthermore, the women of our family have grown accustomed to the ways of students . . . so that they are a help to their husbands . . . they are not used to extravagant expenditure. . . ." Translated in Israel Abrahams, *Hebrew Ethical Wills* (Philadelphia, 1976), pp. 184–185. For more examples of such "archaic endogamy," see the recent work by Henri Bresc: *Un monde méditerranéen: Economie et société en Sicile, 1300–1450,* vol. 2 (Rome, 1986), pp. 684–687. See also numerous studies of Manuel Grau i Monserrat cited in the bibliography of the present study. For family structures in England in the thirteenth century, see V. D. Lipman, *The Jews of Medieval Norwich* (London, 1967), pp. 46–48, 95–112.

10. Edouard Baratier, *La démographie provençale du XIIIe au XVIe siècle* (Paris, 1971), pp. 216–220 and pp. 58–61. Bernhard Blumenkranz, "Un quartier juif au moyen âge: Aix-en-Provence, juillet-septembre 1341," *Archives juives* 19 (1983): 1–10. Professor Noël Coulet insists that it is only the Jewry of the city of the count that is presented in the document. See his "Autour d'un quinzain des métiers de la communauté juive d'Aix en 1437," in *Minorités, techniques et métiers: Actes de la Table ronde du Groupement d'intérêt scientifique Sciences humaines sur l'aire méditerranéenne, Abbaye de Sénanque, octobre 1978* (Aix-en-

Provence, [1980]), pp. 79–104, mostly p. 79. For the city of Carpentras in 1473, we have a similar list where the 69 Jewish households constitute 398 persons (a lower average of 4,3 only). See R. H. Bautier, "Feux, population et structure sociale au milieu du XVe siècle (l'exemple de Carpentras)," *Annales: ESC* 14 (1959): 255–268. Similar small family sizes were discovered in other localities of Provence. See, for the small city of Trets, near Marseilles, F. Menkes, "Une communauté juive en Provence au XIVe siècle: Étude d'un groupe social," *Le moyen âge* 26 (1971): 279–295. See also Monique Wernham, *La communauté juive de Salon de Provence d'après les actes notariés 1391–1435* (Toronto, 1987), pp. 25–41.

11. (A.D.) 381 E16, 25v, 29.8.1306. From a document of 1311, (A.M.) FF 503, 87r, 31.10.1311, we learn that a house owned by a certain Natanetus Macere was confronted *ab una parte cum domo habrae de Draguinhano et ab alia parte cum domo Asseris Negrelli et cum domo heredum Pesati judei condam et cum quadam travercia que non transit, et est sub dominio heredum domini Berengarii Hugolini.*

12. (A.D.) 381 E21 36r–v, 7.10.1311: *Bonus Davinus de Draguiniano judeus maior xxv annis ut asserit filius Abrae de Draguiniano judei.* The words *maior xxv annis ut asserit* are between the lines. In Manosque in 1308 ((A.D.) 56H 912, 69v, 22.4.1308) the legal competence of an inhabitant can be challenged in court if he is less than twenty-five years old, *et per consequens non habere legitimam personam in judicio standi.*

13. See Luke E. Demaitre, *Doctor Bernard Gordon, Professor and Practitioner* (Toronto, 1980), pp. 62–63. See also Marie-Thérèse Lorcin, "Vieillesse et vieillissement vus par les médecins du moyen âge," *Bulletin du Centre d'histoire économique et sociale de la région lyonnaise* 4 (1983): 5–22.

14. See n. 7 above.

15. See (A.D.) 381 E374, 14r–v, 28.12.1318, and my "Structures communautaires juives à Marseille: Autour d'un contrat de 1278," *Provence historique* 28 (1979): 33–45.

16. Bonjudas de Borriano seems to have held some seniority or special status among Bondavid's agents. Not only was he representing Bondavid in the court in our trial in 1316–1317, but we notice him much more than the others, and he was still working for Bondavid in 1329 ((A.D.) 381 E68, 68v–67r). Naturally he also represented Bondavid's son-in-law, Davinus Boneti de Avinione (see, for example, (A.D.) 381 E377, 95r–96v, 23.10.1321 and (A.D.) 391 E2, 15v, 5.7.1322). Mosse Clahi or Cailli worked for the Draguignans already in 1308 (see (A.D.) III B803, 44v, 13.6.1308) and 1310 ((A.M.) FF 503, 111r, 24.1.1310), together that year with Bonetus de Perpinhano. For Bonetus see (A.D.)

381 E373, 15r, 30.1.1310 and (A.M.) FF 504, 108r, 15.11.1311, a year when Mosse Profaig was also his representative ((A.M.) FF 504, 88v, 7.7.1311). For Salves de Sancto Egidio as Bondavid's agent in 1314, see (A.D.) 381 E14, 25v, 14.6.1314. That year Vidas (or Vidonus) de Alesto served too as his agent, as witnessed by several documents, e.g. (A.D.) III B481, 9v–10r, 12.6.1314. Salomonetus Alibi (or Alabi) is mentioned once only, in (A.D.) 381 E377, 139r–v, 28.12.1321. For Crescas Pesat, who served as agent in 1338, see A. Crémieux, "Les juifs de Marseille au moyen âge," cited in n. 21 below.

17. A contract between a Lombard moneylender in Manosque and his factor—Jacob Nigri of the same city—is recorded in (A.B–A) FM 4, 19v, 31.3.1313. Nigri's annual salary was established at six pounds and his daily expenses—when out of town, on commission—at twelve *denarii* (= 1 shilling). A similar contract was drawn up in Manosque more than fourteen years later ((A.D.) 56H 918, 25r–27r, 19.9.1327): in it Benedictus de Fonte promised the important merchant Hugo Agrena *colligere debita sua et in colligendis expensas moderatas facere et de receptis eidem rationem reddere*. For similar contracts between bankers and their agents in Flanders, see R. de Roover, *Money, Banking and Credit in Mediaeval Bruges* (Cambridge, Mass., 1948), pp. 32-33. For loans done by intermediaries, see F. Chartrain, "Neuf cents créances des juifs du Buis (1327–1344)," *Cahiers de la Méditerranée* (Nice), 1983: 11–24.

18. See (A.M.) FF 514, 28r–v, 4.12.1324, where he acted as representative for Astrugus Fenoylhi and his wife Astruga, the heiress of Bona Domina.

19. See Isidore Loeb, "Deux livres de commerce du commencement du XIVe siècle," *REJ* 8 (1884): 161–196; 9 (1884): 21–50, 187–213, esp. pp. 203–204.

20. As in the case of Bonjudas de Borriano with the Draguignan family, Dieulosal de Apta seems to have enjoyed a special status with the de Camera family. His first recorded action on their behalf is found in (A.D.) 381 E373, 9r, 18.2.1309. Another agent, Bonetus de Vivariis, appears in (A.D.) 381 E373, 20r, 16.3.1309, as well as (A.M.) FF 503, 104r and 107v, 12.12.1309 and 15.1.1310 respectively. Abraham de Bellicadro represented them as early as 1305 (see (A.D.) 381 E47, 23v, 14.12.1305). Habrametus de Montepessulano was in their service three years later, as can be seen from (A.D.) III B803, 41v–42r, 16.5.1308. Astrugus de Nemauso, who may have been related to Master Vitalis de Nemauso, was their representative in 1317, as is evident from (A.D.) iii B6, 39r, 5.9.1317. We discover also Bonafos de Cezerista as Astes's representative in (A.D.) 381 E377, 116v, 1.11.1321.

21. Edouard Baratier and Felix Reynaud, *Histoire du commerce de Marseille*, vol. 2 (Paris, 1951), p. 95. In his work about the Jews of

Marseilles in the Middle Ages, A. Crémieux noticed on several occasions the importance of Bondavid and his father as moneylenders. While Crémieux knew about Abraham, he did not mention our legal procedure of 1316–1317 in his work. See his very important study, "Les juifs de Marseille au moyen âge." *REJ* 46 (1903): 1–47, 246–268; 47 (1903): 62–86, 243–261. On Bondavid and his father see 46:26 and 248–250; also 47:247–248. On his real estate possessions, see 46:29. Register (A.M.) FF 512, 26r–27v, 20.3.1322, mentions a house that owed him tax (*directum*).

22. See my article about communal structures in Marseilles mentioned in n. 15 above. Issac Marvani, businessman and syndic of the Jewish community in these years, can probably be identified with *Isaac Marvan ben Jacob ha-Senirimi-Marseilia*, who is the author of a *responsum* published in *Responsa of the Sages of Provence*, ed. Abraham Schreiber (Jerusalem, 5727 = 1967), pp. 171–176.

23. (A.D.) 391 E2, 12v–13r, 17.5.1322.

24. (A.D.) III B19, 8r–9r, 20.12.1325.

25. See (A.D.) III B15 22r and also folio 24r. In 1325 Davinus Boneti de Avinione, *civis Massilie*, appears as Bondavid's son-in-law (e.g., (A.D.) III B17 82r–84r, 21.4.1325, 21.4.1325).

26. See n. 7 above.

27. See for the heirs of Bondavid—the name of Leonet Passapayre is quoted especially—Philippe Mabilly, *Inventaire sommaire des archives communales antérieures à 1790, série BB*, (Marseilles, 1907), pp. 102-103. I owe this reference to my friend Noël Coulet of the Université de Provence, Aix. The Jewish doctor Abraham Bondavin had to answer charges of malpractice in 1389–1390. See Félix Portal, *Un procès en responsabilité médicale à Marseille en 1390* (Marseilles, 1902). Another doctor from Marseilles is Bonjudas Bondavin. He migrated to the island of Sardinia in 1390, where he started a remarkable career and served as chief rabbi of Sardinia in the first decade of the 1400s. See C. Roth, *History of the Jews in Italy* (Tel Aviv,1962), pp. 158–159 (Hebrew); and also Isaac Bloch, "Bonjudas Bondavin," *REJ* 8 (1884): 280–283.

28. See above in chapter 1 and also Crémieux, "Les juifs de Marseille au moyen âge," 46:249–250.

29. The municipal statutes (Pernoud, *Les statuts municipaux de Marseille*, p. 225) expect the *laboratores* to be present every morning in the *platea, que est infra portale Laureti Massilie*, so that whoever needs to hire their services, essentially for agricultural work, could do it *pro podando vel fodendo sive reclaure aut mayencando et aliis operibus necessariis terrritorio Massilie*. In contrast, for Philippe Mabilly, *Les villes de Marseille au moyen âge: Ville supérieure et ville de la prévôté* (Marseilles, 1905), p. 231, *laborator* is a generic term that includes all

manual professions. On the *laboratores* and their place in the tripartite division of medieval society, see Marcel David, "Les laboratores du renouveau économique du XIIᵉ siècle à la fin du XIVᵉ siècle," *Revue historique de droit français et étranger* 37 (1959): 174–195, 295–325. See the recent work by Louis Stouff, *Arles à la fin du moyen-âge*, 2 vols. (Aix-en-Provence and Lille, 1986), 1:294 and esp. pp. 426–431.

30. See (A.D.) 56H 958, document inserted between 15r and 16, dating from 26.3.1302; see also the inquest in 26r-27v: *In primis intendit probare dictus Rostagnus ad sui deffensionem ut supra quod Pontius Michaelis testis receptus per dictam curiam est homo vilis et vilis conditionis, latro et etiam fuit condemnatus annus est elapsus de furto per curiam domini Guillelmi de Villamuris tam in castro Montefurono quam in castro de Vols.*

31. (A.D.) 56H 954, 81r-82r, 30.11.1290: *Defensiones Petri Arnulfi. In primis intendit probare et fidem facere quod Guillelmus Bannerius qui dicitur toluisse testimonium, vilis est homo, stando in tabernis et comedendo bibendo et alia vilia faciendo et ludendo ad taxillas, et erat tempore quo tulit testimonium. . . . Item quod Guillelmus est infamis et erat tempore quo tulit testimonium.*

32. See (A.D.) 56H 910, 34r, 15.6.1327. See also n. 3 to chapter 5.

33. Some *laboratores* about this time might have been people of some wealth and certainly possessed real estate. See, for example, (A.D.) B 819, where real estate of *laboratores* in Marseilles in the years 1317–1318 is mentioned in 10v (Petrus of Brinonia, *Laborator*); 26v (Gaufridus Asam, *Laborator*, who owns three vineyards); 33v, 34v, etc. On 28 January 1329 (see A.D.) 381 E32, 207r-208v), Johannes Alexii, son of a *laborator* in Marseilles, and probably a *laborator* himself, received, as part of the dowry of his wife Rixenda, two vineyards. The court register of Marseilles ((A.D.) III B14, 22v) mentions a loan of £11 10s. given *ex causa mutui* by Paulus Boeri, *laborator* to a couple in that city on 7 May 1318.

34. In Manosque, the defense of Petrus Arnulfi, quoted above, insists on the poverty of his adversary: *quod dictus Guillelmus non habet in bonis usque ad quantitatem L. aureorum et sic est pauper* ((A.D.) 56H 954, 81r-82r, 30.11.1291). Seventy years later, in July 1357, in the same court, Guillelmus Barnifredi, accused of a homicide that occurred in 1348, claimed that the only witness against him, Raymundus Aventi, *testis unus in dicta inquisitione, contra dictum Guillelmum accusatum, pro parte dicte curie receptus est et erat tempore per eum lati testimonii homo pauper valorem triginta aureorum in bonis non habens.* See (A.D.) 56H 988, 28r.

35. See *The Decameron of Giovanni Boccaccio*, trans. Richard Aldington (New York, 1976), p. 45.

36. The *tabernarii* explicitly mentioned in register AD III B7 are Chalaman [Chamam?] Droni (10v, 18r), Andrea Suan (11r), Petrus Asam (17r), Guillelmus de Curia Bonafocius Miramas, Rostagnus de Costa and Franciscus Piscaria (all in 18r). Another place where Petrus was seen on occasion was the "Campus Cabrioli" (10v).

37. See Charles Giraud, *Essai sur l'histoire du droit français au moyen âge*, vol. 2 (Paris, 1846), p. 206: *Item, statuimus quod nullus audeat ludere in tabernis post pulsationem campane communis, et si contra predicta aliquis fecerit, in decem solidis puniatur pro qualibet vice, quorum medietas sit communis et alia accusantis, accusatore nullo modo et tempore celato. Similiter et tabernarii qui eos receperint post pulsationem campane in tabernis, in viginti solidis puniantur, quorum medietas sit communis et alia accusantis, accusatore nullo modo vel tempore celato. Quod si non haberent unde solverent, fustigentur.*

38. Ibid., p. 261: *Item, statuimus ne aliquis famulus stans cum domino pro mercede audeat ludere ad taxillos vel eysaquetos, de die vel de nocte, infra villam vel extra, et si luserit de die, det duos solidos et sex denarios curiae nostrae pro pena: si de nocte, det quinque solidos; et qui tales ludentes in domo sua recolligerit, det decem solidos, et illi qui ludentes ad taxillos vel eysaquetos et illos qui recolligerint ludentes curiae revelarint habeant medietatem penae et curia aliam.*

39. (A.D.) B1704, f. 78v. In an association contract drawn between two barbers in Manosque at the end of 1294 ((A.D.) 56H1092 f. 123r), special attention is given to this vice: *Item fuit etiam actum inter dictos contraentes quod si unus dictorum contraentium iret lusum ad taxillos per villam Manuasce, quod per tempus quod luderet et operare cessiret in dicto operatorio, quod per illum tempus quod cessiret de lucro quod alter faceret nichil debet habere.*

40. Yom Tob ben Abraham al-Ishbili, *Sheelot u-Teshuvot* (Responsa), ed. Joseph Quifah (Jerusalem, 1959), p. 143, *responsum* no. 122 (Hebrew).

41. Richard W. Emery, "Documents concerning Jewish Scholars in Perpignan in the Fourteenth and Fifteenth Centuries," *Michael: On the History of the Jews in the Diaspora* (Tel Aviv) 4 (1976): 27–48, esp. pp. 44–45, document no. 10. See also Pierre Vidal, "Les juifs des anciens comtés de Roussillon et de Cerdagne," *REJ* 15 (1887): 19–55; 16 (1888): 1–23, 170–203—esp. 15:47 ff. There is hardly any study done in archives in southern Europe that has not come up with such contracts. For Italy see Ariel Toaff, *Gli ebrei a Perugia* (Perugia, 1975), pp. 286–290. For Spain see Jean Régné, *History of the Jews in Aragon: Regesta and Documents, 1213–1327* (Jerusalem, 1978), nos. 634, 1338, 2592, 2933; Fritz Baer, *Die Juden im christlichen Spanien*, vol. 1 (Berlin, 1929), p. 444 (no. 304, license to enjoy the *ludum taxillorum*) and p. 481; and recently

Béatrice Leroy, "Le royaume de Navarre et les juifs aux XIVe et XVe siècles, Entre l'accueil et la tolérance," *Sefarad* 38 (1978): 263–292, esp. p. 279; Justiniano Rodríguez Fernández, *La judería de la ciudad de León* (León, 1969), p. 82.

42. Salomon Kahn, "Les juifs de Tarascon au moyen âge," *REJ* 39 (1889): 95–112, 261–298, esp. pp. 266–267. For similar evidence in contemporary rabbinic sources, se also Salomon ben Adreth, *Responsa*, vol. 7 (Jerusalem, 1960), nos. 4 and 244.

43. (A.D.) 56H 955, 12r, 17.12.1298: *Alasatia uxor Johannis Textoris de Manuasca est perjura et fuit in hoc mense novembris et de hoc est fama.*

44. (A.D.) 56H 955, 41r, 2.4.1298.

45. See Adolf Berger, *Encyclopedic Dictionary of Roman Law* (Philadelphia, 1953), s.v.

46. Mansi, *Concilia* 23:22, *de perjuris et de falsis testibus.*

47. Ibid., pp. 772, 1107, for the assemblies of Valencia and Tarragona respectively, and also pp. 560–561, 781, 790, 804, and 850 ff. for other decrees in the same vein.

48. Ibid. 24:1220: *Statuimus ut presbyteri . . . semel in quolibet mense. . . exponant quod perjuri sunt infames et a perhibendo testimonio et omni actu legitimo repellendi.*

49. Ibid. 25:113: *Statuimus ut quicumque in transgressione juramenti manifeste fuerit deprehensi . . . denuncientur intestabiles et infames, nec ad testimonium vel actus legitimos admittantur.*

50. See (A.D.) III B12, 22v, 13.2.1319: *interrogatus quid est fama et quid vox et in quo differant in quo persone faciunt famam ad singulum dixit quod nescit cum sit simplex laycus, sed dixit testis quod dictus Guillelmus habet famam boni et legalis homini.* See also 23v: *Hugo de Severiis . . . interrogatus quid est fama dixit quod id quod gentes dicunt de aliquo communiter, sed quia clericus non est ut dixit ymo laycus ignorat.* In Manosque in the beginning of 1322, the response of Raymunda, the wife of magister Johannes, defined *fama id quod gentes dicunt.* See (A.D.) 56H 973, 10v, 4.12.1322. Other definitions to be found in the same register from Manosque relate to *bona fama* (13v–14r): *bona fama est custodiri ab alienis rapinis et a dictis contrariis et faciendo bonum. Bona fama sit quando aliquid se custodit a malo facere sive dicere.* The notary Andreas Raymundi distinguishes thus between *vox* and *fama*: *dixit quod illud exit ab ore homini credit quod sit vox. Fama est illud quod vulgariter dicitur per plures* (ibid. 38r–v, 27.7.1323).

51. (A.D.) III B2 5v–6r, 31.7.1311: . . . *dictus Guillelmus est homo rixosus et rixatur cum omnibus personis cum quibus habet facere ita quod multi homines sunt in civitate ista quod non locuntur sibi. Et specialiter*

rixatur cum liberis suis prime uxoris percussiendo eos et eiciendo eos de domo sua.

52. For such questions in Manosque, see (A.D.) 56H 973, 40r, 2.8.1323: *Interrogatus quam partem vellet potius obtinere, dixit quod jus habentem* or (A.D.) 56H 963, 40, A (1310): *requisitus quam partem vellet potius optinere, dixit quod ius habentem.*

3. Opposition to Jewish Moneylending: Between Theology and Politics

1. See Judah Rosenthal's study "Asking Interest from the Foreigner," in his *Studies and Sources* (Jerusalem, 1967), 1:253–323 (in Hebrew) and Sigmund Stein, "Interest from the Foreigner," *Journal of Jewish Studies* 1 (1956): 141–164.

2. See J.-L.-A. Huillard-Bréholles, *Historia diplomatica Frederici Secundi*, vol. 4, pt. 1 (Paris, 1844), pp. 10–11: *A nexu tamen presentis constitutionis nostre judeos tantum excipimus, in quibus non potest argui fenus illicitum, nec divina lege prohibitum, quos constat non esse sub lege a beatissimis patribus istituta, quos etiam auctoritate nostre licentie improbum fenus nolumus exercere.* The legislation goes on to limit the amount of interest they could ask. *Sed metam ipsis imponimus, quam eis non licebit transgredi, videlicet ut pro decem unciis per circulum anni integri unam ipsis tantummodo lucrari liceat pro usuris.* For an English translation, see James M. Powell, trans., *The Liber Augustalis, or Constitutions of Melfi, Promulgated by the Emperor Frederick II for the Kingdom of Sicily in 1231* (Syracuse, N.Y., 1971), pp. 12–13.

3. *Summa theologiae* II–II, p. 78: *accipere usuram pro pecunia mutuata est secundum se injustum quia venditur id quod non est, per quod manifeste inaequalitas constituitur, quae iustitiae contrariatur* and ibid: *debemus enim omnem hominem habere quasi proximum et fratrem precipue in statu Evangelii ad quod omnes vocantur.* See also G. Le Bras, "usure," in *Dictionnaire de théologie catholique*, vol. 15 (Paris, 1950), p. 2354. Canonists like Johannes Teutonicus or Raymundus de Penaforte regarded usury as a violation of natural law and therefore denied Jews the right to lend money to Christians. See discussion in the doctoral dissertation of Francis R. Czerwinsky, "The Teachings of the Twelfth and Thirteenth Century Canonists about the Jews" (Ph.D. diss., Cornell University, 1972), pp. 201–241. For this reason, when King Alfonso XI of Castile wanted to banish Jewish usury, he was able

to argue that "usury . . . is a great sin forbidden both by laws of nature and by Scripture." See also L. Poliakov, *Jewish Bankers and the Holy See* (London, 1977), pp. 13–35. See also n. 29 below, where the statement of the Synod of Narbonne (1227) is quoted: *a Domino generaliter prohibeantur usurae*.

4. See John T. Noonan, *The Scholastic Analysis of Usury* (Cambridge, Mass., 1957), p. 17, and James Parkes, *The Jew in the Medieval Community* (New York, 1976), pp. 283–284. For Dante Alighieri's negative view of usury, which sums up a whole medieval tradition, see Giuseppe Ragazzini, *Ebrei e usurai nella società e nel dramma elisabettiani* (Bologna, 1988), pp. 78–79. Ragazzini notes also that while Dante's was a total condemnation of usury and usuries, Shakespeare limited his attention to the Jewish Shylock and did not consider the general problem of usury.

5. See Felix Liebermann, *Die Gesetze der Angelsachsen* (Berlin, 1903), p. 668, no. 37, 1: *Hoc autem dicebat, sepe se audisse in curia regis Francorum, dum ibi moratus esset; nec immerito: usura enim summa radix omnium uiciorum interpretatur.*

6. There is a vast literature about this doctrinal development. To the book by John T. Noonan cited in n. 4 above, one must add Benjamin Nelson's classic, *The Idea of Usury: From Tribal Brotherhood to Universal Otherhood* (Chicago and London, 1969), and its updated bibliography on pp. 255–277 as well as John W. Baldwin's *The Medieval Theories of the Just Price: Romanists, Canonists and Theologians in the Twelfth and Thirteenth Centuries* (Philadelphia, 1959). Also see Terence P. McLaughlin, "The Teaching of the Canonists on Usury (XII, XIII, XIV Centuries)," *Mediaeval Studies* 1 (1939): 81–147; 2 (1940): 1–22; John T. Gilchrist, *The Church and Economic Activity in the Middle Ages* (London, 1969); Raymond de Roover, *La pensée économique des scolastiques: Doctrines et méthodes* (Montréal, 1971); and Bernard Schnapper, "La répression de l'usure et l'évolution économique (XIIIe–XVIe siècles)," *Tijdschrift voor rechtsgescheidenis* 37 (1969): 47–75. The clasics of the nineteenth century are also noteworthy: Max Neumann, *Geschichte des Wuchers in Deutschland* (Halle, 1865) and Wilhelm Endemann, *Studien in der romanisch-kanonistischen Wirtschafts- und Rechtslehre* (Berlin, 1897). See also the recent study by Jacques Le Goff, "The Usurer and Purgatory," in *The Dawn of Modern Banking* (New Haven, 1979), pp. 25–52, which relies mostly on thirteenth-century *exempla*. See the recent book by Jacob Viner, *Religious Thought and Economic Society* (Durham, N. C., 1979), especially the chapter "The Economic Doctrines of the Scholastics," pp. 46–113, as well as Lester K. Little, *Religious Poverty and the Profit Economy in Medieval Europe* (London, 1978), pp. 173 ff.

7. *Dicendum quod leges humanae dimittunt aliqua peccata impunita propter conditiones hominum imperfectorum in quibus multae utilitates impedirentur si omnia peccata districte prohiberentur poenis adhibitis. Et ideo usuras lex humana concessit, non quasi existimans eas esse secundum iustitiam, sed ne impedirentur utilitates multorum. Summa theologiae* II–II, 78, art. 1, ad 3. See Little, *Religious Poverty*, p. 212 for a translation.

8. Giacomo Todeschini, *Un trattato di economia politica francescana: Il "De emptionibus et venditionibus, de usuris, de restitutionibus" di Pietro di Giovanni Olivi* (Rome, 1980).

9. The translation is in John T. Gilchrist, *The Church and Economic Activity*, p. 206. The original reads: *Sane, si quis in illum errorem inciderit, ut pertinaciter affirmare praesumat, excercere usuras non esse peccatum: decernimus, eum velut haereticum puniendum, locorum nihilominus ordinariis et haereticae pravitatis inquisitoribus districtius iniungentes, ut contra eos, quos de errore huiusmodi diffamatos invenerint aut suspectos, tanquam contra diffamatos vel suspectos de haeresi procedere non omittant.* See CorpIurCanClem 5.5; Mansi, *Concilia* 25:411.

10. Joseph Shatzmiller, "Desecrating the Cross: A Rare Medieval Accusation," *Studies in the History of the Jewish People and the Land of Israel* (Haifa) 5 (1980): 159–173, esp. pp. 168–169 (Hebrew).

11. See the recent summary by Klaus Geissler, "Die Juden in mittelalterlichen Texten Deutschlands," *Zeitschrift für bayerische Landesgeschichte* 38 (1975): 163–226, esp. pp. 194–199. See also the data assembled by Moritz Guedemann, *Geschichte des Erziehungswesens und Kultur der abendländischen Juden während des Mittelalters* (Vienna, 1880), 1:127–146, and by Moses Hoffmann, *Der Geldhandel der deutschen Juden während des Mittelalters bis zum Jahre 1350* (Leipzi, 1910), p. 85. On *judaizare* see the article by Kenneth P. Stow, "Papal and Royal Attitudes towards Jewish Moneylending in the Thirteenth Century," *Association for Jewish Studies Review* 6 (1981): 161–184, esp. pp. 178–179. For a similar structure, "Lombardieren," see Raymund de Roover, *Money, Banking and Credit in Mediaeval Bruges* (Cambridge, Mass., 1948), p. 124.

12. *Gaudano grossamente de usure del sangue dei subditi nostri christiani . . . de sangue christiano inrichiti.* See David Jacoby, "Les juifs à Venise," first published in *Venezia, centro di mediazione tra Oriente e Occidente (secoli XV–XVI): Aspetti e problemi: Atti del II Convegno internazionale di storia della civiltà veneziana, Venezia, 1973* (Florence, 1977), vol. 1, then later reprinted in *Recherches sur la Méditerranée orientale du XIIe au XVe siècle: peuples, sociétés, économies.* (London, 1979), esp. p. 173. See also, in general, the comments of Ariel Toaff, "Jewish Banking in Central Italy in the 13th–15th Centuries," in

Jews in Italy: Studies Published on the Occasion of the One Hundredth Anniversary of M. D. Cassuto (Jerusalem, 1987), pp. 109–130, esp. pp. 116–120 (Hebrew).

13. Adolphe Crémieux, "Les juifs de Marseille au moyen âge," *REJ* 47 (1903): 256–257. "Fraus usurarum," "detestabilius," "oin grande malice," "demnables usures," "fraudes, abus et malices," "inquietations et molestations," "propter usuras maledictas." See also Danièle Iancu, *Les juifs en Provence (1475–1501) de l'insertion à l'expulsion* (Marseilles, 1981), pp. 282–285.

14. (A.D.) 56H 948, 33v, 3.1.1276.

15. (A.D.) 56H 965, 22v–23v, 26.7.1312. The dictionaries also have "bloodhound" as a translation of "soira." Professor Noël Coulet suggests that we may decipher not "Soira" but "foira" ("out!" in the imperative) and that we may understand "sagnentas" as "leech," which would be of more significance in the context of moneylending and would resemble the expressions we found in Italy. The first of the above-mentioned explanations would expand both in time and space the medieval tradition of the "Jewish swine" (*Judensau*), which is known to exist only in Germany in the later Middle Ages. See Isaiah Shachar, *The Judensau: A Medieval Anti-Jewish Motif and Its History* (London, 1974). As for the menstruation attributed to Jewish males, see Joshua Trachtenberg, *The Devil and the Jew*, 2d ed. (New York and Philadelphia, 1961), pp. 50–52.

16. (A.D.) 56H 986, 90r, 23.10.1341.

17. Ibid., 131r, 166r–166v, 214r–217r, etc.

18. See Umberto Cassuto, *Gli ebrei a Firenze nell'età del Rinascimento* (2d ed.) (Florence, 1965), pp. 56–59. See also Renata Segre, "Bernardino da Feltre, i Monti di Pietà e i banchi ebraici," *Rivista storica italiana* 90 (1978): 818–833.

19. The York events have been described by many modern scholars. The best account, however, is the most recent one: R. B. Dobson, *The Jews of Medieval York and the Massacre of March 1190*, Borthwick Papers, no. 45 (York, 1974).

20. Quoted from the English translation as given by Joseph Jacobs, *The Jews of Angevin England* (London, 1893), p. 118. The original Latin reads: . . . *conjurarunt adversus Judaeos Eboracenses provinciales plurimi. . . . Hiis auctores ad audendum fuerunt quidam nobiliores impiis foeneratoribus in multam summam debitores, quorum nonnulli cum pro accepta pecunia praedia illis propria apposuissent, grandi inopia premebantur; quidam vero cautionibus propriis obligati, ad satisfaciendum regiis foeneratoribus a fisci exactoribus urgebantur. . . . Historia Rerum Anglicarum Willelmi Parvi . . . de Newburgh*, ed. Hans Clade Hamilton, 2 vols. in 1, (London, 1856), 2:20 (lib. IV, cap. IX).

21. The English translation is from Jacobs, *The Jews of Angevin England*, p. 129. The Latin original is *Caede vero completa, conjurati continuo cathedralem ecclesiam adeuntes, monumenta debitorum, quibus Christiani premebantur, a Judaeis foeneratoribus regiis ibidem reposita, ab exterritis custodibus violenta instantia resignari fecerunt, et tam pro sua quam et aliorum multorum liberatione eadem profane avaritiae instrumenta in medio ecclesiae flammis solemnibus absumpserunt. Historia Rerum Anglicarum* 2:28 (lib. IV, cap. I).

22. Clement inserted the following phrase, which is not to be found in a previous, identical bull of 26 September: *et ut multorum habet assertio, cupiditate propria excecati in ipsorum dispendiis Iudeorum, quorum aliquibus nonnulli Christianorum ipsorum in magnis tenebantur pecuniarum quantitatibus, propria lucra venantes*. See Shlomo Simonsohn, *The Apostolic See and the Jews: Documents, 492–1404* (Toronto, 1988), pp. 396–398.

23. *Magis credo fuisse exordium calamitatum eorum magnam et infinitam pecuniam, quam barones cum militibus, cives cum rusticis ipsis solvere tenebantur*, as quoted by Alfred Haverkampf, "Die Judenverfolgungen zur Zeit des Schwarzen Todes im Gesellschaftsgefüge deutscher Städte," in *Zur Geschichte der Juden im Deutschland des späten Mittelalters und der frühen Neuzeit* (Stuttgart, 1981), p. 30 n. 8. See also Stuart Jenks, "Judenverschuldung und Verfolgung von Juden im 14. Jahrhundert: Franken bis 1349," *Vierteljahrsschrift für Sozial- und Wirtschaftsgeschichte* 65 (1978): 309–356.

24. The document was published by Antonio Pons, *Los judíos del reíno de Mallorca durante los siglos XIII y XIV*, 2d ed. (Palma de Mallorca, 1984), 1:227–228.

25. Frédéric Chartrain, "Le point de non retour: L'endettement de deux communautés rurales dauphinoises envers les préteurs italiens et juifs et l'intervention delphinale," in *Minorités et marginaux en Espagne et dans le midi de la France* (VIIᵉ–XVIIᵉ siècles) (Paris, 1986), pp. 307–338. For similar horror stories, see, e.g., Kathryn Reyerson, "Les opérations de crédit dans la coutume et dans la vie des affaires à Montpellier au moyen âge: Le problème de l'usure," in *Diritto comune e diritti locali nella storia dell'Europa* (Milan, 1980), pp. 189–209, esp. p. 206; Marino Ciardini, *I banchieri ebrei in Firenze nel secolo XV e il Monte di Pietà fondato da Girolamo Savonarola*, 2d ed. (Florence, 1975), esp. document XXXIV, pp. XCI–C.

26. Republished recently by M. Schnerb-Lièvre, *Le songe du vergier*, 2 vols. (Paris, 1982): ". . . je cognois tel, lequel a amprunté d'un Joyf XIIII frans, dezquelx, tant que pour le sort, que pour lez usures, il en a ja poié XIIII cent frans et encore n'est il pas quitte. 10. Et qui voudret diligeaulment enquerir, l'en troyerret, ou royaume de France,

cinquante mille personnes lesquelx sont desherités et mis a poureté par cez feault Juys . . ." (1:356–357 [livre I, chap. clxiii, 9–10]). The text is quoted also in the article by Jules Simonnet, "Juifs et Lombards en Bourgogne," *Mémoires de l'Académie impériale des sciences, arts et belles lettres de Dijon*, 2d ser., 13 (1866): 145–272, esp. p. 176.

27. *Le songe du vergier* 1:356 (livre I, chap. clxiiii, 9): ". . . ils mettent lez Crestians a telle povreté que, dez ce que un Crestian est une foys en leurs mains, a poinez en peret echaper et si ne se puet jamés ressoudre. . . ."

28. CorpIurCan X.5.19.18: *Quanto amplius Christiana religio ab exactione compescitur usurarum, tanto gravius super his Iudaeorum perfidia insolescit, ita, quod brevi tempore Christianorum exhauriunt facultates. Volentes igitur in hac parte prospicere Christianis, ne a Iudaeis immaniter aggraventur, synodali decreto statuimus, ut, si de cetero quocunque praetextu Iudaei a Christianis graves immoderatasve usuras extorserint, Christianorum eis participium subtrahatur, donec de immoderato gravamine satisfecerint competenter. . . .* See also Mansi, *Concilia* 22:1054–1055. The translation I quote is by Jacob R. Marcus, *The Jew in the Medieval World*, 2d ed. (New York, 1972), p. 137. For a slightly different translation, see John T. Gilchrist, *The Church and Economic Activity*, pp. 182–183. See also Robert Chazan, ed., *Church, State and the Jew in the Middle Ages* (New York, 1980), p. 198.

29. See Mansi, *Concilia* 23:21–22 (for Narbonne) and p. 701 for Béziers. In the Narbonne decree we read: *Item quia Judaei usurariis exactionibus plurimum opprimunt Christianos, cum a Domino generaliter prohibeantur usurae: synodali concilio duximus providendum, ne Judaei aliquatenus a christianis immoderatas aliquatenus usuras accipiant. Quod si fecerint, eas restituere ab ecclesia compellantur: videlicet per excommunicationem in Christianos, qui cum eis in commercio vel aliis participationem habebunt.* Béziers (1246) repeated this provision almost verbatim.

30. Mansi, *Concilia* 23:850 (Albi) and p. 992 (Montpellier). Albi decreed: *. . . christianos ad solvendum judeis . . . usuras aliquas . . . non compellat ullus judex ecclesiasticus vel etiam secularis. Statuimus insuper [quod], si sit dubium, an sit aliquid de usuris illis debitis . . . iidem judei veritatem prius dicere juramento super legem Mosaicam astringantur. . . .*

31. Mansi, *Concilia* 23:1175–1176. For the elaborate anti-Jewish legislation in Saintes and Poitiers in 1280 see ibid., pp. 379–380, 383–384. Yet these two councils do not refer to the *Quanto amplius*. Rather they instruct ecclesiastical judges how to deal with Jewish moneylenders.

32. Mansi, *Concilia* 22:1171–1174 (Oxford); 23:239–40 (Castres);

23:336 (Arles); 23:772 (Valencia) and 23:1000 (Mainz). See also the documents assembled by Solomon Grayzel, *The Church and the Jews in the Thirteenth Century*, rev. ed. (New York, 1966), pp. 307–337.

33. Mansi, *Concilia* 23:662–664 (Lyon I), 24:99 (Lyon II), 25:1120–1122 (Aquileia), and 25:1139–1141 (Padua).

34. The church continued to receive individual complaints and grievances, as can be seen from the correspondence of Pope John XXII: see Solomon Grayzel, "References to the Jews in the Correspondence of John XXII," *Hebrew Union College Annual* 23 (Part 2) (1950–51): 37–80. Individuals as well as (monastic) institutions obtained papal letters that ordered Jewish and non-Jewish usurers to restitute all usuries and to be content with the recuperation of the principal they had handed out. Such was the order issued on 7 March 1321 (ibid., p. 63) against the Jew Salman of Basel at the request of John, lord of the castle of Stauffenberg, and such was the order to a group of Jews on 6 October of the same year after grievances about *usurae* that were extorted were presented by the dean of the chapter of St. Andrew of Cologne (ibid., p. 75), to quote only two examples. The pope would consistently menace the Jews with "separation from the communion of the faithful" (*per separationem communionis fidelium*), which is not a mere "boycott," as Grayzel (ibid., p. 75) would have it described, but rather a special ecclesiastical censure applicable to the Jews—the equivalent of excommunication within the church. It could deprive them, notably, from having any status in court while "separated." See my "Jews Separated from the Communion of the Faithful in Christ in the Middle Ages," in *Studies in Medieval Jewish History and Literature*, ed. Isadore Twersky, vol. 1 (Cambridge, Mass., 1979), pp. 307–314, and William C. Jordan, "Christian Excommunication of the Jews in the Middle Ages: A Restatement of the Issues," *Jewish History* 1 (1986):31–38.

35. "De vita et actibus inclytae recordationis regis Francorum Ludovici . . . Auctore Guillelmo Gartonensi," in *Recueil des historiens des Gaules et de la France*, ed. Martin Bouquet, vol. 20 (Paris, 1840), pp. 27–41, esp. p. 34: *De christianis, inquiens, foenerantibus, et de usuris eorum, ad praelatos ecclesiarum pertinere videtur. Ad me vero pertinet de Judaeis, qui jugo servitutis mihi subjecti sunt; ne scilicet per usuras christianos opprimant, et sub umbra protectionis meae talia permittatur ut exerceant, et veneno suo inficiant terram meam. Faciant ipsi praelati quod ad ipsos spectat de suis subditis christianis, et ego volo facere quod ad me pertinet de Judaeis. Dimittant usuras, aut omnino exeant de terra mea, ne eorum sordibus amplius inquinetur.*

36. A. Prudhomme, "Notes et documents sur les juifs du Dauphiné," *REJ* 9 (1884): 231–263, esp. 260–261.

37. Camille Arnaud, *Essai sur la condition des juifs en Provence au moyen âge* (Forcalquier, 1879), pp. 68–69; A. Crémieux, "Les juifs de Marseille au moyen âge," *REJ* 46 (1903): 248. For Marseilles, see R. Pernoud, *Les statuts municipaux de Marseille*, pp. 97–98.

38. Jean Régné, *History of the Jews in Aragon: Regesta and Documents, 1213–1327* (Jerusalem, 1978), documents nos. 4, 9–10, 28, 51. This very important publication reproduces, by the way, Régné's famous "Catalogue des actes de Jaime 1er, Pedro III et Alfonso III, rois d'Aragon, concernant les juifs 1213–1291" and "Catalogue d'actes pour servir à l'histoire des juifs de la couronne d'Aragon sous le règne de Jaime II, 1298–1327," published in the Parisian *REJ* between 1910 (vol. 60) and 1924 (vol. 78). Henceforward I will refer to it as "Régné, *Catalogue*," and quote just the number given by Régné to the documents he presented. James's legislation of 1229 is to be found in a writ sent to his administration in the county of Besalú on 31 March of that year. He insists that the legislation was introduced at the request of the papal legate and of the bishop of Gerona, *a voluntatem et preces Cardinalis et venerabilis in Christo Patris G. Dei gratia Gerundensis Episcopi.* See the document in Enrique Claudio Gibral, *Los judíos en Gerona* (Gerona, 1870), p. 91 (document no. 1). Gibral's book is reproduced now in the magnificent two-volume *Per a una història de la Girona jueva*, published in 1988 under the direction of Professor David Romano (vol. 1, pp. 23–114).

39. Régné, *Catalogue*, no. 152. The same rate of interest was made legal in Valencia in 1241. See Arcado García-Sanz, "El Censal," *Boletin de la Sociedad castellonense de cultura* 37 (1961): 281–310, esp. pp. 282–283.

40. Cecil Roth, *A History of the Jews in England.* 2d ed. (Oxford, 1964), pp. 105–107. The same rate was charged by the Lombards in the fifteenth century. See de Roover, *Money, Banking and Credit in Mediaeval Bruges*, p. 105.

41. See Wolfgang von Stromer and Michael Toch, "Zur Buchführung der Juden im Spätmittelalter," in *Wirtschaftskräfte und Wirtschaftswege: Festschrift für Hermann Kellenbenz*, ed. Jürgen Schneider et al., vol. 1 ([Stuttgart], 1978), pp. 387–410, esp. p. 399.

42. See Stow, "Papal and Royal Attitudes towards Jewish Moneylending," pp. 161–184, esp. p. 165.

43. Léon Gauthier, "Les juifs des Deux-Bourgognes," *REJ* 48 (1904): 208–229; 49 (1904): 1–17, 244–261, esp. 48:226.

44. Moses Hoffmann, *Der Geldhandel der deutschen Juden*, (Leipzig, 1910), pp. 70–74, and Parkes, *The Jew in the Medieval Community*, (New York, 1976), pp. 351–355. See also Max Neumann, *Geschichte des Wuchers*, pp. 319–327, and Markus J. Wenninger, *Man bedarf keiner Juden mehr* (Vienna, Cologne, Graz, 1981), pp. 230–236.

45. James Parkes, *The Jew in the Medieval Community*, pp. 362–364; Salomon Kahn, "Les juifs de la Sénéchaussée de Beaucaire," *REJ* 66 (1913): 186–187.

46. *De instrumentis usurariorum infra quod tempus valeant vel non valeant, . . . non valeant si triennium elapsum a termino prime solutionis . . . nisi querimonia fuisset medio tempore deposita in curia.* See Fernand Benoît, *Recueil des actes des comtes de Provence appartenant à la maison de Barcelone*, 2 vols. (Paris and Monaco, 1925), 2:475–476.

47. See A. Pons, *Los judíos del reíno de Mallorca* 1:216, no. 16: *Quod judei infra quinquennium sua debita petere teneantur.*

48. E. H. Lindo, *The History of the Jews of Spain and Portugal*, 2d ed. (New York, 1970), p. 77. In Montpellier the wording was: *postquam usura equiparata fuerit sorti, deinde usura nullatenus accrescat ulla temporis diuturnitate.* See P. de Saint-Paul, ed., *Thalamus Parvus: Le petit Thalamus de Montpellier* (Montpellier, 1840), p. 50, no. CXVII. The *Coutumes d'Alais* state also that usury may never surpass principal. See McLaughlin, "The Teaching of the Canonists on Usury," *Mediaeval Studies* 1:84 n. 3.

49. See F. R. Czerwinsky, "The Teachings of the Twelfth and Thirteenth Century Canonists" pp. 216–219, and Gilchrist, *The Church and Economic Activity*, pp. 185–189.

50. For Germany see a list of such cases in Moses Hoffmann, *Der Geldhandel der deutschen Juden*, pp. 104–105. See Robert Chazan, *Medieval Jewry in Northern France* (Baltimore and London, 1973), pp. 110–119.

51. Much was written about the emergence of the concept *servitus Judeorum* and the designation of the Jews as *servi camere nostre*. Reference should be made to Guido Kisch, *The Jews in Medieval Germany* (New York, 1970) and to his articles assembled now in *Forschungen zur Rechts- und Sozialgeschichte der Juden in Deutschland während des Mittelalters*, 2 vols. (Sigmaringen, 1978). See also Salo W. Baron's essays, "Plenitude of Apostolic Powers and Medieval Jewish Serfdom" and "Medieval Nationalism and Jewish Serfdom," in *Ancient and Medieval Jewish History: Essays by Salo Wittmayer Baron*, ed. Leon A. Feldman (New Brunswick, N. J., 1972), pp. 284–322. Emperor Louis's interpretation of the meaning of Jewish serfdom is quoted by Wenninger, *Man bedarf keiner Juden mehr*, p. 39: "Ihr [die Juden] uns und dem Reiche mit Leib und Gut gehört und wir damit schaffen, tun und handeln können, was wir wollen und wie es uns gut dünkt."

52. Wenninger, *Man bedarf keiner Juden mehr*, pp. 40–46.

53. Parkes, *The Jew in the Medieval Community*, pp. 367–371.

54. Fritz Baer, *Die Juden im christlichen Spanien*, vol. 2 (Berlin, 1936), p. 209. Trastamara's action was by no means a novelty in the

Castile of his time. On numerous occasions Cortes required and obtained reductions from monarchs. Thus the amount was 25 percent at the Cortes of Burgos in 1315 and at the Cortes of Valladolid ten years later. For more information see Guillermo Castán Lanaspa, "Créditos, deudas y pagos en el área rural castellano-leonesa (siglos XI–XIV)," *Studia historica* 1 (1983): 67–85, esp. p. 72.

55. Régné, *Catalogue*, document no. 2978.

56. José María Sanz Artibucilla, "Los judíos en Aragón y Navarra," *Sefarad* 5 (1945): 337–366, esp. pp. 356–357. See also Ramón Corbella i Llobet, *L'aljama de jueus de Vic*, 2d ed. (Vich, 1984), p. 173 (document no. 6). For Valencia, see José Hinojosa Montalvo, "El préstamo judío en la ciudad de Valencia en la segunda mitad del siglo XIV," *Sefarad* 45 (1985): 315–339, as well as J. R. Magdalena-Nom de Deu's "Juramentos de prestamistas y corredores judíos en Castellón de la Plana (1441–1448)," *Anuario de filología* (Barcelona) 3 (1977): 215–223.

57. Régné, *Catalogue*, document no. 2717.

58. Ibid., document no. 1086.

59. Ibid., document no. 1803.

60. Ibid., document no. 2034.

61. Ibid., document no. 2896.

62. Ibid., document nos. 3195, 3213.

63. Ibid., document no. 3193.

64. Ibid., documents nos. 2915, 2910, 2155. A document issued at Vich as early as 20 March 1278 shows a group of Jews "composing" with the local authorities. They had to pay 360 shillings in order to be acquitted of all accusations. See Corbella i Llobet, *L'aljama de jueus de Vic*, p. 188 (document no. 31).

65. Thomas N. Bisson, *Conservation of Coinage: Monetary Exploitation and Its Restraint in France, Catalonia and Aragon* (Oxford, 1971).

66. Régné, *Catalogue*, document no. 51.

67. Ibid., document no. 1810.

68. Ibid., document no. 2123.

69. Ibid., documents nos. 2130 and esp. 2139.

70. Ibid., document no. 2683.

71. Ibid., document no. 2163.

72. Ibid., documents nos. 2693, 2698, 2707, and 2627.

73. Ibid., document no. 2694.

74. Ibid., document no. 2699.

75. Ibid., document no. 3393.

76. For the theory of restitution, see A.-M. Hamelin, ed., *Un traité de morale économique au XIVe siècle: Le Tractatus de usuris de Maître Alexandre d'Alexandrie*, Analecta Mediaevalia Namurcensia, vol. 14

(Louvain, 1962), pp. 107–114, 186–209. See also Benjamin Nelson, "The Usurer and the Merchant Prince: Italian Businessmen and the Ecclesiastical Law of Restitution, 1100–1150," *The Tasks of Economic History,* 1947, suppl. 7 to Journal of Economic History, pp. 104–122, and John H. Mundy, *Europe in the High Middle Ages, 1150–1309* (New York, 1973), pp. 181–189.

77. John T. Gilchrist, *The Church and Economic Activity*, p. 111. The evidence about "Jewish restitution" is in Richard W. Emery, *The Jews of Perpignan in the Thirteenth Century* (New York, 1959), p. 88.

78. See mostly the fine studies of William C. Jordan, "Jews on Top: Women and the Availability of Consumption Loans in Northern France in the Mid-Thirteenth Century," *Journal of Jewish Studies* 29 (1978): 39–56, esp. pp. 41–42; idem, "Jewish-Christian Relations in Mid-Thirteenth Century France: An Unpublished *Enquête* from Picardy," *REJ* 138 (1979): 47–55; idem, "An Aspect of Credit in Picardy in the 1240's: The Deterioration of Jewish-Christian Financial Relations," *REJ* 142 (1983): 141–152. See also the next note.

79. R. Chazan, *Medieval Jewry in Northern France*, pp. 110 ff.

80. For a campaign carried out in southern France in 1292 by Philip the Fair, where people were called to establish *per sua juramenta quid et quantum sortis est . . . et quantum usure*, see Gustave Saige, *Les juifs du Languedoc antérieurement au XIVᵉ siècle* (Paris, 1881), pp. 227–228.

81. See "Notes de Vyon d'Herouval sur les baptisés et les convers," *Bibliothèque de l'Ecole des chartes*, 6th ser., vol. 3 (1867): 613–620.

82. Léopold Delisle, "De Usuris Judaeorum Ut Videtur circ. Annum 1247," in *Recueil des historiens des Gaules et de la France*, vol. 24 (Paris, 1904), pp. 731–744; idem, "Fragments d'un registre des enquêteurs de Saint Louis," *Comptes rendus de l'Académie des inscriptions et belles-lettres*, 4th ser., 17 (1889): 315–326.

83. See n. 78 above.

84. Jordan, "Jewish-Christian Relations," p. 50, no. 171.

85. Ibid., no. 186.

86. Delisle, "Fragments d'un registre," p. 745, no. 6.

87. *Perret Harmez jura et dit que Menesier a eu de l'ui duzure puis ii ans vi lib. Testis Perret Stoblet. Johan Li Osteliars de Warno les Dames Jura et did que Menesier a eu de lui duzure puis ii ans xxx S. Testis Ferret de Warno les Dames.*

88. Elie Berger, *Layettes du Trésor des chartes*, vol. 4 (Paris, 1902), pp. 452–453. See the discussion by Chazan, *Medieval Jewry in Northern France,* p. 119. I also consulted the document as copied in the Collection Dupuy in the Bibliothèque Nationale in Paris, vol. 532, fols. 88r–90v and 103r–104v.

89. R. Chazan, *Medieval Jewry in Northern France*, pp. 110–111, and Grayzel, *The Church and the Jews in the Thirteenth Century*, pp. 232–35.

90. Chazan, *Medieval Jewry in Northern France*. As king of Navarra, Theobald of Champagne directed a similar question to Pope Alexander IV in 1256. See Pedro Lopez Elum, "Datos sobre la usura en Navarra en los comienzos del siglo XIV," *Príncipe de Viana* 32 (1971): 257–262, esp. pp. 257–258.

91. See Jean Stengers, *Les juifs dans les Pays-Bas au moyen âge* (Brussels, 1950), pp. 49–51; H. Liebeschütz, "Judaism and Jewry in the Social Doctrine of Thomas Aquinas," *Journal of Jewish Studies* 13 (1962): 57–81. I have not seen Henri Pirenne's article "La duchesse Aleyde de Brabant et de regimine judeorum," *Revue néo-scholastique de philosophie* (Louvain) 30 (1928): 193–205, but have consulted his (identical?) lecture in the *Académie Royale de Belgique: Bulletin de la classe des lettres et des sciences morales et politiques*, 5th ser., 14, no. 3 (1928): 43–55. The most recent discussion of the subject is that of Bernhard Blumenkranz. "Le *De Regimine Judaeorum*: ses modèles, son exemple" in Aquinas and Problems of his Time (Louvain-La Haye, 1976): 101–117.

92. A. P. D'Entrèves, *Aquinas: Selected Political Writings* (Oxford, 1965), pp. 84–95, esp. p. 87.

93. I have consulted the documents at the Archives Nationales. They are published in part in the *Layettes du Trésor des chartes*, vol. 3 (Paris, 1875), nos. 4502/08/10–36/41–48 (pp. 473–484). See Chazan, *Medieval Jewry in Northern France*, p. 123 n. 76.

94. Quoted by Chazan, *Medieval Jewry in Northern France*, p. 114.

95. *Le songe du vergier* (n. 26 above).

96. F. Baer, *Die Juden im christlichen Spanien* 2:171–172. The translation is by Lindo, *The History of the Jews of Spain and Portugal*, pp. 143–144.

97. See J. Parkes, *The Jew in the Medieval Community*, pp. 217–220.

98. The letter of Peter of Cluny to King Louis VII (1146), in *Letters of Peter the Venerable*, ed. Giles Constable (Cambridge, 1967), letter 130, pp. 327–330, esp. p. 329: *Non enim de simplici agricultura, non de legali militia, non de quolibet honesto et utili officio horrea sua frugibus, cellant, quantum de his quae ut dixi Christicolis dolose subtrahunt, de his quae furtim a furibus empta, uili praecio res carissimas comparant.*

99. Cecil Roth, *A History of the Jews in England* (Oxford, 1964), p. 69. The text itself is found in M. A. Luard, ed., *Letters of Robert Grosseteste Illustrative of the Social Conditions of His Time* (London, 1891), pp. 33–38.

100. Robert Chazan, "Anti-usury Efforts in Thirteenth Century Narbonne and the Jewish Response," *Proceedings of the American Academy for Jewish Research* 41–42 (1975): 50.

101. F. Baer, *Die Juden im christlichen Spanien* 2:171–172; Yitzhak F. Baer, *A History of the Jews in Christian Spain*, vol. 1, trans. Louis Schoffman (Philadelphia, 1961), pp. 360–362.

102. For similar discussions of the Council of Constanz (1414) and the Diet of Regensburg (1531), see Tamar Bermann, "Produktivierungsmythen und Antisemitismus: Assimilatorische und zionistische Berufsumschichtungsbestrebungen unter den Juden Deutschlands und Österreichs bis 1938" (Ph.D. diss., Ludwig Maximilian University, Munich, 1971), p. 57 n. 42; idem, *Produktivierungsmythen und Antisemitismus: Eine soziologische Studie* (Vienna, 1973).

103. R. Chazan, *Medieval Jewry in Northern France*, p. 112, and particularly Georg Caro, *Sozial- und Wirtschaftsgechichte der Juden im Mittelalter und der Neuzeit*, vol. 1 (Leipzig, 1908), pp. 364–386, and Adolphe Vuitry, *Etudes sur le régime financier de la France avant la révolution de 1789* (Paris, 1978), pp. 315–330.

104. R. Chazan, *Medieval Jewry in Northern France*, p. 121, and C. Roth, *A History of the Jews in England*, pp. 69–70. Matthew Paris, when reporting on the monarch's decree to expel them, similarly describes Louis as having tempered his decision: *qui remanere desiderat negotiator sit vel operator manuum, incumbat mechanicis artificiis* (*Matthaei Parisiensis . . . Chronica Majora*, ed. Henry Richards Luard [London, 1872–1883], 5:361–362).

105. R. Chazan, *Medieval Jewry in Northern France*, p. 103. Similarly, in his last will, dictated in 1302, Robert, the duke of Burgundy, expressed the pious wish "that the Jews stay on my land, principally for reasons of humanity, and that they conduct their commerce legally, without usury and live on their labor." See Léon Gauthier, "Les juifs des Deux-Bourgognes: Etude sur le commerce d'argent aux XIIIᵉ et XIVᵉ siècles," *REJ* 48 (1904): 208–229, esp. p. 218.

106. R. Chazan, *Medieval Jewry in Northern France*, pp. 104 ff.

107. See D'Blossiers Tovey, *Anglia Judaica* (Oxford, 1738), p. 200; A. M. Hyamson, *A History of the Jews in England* (London, 1908), pp. 78–79; and Roth, *A History of the Jews in England*, pp. 70–90.

108. For an English translation of the decree of expulsion, see Chazan, *Church, State and the Jew in the Middle Ages*, p. 318–319.

109. C. Roth, *A History of the Jews in England*, pp. 71–72; Vivian D. Lipman, *The Jews of Medieval Norwich* (London, 1967), pp. 162, 185; B. Lionel Abrahams, "The Expulsion of the Jews from England in 1290," *Jewish Quarterly Review* 7 (1895): 75–100, 236–258, 428–450; idem, "The Condition of the Jews of England at the Time of Their Ex-

pulsion in 1290," *Transactions of the Jewish Historical Society of England* 2 (1894–1895): 75–105.

110. To the above-mentioned studies of Roth, Lipman, and Abrahams ("The Expulsion of the Jews," pp. 250–258), one must add Peter Elman's article, "The Economic Causes of the Expulsion of the Jews in 1290," *Economic History Review* 7 (1937): 145–154. Also see the recent and most instructive article of R. B. Dobson, "The Decline and Expulsion of the Medieval Jews of York," *Transactions of the Jewish Historical Society of England* 26 (1979): 40–41, where he maintains that the Italian banking firms pushed aside the Jew, in opposition to the opinion expressed by H. G. Richardson, *The English Jewry under Angevin Kings* (London, 1960), pp. 213–233. See also Bennett D. Ovrut, "Edward I and the Expulsion of the Jews," *Jewish Quarterly Review* 67 (1977): 224–235.

111. See Wenninger, *Man bedarf keiner Juden mehr*, pp. 175–176. See also the doctoral dissertation, in Hebrew, of Ben-Zion Degany, "The Anti-Jewish Public Opinion as a Factor towards the Expulsion of the Jews from German Towns (1440–1530)" (Hebrew University, Jerusalem, 1982), pp. 107–115; 166–176.

112. See R. Chazan, *Medieval Jewry in Northern France*, p. 185, and Lucien Lazard, "Les juifs de Touraine," *REJ* 17 (1888): 210–234, esp. pp. 225–226.

113. See a list of English cities in Abrahams, "The Expulsion of the Jews," p. 90, and for France see Parkes, *The Jew in the Medieval Community*, p. 335.

114. Dr. Vincent, "Les juifs du Poitou au bas moyen âge," *Revue d'histoire économique et sociale* 18 (1930): 265–313, esp. pp. 277–278.

115. Wenninger, *Man bedarf keiner Juden mehr*, pp. 126–130.

116. "Le moult esmeu de pitie et de compassion," as quoted by Manya Lifschitz-Golden, *Les juifs dans la littérature française du moyen âge* (New York, 1967), pp. 176–177.

117. The translation is that of Jacob R. Marcus, *The Jew in the Medieval World*. 2d ed. (New York, 1972), p. 24.

118. Adolphe Crémieux, "Les juifs de Marseille au moyen âge," *REJ* 47 (1903): 256–259: "Molestent, fatiquent, et travaillent lesdit debiteurs chretiens par emprisonnement, excommunient et autrement dont iceux debiteurs sont apeurez et la plupart destruiz." On the Forbins, see Paul Amargier and Pierre Guiral, *Histoire de Marseille* (Paris, 1983), pp. 131–136; Roger Duchène, *Et la Provence devint française* (Paris, 1983), pp. 122–135; and Marquis de Forbin, "L'union de la Provence à la France 11 décembre 1481," *Mémoires de l'Académie de Vaucluse*, 1981:19–112.

119. Crémieux, "Les juifs de Marseille," *REJ* 46:258: "La pluspart desquels juifz ne vivent fors que des usures et larrencins qu'ils font tousjours et prennent sur les chrétiens et chrétiennes."

120. Salomon Kahn, "Les juifs de Tarascon au moyen âge," *REJ* 39 (1899): 95–112, 261–298, and esp. pp. 293–295: ". . . des grans abuz, usures, rapines et autres trompteries que faisoient et commectoyent les juif. . . . commenctans usures rapines et autres maulx innumérables . . . au moyen de quoy par lesdits usures, les pauvres Chrestiens sont grandement endommaigez et est leur destruction. . . ."

121. Wenninger, *Man bedarf keiner Juden mehr*, pp. 146–147 and 147 ff.: "Mannigfaltig boser gefahrlicher und behender wucherlicher gegen ewern mitburgen und andern geubt."

122. The translation is Chazan's in *Church, State and the Jew in the Middle Ages*, p. 214. For the Béziers decision, see Charles Giraud, *Essai sur l'histoire du droit français au moyen âge* (Paris, 1846), 2:37–39.

123. I had the opportunity to consult these registers in the "Casa de la Cultura" in the summer of 1983. Frequent usage of *lucrum* is present in register 28 (year 1309) and still prevailed in register 47 (years 1327–1328). On the notarial registers of Castelló d'Empuries, see Eric Mirambell Belloc, "Els protocols notarials histórics de Castelló d'Empuries Separates," *Annals de l'Institut d'estudis empordanensos*, 1977:217–231.

124. R. W. Emery, *The Jews of Perpignan*, p. 87, also p. 54.

125. Arcadio García-Sanz, "Los intereses en los préstamos de los judíos de Vich durante la primera mitad del siglo XIV," *Ausa* 4 (1961–1963): 247–253.

126. Enrico Fiumi, *Storia economica e sociale di San Gimignano* (Florence, 1961), p. 87 n. 286.

127. Gino Luzzatto, *I banchieri ebrei in Urbino nell'età ducale* (Padua, 1902), pp. 51–52: *Quod intendit tenere in vestra civitate Urbino bancum et mutuare sub usuris omnibus . . . volentibus mutuo sub usuris accipere.*

128. Ibid., p. 52–53. *Contraxerunt societatem . . . banchum in civitate Urbini et mutuandi pecunias sub usuris and lucrum . . . quibuscumque petentibus et volentibus pecunias sub usuris mutuare.*

129. Shlomo Simonsohn, *The Jews of the Duchy of Milan*, vol. 1 (Jerusalem, 1982), p. 9. For example, the council of Vigevano stated that *quod inter cetera negotia dicti comunis fuit et est quod apparuit quidam Salamon de Gallis filius quondam abrae hebrey, qui vellet venire ad standum in terra Viglevani cum eius familia ad mutuandum suas pecunias ad fenus et usuram accipere.* For Florence, see Marino Ciardini, *I banchieri ebrei in Firenze nel secolo XV e il Monte di Pietà fondato da Girolamo Savonarola* (Florence, 1975), documenti II (pp. x–xvi) and passim.

130. Simonsohn, *The Jews of the Duchy of Milan* 1:51–53: . . . *dicens se nolebat intromittere de usuris nec in causis usurarum.*

131. John H. Mundy, "Un usurier malheureux," *Annales du Midi* 68 (1956): 217–228.

132. Mavis Mate, "The Indebtedness of Canterbury Cathedral Priory, 1215–1299," *Economic History Review*, 2d ser., 26 (1973): 183–197, esp. pp. 184–185.

133. Camille Arnaud, *Essai sur la condition des juifs en Provence au moyen âge* (Forcalquier, 1879), pp. 67–68: *Statuimus quod iudei possint usuras IV solidorum pro libra quolibet mense recipere . . . et non ultra.* I have corrected *solidi* to *denarii*—otherwise it would indicate a rate of almost 250 percent.

134. Ibid., p. 69. See also A. Crémieux, "Les juifs de Marseille," *REJ* 46:251: *Rex . . . prohibet judeis . . . dicte civitatis . . . [ne de] cetero ipsi judei recipiant pro (sic!) usuras Christianas ultra florenos vigintiquinque pro centennario.*

135. See R. Pernoud, *Les statuts municipaux de Marseille*, pp. 97–98, and Crémieux, "Les juifs de Marseille," *REJ* 46:248 n. 3: *Presenti constituto firmamus ut omnes judices curiarum Massilie teneantur quod compellant aliquem vel aliquos ad solvendum usuras creditoribus seu condempnent ultra tres denarios per lib. ad racionem mensis et quod omnes dictos creditores contentos esse faciunt et compellant dicta quantitate usurarum dictarum, quod quidem locum habere volumus in illis casibus quando aliquis certas usuras alicui se daturum promittit sive convenit. Et si qua pena in dictis contractibus opposita fuerit redigatur ad formam dictarum usurarum et eodem modo eadem judicetur. Huic de novo addimus quod mortuo debitore qui tenebatur prestare dictas usuras seu erat obligatus in hujus modi usuris seu penis solvendis, statim cesset cursus usurarum et penarum supradictarum, ita quod pro tempore currenti post mortem dicti debitoris heredes debitoris vel ejus bona non teneantur nec nomine usurarum vel penarum hujusmodi nec aliquid adjudicetur pro dicto tempore contra heredes dicti debitoris vel contra aliquas personas que pro dicto debitore se obligassent. Et hec supradicta intelligimus nisi post mortem dicti debitoris esse facta renovacio dicti debiti cum predictis heredibus vel aliis pro eis cum repeticione predictarum usurarum vel penarum.*

4. Indebtedness in Medieval Society: Need, Habit, and Equanimity

1. How such registers were handeld can be seen in the Hebrew registers of Héliot of Vesoul of the first quarter of the fourteenth century,

preserved at the archives of the Côte-d'Or in Dijon. See Isidore Loeb's "Deux livres de commerce du commencement du XIVe siècle," *REJ* 8 (1884): 161–196; 9 (1884): 21–50, 187–213; as well as Moise Schwab's "Une page des Livres de commerce de la banque Héliot a Vesoul" REJ 68 (1914): 222–234. A very impressive Hebrew register from Florence, describing the activities of a Jewish pawnbroker's firm in 1474–1475, survived in the Archivio di Stato of that city and was described by Umberto Cassuto in his *Gli ebrei a Firenze nell'età del Rinascimento* (Florence, 1918; 2d ed., 1965), pp. 160–167. See also pp. 168–171 for Cassuto's description of yet another register preserved at the library of the Vatican. Prof. Michael Toch of the Hebrew University discovered in German archives a few leaves from such a register. See Wolfgang von Stromer and Michael Toch, "Zur Buchführung der Juden im Spätmittelalter," in *Wirtschaftskräfte und Wirtschaftswege: Festschrift für Hermann Kellenbenz*, ed. Jürgen Schneider et al., vol. 1 ([Stuttgart], 1978), pp. 387–410 and appendixes, as well as Michael Toch, "Geld und Kredit in einer spätmittelalterlichen Landschaft," *Deutches Archiv für Erforschung des Mittelalters* 38 (1982): 499–550. See also the fine recent studies of Prof. Daniel Carpi, "The Account Book of a Jewish Moneylender in Montepulciano (1409–1410)," *Journal of European Economic History* 14 (1985): 501–513, and "Towards the History of the Jewish Moneylenders in Montepulciano at the Turn of the Fifteenth Century," in *Jews in Italy: Studies Published on the Occasion of the One Hundredth Birthday of M. D. Cassuto* (Jerusalem, 1987), pp. 231–274 (Hebrew). Similarly, J. Millás i Vallicrosa discovered remnants of an account book from Girona of about 1330. See his "Petita lista d'un prestamista jueu," *Estudis Universitaris Catalans* 12 (1927): 65–67. For the notebook of a notary engaged by Jewish pawnbrokers in southern Italy at the end of the fifteenth century, see the recent publication of Filena Patroni Griffi, *Il banco di pegni di Cava dei Tirreni del 1495* (Cava dei Tirreni, 1985).

2. Richard W. Emery, *The Jews of Perpignan in the Thirteenth Century: An Economic Study Based on Notarial Records* (New York, 1959), p. 39.

3. Ibid., pp. 40–48, esp. p. 47.

4. Ibid., pp. 48–51.

5. Ibid., esp. p. 51.

6. Ibid., p. 39.

7. Ibid., pp. 61–66, esp. p. 62.

8. Mathias Delcor, "Les juifs de Puigcerdà au XIIIe siècle," *Sefarad* 26 (1966): 32–37.

9. Louis Stouff, "Activités et professions dans une communauté juive de Provence au bas moyen âge—La juiverie d'Arles, 1400–1450," in *Minorités, techniques et métiers: Actes de la Table ronde du Groupe-*

ment d'intérêt scientifique Sciences humaines sur l'aire méditerranéenne, Abbaye de Sénanque, octobre 1978 (Aix-en-Provence, [1980]), pp. 57–77, esp. p. 62, and now his *Arles à la fin du moyen-âge*, vol. 2 (Aix-en-Provence and Lille, 1986), p. 751.

10. For the Catalan city Santa Coloma de Queralt, Professor Yom Tov Assis obtained remarkably similar results, concerning the duration of loans. His detailed study, published recently, covers the years 1293–1299 and is based on an extensive study of no fewer than 3,468 acts. See Yom Tov Assis, *The Jews of Santa Coloma de Queralt* (Jerusalem, 1988), pp. 70–74. Unfortunately the book came out when the present study was already being considered for publication. I could not make as much use of it as I would have liked.

11. Monique Wernham, *La communauté juive de Salon-de-Provence d'après les actes notariés 1391–1435* (Toronto, 1987), pp. 147–158.

12. Noël Coulet, "Autour d'un quinzain des métiers de la communauté juive d'Aix en 1437," in *Minorités, techniques et métiers: Actes de la Table ronde du Groupement d'intérêt scientifique Sciences humaines sur l'aire méditerranéenne, Abbaye de Sénanque, octobre 1978* (Aix-en-Provence, [1980]), pp. 79–104.

13. Ibid., pp. 91–95. Similar results were obtained very recently for Tudela, Navarra in 1382. See Juan Carrasco Pérez, "Prestamistas judíos de Tudela a fines del siglo XIV," *Miscelánea de estudios árabes y hebráicos* 29 (1980): 87–109.

14. Louis Stouff, "Activités et professions," p. 65, and *Arles à la fin du moyen âge*, p. 764.

15. M.-Z. Isnard, *Livre des privilèges de Manosque* (Paris, 1894), pp. 66–71. See also Cecil Roth, *The Jews of Medieval Oxford* (Oxford, 1951), p. 35. Such is finally the impression one gets after considering the forty cases of pawnbroking discovered by Yom Tov Assis in Santa Coloma de Queralt. See Assis, *The Jews of Santa Coloma de Querlat*, pp. 87–91.

16. Rodrigue Lavoie, "Endettement et pauvreté en Provence d'après les listes de la justice comtale," *Provence historique* 23 (1973): 201–216, esp. p. 210.

17. Similar results were obtained in a recent study by the Polish historian Danuta Poppe, *Economie et société d'un bourg provençal au XIVe siècle; Reillanne en haute Provence* (Wroclaw, Warsaw, Krakow, Gdansk, 1980), pp. 159–67.

18. Lavoie, "Endettement et pauvreté, pp. 213–215.

19. Christian Castellani, "Le rôle économique de la communauté juive de Carpentras au début du XVe siècle," *Annales: ESC* 3 (1972): 583–611. Precious information, drawn from the archives of Navarre, can be found in the numerous studies by Béatrice Leroy. See, for example,

her "Le royaume de Navarre e les juifs aux XIVe et XVe siècles: Entre l'accueil et la tolérance," *Sefarad* 38 (1978): 263–292, as well as in her recent book (written with Mercedes García-Arendal), *Moros y judíos en Navarra en la baja edad media* (Madrid, 1984), pp. 169–174. Equally fascinating are the discoveries of Juan Carrasco Pérez. See his "Prestamistas judíos de Tudela a fines del siglo XIV," cited in n. 13 of this chapter; "El libro del Bedinage de Estella (1328–1331)," *Miscelánea de estudios árabes y hebráicos* 30 (1981): 109–120; "Acerca del préstamo judío en Tudela a fines del siglo XIV," *Príncipe de Viana* (Pamplona) 166–167 (1982): 909–948; and "Los judíos de Viana y Laguardia (1350–1408): Aspectos sociales y económicos," in *Vitoria en la edad media* (Vitoria and Gasteiz, 1982), pp. 419–447.

20. (A.D.) 56H 907 A, 22r, 7.4.1294. Almost all court registers of Manosque from this period reveal such lists of indebtedness. Thus, in the previously cited register, on folio 31v, one of the five creditors of Raymundus de Fonte is a Jew, Mosse de Grassa. The others are Raymundus's wife, who claims her dowry; his two brothers; and two inhabitants of Manosque. Of Guillelmus Upegonis's four creditors (55r–v), Jauseph (de Alesto) was the only Jew. The others were his mother (*ratione dotis*), the Florentine Simon de Bieco, and Jacob Michael. In the case of Guillelmus Bonus Par (127r–128r), we have nine creditors, only one of whom, Regina, was Jewish. Finally, one Jewish creditor, Salvetus, figures among the four creditors of Master Oliveri (148r–v), while in the case of Jacob Michael (153r), two of the three creditors are Jewish.

21. (A.D.) 56H 904, 108v–109r, 23.10.1287.

22. For Ebrardus Gibosi, see (A.D.) 56H 904, 93v–96v, 26.6.1289.

23. For R. Sartoris, see (A.D.) 56H 904, 97v–98v, 10.2.1289.

24. For B. Malipili, see (A.D.) 56H 904, 107v–108r, 3.9.1289.

25. Patricia M. Barnes, "The Anesty Case," in *A Medieval Miscellany for Doris Mary Stenton*, ed. P. M. Barnes and C. F. Slade (London, 1962), pp. 1–24. For a translation into English see Joseph Jacobs, *The Jews of Angevin England* (London, 1893), pp. 38–42.

26. *Et ad festum santi Martini quando replacitavi in curia predictorum judicum tunc prestitit mihi Jacobus Judeus de Niuport lxx solidos libram pro denariis per ebdomadam, quos tenui xiij denarios. Et ad eundem terminum prestiti mihi Benedictus Judeus Lundonie x solidos pro denariis per ebdomadam, quos tenui iij annis, de quibus pro usura reddidi xxvj solidos.* I changed "usance" in Jacob's translation to "usury." Barnes, "The Anesty Case," p. 22 and Jacobs, *The Jews of Angevin England*, p. 40.

27. See Mavis Mate, "The Indebtedness of Canterbury Cathedral Priory, 1215–1295," *Economic History Review* 26 (1973): 187.

28. Castellani, "Le rôle économique," p. 607.

29. See my study, "Desecrating the Cross: A Rare Medieval Accusation," *Studies in the History of the Jewish People and the Land of Israel* (Haifa) 5 (1980): 159–173 (in Hebrew).

30. Ariel Toaff, *The Jews in Medieval Assisi, 1305–1487* (Florence, 1979), p. 45 n. 147: *Et impugnatur error eorum qui dicunt civitatem stare non posse sine usurario manifesto.*

31. Although the polemics of Meir ben Simeon are not yet fully published, there is much scholarly discourse concerning Meir and his polemics. I refer the reader to a few recent contributions where further bibliography can be found: S. Stein, *Jewish-Christian Disputations in Thirteenth Century Narbonne* (London, 1964); idem, "A Disputation on Moneylending between Jews and Gentiles in Me'ir ben Simeon's Milhemet Misvah," *Tarbiz* 45 (1976): 296–302 (in Hebrew). See also Robert Chazan, "Anti-usury Efforts in Thirteenth Century Narbonne and the Jewish Response," *Proceedings of the American Academy for Jewish Research* 41–42 (1973–1974): 47–67; "A Jewish Plaint to Saint Louis," *Hebrew Union College Annual* 45 (1974): 287–305 "Archbishop Guy Fulcodi of Narbonne and His Jews," *REJ* (1973): 587–594; and "Confrontation in the Synagogue of Narbonne: A Christian Sermon and a Jewish Reply," *Harvard Theological Review* 67 (1974):437–457. The texts that I will quote herewith were recently transcribed by William K. Herskowitz, "Judeo-Christian Dialogue in Provence as Reflected in Milhemet Mitzva of R. Meir Hameili" (Ph.D. diss., Yeshiva University, New York, 1974). For Meir's economic polemics see the recent study by Giacomo Todeschini, "Teorie economiche degli ebrei alla fine del medioevo: Storia di una presenza consapevole," *Quaderni storici* 52 (1983): 181–225, esp. pp. 203–206.

32. As suggested by Chazan, "Anti-usury Efforts," p. 61.

33. See Herskowitz, "Judeo-Christian Dialogue," pp. 99, 115, 155.

34. Ibid., p. 99. I have used in part the translation of Chazan, "Anti-usury Efforts," p. 61.

35. See, for Pavia, Shlomo Simonsohn, *The Jews in the Duchy of Milan*, vol. 2 (Jerusalem, 1982), p. 868, no. 2089: "e maxime ne fano mali li poveri che non avendo modo alcuno de compararse del pane se non cum impegnare qualche cosa de loro, per non ritrovar ne ebreo ne christiano che cum el loro medesimo li sovengano se habiano a morire de fame." For Siena, see Sofia Boesch Gajano, "Il comune di Siena e il prestito nei secoli XIV e XV," in *Aspetti e problemi della presenza ebraica nell'Italia centro-settentrionale*, Quaderni dell'Istituto di scienze storiche dell'Università di Roma, no. 2 (Rome, 1983), pp. 175–225, esp. p. 209 n. 89; *sic pauperes et alii, nonnullis necessitatibus astricti non valentes nec rerum suarum emptores invenire nec qui eis sub pignoribus*

mutuare velint, ad varias murmorationes perveniant. For Florence, see M. Ciardini, *I banchieri ebrei in Firenze nel secolo XV e il Monte di Pietà fondato da Girolamo Savonarola* (Borgo S. Lorenzo, 1907; reprint, Florence, 1975), p. 68: "Le cose, riferi, sono ridotte in grande estremità, et in tal luogo, che i poveri nessun credito hanno ne possono alle loro necessità sovvenire se non, o con accattare da ebrei in su loro pegni, o vendendo le cose con gran perdita, o facendo coi cristiani tali contratti, come in moltissimi luoghi della giurisdizione del Comune si fa, e che in tutto ne segue la loro ruina e sono molto più dannosi e di maggiore infamia che quei che si fanno per mezzo degli ebrei."

36. Chazan, "A Jewish Plaint to Saint Louis," p. 61, and see also Marc Saperstein, *Decoding the Rabbis: A Thirteenth-Century Commentary on the Aggadah* (Cambridge, Mass., 1980), p. 165, for Raymond Tranceval's rebellion.

37. Herskowitz, "Judeo-Christian Dialogue," p. 99. While there is no doubt that we have a reference to a genuine case here, we are left with the dilemma as to who this official (*pakid*) could be. Jews did occupy government positions in southern France in the twelfth century. See G. Saige, *Les juifs du Languedoc antérieurement au XIVe siècle* (Paris, 1881), pp. 13–18. There were Jews who held such offices in places like Béziers and Carcassonne. In *The Itinerary of Benjamin of Tudela*, ed. Marcus Nathan Adler (London, 1907), p. 48, the famous traveler called the courtier Abba Mari bar Isaac at Saint-Gilles by the same Hebrew title of *pakid* that we find in Meir's polemics. In the 1240s, there flourished at Béziers a highly appreciated Jewish courtier, whose praise is sung by Isaac ben Yedaiah. This courtier was involved, as almost all were, in the administration of financing. "Like Adoniram overseeing the taxes, so he supervised all matters involving large sums of money." See M. Saperstein, *Decoding the Rabbis*, pp. 162, 159–67, Professor Saperstein suggests the plausible identification of this courtier of Béziers with Astrugetus Judeus, who appears as an *officialis domini regis* in Latin documents for the royal administration of the 1240s. For similar *consortia* of Jewish moneylenders, who in the 1170s provided loans to Henry II of England, see H. G. Richardson, *The English Jewry under Angevin Kings* (London, 1960), pp. 61–66.

38. On Jacob ben Elijah of Venice, see my article, "Paulus Christiani, un aspect de son activité anti-juive," in *Hommage à Georges Vajda* (Louvain, 1980), pp. 203–217 and the bibliography there. The Hebrew text was first published by Joseph Kobak in *Jeschurun* (Lemberg) 6 (1868): 1–34. An English translation of that paragraph is in Leon Poliakov's *Jewish Bankers and the Holy See* (London and Boston, 1979), pp. 234–236. The fact that ecclesiastics were among the moneylenders' cli-

ents assisted them in overcoming moral scruples about their profession. This point was made in the excellent study of Enrico Fiumi, "L'attività usuraria dei mercati sangimignanesi nell'età comunale," *Archivio storico italiano* 119 (1961): 145–162.

39. On the Italian merchants, see E. Jordan, *De Mercatoribus Camerae Apostolicae* (Condate Rhedonum [i.e., Rennes], 1909), pp. 117–128, and for the thirteenth century, Yves Renouard, *Les relations des papes d'Avignon et des compagnies commerciales et bancaires de 1316 à 1378* (Paris, 1941), esp. pp. 86–117 and p. 197, where the author states: "le premier caractère qui frappe . . . c'est la préférence presque exclusive . . . [des] compagnies toscanes. . . ."

40. *Populus vivere non poterat sine mutuo nec terre excoli nec ministria vel mercimonia exerceri.* See William Cornot, "De Vita et Actibus . . . Ludovici," in *Recueil des historiens des Gaules et de la France*, ed. Martin Bouquet, 24 vols. (Paris, 1737–1904), vol. 20 (1840), p. 34. This text is quoted fully by Solomon Grayzel in *The Church and the Jews in the Thirteenth Century* (New York, 1966), p. 46 n. 25 and translated by Robert Chazan in *Church, State and the Jew in the Middle Ages* (New York, 1980), p. 217. About Italian bankers, see also Jacques Le Goff, "The Usurer and Purgatory," in *The Dawn of Modern Banking* (New Haven and London, 1979).

41. Simonsohn, *The Jews in the Duchy of Milan* 1: 51–53, no. 63. The podestà is quoted as saying, *quod erat utile rei publice ut plures hebrey et alie persone huc venirent habitaturum.*

42. See Ariel Toaff, *Gli ebrei a Perugia* (Perugia, 1975), p. 19: *Cum persone ipsorum Iudeorum sint valde utiles et necessari in civitate Perusii tam ipsi comuni Perusii quam specialibus personis civitatis predicte et burgorum ipsius et maxime in occasione habende pecunie et recipiende sub mutuo ab eisdem pro guerra et aliis rebus et necessitatibus occurrentibus.*

43. Robert Davidsohn, *Forschungen zur Geschichte von Florenz*, vol. 2 (Berlin, 1900), pp. 328–329. See also the elaboration of Vittore Colorni in his "Prestito ebraico e comunità ebraiche nell'Italia centrale e settentrionale con particolare riguardo alla comunità di Mantova," republished in his *Judaica Minora* (Milan, 1982), p. 231.

44. See Francesca Bocchi, "I debiti dei contadini (1235): Note sulla piccola proprietà terriera nella crisi del feudalismo," in *Studi in memoria di Luigi dal Pane* (Bologna, 1982), pp. 169–209.

45. Elain Clark, "Debt Litigation in a Late Medieval English Vill," in *Pathways to Medieval Peasants*, ed. J. A. Raftis (Toronto, 1981), pp. 247–279.

46. See L. H. Butler, "Archbishop Melton: His Neighbors and His Kinsmen," *Journal of Ecclesiastical History* 2 (1951): 54–68; Ralph B. Pugh, "Some Medieval Moneylenders," *Speculum* 43 (1968): 274–289.

47. Y. T. Assis, *The Jews of Santa Coloma de Queralt, pp. 40–44.* For non-Jewish moneylenders in Padua, see Antonio Ciscato, *Gli ebrei in Padova (1300–1800)* (Padua, 1901), pp. 15–18.

48. C. R. Cheney, *Episcopal Visitations of Monasteries in the Thirteenth Century,* 2d ed. (Manchester, 1983), pp. 11–12; Noël Coulet, *Les visites pastorales* (Turnhout, 1977), pp. 14–15. I consulted the text as published in Mansi, *Concilia* 24: 650–766, esp. pp. 711–714, and the French translation of the Latin entitled "Visites du diocèse de Cahors par Simon de Beaulieu archevêque de Bourges, 1285/6–1290/1," *Bulletin de la Société des études du Lot* 25 (1900): 279–327, esp. pp. 291–295.

49. See Philippe Wolff, "Le problème des Cahorsins," *Annales du Midi* 62 (1950): 229–238. Prof. Wolff, who demonstrates that *Cahorsins* is not just a label attached to any moneylender, brings forth the example of a usurer, Guiral Trapas, who came from the small city Crécy and who had interests in England (London, Gloucester, Southampton, Canterbury, Salisbury, and Stamford) and also in Spain (Burgos, Palencia, and Toledo).

50. Armando Sapori, "Usura nel dugento a Pistoia," in his *Studi di storia economica,* vol. 1 (Florence, 1955), esp. pp. 181–189.

51. The proceedings of the investigation were published by A. Blanc, *Le livre de comptes de Jacme Olivier* (Paris, 1899), pp. 333–344. Similar campaigns took place in Bruges and Flanders. In 1304, twenty-one people were investigated, and in 1310, nineteen. See R. de Roover, *Money, Banking and Credit in Mediaeval Bruges* (Cambridge, Mass., 1948), pp. 160–165.

52. See John H. Mundy, *Liberty and Political Power in Toulouse, 1050–1230* (New York, 1954), pp. 81–83 and passim, and also his study "Un usurier malheureux," *Annales du Midi* 68 (1956): 217–225. See also Mireille Castaing-Sicard, "Le prêt à intérêt à Toulouse aux XIIe et XIIIe siècles," *Bulletin philologique et historique (jusqu'à 1715) du Comité des travaux historiques et scientifiques* (Paris), 1952–53: 273–278.

53. Richard W. Kaeuper, *Bankers to the Crown: The Riccardi of Lucca and Edward I* (Princeton, 1973).

54. Ibid., pp. 27–46. The quotation is from p. 32.

55. Anna Maria Patrone, *Le casane astigiane in Savoia* (Turin, 1959).

56. Léon Gauthier, *Les Lombards dans les deux Bourgognes* (Paris, 1907).

57. Charles de La Roncière, *Un changeur florentin du trecento: Lippo di Fede del Sega* (Paris, 1973).

58. See, for example, the notarial act in (A.D.) 381 E32, 115v–116v, 21.8.1326, where the names of three Florentines are mentioned: Fabrionus Berti, Lambertus Philippi, and Peyronus Comi. They must have belonged to the same company.

59. For the Comtat Venaissin, see H. Chobaut, "Deux documents sur les marchands italiens établis dans le Comtat Venaissin au début du XIVe siècle," *Annales d'Avignon et du Comtat Venaissin* 15 (1929): 117–128. For upper Provence I refer to a notarial deed done in Manosque on 25 August 1313, to be found in the Archives des Basses-Alpes, Fonds Meyer, 4, fol. 21v.

60. See the previous note.

61. See my *Recherches sur la communauté juive de Manosque au moyen âge (1241–1329)* (Paris and The Hague, 1973), pp. 26–31, 149–164.

62. In Aix-en-Provence, in 1336, in contrast, we discover that the Dulcini family, one of the most distinguished in the Jewish community, did a lot of business with such social classes. See my study, "Documents de la communauté d'Aix en Provence," in *Michael: On the History of the Jews in the Diaspora* (Tel Aviv) 4 (1976): 414–445, esp. pp. 420–422.

63. See M. Mate, "The Indebtedness of Canterbury Cathedral Priory," pp. 183–187.

64. See R. Lavoie, "Endettement et pauvreté," pp. 201–205.

65. See nn. 20–24 of the present chapter.

66. A most welcome study is the recent article of Juan Carrasco Pérez, "Crédito agrícola y deuda mudéjaren el reíno de Navarra (1436–1441): Notas para su estudio," in *Homenaje al Profesor Dr. Dario Cabarulas Rodríguez* (Granada, 1986), of which my esteemed friend sent me the prepublication galley proofs.

67. See Judah Rosenthal, "A Religious Disputation between the Scholar Menahem and the Convert and Dominican Friar Paolo Christiani," *Hebrew Thought in America* 3 (1974): 61–71, esp. p. 68 (Hebrew).

68. Joseph Kimhi, *The Book of the Covenant*, trans. Frank Talmage (Toronto, 1972), pp. 34–35.

69. For the translation see Poliakov, *Jewish Bankers and the Holy See*, pp. 234–236. I have altered it slightly. For a loan given on 23 December 1310 by the Jews of Bédarrides to the bishop of Avignon, *pro solutione pecunie per dictum dominum episcopum domino nostro*

summo pontifici debite, see Romolo Caggase, *Roberto d'Anio e i suoi tempi* (Florence, 1920), p. 303 n. 4.

70. See for example, G. G. Coulton, *Medieval Panorama* (New York, 1974), pp. 328–329. See also the case of the Jew Moreau Baruc who was brought to court in Paris in May 1387 for having insulted Christians by saying that they are worse usurers than the Jews, in Roger Kohn, "Les Juifs de la France du Nord à travers les archives du parlement de Paris (1359?–1394)" REJ 141 (1982):5–138, document 216 (p. 104).

71. See chapter 3, n. 2.

72. See n. 40 in this chapter.

73. Herskowitz, "Judeo-Christian Dialogue," p. 195. I thank my friend Professor Walter Goffart of the University of Toronto for helping me translate this text, and many others, into English.

74. See the text reproduced in Guido Kisch, *Jewry-Law in Medieval Germany* (New York, 1949), p. 101: "Es stet geschreben in dem dritten buche Moysi, in dem XXV capitel, das got sprach also: din gelt saltu nicht umgeben zeu Wucher wider dynen ebenmenschen, nach dyne fruchte. Von gotes rechte sal kein iude wucher nemen von iuden nach von cristen, sundern got hat es yn erleubt von den heyden, da ehr sprach: ir solt nicht wucher nhemenn von keynen menschenn, sunder von den fromden, wan dye heyden sint fromde bon gote und beten fromde gote an, das sint dye abgote, das thun dye cristen nicht, dye beten an den untotlichenn ewigen got also dy iuden. Nhw ist ir ordnung aber anders geschichkt, das sye zeu lande nicht mogen eygens gehabe, nach erbliche guter besitzen, wan man yn des nicht statet, und hetten sye dye, so gesche yn von den luten schade darzeu: erbeiten sye dye hantwerge, des ledin dye zeunfte und hantwercksmeyster nicht, und musten irer geselschaft enperen, und dye lute lissen sy nicht arbeyten: triben sy dan koufmanschaft, so koufte nymant gerne weder sye. Und darumb so musen sye wuchern, und dit ist ir behelffen; aber dy cristenn wucherer haben kein behelffen wan es ist ir girheit und ir vorzewifelte bossheit." See also the documents on pp. 97 and 103. The translation I quote is that of Guido Kisch in his *The Jews in Medieval Germany: A Study of Their Legal and Social Status.* 2d ed. (New York, 1970), pp. 193–194.

75. Kisch, *The Jews in Medieval Germany*, p. 193.

76. See Peter Abelard, *Dialogue of a Philosopher with a Jew and a Christian*, trans. Pierre J. Payer (Toronto, 1979), p. 33.

77. For a translation, see R. Chazan, *Church, State and the Jew in the Middle Ages*, pp. 103–104.

78. For a translation, see James Parkes, *The Jew in the Medieval Community*, 2d ed. (New York, 1976), p. 338.

79. *Matthaei Parisiensis . . . Chronica Majora*, ed. Henry Richards Luard (London, 1872–1883), 5: 404–405: *Quae conditio gravior est quam judeorum quia quandoque sortem judeo attuleris recipiet benigne cum tanto lucro quod temporali tanto se commensurat.* See also Herbert Loewe, *Starrs and Jewish Charters Preserved in the British Museum* (London, 1932), 2: cvi and the translation by H. Michaelson, *The Jews in Early English Literature* (Amsterdam, 1926), p. 30.

80. Herskowitz, "Judeo-Christian Dialogue," p. 194.

81. The translation is by Parkes, *The Jew in the Medieval Community*, pp. 336–337.

82. See the English translation in L. Poliakov, *The History of Anti-Semitism*, vol. 1, translated from the French by Richard Howard (London, 1974), p. 80. The original French reads: "Toute pauvre gent se plaint / Car Juifs furent débonnaires / Beaucoup plus en faisant leurs affaires / Que ne sont maintenant les chrétiens. / Garanties ils demandent et liens, / Gages demandent et tout extorquent / Que les gens plument et écorchent . . . / Mais si les Juifs demeurés / Fussent au royaume de France, / Chrétiens moult grande aidance / Eussent eu, qu'ils n'ont plus." "Chronique rimée attribuée à Geffroi de Paris," in *Recueil des historiens des Gaules et de la France*, ed. Martin Bouquet, vol. 22 (Paris, 1840), p. 119, lines 3121–3127, 3762–3765.

83. The charter of 1315 can be found in *Ordonnances des roys de France de la troisième race*, ed. Eusèbe de Laurière et al. (Paris, 1723), 1: 595–597. An example of how public complaint made the government annul a decision to ban Jewish moneylenders comes from Florence, Tuscany. There, on 26 January 1406, a decision was made in this sense against the Jews, "enemies of the Cross, of our Lord Jesus Christ, and of all Christians." In August of the same year, however, the government of the Florentine republic received complaints from the villages of the *contado*, who were also willing to raise a special contribution of two thousand florins to help the city council change its mind. And so it happened that the decree was revoked and the activities of Jewish moneylenders were made legitimate in eleven villages of the *contado*. See M. Ciardini, *I banchieri ebrei in Firenze nel secolo XV e il Monte di Pietà fondato da Girolamo Savonarola*, 2d ed. (Florence, 1975), pp. 25–26.

84. Salomon Kahn, "Les juifs de la Sénéchaussée de Beaucaire," *REJ* 65 (1913): 181–195; 66 (1913): 75–97, esp. pp. 83–84.

85. "[usurae] quae in anno sortem principalem excedunt." See Kahn, "Les juifs de la Sénéchaussée de Beaucaire," p. 191.

86. Stouff, "Activités et professions," p. 66.

87. Barnes, "The Anesty Case," p. 14.

88. See Manuel Grau i Monserrat, "Instrumenta Judeorum," *Amics de Besalú* 5 (1983): 129–179; Immaculada Ollich i Castanyer, "Aspects econòmics de l'activitat dels jueus de Vic, segon els 'Libri iudeorum' (1266–1278)," *Miscel·lànea Textos Medievals* 3 (1985): 7–118.

89. For bibliography on "ma'arufia," see the *Encyclopaedia Judaica* (Jerusalem, 1973), 11: 640–641. Also one must refer to Moses Hoffmann, *Der Geldhandel der deutschen Juden während des Mittelalters* (Leipzig, 1910), pp. 94–100, and Ben-Zion Dinur, *Israel in the Diaspora* (Tel Aviv and Jerusalem, 1966), vol. 2, book 2, pp. 250–251, where the major documents are presented. See also S. Eidelberg, "Ma'arufia in Rabbenu Gershom's Responsa," *Historia Judaica* 15 (1953): 59–66, and his *The Responsa of Rabbenu Gershom Meor Hagolah* (New York, 1955), pp. 159–163. Also useful are Irving A. Agus, *The Heroic Age of Franco-German Jewry* (New York, 1969), pp. 78–86, and the same author's *Urban Civilization in Pre-Crusade Europe* (New York, 1968), vols. 1 and 2, index. As to the etymology of the term, I should add that in modern Arabic, according to my faint knowledge of it, the noun *ma'aruf* signifies a favor (*gratia* in Latin). A *ma'arufia* might therefore be someone who receives favors. See also the following note.

90. For the "migration" of commercial terminology from the Orient, see Abraham Grossman, "Family Lineage and Its Place in Early Ashkenazic Jewish Society," in *Studies in the History of Jewish Society in the Middle Ages and in the Modern Period* (presented to Prof. Jacob Katz) (Jerusalem, 1980), p. 13 n. 46, and his "The Migration of the Kalonymos Family from Italy to Germany," *Zion* 3–4 (1975): 170 n. 46.

91. Agus, *Urban Civilization* 1:210.

92. Eidelberg, "Ma'arufia," p. 65.

93. Ibid.

94. Ibid. For later examples, see pp. 61–62, and Eliezer ben Yehuda, *A Complete Dictionary of Ancient and Modern Hebrew* (New York, 1960), 4:3196.

95. A recent and most penetrating book about the Jewish pietists in medieval Germany is Ivan S. Marcus, *Piety and Society* (London, 1981). It contains a discussion of modern research on this subject. In this chapter I shall quote from the Berlin edition (1891–1893) of Jehuda Wistinetzki, ed., *Das Buch der Frommen (Sefer hasidim)*, reissued in 1924 in Frankfurt am Main and later in Jerusalem (henceforward referred to as *Sefer hasidim*).

96. *Sefer hasidim*, p. 301.

97. Eliezer ben Nathan, *Even ha-Ezer Sefer Raban*, 2d ed., Jerusalem, 1975), pp. 77, no. 104. My interpretation is founded on the fact

that the man did not ask his colleague simply to lend money to his *ma'arufia* but to lend money to his *ma'arufia* at a certain rate of interest (*be-khakh ve-khakh ribbit le-shavua*).

98. *The Responsa of Meir of Rothenburg* (Berlin, 1891; reprint, Jerusalem, 1968), p. 20, no. 55, as quoted by Dinur, *Israel in the Diaspora*, vol. 2, book 2, p. 251.

99. See Wolfgang von Stromer and Michael Toch, "Zur Buchführung der Juden im Spätmittelalter," in *Wirtschaftskräfte und Wirtschaftswege: Festschrift für Hermann Kellenbenz*, ed. Jürgen Schneider et al., vol. 1 ([Stuttgart], 1978), pp. 387–410, and Michael Toch, "Business Techniques of Medieval German Jews: New Evidence from South Germany," in *Proceedings of the Eighth World Congress of Jewish Studies*, Div. B (Jerusalem, 1982), pp. 47–50. According to Toch's interpretation, some of the loans were given "for thirty weeks." I wonder whether this should not be read rather as *bi-leshon Shevnot*, "on the power of oath."

100. *Sefer hasidim*, p. 202.

101. See Jean Régné, *History of the Jews in Aragon* (Jerusalem, 1978), no. 336. Noteworthy is the information from Marseilles for 3.6.1321 (381 E 376) that *magister Elia, medicus judeus* of Marseilles, cannot be present at court when the witnesses take oath, *et dictum judeum respondisse quod non poterat venire propter festum pentecostas judey*. See also the recent study of Jacob Katz, *The Sabbath Gentile* (Jerusalem, 1983), which has as its subtitle *The Socio-Economic and Halakhic Background to the Employment of Gentiles on Jewish Sabbath and Festivals*.

102. Quoted by Irving Agus, *Rabbi Meir of Rothenburg*, 2d ed. (New York, 1970), 1: 25 n. 54.

103. Asher ben Yehiel, *Responsa* (Jerusalem, 1971), chapter 23, *responsum* no. 4 (Hebrew).

104. Eliezer ben Nathan, *Even ha-Ezer*, p. 205. A similar situation (the same?) is depicted in the *Responsa* of Meir of Rothenburg (Prague, 1895), no. 664.

105. An echo of such a relationship of honor or confidence—this time in the real world—is found in the business registers of the bank of the Jew Heliot of Vesoul. On one of the pages that recorded his banking activities in the first years of the fourteenth century, there is an entry that reveals confusion about the sum of money a Christian customer deposited, but the customer stated "that he will accept our word for it." I have it on the authority of Isidore Loeb, "Deux livres de commerce du commencement du XIVe siècle," *REJ* 9 (1884): 41.

5. Shylock Reconsidered: Bondavid Seen by His Friends

1. I reconstituted the possible tenor of the article from the subsidiary questions in folio 49Ar, as well as from the testimony of Petrus Bonifilii in 44v. *Quod dictus Bondavinus fuit rogatus per aliquas personas compositionem facere cum dicto Laurentio.*

2. The reconstitution of the possible tenor of article 3 comes from folio 42r: *Quod dictus Bondavinus pluribus hominibus fecit gratiam de debitis suis prolungando partem debiti. Debitoribus restituendo et instrumenta seu mandamenta gratiose reddendo debitoribus.*

3. The article is reconstituted from testimony, mainly from three witnesses: Hugo Mercerii, 31v; Montolivus de Montolivo, 28r; and Petrus Bermundi de Sancto Felicii, 37v: *Item quod dictus Bondavid est homo bonus, pacificus et quietus et legalis, bone fame et bone opinionis et numquam consuevit aliquem defraudare nec decipere verbo facto vel opere nec debita persoluta alias repetere. Et de predicti fama esse in civitate Massilie inter notos et vicinos.* Compare the article presented by a couple in Manosque about June 1323, where we read: *Et primo intendunt probare quod ipsi sunt et erant tempore contra eos inquisitio supradicta (facta?) homines bone fame et bone opinionis et tale habentur et habebantur inter notos et vicinos, et quod a similibus criminibus perpetrandis abstinere consueverunt.* (A.D.) 56H 973, 35v, 16.[6].1323. Register (A.D.) 56H 973 contains, almost exclusively, such *tituli* and *defensiones.* See also (A.D.) 56H 980, 34r, 15.6.1327, where Bertrandus Assis of Manosque, in a case of human slaughter, is acquitted in the court, because the judge considers him to be *bone fame et opinionis et numquam rixari seu plagias facere . . . usus fuit . . . immo pacificus,* while his adversary was known *fuisse et extitisse hominem male fame et male opinionis et in malis societatibus conversantem, pauperem. . . .* For similar language at the court of Bologna, in 1289, see Ottavio Mazzoni Tosselli, *Racconti storici estratti dell'archivio criminale di Bologna* (Bologna, 1866), p. 482: *Domininus Bernabo est homo bonae famae et opinionis, conversat cum mercatoribus et cambiatoribus, et non audivit umquam ipsum Bernabonum conversari cum aliqua cativa persona et schivat libenter brigas.*

4. See F. Perry, *Saint Louis: The Most Christian King* (New York and London, 1901), pp. 255–256.

5. (A.M.) register FF 507. The document is from the year 1321. There is no pagination in the register.

6. For the real-estate holdings of another probable member of the Bermundi family, see (A.D.) B 1936, 63v–64r. These included, among others, six houses in the *jusataria*.

7. (A.D.) 381 E 30, 89v–90r, 20.12.1319.

8. (A.D.) 381 E 14, 82r–83r, 23.10.1320 and (A.D.) III B19, 31r–37r, [29].1.1326.

9. See André Vauchez's introduction to Jacques Cambell, ed., *Enquête pour le procès de canonisation de Dauphine de Puimichel, comtesse d'Ariano* (Turin, 1978), p. X.

10. For the social milieux of Marseilles and its eminent families, I mainly consulted Georges Lesage, *Marseille angevine* (Paris, 1950) and Philippe Mabilly, *Les villes de Marseille au moyen âge: Ville supérieure et ville de la prévôté* (Marseilles, 1905), pp. 186–200. Both authors tried to establish files for leading families in the city. See also Felix Portal, *La république marseillaise du XIIIᵉ siècle (1200–1263)* (Marseilles, 1907).

11. On the Baux family, see Edwin Smyrl, "La famille des Baux," *Cahiers du centre d'études des sociétés méditerranéennes* (Aix-en-Provence), 2 (1968): 7–108; Edouard Baratier, *Enquêtes sur les droits et revenus de Charles Ier d'Anjou en Provence, 1252–1278* (Paris, 1969), pp. 163–165; and Mireille Zarb, *Les privilèges de la ville de Marseille du Xe siècle à la révolution* (Paris, 1961), p. 74. See also L. Barthélémy, *Inventaire chronologique et analytique des chartes de la maison des Baux* (Marseilles, 1882); F. Portal, *La république marseillaise*, pp. 57–59, 351–373, 406–410, and M. Z. Isnard, *Inventaire sommaire chronologique des chartes, lettres patentes, lettres missives et titres divers antérieurs à 1500* (Marseilles, 1939), pp. 38–39, 56.

12. For the Bonvini family, see Lesage, *Marseille angevine*, pp. 117–118 and also 106–123. For the location of their house in the city in 1318 see (A.D.) 819, 59v.

13. On the Sardis and Saint-Félix, see Mabilly, *Les villes de Marseille*, pp. 240–241. Bertrand Sardi was one of the founders of the confraternity "Saint Esprit," thus supporting municipal independence. See Portal, *La république marseillaise*, p. 30.

14. Monteolivus de Monteolivo undoubtedly deserves a special political biography. The communal deliberations of Marseilles would provide enough data for one. For the purposes of my brief biography of Monteolivus, which depicts just the highlights, I consulted the very detailed *Inventaire sommaire des archives communales antérieures à 1790* (Marseille, 1907) by Philippe Mabilly, pp. 1–57. For the elements of his biography see especially pp. 3–4, 19, 22, 31–32. I also collected some data from Lesage, *Marseille angevine*, pp. 167–169.

15. For the importance of this position, see Edouard Baratier and Félix Reynaud, *Histoire du commerce de Marseille*, vol. 2 (Paris, 1951), pp. 149–163), and Georges Lesage, *Marseille angevine*, p. 152.

16. There is a vast scholarly literature on the subject. For southern France see the two recent monographs by Michel Hébert, *Tarascon au XIVe siècle* (Aix-en-Provence, 1979) and Jan Rogozinski, *Power, Caste and Law; Social Conflict in Fourteenth Century Montpellier* (Cambridge, Mass., 1982). Also Jacques Le Goff, *Marchands et banquiers du moyen âge* (Paris, 1972), pp. 42 ff. is, as always, very suggestive.

17. See G. Lesage, *Marseille angevine*, pp. 117–118 and 381 E 32, 219r, 2.2.1327, where Bartholomeus Bonvini, son of the deceased Raymundus, sells a house to Petrus Ronsani.

18. See Lesage, *Marseille angevine*, pp. 66–69, and Mabilly, *Inventaire*, p. 19. In 1318, when his daughter Margarita married a *draperius* named Guillelmus Eguserii, Ricavus and his wife Bertranda endowed her with the considerable sum of four hundred pounds. See (A.D.) 381 E29, 5v and 102r. For the location of a house of his in the "Carreria de Jerusalem," see (A.D.) B 819, 4r.

19. See Mabilly, *Inventaire*, p. 20.

20. Ibid., p. 2.

21. See *Processus Canonizationis et Legendae Variae Sancti Ludovici, O.F.M.*, Analecta Franciscana, vol. 7 (Quaracchi, 1951), pp. 1–5.

22. (A.D.) B 819, 31r, January 1318: *Marquesius de Jerusalem filius domini Vivaudi de Jerusalem . . . dixit et asseruit dictum dominum Vivaudum patrem suam absentem esse a civitate Massilie . . . et ivisse ad dominum nostrum regem una cum Petro Bermundi de Sancto Felicio ut ambaxatores pro civitate Massilie et pro magnis et arduis negotiis civitatis predicte.*

23. (A.D.) 381 E 379, 99r–v, 10.10.1324. The honor had been bestowed upon him on 8.1.1319. Petrus registered it officially, for reasons which we do not understand, five years later on 10 October 1324. On a similar honor bestowed on Auguillet Mars, see Lesage, *Marseille angevine*, p. 166.

24. For these families, see G. Lesage, *Marseille angevine*, pp. 113–124; Ph. Mabilly, *Les villes de Marseille*, pp. 186–209 and 46; Régine Pernoud, *Les statuts municipaux de Marseille* (Monaco and Paris, 1949), pp. 297–302; and Baratier and Reynaud, *Histoire du commerce* 2:63–89. For the committee chosen in 1307 to promote the canonization of Louis of Anjou, see *Processus Canonizationis et Legendae*, p. 1: *discreti viri magister Raymundus Egidii et Raymundus Viridis, Massilienses canonici, necnon et nobiles viri dominus Gauffridus Ricavi, miles, Petrus Bermundi de Sancto Felicio, domicellus, et Hugo de Fonte, cives Massil-*

ienses, procuratores, prosequutores, instructores et promotores per predictum dominum episcopum et eciam per generale Consilium civitatis Massilie . . . constituti. . . .

25. Mabilly, *Les villes de Marseille*, p. 161. Considering my own findings in the archives of Manosque, I would suggest a lower sum of about one hundred and thirty pounds. See *Recherches sur la communauté juive de* Manosque, p. 105.

26. A loan of twelve pounds Bondavid extended to Raymundus Payrolerii in 1310 is recorded in (A.M.) FF 503, 88r.

27. See Francesco de Bofarull y Sans, *Los judíos en el territorio de Barcelona* (Barcelona, 1910), p. 111 and (A.D.) 56H 907, 44r, 4.2.1296, where Bertrandus Scoferii refuses to pay off a debt to a Florentine, *quia dominum noster rex Karolus secundus prorogavit debita Bertrandi Scoferii predicti usque ad duos annos.* The Jewish doctor, Master Leo, asked his (Jewish) creditors for a *prorogatio* of ten years. He wanted to get a similar *prorogatio* from the Florentine moneylender Donatus de Florentia, *habitator Apte.* See (A.D.) 56H 904, 71r–v, 24.2.1289.

28. See Jean Régné, *History of the Jews in Aragon* (Jerusalem, 1978), nos. 5, 269, 279, 338, 410.

29. See A. Cordoner y Planas and Francisca Verdrell Gallostia, "Aportaciones al estudio de la familia Abenardut Médicos Reales," *Sefarad* 7 (1947): 303–348, esp. p. 339, as well as Jose Rius Serra, "Aportaciones sobre médicos judíos en Aragón en la primera mitad del siglo XIV," *Sefarad* 12 (1952): 337–350, esp. p. 247.

30. For a growing sense of dissatisfaction with legislation at the beginning of the thirteenth century and in the fourteenth century, see Robert I. Burns, "Canon Law and the Reconquista: Convergence and Symbiosis in the Kingdom of Valencia under Jaume the Conqueror, 1213–1276," *Proceedings of the Fifth International Congress of Medieval Canon Law, 1976* (Vatican City, 1980), esp. pp. 387–389. See also M. T. Clanchy, *From Memory to Written Record: England, 1066–1307* (Cambridge, Mass., 1979), especially the second part, pp. 149 ff., where literate and "anti-literate" mentalities are discussed.

31. On the virtues of the ideal medieval man, see Charles V. Langlois, *La vie en France au moyen âge* (Paris, 1926), where he presents Philippe de Navarre's thirteenth-century treatise, "Les quatre âges de l'homme." See also Achille Luchaire's work, *Social France at the Time of Philip Augustus* (New York, n.d.), pp. 333–350, and most recently, Georges Duby, *William Marshall: The Flower of the Chivalry*, trans. Richard Howard (New York, 1985).

32. See the data in my article, "Paulus Christiani, un aspect de son activité anti-juive," in *Hommage à Georges Vajda* (Louvain, 1980), pp. 203–217.

33. For the English translation, see John T. Gilchrist, *The Church and Economic Activity in the Middle Ages* (New York, 1969), p. 206. For the original, see CorpIurCanClem 5.5: *Ex gravi ad nos insinuatione pervenit, quod quorundum communitates locorum in offensam Dei et proximi, ac contra iura divina pariter et humana usurarium approbantes quodammodo pravitatem, per statuta sua iuramento quandoque firmata usuras exigi et solvi nedum concedunt, sed ad solvendas eas debitores scienter compellunt, ac iuxta ipsorum continentiam statutorum gravia impondendo, plerumque usuras repetentibus onera, aliisque utendo super his diversis coloribus et fraudibus exquisitis, repetitionem impediunt earundem. Nos igitur, perniciosis his ausibus obviare volentes, sacro approbante concilio statuimus, ut, quicunque communitatum ipsarum potestates, capitanei, rectores, consules, iudices, consiliarii aut alii quivis officiales statuta huiusmodi de cetero facere, scribere vel dictare, aut quod solvantur usurae, vel quod solutae, quum repetuntur, non restituantur plene ac libere, scienter iudicare praesumserint sententiam excommunicationis incurrant, eandem etiam sententiam incursuri, nisi statuta huiusmodi hactenus edita de libris communitatum ipsarum (si super hoc potestatem habuerint) infra tres menses deleverint, aut si ipsa statuta sive consuetudines, effectum eorum habentes, quoquo modo praesumpserint observare.*

34. The council of Brussels asked the duke of Brabant in 1319 to present a question to the University of Paris concerning the applicability of the canon *Ex gravi* to their activities. See Georges Bigwood, *Le régime juridique et économique du commerce de l'argent dans la Belgique du moyen âge* (Brussels, 1921), pp. 459–460. For legislation in Marseilles, see Régine Pernoud, *Les statuts municipaux*, pp. 232–233. In the book itself this new legislation is called *De usuris*. In the list of chapter that opens the manuscript, Pernoud used the title that is more proper, *Revocatio statutorum de usuris*. It reads, *In nomine domini nostri, Jesu-Christi, Amen. Cum in detestationem usurarie pravitatis, summus pontifex Clemens V in Consilio Vianensi statuerit ut quicumque communitatum potestates, Capitanei, rectores, judices, consules, consiliarii aut alii quiuis officiales sententiam excommunicationis incurrant nisi statuta hactenus edita usuras exigi et solui concedencia seu repetitionem impediencia earundem de libris communitatum ipsarum si potestatem super hoc habuerint infra tres menses deleverint. Nos volentes ut christiani fideles mandatis apostolicis, ut convenit, obedire et predictam excommunicationis sententiam modis omnibus evitare, statutum, positum in secundo libro statutorum hujus civitatis Massilie, sub rubrica pro qua quantitate usure adjudicentur quod incipit presenti statuto etc., in eo quod usuras exigi et solvi concedit tacite vel expresse, nec non et omnia alia statuta in dicto libro posita seu comprehensa usuras exigi et solvi concedencia*

tacite vel expresse, seu repeticone impedencia earundem quantum ad id presenti statuto delemus, corrigimus et funditus irritamus. In ceteris vero capitulis, in dictis statutis comprehensis, ea statuta in sui robore volumus perdurare.

Predictum siquidem statutum noviter factum, lectum fuit et publicatum per me Bartholomeus de Salinis notarium publicum Massilie, in consilio generali civitatis vicecomitalis Massilie, in aula regii Palacii, ad vocem preconis et sonum campane more solito congregato, et per id consilium confirmatum honorabili viro domino Raymundo de Villanova, milite, existente Vicario dicte civitatis inibi, anno domino millesimo trecentesimo septimo decimo, indictione prima die quarto decimo februarii. Ego idem Bartholomeus de Salinis, notarius hec scripsi.

35. For a history of the publication of the Clementines, see Charles Joseph Hefele and H. Leclercq, *Histoire des conciles*, vol. 6 (Paris, 1915), pp. 664–665; and, more particularly, Franz Ehrle's studies, "Ein Bruchstück der Acten des Concils von Vienne," *Archiv für Literatur- und Kirchengeschichte des Mittelalters* 4 (1888): 361–470, and "Zur Geschichte der Vienner Concilsdecrete und der Clementiner," ibid., pp. 452 ff.

36. See G. Lesage, *Marseille angevine*, pp. 161–163.

37. On Saint Louis of Anjou, his legend, and his miracles, see *Processus canonizationis et legendae varie sancti Ludovici* (Quaracchi 1951); the monograph of Margaret R. Toynbee, *S. Louis of Toulouse and the Process of Canonisation in the Fourteenth Century* (Manchester, 1929); M.-H. Laurent, *Le culte de s. Louis d'Anjou à Marseille au XIVe siècle* (Rome, 1954); and the numerous studies of Jacques Paul, most notably "Le rayonnement géographique du pèlerinage au tombeau de Louis d'Anjou," in *Le pèlerinage*, Cahiers de Fanjeaux, vol. 15 (Toulouse, 1980), pp. 137–158; "Le 'Liber miraculorum' de saint Louis d'Anjou," *Archivum Franciscanum Historicum* 69 (1976): 209–219; and "Témoignage historique et hagiographique dans le procès de canonisation de Louis d'Anjou," *Provence historique* 23 (1973): 305–317.

Conclusion

1. For the general picture see Guy Bois, *Crise du féodalisme* (Paris, 1981); the famous article by Edouard Perroy, "A l'origine d'une économie contractée: La crise du XIV siècle," *Annales: ESC* 4 (1949): 167–182; and recently John Day, *The Medieval Market Economy* (Oxford, 1987), pp. 90–107, 185–224. The work of my teacher Georges Duby is of much importance, as is well known. See his *La société aux XIe et XIIIe siècles dans la région mâconnaise*, 2d. ed., Paris, 1971, as well as his *Rural*

Economy and Country Life in the Medieval West, translated by C. Postan, Columbia, S.C., 1968.

2. Georges Lesage, *Marseille angevine* (Paris, 1950), p. 185. The immediate reason for the inquiry was the diminution of income to the city from taxation (*annonaria*), but, as Lesage noticed, the individual consulted broadened the scope of the discussion. The document reads: *Guido de Terruti. . . testis . . . dixit . . . se ignorare nec credit quod possit de facili prasentialiter reparari seu restitui ad statum pristinum quia civitas Massilie non esse in ita bono statu sicut erat tempore quo integre persolvebantur census predicti. . . . Bernardus Garnerii . . . credit et existimat quod deterioratio et diminutio dictorum reddituum provenit.*

3. See ibid., pp. 163–165.

Appendix 1

1. MS. has also: "contra."

2. Notary's reference: "Quere supra ad tale signum."

3. Underlined in the original.

4. Reference of the notary at the bottom of the MS: "Quere infra ad tale signum in tertio folio."

5. MS: "cum cum."

6. MS: For "esse" or "et se"?

7. MS: "de quodam de quodam."

8. MS: "ipse ipse."

9. *Sic* for "faciendo"? Obviously the notary omitted at this place some words or sentences.

10. MS: "super super."

11. MS: "qui qui."

12. Or: "sacerdotis."

13. It would seem that the notary omitted some words or phrases at this place.

14. The MS has clearly "habet" and "facit" in this quotation.

15. For "Boniuzas," in all probability.

Appendix 2

1. Barred: "et corpore."

2. This last item is written on the margins. A note of about fifteen words, in upper margin of the page, concerning "dicta uxor [mea],' 'is illegible.

3. Barred: "Quingentas Solidos." "C. Librass" written instead over the line.

4. MS: "denio" or "demo."

5. Barred: "xxv librarum." "C. librarum" written instead over the line.

6. Barred: "et xxv libras dicte monete in peccunia."

7. Undecipherable: a note of about fifteen words scribbled at the margins of the page. It concerns "Salomonetus" and somehow conditions the bequest of the house on his willingness to live in it, if the deciphering of "si vellet in morari" is correct.

8. Barred: "Astes judeam carissimam uxorem meam filiam Davini de Massilia judei condam."

Bibliography

The following two journal titles are abbreviated in this Bibliography:
Annales: ESC = *Annales: Economies, sociétés, civilisations*
REJ = *Revue des études juives*

Abrahams, B. Lionel. "The Condition of the Jews of England at the Time of Their Expulsion in 1290." *Transactions of the Jewish Historical Society of England* 2 (1894–1895):75–105.
———. "The Expulsion of the Jews from England in 1290." *Jewish Quarterly Review* 7 (1895):75–100, 236–258, 428–450.
Abrahams, Israel, trans. *Hebrew Ethical Wills*. Philadelphia, 1976.
Abrahams, Israel, H. P. Stokes, and Herbert Loewe. *Starrs and Jewish Charters Preserved in the British Museum*. 3 vols. London, 1930–1932.
Adler, Marcus Nathan, ed. *The Itinerary of Benjamin of Tudela*. London, 1907.
Adler, Michael. *Jews in Medieval England*. London, 1939.
Agus, Irving. *Urban Civilization in Pre-Crusade Europe*. 2 vols. New York, 1968.
———. *The Heroic Age of Franco-German Jewry*. New York, 1969.
———. *Rabbi Meir of Rothenburg*. 2d ed. New York, 1970.
Amargier, Paul, and Pierre Guiral. *Histoire de Marseille*. Paris, 1983.
Antoniazzi-Villa, Anna. "A proposito di ebrei, francescani, Monti di Pietà: Bernardino de Bustis e la polemica antiebraica nella Milano di fine 1400." In *Il francescanesimo in Lombardia: Storia e arte*, pp. 49–52. Milan, 1983.
Arbaud, Dumas. *Etude historique sur la ville de Manosque au moyen âge*. Digne, 1864.
Arnaud, Camille. *Histoire de la viguerie de Forcalquier*. 2 vols. Marseilles, 1874–1875.
———. *Essai sur la condition des juifs en Provence au moyen âge*. Forcalquier, 1879.

Asher ben Yehiel. *Responsa*. Jerusalem, 1971. Hebrew.

Assis, Yom Tov. "The Financial Activities of Catalan Jews: Santa Coloma de Queralt (1293–1294)." In *Proceedings of the Eighth World Congress of Jewish Studies*, pp. 33–38. Jerusalem, 1982. Hebrew.

———. *The Jews of Santa Coloma de Queralt: An Economic and Demographic Case Study of a Community at the End of the Thirteenth Century*. Jerusalem, 1988.

Aubenas, Roger. *Cours d'histoire du droit privé des pays de droit écrit (XIIIe–XVIe siècle)*. 7 vols. Aix-en-Provence, 1961.

———. *Recueil des lettres des officialités de Marseille et d'Aix*. 2 vols. Paris, 1937–1938.

Baer, Fritz. *Die Juden im christlichen Spanien*. 2 vols. Berlin, 1929–1936.

Baer, Yitzhak. *A History of the Jews in Christian Spain*. Translated by Louis Schoffman. 2 vols. Philadelphia, 1961–1966.

Baldwin, John W. *The Medieval Theories of the Just Price: Romanists, Canonists and Theologians in the Twelfth and Thirteenth Centuries*. Philadelphia, 1959.

Baratier, Edouard. *Enquêtes sur les droits et revenus de Charles Ier d'Anjou en Provence, 1252–1278*. Paris, 1969.

———. *La démographie provençale du XIIIe au XVIe siècle*. Paris, 1971.

Baratier, Edouard, and Félix Reynaud. *Histoire du commerce de Marseille de 1291 à 1480*. Vol. 2. Paris, 1951.

Barnes, Patricia M. "The Anesty Case." In *A Medieval Miscellany for Doris Mary Stenton*, edited by P. M. Barnes and C. F. Slade, pp. 1–24. London, 1962.

Baron, Salo W. "Plenitude of Apostolic Powers and Medieval Jewish Serfdom" and "Medieval Nationalism and Jewish Serfdom." In *Ancient and Medieval Jewish History: Essays by Salo Wittmayer Baron*, edited by Leon A. Feldman, pp. 284–322. New Brunswick, N.J., 1972.

———. *A Social and Religious History of the Jews*. 18 vols. New York and Philadelphia, 1952–1983.

Barthélémy, L. *Inventaire chronologique et analytique des chartes de la maison des Baux*. Marseilles, 1882.

———. *Les médecins à Marseille avant et pendant le moyen âge*. Marseilles, 1883.

Bautier, Robert H. "Feux, population et structure sociale au milieu du XVe siècle (l'exemple de Carpentras)." *Annales: ESC* 14 (1959):255–268.

Bautier, Robert Henri, and Janine Sornay. *Les sources de l'histoire économique et sociale du moyen âge: Provence–Comtat Venaissin–Dauphiné–Etats de la Maison de Savoie*. 3 vols. Paris, 1971–1974.

Beardwood, Alice. *The Trial of Walter Langton, Bishop of Lichfield, 1307–1312*. Transactions of the American Philosophical Society, n.s., vol. 54, pt. 3. Philadelphia, 1964.

Becker, M. "Gualtieri di Brienne e la regolamentazione dell'usura a Firenze." *Archivo Storico Italiano* 94 (1956):734–740.

Benoît, Fernand. *Recueil des actes des comtes de Provence appartenant à la maison de Barcelone*. 2 vols. Paris and Monaco, 1925.

Berger, Adolf. *Encyclopedic Dictionary of Roman Law*. Transactions of the American Philosophical Society, n.s., vol. 43, pt. 2 Philadelphia, 1953.

Berger, David. *The Jewish-Christian Debate in the High Middle Ages*. Philadelphia, 1979.

Berger, Elie. *Layettes du Trésor des chartes*. Vol. 4. Paris, 1902.

Bermann, Tamar. "Produktivierungsmythen und Antisemitismus: Assimilatorische und zionistische Berufsumschichtungsbestrebungen unter den Juden Deutschlands und Österreichs bis 1938." (Ph.D. diss., Munich, 1971.

———. *Produktivierungsmythen und Antisemitismus: Eine soziologische Studie*. Vienna, 1973.

Berthier, A. "Aspects juridiques et sociaux de l'histoire de Marseille au XIVe siècle (1309–1423) d'après les registres de la Cour du Palais et des Cours des Appellations." Thèse de l'Ecole des Chartes, Paris, 1970.

Bigwood, Georges. *Le régime juridique et économique du commerce de l'argent dans la Belgique du moyen âge*. Mémoires de l'Académie royale de Belgique, Classe des lettres et des sciences morales et politiques, 2d ser., vol. 14. Brussels, 1921–1922.

Bisson, Thomas N. *Conservation of Coinage: Monetary Exploitation and Its Restraint in France, Catalonia and Aragon*. Oxford, 1971.

Blanc, A. *Le livre de comptes de Jacme Olivier*. Paris, 1899.

Blancard, Louis. *Inventaire sommaire des Archives départementales antérieures à 1790, Bouches-du-Rhône, Archives civiles, Série B*. 2 vols. Paris, 1865–1879.

———. *Documents inédits sur le commerce de Marseille au moyen âge*. Marseilles, 1884–1885.

Bloch, Isaac. "Bonjudas Bondavin." *REJ* 8 (1884):280–283.

Blumenkranz, Bernhard. *Histoire des juifs en France*. Toulouse, 1972.

———. *Bibliographie des juifs en France*. Toulouse, 1974.

———. "Un quartier juif au moyen âge: Aix-en-Provence, juillet-septembre 1341." *Archives juives* 19 (1983):1–10.

———. "Le *De regimine judaeorum*: ses modèles, son exemple." In *Aquinas and Problems of his Time*, pp. 101–117. Louvain and The Hague, 1976.

Blumenkranz, Bernhard, and Geneviève Chazelas. "Un dossier sur les juifs du Languedoc médiéval dans la collection Doat." *Archives juives* 5 (1968–1969):32–40, 47–48.

Boccaccio, Giovanni. *The Decameron*. Translated by Richard Aldington. New York, 1976.

Bocchi, Francesca. "I debiti dei contadini (1235): Note sulla piccola proprietà terriera nella crisi del feudalismo." In *Studi in memoria di Luigi dal Pane*, pp. 169–209. Bologna, 1982.

Boesch Gajano, Sofia. "Il comune di Siena e il prestito nei secoli XIV e XV." In *Aspetti e problemi della presenza ebraica nell'Italia centro-settentrionale*, pp. 175–225. Quaderni dell'Istituto di scienze storiche dell'Università di Roma, no. 2. Rome, 1983.

de Bofarull y Sans, Francisco. *Los judíos en el territorio de Barcelona (siglos X al XIII)*. Barcelona, 1910.

Bois, Guy. *Crise du féodalisme*. Paris, 1981.

Bouquet, Martin, ed. *Recueil des historiens des Gaules et de la France*. 24 vols. Paris, 1737–1904.

Bourilly, V.-L. *Essai sur l'histoire politique de la commune de Marseille, des origines à la victoire de Charles d'Anjou (1264)*. Aix-en-Provence, 1925.

Bresc, Henri. *Un monde méditerranéen: Economie et société en Sicile, 1300–1450*. 2 vols. Rome, 1986.

Breur, Mordechai, ed. *Sefer Nizzahon Yashan*. Jerusalem, 1978. Hebrew.

Brezzi, Paulo, and Lee Egmont, eds. *Sources of Social History: Private Acts of the late Middle Ages*. Toronto, 1984.

Bruel, Alexandre. "Notes de Vyon d'Herouval sur les baptisés et les convers." *Bibliothèque de l'Ecole des chartes*, 6th ser., vol. 3 (1867): 613–620.

Brun, Robert. *La ville de Salon au moyen âge*. Aix-en-Provence, 1924.

Buber, Salomon, ed. *Schaare Zion: Beitrag zur Geschichte des Judentums bis zum Jahre 1372 von Rab. Isaac de Lattes*. Jaroslaw, 1885. Hebrew.

Burns, Robert I. "Canon Law and the Reconquista: Convergence and Symbiosis in the Kingdom of Valencia under Jaume the Conqueror, 1213–1276." In *Proceedings of the Fifth International Congress of Medieval Canon Law, 1976*. Vatican City, 1980.

Busquet, Raoul, and Régine Pernoud. *Histoire du commerce de Marseille*. Vol. 1. Paris, 1949.

Butler, L. H. "Archbishop Melton: His Neighbors and His Kinsmen." *Journal of Ecclesiastical History* 2 (1951):54–68.

Caggase, Romolo. *Roberto d'Anio e i suoi tempi*. Florence, 1920.

Cambell, Jacques, ed. *Enquête pour le procès de canonisation de Dauphine de Puimichel, comtessa d'Ariano*. Turin, 1978.

Cantera Burgos, Francisco. "La usura judía en Castilla." *La ciencia tomista* 43 (1931):5–26.

Caro, George. *Sozial- und Wirtschaftsgechichte der Juden im Mittelalter und der Neuzeit*. Vol. 1. Leipzig, 1908.

Carpi, Daniel. "The Account Book of a Jewish Moneylender in Montepulciano (1409–1410)." *Journal of European Economic History* 14 (1985):501–513.

———. "Towards the History of the Jewish Moneylenders in Montepulciano at the Turn of the Fifteenth Century." In *Jews in Italy: Studies Published on the Occasion of the One Hundredth Birthday of M. D. Cassuto*, pp. 231–274. Jerusalem; 1987. Hebrew.

Carrasco Pérez, Juan. "Prestamistas judíos de Tudela a fines del siglo XIV." *Miscelánea de estudios árabes y hebráicos* 29 (1980):87–109.

———. "El libro del Bedinage de Estella (1328–1331)." *Miscelanea de estudios árabes y hebráicos* 30 (1981):109–120.

———. "Acerca del préstamo judío en Tudela a fines del siglo XIV." *Principe de Viana* (Pamplona) 166–167 (1982):909–948.

———. "Los judíos de Viana y Laguardia (1350–1408): Aspectos sociales y economicos." In *Vitoria en la edad media*, pp. 419–447. Vitoria and Gasteiz, 1982.

———. "Crédito agrícola y deuda mudejaren el reíno de Navarra (1436–1441): Notas para su estudio." In *Homenaje al Profesor Dr. Dario Cabarulas Rodríguez*. Granada, 1986.

Carrete Parrondo, Carlos. *Fontes Iudaeorum Regni Castellae*. 3 vols. Salamanca, 1981–1985.

Casas i Nadal, Montserrat. "El 'Liber Judeorum' de Cardona (1330–1334): Edició I Estudi." In *Miscel·lània de textos medievals* (Barcelona) 3 (1985):119–351.

Cassandro, Michele. *Gli ebrei e il prestito ebraico a Siena nel cinquecento*. Milan, 1979.

Cassuto, Umberto. *Gli ebrei a Firenze nell'età del Rinascimento*. 2d ed., Florence, 1965.

Castaing-Sicurd, Mireille. "Le prêt à intérêt à Toulouse aux XIIe et XIIIe siècles." *Bulletin philologique et historique (jusqu'à 1715) du Comité des travaux historiques et scientifiques* (Paris), 1952–53:273–278.

———. *Les contrats dans le très ancien droit Toulousain (Xe–XIIIe siècle)*. Toulouse, 1959.

Castán Lanaspa, Guillermo. "Créditos, deudas y pagos en el área rural castellano-leonesa (siglos XI–XIV)." *Studia historica* 1 (1983): 67–85.

Castellani, Christian. "Le rôle économique de la communauté juive de Carpentras au début du XVe siècle." *Annales: ESC* 3 (1972) 583–611.

Chartrain, Frédéric. "Neuf cents créances des juifs du Buis (1327–1344)." *Cahiers de la Méditerranée*. (Nice), 1983:11–24.

———. "Le point de non-retour: L'endettement de deux communautés rurales dauphinoises envers les prêteurs italiens et juifs et l'intervention delphinale." In *Minorités et marginaux en Espagne et dans le midi de la France (VIIᵉ–XVIIIᵉ siècles)*, pp. 307–338. Paris, 1986.

Chazan, Robert. "Archbishop Guy Fulcodi of Narbonne and His Jews." *REJ* 132 (1973):587–594.

———. *Medieval Jewry in Northern France*. Baltimore and London, 1973.

———. "Confrontation in the Synagogue of Narbonne: A Christian Sermon and a Jewish Reply." *Harvard Theological Review* 67 (1974): 437–457.

———. "A Jewish Plaint to Saint Louis." *Hebrew Union College Annual* 45 (1974):287–305.

———. "Anti-usury Efforts in Thirteenth Century Narbonne and the Jewish Response." *Proceedings of the American Academy for Jewish Research* 41–42 (1973–1974): 47–67.

———. ed. *Church, State and the Jew in the Middle Ages*. New York, 1980.

Cheney, C. R. *Episcopal Visitations of Monasteries in the Thirteenth Century*. 2d ed. Manchester, 1983.

Chiffoleau, Jacques. *Les justices du pape: Délinquance et criminalité dans la région d'Avignon au XIVᵉ siècle*. Paris, 1984.

Chobaut, H. "Deux documents sur les marchands italiens établis dans le Comtat Venaissin au début du XIVᵉ siècle." *Annales d'Avignon et du Comtat Venaissin* 15 (1929):117–128.

Chomel, Vital. "Communautés rurales et *casanae* lombardes en Dauphiné (1346): Contribution au problème de l'endettement dans les sociétés paysannes du sud-est de la France au bas moyen âge." *Bulletin philologique et historique (jusqu'à 1715) du Comité des travaux historiques et scientifiques* (Paris), 1951–1952:225–247.

Ciardini, Marino. *I banchieri ebrei in Firenze nel secolo XV e il Monte di Pietà fondato da Girolamo Savonarola*. Borgo S. Lorenzo, 1907. Reprint. Florence, 1975.

Ciscato, Antonio. *Gli ebrei in Padova (1300–1800)*. Padua, 1901.

Clanchy, M. T. *From Memory to Written Record: England, 1066–1307*. Cambridge, Mass., 1979.

Clark, Elain. "Debt Litigation in a Late Medieval English Vill." In *Pathways to Medieval Peasants*, edited by J. A. Raftis, pp. 247–279. Toronto, 1981.

Collier, Raymond. "Excommunications à Moustiers- Sainte-Marie (Basses-Alpes) au début du XVe siècle." *Bulletin philologique et historique (jusqu'à 1610) du Comité des travaux historiques et scientifiques (Paris), 1962*:565–579.

Colorni, Vittore. *Judaica Minora: Saggi sulla storia dell'ebraismo italiano dall'antichità all'età moderna*. Milan, 1983.

———. "Prestito ebraico e comunità ebraiche nell'Italia centrale e settentrionale con particolare riguardo alla comunità di Mantova." Republished in his *Judaica Minora*. Milan, 1983.

Constable, Giles, ed. *Letters of Peter the Venerable*. Cambridge, Mass., 1967.

Corbella i Llobet, Ramón. *L'aljama de jueus de Vic*. 2d ed. Vich, 1984.

Cordoner y Planas, A., and Francisca Verdrell Gallostia. "Aportaciones al estudio de la familia Abenardut Médicos Reales." *Sefarad* 7 (1947):303-348.

Cornot, William (Carnotensis, Guillelmus). "De Vita et Actibus Regis Francorum Ludovici." In *Recueil des historiens des Gaules et de la France*, edited by Martin Bouquet, 20:27–41. Paris, 1840.

Coulet, Noël. *Les visites pastorales*. Turnhout, 1977.

———. *Aix-en-Provence: Espace et relations d'une capitale (milieu XIVe s. -milieu XVe s.)*. 2 vols. Aix-en-Provence, 1988.

———. "Autour d'un quinzain des métiers de la communauté juive d'Aix en 1437." In *Minorités, techniques et métiers: Actes de la Table ronde du Groupement d'intérêt scientifique Sciences humaines sur l'aire méditerranéenne, Abbaye de Sénanque, octobre 1978*, pp. 79–104. Aix-en-Provence, [1980].

Coulton, G. G. *Medieval Panorama*. New York, 1974.

Crémieux, Adolphe. "Les juifs de Marseille au moyen âge." *REJ* 46 (1903):1–47, 246–268; 47 (1903):62–86, 243–261.

Czerwinsky, Francis R. "The Teachings of the Twelfth and Thirteenth Century Canonists about the Jews." Ph.D. diss., Cornell University, 1972.

David, Marcel. "Les laboratores du renouveau économique du XIIᵉ siècle à la fin du XIVᵉ siècle." *Revue historique de droit français et étranger* 37 (1959):174–195, 295–325.

Davidsohn, Robert. *Forschungen zur Geschichte von Florenz*. 4 vols. Berlin, 1896–1908.

Day, John, *The Medieval Market Economy*. Oxford, 1987.

Degany, Ben-Zion. "The Anti-Jewish Public Opinion as a Factor towards the Expulsion of the Jews from German Towns (1440–1530)." Ph.D. diss., Hebrew University, Jerusalem, 1982. Hebrew.

Delcor, Mathias. "Les juifs de Puigcerdà au XIIIe siècle." *Sefarad* 26 (1966):32–37.

Delisle, Léopold. "Fragments d'un registre des enquêteurs de Saint Louis," *Comptes rendus de l'Académie des inscriptions et belles-lettres* 17 (1889):315–326.

———. "De Usuris Judaeorum Ut Videtur circ. Annum 1247." In *Recueil des historiens des Gaules et de la France* 24:731–744. Paris, 1904.

Demaitre, Luke E. *Doctor Bernard Gordon, Professor and Practitioner.* Toronto, 1980.

D'Entrèves, A. P. *Aquinas: Selected Political Writings.* Oxford, 1965.

Didier, Arturo. "Un banco di pegni di ebrei a Teggiano." *Rassegna storica salernitana* 4 (1987):185–195.

Dinur, Ben-Zion. *Israel in the Diaspora.* 10 vols. Tel Aviv and Jerusalem, 1966–1971. Hebrew.

Dobson, R. B. *The Jews of Medieval York and the Massacre of March 1190.* Borthwick Papers, no. 45. York, 1974.

———. "The Decline and Expulsion of the Medieval Jews of York." *Transactions of the Jewish Historical Society of England* 26 (1979): 34–52.

Duby, Georges. *Rural Economy and Country Life in the Medieval West.* Translated by C. Postan. Columbia, S.C., 1968.

———. *La société aux XIe et XIIe siècles dans la région mâconnaise.* 2d ed. Paris, 1971.

———. *William Marshall: The Flower of the Chivalry.* Translated by Richard Howard. New York, 1985.

Duchène, Roger. *Et la Provence devint française.* Paris, 1983.

Ehrle, Franz. "Ein Bruchstück der Acten des Concils von Vienne." *Archiv für Literatur- und Kirchengeschichte des Mittelalters* 4 (1888): 361–470.

Eidelberg, Shlomo. "Maarufia in Rabbenu Gershom's Responsa." *Historia Judaica* 15 (1953):59–66.

———. *The Responsa of Rabbenu Gershom Meor Hagolah.* New York, 1955. Hebrew.

———. "More on *Hezkat Yishuv*." *Tarbiz* 49 (1980):432–434. Hebrew.

Eliezer ben Nathan. *Even ha-Ezer Sefer Raban.* 2d ed. Jerusalem, 1975. Hebrew.

Eliezer ben Yehuda. *A Complete Dictionary of Ancient and Modern Hebrew.* Vol. 4. New York, 1960.

Elman, Peter. "The Economic Causes of the Expulsion of the Jews in 1290." *Economic History Review* 7 (1937):145–154.

Emery, Richard W. *The Jews of Perpignan in the Thirteenth Century: An Economic Study Based on Notarial Records.* New York, 1959.

——. "Documents concerning Jewish Scholars in Perpignan in the Fourteenth and Fifteenth Centuries." *Michael: On the History of the Jews in the Diaspora* (Tel Aviv) 4 (1976):27–48.

——. "Le prêt d'argent juif en Languedoc et Roussillon." In *Juifs et judaïsme de Languedoc*, pp. 85–96. Cahiers de Fanjeaux, vol. 12. Toulouse, 1977.

Endemann, Wilhelm. *Studien in der romanisch-kanonistischen Wirthschafts- und Rechtslehre.* Berlin, 1874.

Esmein, E. *A History of Continental Criminal Procedure.* Translated by John Simpson. New York, 1968.

Fiumi, Enrico. *Storia economica e sociale di San Gimignano.* Florence, 1961.

——. "L'attività usuraria dei mercati sangimignanesi nell'età comunale." *Archivio storico italiano* 119 (1961):145–162.

Forbin, Marquis de. "L'union de la Provence à la France, 11 décembre 1481." *Mémoires de l'Académie de Vaucluse*, 1981:19–112.

Fournier, Pierre-Fr., and Pascal Guébin. *Enquêtes administratives d'Alfonse de Poitiers: Arrêts de son parlement tenu à Toulouse et textes annexes, 1249–1271.* Paris, 1959.

García-Sanz, Arcadio. "Los intereses en los préstamos de los judíos de Vich durante la primera mitad del siglo XIV." *Ausa* 4 (1961–1963): 247–255.

——. "El Censal." *Boletín de la sociedad castellonense de cultura* 37 (1961): 281–310.

Gasnos, X. *Etude historique sur la condition des juifs dans l'ancien droit français.* Angers, 1897.

Gasparri, Françoise. "Juifs et Italiens à Orange au XIVe siècle: Métirs comparés." In *Minorités, techniques et métiers: Actes de la Table ronde du Groupement d'intérêt scientifique Sciences humaines sur l'aire méditerranéenne, Abbaye de Sénanque, octobre 1978*, pp. 47–56. Aix-en-Provence, [1980].

——. *La principauté d'Orange au moyen âge.* Paris, 1985.

Gauthier, Léon. "Les juifs des Deux-Bourgognes: Etude sur le commerce d'argent aux XIIIe et XIVe siècles." *REJ* 48 (1904):208–229; 49 (1904): 1–17, 244–261.

——. *Les Lombards dans les Deux-Bourgognes.* Paris, 1907.

Geissler, Klaus. "Die Juden in mittelalterlichen Texten Deutschlands." *Zeitschrift für bayerische Landesgeschichte* 38 (1975):163–226.

Gibral, Enrique Claudio. *Los judíos en Gerona*. Gerona, 1870. Reprinted in *Per a una história de la Girona jueva*, edited by David Romano, 1:23–114. Gerona, 1988.

Gilchrist, John T. *The Church and Economic Activity in the Middle Ages*. New York, 1969.

Giraud, Charles. *Essai sur l'histoire du droit français au moyen âge*. 2 vols. Paris, 1846.

Grabois, Arieh. "Du crédit juif à Paris au temps de Saint Louis." *REJ* 129 (1970):5–22.

Grau i Monserrat, Manuel. "La comunitat hebraica d'Olot (segle XIV)." *Amics de Besalú, II Assemblea d'Estudis del seu Comtat*, pp. 53–84. Olot (Girona), 1973.

———. "Familias judías de Besalú (siglos XIII–XIV), I, Bonanasc, Sultan y Bellcaire." *Anuario de Filología* 5 (1979):125–183.

———. "Los judíos y la nobleza en el antiguo condado de Besalú (siglo XIV)." *Annals 1978 – Patronat d'Estudis Històrics d'Olot i Comarca*, 1979:51–120.

———. "Aportacions documentals sobre la comunitat jueva de Camprodon (segles XIII–XV)." *Amics de Besalú, IV Assemblea d'Estudis del seu Comtat* 2:111–145. Olot (Girona), 1980.

———. "Els jueus a Bàscara (Girona)." *Anuario de Filología* 8 (1982): 157–168.

———. "Instrumenta Judeorum (1327–1328)." *Amics de Besalú* 5 (1983):129–179.

Grayzel, Solomon. "References to the Jews in the Correspondence of John XXII." *Hebrew Union College Annual* 23 (Part 2) (1950–51):37–80.

———. *The Church and the Jews in the Thirteenth Century*. Rev. ed. New York, 1966.

Grossman, Abraham. "The Migration of the Kalonymos Family from Italy to Germany." *Zion* 3–4 (1975):154–185.

———. "Family Lineage and Its Place in Early Ashkenazic Jewish Society." In *Studies in the History of Jewish Society in the Middle Ages and in the Modern Period* (presented to Prof. Jacob Katz), pp. 9–23. Jerusalem, 1980. Hebrew.

Guedemann, Moritz. *Geschichte des Erziehungswesens und Kultur der abendländischen Juden während des Mittelalters*. 3 vols. Vienna, 1880.

Guillemain, Bernard. *Les recettes et les dépenses de la Chambre apostolique pour la quatrième année du pontificat de Clément V (1308–1309)*. Rome, 1978.

Hamelin, A.-M., ed. *Un traité de morale économique au XIVe siècle: Le*

Tractatus de usuris de Maître Alexandre d'Alexandrie. Analecta Mediaevalia Namurcensia, vol. 14. Louvain, 1962.

Hamilton, Hans Clade. *Historia Rerum Anglicarum Willelmi Parvi . . .
de Newburgh*. 2 vols. in 1. London, 1856.

Haverkampf, Alfred. "Die Judenverfolgungen zur Zeit des Schwarzen
Todes im Gesellschaftesgefüge deutscher Städte." In *Zur Geschichte
der Juden im Deutschland des späten Mittelalters und der frühen
Neuzeit*, pp. 27–93. Stuttgart, 1980.

Hebert, Michel. *Tarascon au XIVe siècle*. Aix-en-Provence, 1979.

Hefele, Charles Joseph, and H. Leclercq. *Histoire des conciles*. Vol. 6.
Paris, 1915.

Helmholz, R. H. "Usury and the Medieval English Church Courts."
Speculum 61 (1986):364–380.

Hernando, Joseph. "El problema del crèdit i la moral a Catalunya (segle
XIV)." In *La Societat Barcelonina a la baix edat mitjana*, pp. 113–
136. Barcelona, 1982–1983.

Herskowitz, William K. "Judeo-Christian Dialogue in Provence as Reflected in Milhemet Mitzva of R. Meir Hameili." Ph.D. diss., Yeshiva University, New York, 1974.

Hinojosa Montalvo, José. "Los judíos del reíno de Valencia durante
el siglo XV." *Anales de la Universidad de Alicante* 3 (1984):
143–181.

———. "El préstamo judío en la ciudad de Valencia en la segunda mitad
del siglo XIV." *Sefarad* 45 (1985):315–339.

Hoffman, Moses. *Der Geldhandel der deutschen Juden während des Mittelalters bis zum Jahre 1350*. Leipzig, 1910.

Huillard-Bréholles, J.-L.-A. *Historia Diplomatica Frederici Secundi*.
Vol. 4, part 1. Paris, 1844.

Hyamson, A. M. *A History of the Jews in England*. London, 1908.

Iancu, Danièle. "L'expulsion des juifs de Provence à la fin du XVe
siècle: Données et problématique." *Senefiance* 5 (1978):225–237.

———. *Les juifs en Provence (1475–1501) de l'insertion à l'expulsion*.
Marseilles, 1981.

Ibanès, Jean. *La doctrine de l'Eglise et les réalités économiques au XIIIe
siècle*. Paris, 1967.

Isnard, M. Z. *Livre des privilèges de Manosque*. Paris, 1894.

———. *Inventaire sommaire chronologique des chartes, lettres patentes,
lettres missives et titres divers antérieurs à 1500*. Marseilles, 1939.

Jacobs, Joseph. *The Jews of Angevin England*. London, 1893.

Jacoby, David. "Les juifs à Venise au XIVe siècle." In his *Recherches
sur la Méditerranée orientale du XIIe au XVe siècle: peuples, sociétés,
économies*. London, 1979. First published in *Venezia, centro di me-*

diazione tra Oriente ed Occidente (secoli XV–XVI): Aspetti e problemi: Atti del II Convegno internazionale di storia della civiltà veneziana, Venezia, 1973. Vol. 1. Florence, 1977.

Jenkinson, Hilary. "William Cade, a Financier of the Twelfth Century." *English Historical Review* 110 (1913):209–227, 731–732.

——. *Calendar of the Plea Rolls of the Exchequer of the Jews.* Vol. 3. London, 1929.

Jenks, Stuart. "Judenverschuldung und Verfolgung von Juden im 14. Jahrhundert: Franken bis 1349." *Vierteljahrsschrift für Sozial- und Wirtschaftsgeschichte* 65 (1978):309–356.

Jordan, E. *De Mercatoribus Camerae Apostolicae.* Condate Rhedonum [i.e., Rennes], 1909.

Jordan, William C. "Jews on Top: Women and the Availability of Consumption Loans in Northern France in the Mid-Thirteenth Century." *Journal of Jewish Studies* 29 (1978):39–56.

——. "Jewish-Christian Relations in Mid-Thirteenth Century France: An Unpublished *Enquête* from Picardy." *REJ* 138 (1979):47–55.

——. *Louis IX and the Challenge of the Crusade.* Princeton, 1979.

——. "An Aspect of Credit in Picardy in the 1240's: The Deterioration of Jewish-Christian Financial Relations." *REJ* 142 (1983): 141–152.

——. "Christian Excommunication of the Jews in the Middle Ages: A Restatement of the Issues." *Jewish History* 1 (1986):31–38.

Kaeuper, Richard W. *Bankers to the Crown: The Riccardi of Lucca and Edward I.* Princeton, 1973.

Kahn, Salomon. "Les juifs de Tarascon au moyen âge." *REJ* 39 (1899): 95–112, 261–298.

——. "Documents inédits sur les juifs de Montpellier au moyen âge." *REJ* 19 (1889):259–281; 22 (1891):264–279; 23 (1891):265–278; 28 (1894):131–132.

——. "Les juifs de la Sénéchaussée de Beaucaire." *REJ* 65 (1913):181–195; 66 (1913):75–97.

Katz, Jacob. *The Sabbath Gentile.* Jerusalem, 1983. Hebrew.

Kimhi, Joseph. *The Book of the Covenant.* Translated by Frank Talmage. Toronto, 1972.

Kirschenbaum, Aaron. "Jewish and Christian Theories of Usury in the Middle Ages." *Jewish Quarterly Review* 75 (1985):270–289.

Kisch, Guido. *Jewry-Law in Medieval Germany.* New York, 1949.

——. *The Jews in Medieval Germany: A Study of Their Legal and Social Status.* 2d ed. New York, 1970.

——. *Forschungen zur Rechts- und Sozialgeschichte der Juden in Deutschland während des Mittelalters.* 2 vols. Sigmaringen, 1978.

Kobak, Joseph Isaac. "The Epistle of R. Jacob of Venice." *Jeschurun: Zeitschrift für die Wissenschaft des Judenthums* (Lemberg) 6 (1868): 1–34. Hebrew.

Kohn, Roger. "Les juifs de la France du Nord à travers les archives du parlement de Paris (1359?–1394)" *REJ* 141 (1982):5–138.

Kriegel, Maurice. "Mobilisation politique et modernisation organique: Les expulsions de juifs au bas moyen âge." *Archives des sciences sociales des religions* 46 (1978):5–20.

———. "La prise d'une décision: L'expulsion des juifs d'Espagne en 1492." *Revue historique* 260 (1978):49–90.

———. *Les juifs à la fin du moyen âge dans l'Europe méditerranéenne.* Paris, 1979.

de Laborde, Joseph. *Layettes du Trésor des chartes.* Vol. 3. Paris, 1875.

Lane, Frederick C. "Investment and Usury in Medieval Venice." *Explorations in Entrepreneurial History*, 2d ser., 2 (1964–1965):3–15.

Langholm, Odd. *The Aristotelian Analysis of Usury.* Bergen, 1984.

Langlois, Charles V. *La vie en France au moyen âge.* Paris, 1926.

Langmuir, Gavin I. "The Jews and the Archives of Angevine England: Reflections on Medieval Antisemitism." *Traditio* 19 (1963)1:83–243.

de La Roncière, Charles. *Un changeur florentin du trecento: Lippo di Fede del Sega.* Paris, 1973.

Laurent, M.-H. *Le culte de s. Louis d'Anjou à Marseille au XIVe siècle.* Rome, 1954.

de Laurière, Eusèbe Jacob, et al., eds. *Ordonnances des roys de France de la troisième race.* 22 vols. Paris, 1723–1849.

Lavoie, Rodrigue, "Endettement et pauvreté en Provence d'après les listes de la justice comtale." *Provence historique* 23 (1973):201–216.

Lazard, Lucien. "Les juifs de Touraine." *REJ* 17 (1888):210–234.

Le Bras, G. "Usure, l'époque classique." *Dictionnaire de théologie catholique*, vol. 15 (Paris, 1950), p. 2354.

Le Goff, Jacques. *Marchands et banquiers du moyen âge.* Paris, 1972.

———. "The Usurer and Purgatory." In *The Dawn of Modern Banking.* New Haven and London, 1979.

———. *La naissance du Purgatoire.* Paris, 1981.

———. *La bourse et la vie.* Paris, 1986. Translated by Patricia Ranum as *Your Money or Your Life: Economy and Religion in the Middle Ages.* New York, 1988.

León Tello, Pilar. *Judíos de Toledo.* 2 vols. Madrid, 1979.

Leroy, Béatrice. "Les comptes d'Abraham Euxoep au début du XVe siècle." *Príncipe de Viana* 146–147 (1977):177–205.

———. "Le royaume de Navarre et les juifs aux XIVe et XVe siècles: entre l'accueil et la tolérance." *Sefarad* 38 (1978) 263–292.

——. "La vie économique des juifs de Navarre au XIVe siècle." In *Jews and Conversos: Studies in Society and the Inquisition*, edited by Yosef Kaplan, pp. 39–61. Jerusalem, 1981.

——. "Recherches sur les juifs de Navarre à la fin du moyen âge." *REJ* 140 (1981):319–432.

——. "De l'activité d'un juif de Navarre, fin du 14e siècle." *Archives juives* 17 (1981):1–6.

——. *The Jews of Navarre in the late Middle Ages*. Jerusalem, 1985.

Leroy, Béatrice, and Mercedes García-Arendal. *Moros y judíos en Navarra en la baja edad media*. Madrid, 1984.

Lesage, Georges. *Marseille angevine*. Paris, 1950.

Liebermann, Felix. *Die Gesetze der Angelsachsen*. Berlin, 1903.

Liebeschütz, Hans. "Judaism and Jewry in the Social Doctrine of Thomas Aquinas." *Journal of Jewish Studies* 13 (1962):57–81.

Lifschitz-Golden, Manya. *Les juifs dans la littérature française du moyen âge: Mystères, miracles, chroniques*. New York, 1967.

Lindo, E. H. *The History of the Jews of Spain and Portugal*. 2d ed. New York, 1970.

Lipman, Vivian D. *The Jews of Medieval Norwich*. London, 1967.

Little, Lester K. *Religious Poverty and the Profit Economy in Medieval Europe*. London, 1978.

Loeb, Isidore. "Deux livres de commerce du commencement du XIVe siècle." *REJ* 8 (1884):161–196; 9 (1884):21–50, 187–213.

——. "Les expulsions des juifs de France au XIVe siècle." In *Jubelschrift zum siebzigsten Geburtstage des Prof. Dr. H. Graetz*. Breslau, 1887. pp. 39–56.

——. "Le procès de Samuel Ibn Tibbon, Marseille, 1255." *REJ* 15 (1887):70–98; 16 (1888):124–37.

Lopez Elum, Pedro. "Datos sobre la usura en Navarra en los comienzos del siglo XIV." *Príncipe de Viana* 32 (1971):257–262.

Lorcin, Marie-Thérèse. "Vieillesse et vieillissement vus par les médecins du moyen âge." *Bulletin du Centre d'histoire économique et sociale de la région lyonnaise* 4 (1983):5–22.

Luard, Henry Richards, ed. *Matthaei Parisiensis, Monachi Sancti Albani, Chronica Majora*. 7 vols. London, 1872–1883.

Luard, M. A., ed. *Letters of Robert Grosseteste Illustrative of the Social Conditions of His Time*. London, 1891.

Luchaire, Achille. *Social France at the Time of Philip Augustus*. Translated by Edward B. Krehbiel. New York, n.d.

Luzzatto, Gino. *I banchieri ebrei in Urbino nell'età ducale*. Padua, 1902.

——. "Tasso d'interesse e usura a Venezia nei secoli XIII–XV." In *Miscellanea in onore di Roberto Cessi* 1:191–202. Rome, 1958.

Mabilly, Philippe. *Les villes de Marseille au moyen âge: Ville supérieure et ville de la prévôté, 1257–1348.* Marseilles, 1905.

——. *Inventaire sommaire des archives communales antérieures à 1790.* Marseilles, 1907.

McLaughlin, T. P. "The Teaching of the Canonists on Usury (XII, XIII, XIV Centuries)." *Mediaeval Studies* 1 (1939):81–147; 2 (1940):1–22.

Magdalena-Nom de Deu, J. R. "Juramentos de prestamistas y corredores judíos en Castellón de la Plana (1441–1448)." *Anuario de filología* (Barcelona) 3 (1977):215–223.

Malaussena, Paul-Louis. *La vie en Provence orientale aux XIVe et XVe siècles.* Paris, 1969.

Mansi, Giovanni Domenico, et al., eds. *Sacrorum Conciliorum Nova et Amplissima Collectio.* 53 vols. Florence and Rome, 1757–1927.

Marcus, Jacob R. *The Jew in the Medieval World.* 2d ed. New York, 1972.

Marcus, Ivan S. *Piety and Society.* London, 1981.

Mate, Mavis. "The Indebtedness of Canterbury Cathedral Priory, 1215–1299." *Economic History Review,* 2d ser., 26 (1973):183–197.

Mazzoni Tosselli, Ottavio. *Racconti storici estratti dell'archivio criminale di Bologna.* Bologna, 1866.

Meir ben Baruch of Rothenburg. *The Responsa of Meir of Rothenburg.* Berlin, 1891. Reprint. Jerusalem, 1968. Hebrew.

Menache, Sophia. "Faith, Myth and Politics—the Stereotype of Jews and their Expulsion from England and France." *Jewish Quarterly Review* 75 (1985):351–374.

Menkes, F. "Une communauté juive en Provence au XIVe siècle: Étude d'un groupe social." *Le moyen âge* 26 (1971):279–295.

Merhavia, H. "Concerning the Date of A. Meir ben Simon's Milhemet Mizva." *Tarbiz* 45 (1976):296–331. Hebrew.

Michaelson, H. *The Jews in Early English Literature.* Amsterdam, 1926.

Millás i Vallicrosa, J. "Petita lista d'un Prestamista Jueu." *Estudis Universitaris Catalans* 12 (1927):65–67.

Mirambell Belloc, Eric. "Els protocols notarials històrics de Castellò d'Empuries Separates." *Annals de l'Institut d'estudis empordanensos,* 1977:217–231.

Molho, Antony. "A Note on Jewish Moneylending in Tuscany in the Late Trecento and Early Quattrocento." In *Renaissance Studies in Honor of Hans Baron.* Edited by Antony Molho and John A. Tedeschin, pp. 101–117. Florence and De Kalb, Ill., 1971.

Müller, Ewald. *Das Konzil von Vienne, 1311–1312: Seine Quellen und seine Geschichte.* Münster in Westfalen, 1934.

Mudeller, Reinhold C. "Les prêteurs juifs de Venise au moyen âge." *Annales:ESC* 30 (1975):1277–1302.

Mundy, John H. *Liberty and Political Power in Toulouse, 1050–1230.* New York, 1954.

———. "Un usurier malheureux." *Annales du Midi* 68 (1956):217–228.

———. *Europe in the High Middle Ages, 1150–1309.* New York, 1973.

Nahon, Gérard. "Les juifs dans les domaines d'Alfonse de Poitiers, 1241–1271." *REJ* 125 (1966):167–211.

———. "Le crédit et les juifs dans la France du XIIIe siècle." *Annales: ESC* 24 (1969):1121–1148.

———. "Les ordonnances de saint Louis sur les juifs." *Les nouveaux cahiers* 6 (1970):18–35.

———. "Documents sur les juifs de Normandie médiévale au Public Record Office de Londres." *Archives juives* 11 (1975):3–10.

———. "Condition fiscale et economique des juifs." *Cahiers de Fanjeaux* 12 (*Juifs et judaïsme de Languedoc*) (1977):51–84.

Nelson, Benjamin. "The Usurer and the Merchant Prince: Italian Businessmen and the Ecclesiastical Law of Restitution, 1100–1150." *The Tasks of Economic History*, 1947, suppl. 7 to *Journal of Economic History*, pp. 104–122.

———. *The Idea of Usury: From Tribal Brotherhood to Universal Otherhood.* Chicago and London, 1969.

Neumann, Max. *Geschichte des Wuchers in Deutschland bis zur Begründung des heutigen Zinsgesetzes 1654.* Halle, 1865.

Newman, Louis I. *Jewish Influence on Christian Reform Movements.* New York, 1925.

Noonan, John T. *The Scholastic Analysis of Usury.* Cambridge, Mass., 1957.

Ollich i Castanyer, Immaculada. "Aspects Econòmics de l'Activitatdels Jueus de Vic, segon els 'Libri judeorum' (1266–1278)." *Miscellànea de Textos Medievals* (Barcelona) 3 (1985):7–118.

Ovrut, Bennett, D. "Edward I and the Expulsion of the Jews." *Jewish Quarterly Review* 67 (1977):224–235.

Painter, Sidney. *William Marshall.* Baltimore, 1933.

———. *French Chivalry.* New York, 1940.

Papon, J. P. *Histoire générale de la Provence.* 4 vols. Paris, 1775–1786.

Parkes, James. *The Jew in the Medieval Community.* 2d ed. New York, 1976.

Patres Collegii S. Bonaventurae. *Processus canonizationis et Legendae Variae Sancti Ludovici, O.F.M.* Analecta Franciscana, vol. 7. Quaracchi, 1951.

Patrone, Anna Maria. *Le casane astigiane in Savoia.* Turin, 1959.

Patroni Griffi, Filena. *Il banco di pegni di Cava dei Tirreni del 1495.* Cava dei Tirreni, 1985.

Paul, Jacques. "Témoignage historique et hagiographique dans le procès de canonisation de Louis d'Anjou." *Provence historique* 23 (1973):305–317.

——. "Le 'Liber miraculorum' de saint Louis d'Anjou." *Archivum Franciscanum Historicum* 69 (1976):209–219.

——. "Le rayonnement géographique du pèlerinage au tombeau de Louis d'Anjou." In *Le pèlerinage*, pp. 137–158. Cahiers de Fanjeaux, vol. 15. Toulouse, 1980.

Pernoud, Régine. *Les statuts municipaux de Marseille.* Monaco and Paris, 1949.

Perroy, Edouard. "À l'origine d'une économie contractée: Les crises du XIVe siècle." *Annales:ESC* 4 (1949):167–182.

Perry, F. *Saint Louis: The Most Christian King.* New York and London, 1901.

Peter Abelard. *Dialogue of a Philosopher with a Jew and a Christian.* Translated by Pierre J. Payer. Toronto, 1979.

Pirenne, Henri. "La duchesse aleyde de Brabant et de régimine judeorum." *Académie Royale de Belgique: Bulletin de la classe des lettres et des sciences morales et politiques*, 5th ser., 14, no. 3 (1928): 43–55.

Poliakov, Léon. *The History of Anti-Semitism.* 2 vols. Translated by Richard Howard and Natalie Gerardi. London, 1974.

——. *Jewish Bankers and the Holy See from the Thirteenth to the Seventeenth Century.* Translated by Miriam Kochan. London and Boston, 1977.

Pons, Antonio. *Los Judíos del Reíno de Mallorca durante los siglos XIII y XIV.* 2 vols. Palma de Mallorca, 1984.

Poppe, Danuta. *Economie et société d'un bourg provençal au XIVe siècle, Rhillanne en haute Provence.* Wroclaw, Warsaw, Krakow, Gdansk, 1980.

Portal, Félix. *Un procès en responsabilité médicale à Marseille en 1390.* Marseilles, 1902.

——. *La république marseillaise du XIIIe siècle (1200–1263).* Marseilles, 1907.

Powell, James M., trans. *The Liber Augustalis, or Constitutions of Melfi, Promulgated by the Emperor Frederick II for the Kingdom of Sicily in 1231.* Syracuse, N.Y., 1971.

Prestwich, Michael. "Italian Merchants in Late Thirteenth and Early Fourteenth Century England." In *The Dawn of Modern Banking*, pp. 77–104. New Haven and London, 1979.

Prudhomme, A. "Notes et documents sur les juifs du Dauphiné." *REJ* 9 (1884):231–263.

Pugh, Ralph B. "Some Medieval Moneylenders." *Speculum* 43 (1968):274–289.

Quifah, Joseph David, ed. *Responsa of Yomtob ben Abraham al-Ishbili.* Jerusalem, 1959. Hebrew.

Ragazzini, Giuseppe. *Ebrei e usurai nella società e nel dramma elisabettiani.* Bologna, 1988.

Ramírez Vaquero, Eloisa. "Cartas tornadas y quenaces." *Sefarad* 44 (1984):75–141.

Ravid, Benjamin. "Moneylending in Seventeenth Century Jewish Vernacular Apologia." In *Jewish Thought in the Seventeenth Century*, edited by Isadore Twersky and Bernard Septimus, pp. 257–283. Cambridge, Mass., 1987.

Régné, Jean. *Etude sur la condition des juifs de Narbonne du Ve au XIVe siècle.* 2d ed. Marseilles, 1981.

———. *History of the Jews in Aragon: Regesta and Documents, 1213–1327.* Edited by Y. T. Assis and A. Gruzmann. Jerusalem, 1978.

Renan, Ernest. *Les écrivains juifs français du XIVe siècle.* Paris, 1893. Extract of *L'histoire littéraire de la France*, vol. 31.

Renouard, Yves. *Les relations des papes d'Avignon et des compagnies commerciales et bancaires de 1316 à 1378.* Paris, 1941.

Reyerson, Kathryn. "Les opérations de crédit dans la coutume et dans la vie des affaires à Montpellier au moyen âge: Le problème de l'usure." In *Diritto comune e diritti locali nella storia dell'Europa: Atti del Convegno di Varenna*, pp. 189–209. Milan, 1980.

———. *Business, Banking and Finance in Medieval Montpellier.* Toronto, 1985.

Richardson, H. G. *Calendar of the Plea Rolls of the Exchequer of the Jews.* Vol. 4. London, 1972.

———. *The English Jewry under Angevin Kings.* London, 1960.

Rigg, J. M. *Calendar of the Plea Rolls of the Exchequer of the Jews.* Vol. 1. 2d ed. London, 1971.

Rius Serra, José. "Aportaciones sobre médicos judíos en Aragón en la primera mitad del siglo XIV." *Sefarad* 12 (1952):337–350.

Rivkind, Isaac. *The Fight against Gambling among the Jews: A Study of Five Centuries of Jewish Poetry and Cultural History.* New York, 1946. Yiddish.

Robert, Ulysse. "Catalogue d'actes relatifs aux juifs pendant le moyen âge." *REJ* 3 (1981):211–224.

Rodríguez Fernández, Justiniano. *La judería de la ciudad de León.* León, 1969.

Rogozinski, Jan. *Power, Caste and Law: Social Conflict in Fourteenth Century Montpellier.* Cambridge, Mass., 1982.

Romano, David. "Protócolos judíos de Cardona (siglo XIV)." *Sefarad* 32 (1972):371–372.

——. "Les juifs de la couronne d'Aragon avant 1391." *REJ* 141 (1982):169–182.

——, ed. *Per a una historià de la Girona jueva*. Vols. 1–2. Girona, 1988.

——. "Prestadores judíos en los estados hispánicos medievales." *Estudios Mirandeses* 8 (1988): 117–126.

de Roover, Raymond, *Money, Banking and Credit in Mediaeval Bruges*. Cambridge, Mass., 1948.

——. *The Rise and Decline of the Medici Bank*. New York, 1966.

——. *La pensée économique des scolastiques: Doctrines et méthodes*. Montréal, 1971.

Rosenthal, Judah. *Studies and Sources*. 2 vols. Jerusalem, 1967. Hebrew.

——. "A Religious Disputation between the Scholar Menahem and the Convert and Dominican Friar Paolo Christiani." *Hebrew Thought in America* 3 (1974):61–71.

Roth, Bezalel (Cecil). *A History of the Jews in Italy*. Tel Aviv, 1962. Hebrew.

Roth, Cecil. *A History of the Jews in England*. 2d ed. Oxford, 1964.

——. *The Jews of Medieval Oxford*. Oxford, 1951.

Rutkowska-Plachcinska, Anna. *Salon-de-Provence: Une société urbaine du bas moyen âge*. Wroclaw, Warsaw, etc., 1982.

Saige, Gustave. *Les juifs du Languedoc antérieurement au XIVe siècle*. Paris, 1881.

de Saint-Paul, P., ed. *Thalamus Parvus: Le petit Thalamus de Montpellier*. Montpellier, 1840.

Salvioli, Giuseppe. "La dottrina dell'usura secondo i canonisti e i civilisti italiani dei secoli XIII e XIV." In *Studi giuridici in onore di Carlo Fedda*. 2:261–272. Naples, 1906.

Santschi, Elisabeth. "Aspects de la justice en Crète vénitienne d'après les memoriali du XIVe siecle." *Kretika Chronica* (Heraklion) 2 (1972):294–324.

——. "Contribution à l'étude de la communauté juive en Crète vénitienne au XIVe siècle, d'après des sources administratives et judiciaires." *Studi veneziani* 15 (1973):177–211.

Sanz Artibucilla, José María. "Los judíos en Aragón y Navarra." *Sefarad* 5 (1945):337–366.

Saperstein, Marc. *Decoding the Rabbis: A Thirteenth-Century Commentary on the Aggadah*. Cambridge, Mass., 1980.

Sapori, Armando. "Usura nel dugento a Pistoia." In his *Studi di storia economica* 1:181–189. Florence, 1955.

——. *The Italian Merchant in the Middle Ages*. Translated by Patricia Ann Kennen. New York, 1970.

Schäfer, Karl Heinrich. *Die Ausgaben der apostolischen Kammer unter Johann XXII.* Paderborn, 1911.

Schaub, Franz. *Der Kampf gegen den Zinswucher ungerechten Preis und unlautern Handel im Mittelalter.* Freiburg im Breisgau, 1905.

Schnapper, Bernard. "La répression de l'usure et l'évolution économique (XIIIe–XVIe siècles)." *Tijdschrift voor rechtsgescheidenis* 37 (1969):47–75.

Schnerb-Lièvre, M. *Le songe du vergier.* 2 vols. Paris, 1982.

Schreiber, Abraham, ed. *Responsa of the Sages of Provence.* Jerusalem, 5727 [= 1967]. Hebrew.

Secall i Grüel, Gabriel. *Els Jueus de Valls in la seva poca.* Valls, 1980.

———. "Algunos aspectos de la judería de Valls según un Liber Judeorum (1342–1344)." *Sefarad* 44 (1984):144–178.

Segre, Renata. "Testimonianze documentarie sugli ebrei negli stati Sabaudi (1297–1398)." *Michael: On the History of the Jews in the Diaspora* 4:273–413. Tel Aviv, 1976.

———. "Bernardino da Feltre, i Monti di Pietà e i banchi ebraici." *Rivista storica italiana* 90 (1978):818–833.

———. *The Jews in Piedmont.* Vol. 1. Jerusalem, 1986.

Shachar, Isaiah. *The Judensau: A Medieval Anti-Jewish Motif and Its History.* London, 1974.

Shachar, Shulamit. "The Jews in the Eyes of Court Writers and Their Status by Royal Decrees in the Reign of Charles V of France." *Zion* 33 (1960):1–14. Hebrew.

Shatzmiller, Joseph. "Petite épitre de l'excuse." *Sefunot* 10 (1966):9–52. Hebrew.

———. *Recherches sur la communauté juive de Manosque au moyen âge, 1241–1329.* Paris and The Hague, 1973.

———. "Une experiénce universitaire méconnue: Le studium de Manosque, 1245–1247." *Provence historique* 24 (1974):468–490.

———. "Documents de la communauté d'Aix-en-Provence (1336)" *Michael: On the History of the Jews in the Diaspora* (Tel Aviv) 4 (1976):414–445.

———. "Structures communautaires juives à Marseille: Autour d'un contrat de 1278." *Provence historique* 28 (1979):33–45.

———. "Desecrating the Cross: A Rare Medieval Accusation." *Studies in the History of the Jewish People and the Land of Israel* (Haifa) 5 (1980):159–173. Hebrew.

———. "Jews Separated from the Communion of the Faithful in Christ in the Middle Ages." In *Studies in Medieval Jewish History and Literature,* edited by Isadore Twersky, 1:307–314. Cambridge, Mass., 1979.

――――"Paulus Christiani, un aspect de son activité anti-juive." In *Hommage à Georges Vajda*, pp. 203–217. Louvain, 1980.

Silvestri, Alfonso. "Gli ebrei nel regno di Napoli durante la dominazione aragonese." *Campania Sacra* 18 (1987):21–77.

Simon de Beaulieu. "Visites du diocèse de Cahors par Simon de Beaulieu, archevêque de Bourges, 1285–6, 1290–1." *Bulletin de l'Académie impériale des sciences, arts et belles-lettres de Dijon.* 2d ser., 13 (1866):145–272.

Simonnet, Jules. "Juifs et Lombards en Bourgogne." *Mémoires de l'Académie impériale des sciences, arts et belles-lettres de Dijon,* 2d ser., 13 (1866): 145–272.

Simonsohn, Shlomo. "On the History of the Rieti Banking Family in Tuscany." *Studies in the History of the Jewish People and the Land of Israel* 4 (1978):183–203. Hebrew.

――――. *The Jews of the Duchy of Milan.* 4 vols. Jerusalem, 1982.

――――. *The Apostolic See and the Jews: Documents, 492–1404.* Toronto, 1988.

Sivéry, Gérard. "Mouvements de capitaux et taux d'intérêt en Occident au XIIIe siècle." *Annales:ESC* 38 (1983):137–150.

Smyrl, Edwin. "La famille des Baux." *Cahiers du centre d'études des sociétés méditerranéennes* (Aix-en-Provence) 2 (1968):7–108.

Soloveitchik, Haym. *Pawnbroking: A Study of the Interrelationship between Halakha, Economic Activity and Communal Self-Image.* Jerusalem, 1985. Hebrew.

――――. *Halacha and Economy in the Middle Ages.* 2 vols. Jerusalem, 1973. Hebrew.

Stein, Sigmund. "Interest from the Foreigner." *Journal of Jewish Studies* 1 (1956):141–164.

――――. *Jewish-Christian Disputations in Thirteenth Century Narbonne.* London, 1964.

――――. "A Disputation on Moneylending between Jews and Gentiles in Me'ir ben Simeon's Milhemet Misvah." *Tarbiz* 45 (1976):296–302. Hebrew.

Steinschneider, Moritz. *Die hebräischen Übersetzungen des Mittelalters und die Juden als Dolmetscher.* Berlin, 1893.

――――. *Gesammelte Schriften.* Berlin, 1925.

Stengers, Jean. *Les juifs dans les Pays-Bas au moyen âge.* Brussels, 1950.

Stouff, Louis. "Un aspect de la haute-provence à la fin de la période médiévale: Peuplement, économie et societé de quelques villages de la Montagne de Lure, 1250–1450." *Cahiers du Centre d'études des sociétés méditerranéennes* 1 (1966):35–109.

――――. "Les registres de notaires d'Arles (début XIVe siècle–1460).

Quelques problèmes posés par l'utilisation des archives notariales." *Provence historique* 25 (1975):305–324.

———. "Activités et professions dans une communauté juive de Provence au bas moyen âge—La juiverie d'Arles, 1400–1450." In *Minorités, techniques et métiers: Actes de la Table ronde du Groupement d'intérêt scientifique Sciences humaines sur l'aire méditerranéenne, Abbaye de Sénanque, octobre 1978*, pp. 57–77. Aix-en-Provence, [1980].

———. *Arles à la fin du moyen âge*. 2 vols. Aix-en-Provence and Lille, 1986.

Stow, Kenneth R. "Papal and Royal Attitudes towards Jewish Moneylending in the Thirteenth Century." *Association for Jewish Studies Review* 6 (1981):161–184.

Strayer, Joseph. *The Administration of Normandy under Saint Louis*. Cambridge, Mass., 1932.

von Stromer, Wolfgang, and Michael Toch. "Zur Buchführung der Juden im Spätmittelalter." In *Wirtschaftskräfte und Wirtschaftswege: Festschrift für Hermann Kellenbenz*, edited by Jürgen Schneider et al., 1:387–410. Beiträge zur Wirtschaftsgeschichte, vol. 4. [Stuttgart], 1978.

Toaff, Ariel. *Gli ebrei a Perugia*. Perugia, 1975.

———. *The Jews in Medieval Assisi, 1305–1487*. Florence, 1979.

———. "Jewish Banking in Central Italy in the 13th–15th Centuries." In *Jews in Italy: Studies Published on the Occasion of the One Hundredth Birthday of M. D. Cassuto*, pp. 109–130. Jerusalem, 1987. Hebrew.

Toch, Michael. "Geld und Kredit in einer spätmittelalterlichen Landschaft." *Deutches Archiv für Erforschung des Mittelalters* 38 (1982):499–550.

———. "Business Techniques of Medieval German Jews: New Evidence from South Germany." In *Proceedings of the Eighth World Congress of Jewish Studies*, Div. B, pp. 47–50. Jerusalem, 1982. Hebrew.

Todeschini, Giacomo. *Un trattato di economia politica francescana: Il "De emptionibus et venditionibus, de usuris, de restitutionibus" di Pietro di Giovanni Olivi*. Rome, 1980.

———. "Teorie economiche degli ebrei alla fine del medioevo: Storia di una presenza consapevole." *Quaderni storici* 52 (1983):181–225.

Tovey, D'Blossiers. *Anglia Judaica*. Oxford, 1738.

Toynbee, Margaret R. *S. Louis of Toulouse and the Process of Canonisation in the Fourteenth Century*. Manchester, 1929.

Trachtenberg, Joshua. *The Devil and the Jews: The Medieval Conception of the Jew and Its Relation to Modern Antisemitism*. 2d ed. New York and Philadelphia, 1961.

Tucoo-Chala, P., ed. *Minorités et marginaux en Espagne et dans le midi de la France (VIIe-XVIIIe siècles)*. Paris, 1986.

Twersky, Isadore. "Aspects of the Social and Cultural History of Provençal Jewry." *Journal of World History* 11 (1968):185–207.

Urbach, Ephriam. *The Tosaphists: Their History, Writings and Methods.* 2 vols. 4th ed. Jerusalem, 1980. Hebrew.

Vidal, Pierre. "Les juifs des anciens comtés de Roussillon et de Cerdagne." *REJ* 15 (1887):19–55; 16 (1888):1–23, 170–203.

Vincent, Dr. "Les juifs du Poitou au bas moyen âge." *Revue d'histoire économique et sociale* 18 (1930):265–313.

Viner, Jacob. *Religious Thought and Economic Society.* Durham, N.C., 1979.

Vuitry, Adolphe. *Etudes sur le régime financier de la France avant la révolution de 1789.* Paris, 1978.

Wenninger, Markus J. *Man bedarf keiner Juden mehr.* Vienna, Cologne, Graz, 1981.

Wernham, Monique. *La communauté juive de Salon-de-Provence d'après les actes notariés, 1391–1453.* Toronto, 1987.

Wistinetzki, Jehuda, ed. *Das Buch der Frommen (Sefer hasidim).* 2d ed. Frankfurt am Main, 1924. Hebrew.

Wolff, Philippe. "Le problème des Cahorsins." *Annales du Midi* 62 (1950):229–238.

Zarb, Mireille. *Les privilèges de la ville de Marseille du Xe siècle à la Révolution.* Paris, 1961.

Index

Aaron ha-Hedri (Aaron de Camera), 28, 33, 108
Abelard, Peter, 96
Abraham de Aquis, 28
Abraham de Bellicadro, 33
Abraham de Castellana, 20
Abraham de Draguigan, 8, 10, 11, 108; will of, 29, 32, Appendix 2
Abraham of Grasse, 16
Abrahim Arapinaz, 56
Acciaiuoli company (Florence), 88
Acre, fall of, 125
Adelaide of Brabant, countess, 61, 63
Aix-en-Provence: delays in repayments of debts in, 10; Jewish population, 31; notarial records, analysis of, 75
Alais, 54
Alasacia Rogerie, 16
Albert the Great, 45
Albi, 51–52
Albigensian War, anti-usury campaign during, 69
Albrecht, king of Germany, 66
Alcalá de Hénares, reform laws enacted at, 63
Alfonso X, king of Castile, 54
Alfonso XI, king of Castile, 62, 63
Alphonse of Poitiers, 59, 60
Altama vel Nigduy (excommunication) of Jewish moneylenders, 55
"Amelioration" of Jews, 63–65
Andreas Bonvini, 109, 110, 111, 118
Angevins, 109
Angy, 66
Anjou, expulsion of Jews from, 65
Anselm of Canterbury, 45
Anselm of Lucca, 45

Aquileia, 52
Aquinas, Saint Thomas, 45, 61, 63, 95
Aragon, 55–58; fines levied for usury in, 56–58; interest rate established in, 53, 55; Jewish communities accused of usury by monarchy, 57–58; laws against usury, 55–56; oath taken by Jews in, 55–58
Archambaud of Bourbon, count, 62–64
Archives des Bouche-du-Rhône, Provence (Marseilles) 2, 105
Aristocracy, loans sought from Christians by, 73
Arles, 52; ecclesiastical court, 13; expulsion of Jews from, 67; moneylending from Jews, analysis of, 75–76; notarial records, 74; statutes on possession of promissory notes, 15
Arnaud de Baux, 108, 109, 116, 118
Asher ben Yehiel, 102
Assis, Yom Tov, 86
Astrugus de Nemanso, 33
Attitudes toward moneylending, 43–44, 67–68, 70, 79–84
Aubenas, Roger, 13
Augier de Mar, 112
Avraham of Aix, 28

Banking houses: in Italy, 89; Jewish, attack on, 48
Baratier, Edouard, 34
Barcelona, 56, 57
Bardi company (Florence), 88
Barral de Baux, 109
Bartholomeo de Geminis, 41

Baux family, 109
Beaucaire, 98–99
ben Simeon, Meir. *See* Meir ben Simeon of Narbonne
Beniounus de Sarrato, 16
Bermundi family, 110
Bernandus Assis, 36
Bernard of Parma, 24
Bernardino da Feltre, 48
Bernardino of Siena, Saint, 80
Berthold of Regensberg, 47
Bessalu, 99
Betrandus Feda, 36
Béziers, 51
Black Death (1348–1349), 72; Jews accused of, 49
Boccaccio, Giovanni, *Decameron*, 37
Bocchi, Francesca, 84
Bonafos de Cezerista, 33
Bonafos Juceff, 57
Bonafos of Manosque, 20
Bondavid of Draguignan: accusations of usury against, 24; age at time of trial, 32; character of, 112–118; characteristics as moneylender, 116–117; children of, 29–30; code of behavior, 117; family history, 29–31; financial record of, 21; financial standing, 34; inquest against (1328), 24; loan to Laurentius, 6, 7; *mandamenta* issued for, 10, 11, 12; out-of-court settlement refused by, 22, 25–26; personal history of, 28–35; praise of witnesses for, 112–118; value of sixty shillings to, 9, 11. *See also* Bondavid of Draguignan, trial of
Bondavid of Draguignan, trial of (Marseilles, 1317), 2, 5–26, 123–124, Appendix 1; character witnesses, 7; chronology, 104–105; collateral not mentioned in, 6; credibility of Petrus Guizo, 35–40; credibility of testimonies of witnesses, 40–42; date of final decision, 6; documentation of proceedings, 105–107; no evidence of usurious interest in, 22; statements of Bondavid's opponents, 119; value of money involved, 87–89; witnesses' attitudes toward Jewish moneylenders, 103;

witnesses' attitudes toward moneylending, 70, 71–72; witnesses called by Bondavid, 107–112; witnesses' testimony on character of Bondavid, 107, 112–118
Bondavinus Abrahami, 29
Bondavinus Abramati, 34
Bonetus Aurioli, 22, 104, 106, 112, 114, 117
Bonetus de Vivarius, 33
Bonfos Vidal, 56
Bonefellii, 117
Bontosius Mercerii, 16
Bonvini family, 110
Bontinus, 16, 21

Cahorsins, 97
Carpentras, 77
Castellane, size of loans made in, 77
Castres, 52
Catalonia, 68, 102
Charles II, 23; edict on usurers, 23, 24
Charles II, count, 65
Charles VIII, 67
Chartrain, Frédéric, 49–50
Chazan, Robert, 81
Christian moneylenders. *See* Moneylenders, non-Jewish
Chronica Majora, 97
Civil authorities: campaigns against usurers, 55; interest rates established by, 53–54; Jewish moneylending and, 52–53
Clark, Elain, 85
Clavarius, 9
Clement IV, pope, 49
Clement V, pope, 121
Corderii family, 31
Cortes of Burgos, 55
Costello family, 31
Coulet, Noël, 10, 75
Council of Marseilles, 70
"Council of the Hundred" (Florence), 81
Council of Vienne (1311–1312), 52, 79; delay in publication of canons, 121; *Ex gravi* canon, 70, 119–122, 124; on usury, 46
Courts, ecclesiastical. *See* ecclesiastical courts

Credit system, 55; recognition of
need for, 67, 95
Creditors. *See* Moneylenders
Creisonus, 48

David de Villaforti, 14
Davidsohn, Robert, 84
Debtors, appeals for help, 49–51
Debts/indebtedness, 71–103; analysis
of causes of, 77–78; cancellation
of, 55; chronic, 77; partial reduction of, by authorities, 54–55; repayment of, 9–14; as widespread,
79. *See also* Loans
de Draguignanos. *See* Draguignan
family
Delcore, Mathias, 74
Delinquency in payment of debts,
fines imposed for, 76
Delisle, L., 59
de Tornameira, P., 17
Deulosal de Apta, 33
Draguignan family, 29–34. *See also*
Abraham of Draguignan; Bondavid of Draguignan
*Dream of the Shepherd, The (Le
songe du vergier)*, 50–51, 62, 65,
99
Duby, Georges, 117
Dulcini family, 31

Ecclesiastical courts, Jewish money-
lenders and, 12–13
Economic system, European: in
fourteenth century, 124–125; in
thirteenth century, 124, 125
Edward I, 88; *Statutum de Judaismo*,
64
Edward the Confessor, 45
Eliezer Aben Ardut, 116
Eliezer ben Nathan of Mainz, 101,
102–103
Elisendis de Abada, 13
Emery, Richard W., 1–2, 39, 68, 91
England: expulsion of Jews from,
64, 66, 85; interest rate
established in, 53–54; Italian
moneylenders and, 88; non-Jewish
moneylenders in, 85
Enrique II, 55
Epinouze, 49, 54
Erfurt, attacks against Jews in, 49

Essex, 85
Eugenius III, pope, 54
Europe, eastern, interest rates established in, 54
Ex gravi (Council of Vienne decree),
46, 70, 119–122; canonization of
Louis XI in relation to, 121–122;
delay in publication of, 121; economic system and, 124; Marseilles
implementation of, 119–122
Excommunication (*Atlana vel
Nigduy*) of Jewish moneylenders,
55
Expulsion of Jews: "amelioration"
of Jews as prelude to, 62–65;
from England, 64; justification
for, 65; politics of, 65–67; presented as act of benevolence, 66

Fama (common knowledge), 24, 41
Financial records, notarial, quantita-
tive analysis of, 72–79
Fines: on delinquent debtors, 76; for
usury, 56–58
Florence, 81; attacks against Jewish
bank in, 48, 49
"For What Amount of Usury Should
One Be Brought to Court" statu-
ate (Marseilles), 70
Fossonos Caracause, 20
Foulque de Neuilly, 47
Foulques, bishop of Toulouse, 69, 87
France, 58–62; "amelioration" of
Jews, 65; campaigns against
usury, 58–62; claims against Jew-
ish usurers, 59–61; Florentines in,
89; restitution by Jewish money-
lenders in, 58–59; restitution for
usury in, 58–61; surplus money
created by restitutions, 61
Franciscus Ricolf, 49
Frederick II of Sicily, 44

Gambling, 37–39
Gauthier, Léon, 89
Geoffrey of Paris, 98
Germany: attitudes toward Jewish
moneylenders, 47; interest rate
established in, 54
Gershom ben Judah of Mainz, 100
Gillelmus de Castronovo, viscount,
73

Girardus de Monteolivo, 108, 110
Good-faith agreements, drawbacks
  of, 17–18
Goudron, non-Jewish moneylenders
  in, 86–87
Gratian, 45, 51
Grau, Manuel, 99
Grenoble, 50
Grossteste, Robert, 63, 97
Guido Burgondionis, 6, 14
Guilelmus Gaufridus, 36
Guillaume de la Brue, archbishop,
  63, 87, 88
Guillelmus Arpanini, 50
Guillelmus Berthelani, 50
Guillelmus Brindin, 116
Guillelmus Furnerus, 20
Guillelmus Gasqueti, 107, 115, 118
Guillelmus Stephani, 39, 115
Guillelmus Tortella, 41
Guillelmus Ymberti, 25

Habraam Maymo, 56
Habramonus de Montepessulano, 33
Halayame, Rabbi, 56
Henry III, 69
Huesca, 56, 58
Huga Briona, 18
Hugo Bernardi, 36, 105
Hugo de Giminis, 39
Hugo Guacelini, 113
Hugo Mercerii, 118, 119
Hugo Michaelis, 23
Hugues de Baux, 109
Humbert II, 50

Indebtedness. See Debts/
  indebtedness
Infamis, witnesses's definitions of, 41
Innocent III, pope, 54
Innocent IV, pope, 97; manifest usu-
  rers defined by, 23–24
Interest: distinguished from usury,
  43–44; "moderate" rate of, 53;
  partial remittance of, 116, 117;
  versus principal, 68
Isaac Corderii, 18
Isaac de Albanato, 12
Isaac de Costello, 31
Isaac son of Juda de Lates, 29
Isaac son of Resplanda, 39–40
Italy: acknowledgment of usury in,

68–69; attitudes about moneylending in, 83–84; non-Jewish
  moneylenders, 88–90

Jacoba (widow of Guillelmus Ym-
  berti), 25
Jacob Angelicus, 116
Jacob ben Elijah of Venice, 82–83,
  93, 94–95; 116
Jacob de Baherias, 48
Jacob de Lunello, 39
Jacob de Sancta Maria, 38
Jacob di Consiglio, 81
Jacob Poncii, 17, 18
James I of Aragon, 53, 56, 116
James II of Aragon, 58
Jehuda Hasid, 101
Jewish communities, as source of
  income for monarchs, 55–58
Jewish cultural renaissance, 28–29
Jewish moneylenders. See Money-
  lenders, Jewish
"Jewish serfdom," 54
Jews: "amelioration" of, 62–65; at-
  tacks against, 47–49; Black Death
  attributed to, 49; designated "serfs
  of the royal chamber," 54–55; ex-
  pulsion of (*see* Expulsion of Jews).
  See also Moneylenders, Jewish
Johannes Bartholome de Sex Furnis,
  24
Johannes Blegerii, 17
Johannes Caponi, 42
Johannes Ferlays, 50
Johannes Floquerius, 14
Johannes Girando, 115
Johannes Montaneys, 34
Johannes Perrerii, 50
John XXII, pope, 121
Jordan, William Chester, 59
Josef Benveniste of Barcelona, 56
Joseph de Alesto, 47
Joseph Kimhi, 94
Juceff Vitalis, 13
Judaizare, 47

Kaeuper, Richard W., 88
Kalonymos ben Kalonymos of Arles,
  28
Kisch, Guido, 96
Konstanz, 54

Langton, Walter, 85

La Rochelle, 66
La Roncière, Charles de, 89
Lateran Council, legislation on usury, 51
Laurentius Daunazati, 90
Laurentius Girardi, 37, 104, 108, 117; association with Petrus Guizo, 37; charge against Bondavid, 5; *interrogatoria* to witnesses, 21, 22; obligatory note of, 6; promissory note not in possession of, 14–15; quitclaim not presented by, 6, 17, 19; refusal to compromise, 22. *See also* Bondavid of Draguignan, trial of
Lavoie, Rodrigue, 76–77, 91, 92
Legal documents, medieval attitudes toward, 117
Legislation against usury, 51–55; by civil authorities, 53–55; *ex gravi* decree, 46, 70, 119–122; "For What Amount of Usury Should One Be Brought to Court" statuate (Marseilles), 70; by Lateran Council, 51–52
Le Goff, Jacques, 43–44
Leonetus, 16
Leo of Moustiers, 31
Lérida, 57, 58
Levi ben Gershom, 28
Loans: duration of, in Arles, 74–75; security not required for, 6; social distribution, Perpignan, 72–74; typical situation, 6. *See also* Debts/indebtedness; Moneylenders *headings*
Lombards, 91, 93
Louis VII, king of France, 62
Louis IX, king of France (Saint Louis), 52, 54, 59, 60, 61, 81, 83, 95, 107, 112, 121; attempts to change economic behavior of Jews, 64; canonization of, in relation to promulgation of *Ex gravi* canon, 121–122; Meir ben Simeon on, 80
Louis X, king of France, 98
Louis of Bavaria, 55
Lyon, 52

Ma'arufia (preferred customer), 100–103; trial of Bondavid in relationship to, 103

Mabilly, Philippe, 8, 113
Mainz, 52
Majorca, 57
Mandamenta, Jews of Marseilles and, 10–11
Manifest usurers: legal definitions of, 23–24; Marseilles courts on, 22–25; Pope Innocent IV on, 23–24; versus usurers, 24
Manifestus usurarius. See Manifest usurers
Manosque, 20, 46, 76, 89; court records, 2, 7, 46, 47; indebtedness in, analysis of causes of, 77–78; Italian moneylenders in, 90; legislation on nonpayment of debts, 12; percentage of Jewish moneylenders, 92–93; seizure orders in registers of, 12
Mansi, 52
Maria of Monteolivo, 108
Marseilles: Archives des Bouches-du-Rhône in, 2, 105; attacks on Jewish moneylending, 47; attempts to expel Jews from, 66–67; claiming unpaid debts in, 9–14; council on possession of promissory notes, 15; court records, 8; ecclesiastical court of, 12–13; economy of (1317), 124, 125; economy of (1342), 124–125; *ex gravi* canon incorporated in legislation of (1318), 119–122; "For What Amount of Usury Should One Be Brought to Court" statute, 70; interest rate established in, 53; Jews of, 31, 32–33; municipal government, 111–112; prices in (1295–1325), 8; notarial registers, 29; "probation by one witness" statute, 6–7, 19; statutes regarding unpaid debts, 10; usury in, during Bondavid's time, 69–70. *See also* Provence
Marvani family, 11, 31
Mate, Mavis, 69, 91
Matheldus Cocellere, 48
Meir ben Simeon of Narbonne, 63, 80–81, 82, 83, 87, 91, 95, 97–98; *Milhemeth Mitsvah*, 80
Meir of Rothenberg, 102
Meissener Rechtsbuch, 96
Melton, William, 85

Merchant of Venice (Shakespeare), 1, 71
Monernii, G., 6
Moneylenders: attitudes toward, 43–44, 67–70, 71, 79–84; dishonesty of, 20–22; fraudulent possession of promissory notes by, 14–20; means of benefitting clients, 116; restrictive legislation applied to, 46; usury never admitted to by, 23. *See also* Moneylenders, Jewish; Moneylenders, non-Jewish; Usurers
Moneylenders, Jewish: ambivalence toward, 67–68, 70; "amelioration" of, 63–65; in Aragon, 55–58; arguments in defense of, 95–97; attitudes toward, 47, 71, 72, 79–84; civil authorities and, 53; in France, 58–61; French treatise on (1373), 50–51; government profit from, 47; image of, 1, 71, 123; loans to Christians in Perpignan, 72–74; opposition to, 43–70; preferred customers (*ma'arufia*) and, 99–103; recognition of contribution of, 67, 72, 81, 95; restrictive legislation applied to, 44–45; Shylockian image of, 1, 71, 123
Moneylenders, non-Jewish, 84–90; in Aix, 75; in England, 85; interest charges of, 97; in Italy, 88–91; little documentation found on, 86; loans to aristocracy, 73. *See also* Moneylenders
Moneylending, shifting attitudes toward, 67–70, 71. *See also* Moneylenders *headings*
Monteolivus de Monteolivo, 110–111, 119, 125
Montpellier, 51–52, 53, 54
Moras, 50
Mordacais Sacerloti of Marseilles, 23, 24–25
Mosse Anglicus, 13, 16, 17
Mosse of Grassa, 14
Muca Abnalcavit, 56

Narbonne, 51
Niort, 66
Notarial records: of Arles, 74; of Manosque, 90; of Marseilles, 29; of Perpignan, 72–74; preserved portions of, 72; promissory notes, 6; quantitative analysis of, 72; of trial of Bondavid of Draguignan, 105–107
Notaries: not required for pawnbroking, 76; term *usara* usually not used by, 68; wages, 9
Nuremburg, 64

Oxford, 52

Padua, 52
Pascal de Mayranicis, 114–115
Patrone, Anna Maria, 89
Paulus Christiani, 93
Pavia, 81
Pawnbroking, 76
Pedro IV, 54
Perpignan, 68, 91, 116; act of 1415, 39; notarial registers, 72–74
Perugia, 83–84
Peruzzi company (Florence), 88
Peter Cantor, 45
Peter the Venerable, 62–63
Petrus Arnulfi, 36
Petrus Bartholi, 115–116
Petrus Bermundi of Saint-Félix, 108, 111, 112, 118
Petrus Bollimeni, 116
Petrus Bonifili, 106, 117
Petrus Columbi, 114, 115, 118
Petrus Dalmati, 17
Petrus de Trella, 114
Petrus Ebrari, 13
Petrus Elsiarii, 29
Petrus Ferreri, 115
Petrus Ferrerini, 113
Petrus Gibosi, 90–91
Petrus Guizo, 40–41, 104; association with Laurentius, 37; character of, 7, 35–38; 41–42; gambling addiction of, 37–38; life of, 27; oath against gambling broken by, 39; testimonies of witnesses on character of, 5, 36–40; testimony of, 6, 7; value of sixty shillings to, 9
Petrus Joannus Olivi, *Treatise about Purchases and Sales, Usuries, and Restitution*, 46
Petrus Pellegrini, 17
Petrus Vitalis, 114
Philip Augustus, 54, 66
Pia, 74, 84

Pistoia, 87
Poitiers, 66
Political treatise (1373), 50–51, 62
Pontius Michaelis, 36
Popes. *See* Clement IV; Clement V; Innocent III; Innocent IV; John XXII
Postponement of repayment, 116–117
Preferred customers (*ma'arufia*), 99–103
Profacius Deulocrescas, 30, 34
Prolongationes, 116–117
Promissory notes: faudulent possession of, by moneylenders, 14–20; possession of, 14
Provence, 69–70; expulsion of Jews from, 47; fines on delinquent debtors, analysis of, 76; interest rate established in, 53; Italian moneylenders in, 89–90; Jews of, 28, 33; wages in (fourteenth century), 9. *See also* Aix-en-Provence; Marseilles
Pugh, Ralph B., 85
Puigcerda, 74
Purgoldt, Johannes, 96
Pryénées-Orientales, 74, 75

Quanto amplius, 51, 52
Quitclaim, 19

Rationnaire général, 9
Raymond VIII, 81
Raymond Berenger, count of Provence, 54, 69
Raymond de Baux, 109
Raymond Gasqueti, 19
Raymond Trancéval of Beziers, 81
Raymundus Dagulla, 36, 42
Raymundus de Alesto, 39, 41, 105
Raymundus de Fonte, 14
Raymundus Egidii, 112, 113
Raymundus Payrolerii, 116
Raymundus Viridis, 112, 113
René I, king of Provence, 69–70
Repayment of debts, 9–14; in Aix-en-Provence, 10; failure in, 12–14; *mandamenta* issued for, 9–12; in Marseilles, 10; witnesses to 9, 17, 18
Ricavi family, 110

Ricavus Ricavi, 108
Riccardi of Lucca, 88
Richard of Anesty, 78–79
Rivoire, 49, 54
Robert de Courcon, 47
Robert de Curzon, 45
Rostagnus Juliani, 24
Rostagnus Pandulfi, 335
Rostang Pugani, 116

Saintes, 66
Saint-Jean-d'Angély, 66
Saint-Laurent-de-la-Salanque, 74
Saint-Maixent, 66
Saint-Pierre-sur-Dives, 66
Saint-Symphorien-d'Ozon, 53
Salomon de Lunello, 17
Salomonetus son of Crescas de Bellicadro, 34
Salon, occupational background of borrowers, 75
Salves Corderii, 108
Salvet Marvani, 13
San Gimignano, 68, 84
Santa Coloma de Querlat, 86
Sapori, Armando, 87
Sardi family, 110
Scholastics, 46
Security, moneylender's attitude toward, 116, 117
Sefer hasidim, 101–102, 114
Segnoretus, 18
Segnoretus Sartor, 21
Shakespeare, William, *The Merchant of Venice*, 1, 71
Siena, 81
Simon David, 46
Simon Davit, 80
Simon de Beaulieu, archbishop of Bourges, 86
Simon de Crilada, 47–48
Simon de Montfort, 55
Societas Riccardorum, 88–89
Sperandeus, 20
Stephanonus Sonnerii of Epinouze, 50
Stephanus Ganelli, 40
Stephaus Giraudi, 24
Stouff, Louis, 74, 75–76, 99

Tarascon, expulsion of Jews from, 67

Tarragona, 40, 56
Teruel, 57
Theobald, count of Champagne, 61
Tholomeus de Portali, 88
Thomas Aquinas, Saint, 45, 61, 63, 95
Toledo, 13
Tortosa, 57
Toulouse, campaign against usurers in, 87–88

Ulrich of Liechtenstein, 47
Usura (word), 67–70; avoidance of use in notarial documents, 68; canon-law definition, 68; connotations, 68; disappearance of term from records, 69, 70; usage in Marseilles, 69–70; usages of, 67–70
Usurare (word), usage of, 68
Usurarius (word), legal meaning of, 22–23
Usurers: declaration as, 23; Jews equated with, 47; versus manifest usurers, 24; procedure for discovering, 24. *See also* Manifest usurers
Usury: ecclesiastical opposition to, 46; fines levied for, 56–58; Gratian's definition of, 45, 51; "immoderate," 51; versus interest (thirteenth century), 43–44; Marseilles legislation on (1318), 119–122; restrictive legislation, 49–55; shifting attitudes toward,

67–70; suppression of, 69, Thomas Aquinas on, 45–46. *See also Usura* (word)

Valencia, 40, 52, 56
Vich, 13, 68, 99–100
Vidal Abulbaca, 56
Vidal Astruc, 13
Vidal Baron, 56
Vidal Gallipapa, 57
Vidalon Barba, 21
Villefranche, 66
Vincencius Maurelli, 20–21
Vivandus de Jerusalem, 111

Walter von der Vogelweide, 47
"War of the Great Count," 81
Wenzel, king of Germany, 55
Wernham, Monique, 75
William Carnot, 52
William de Sackville, 78
William of Auxerre, 45
William of Chartres, 62, 83, 95
William of Newburgh, 48–49
Winchester, countess of, 63
Witnesses: in trial of Bondavid (*see* Bondavid of Draguignan, trial of); to repayment of debts, 17–18

Yedaya ha-Penini Bedresi, 28
York, Jews of, 48
Yosef ibn Kaspi, 28

Zaragoza, 58

Designer:	U.C. Press Staff
Compositor:	A-R Editions, Inc.
Text:	10/12 Times Roman
Display:	Goudy
Printer:	Braun-Brumfield, Inc.
Binder:	Braun-Brumfield, Inc.